CLICK ON 2

Teacher's Book

Virginia Evans - Neil O'Sullivan

Express Publishing

Contents

READING	WRITING	LISTENING & SPEAKING	COMMUNICATION
A Real-Life Person	letter to family/friend about daily routine at summer camp (project) Julie's typical day (article)	listening for specific information; expressing preferences Pronunciation: word stress	giving personal information
The Cottingley Fairies (diary)	biography - Arthur Conan Doyle (project) writing a diary	listening for lexical items & verb phrases; talking about past habits/routines Pronunciation: /e/ silent or pronounced (-ed ending)	talking about past activities
European theme parks	article describing your favourite possession (project) letter to the lost property office	listening for specific information; picture-prompted multiple choice; talking about activities you have (not) done Pronunciation: /ɛ/ - /eə/	describing lost property
Lost in the Desert	story; (project) beginning/ending of a story	listening to position people in picture; listening for gist; talking about past activities Pronunciation: silent /t/	at the doctor's
The World of Fashion in the Year 2200	letter to a friend about your weekend plans (project) letter of complaint	filling in order forms; talking about your plans; prioritising Pronunciation: homophones	buying clothes
Food, Fun & Celebration around the World	article about a festival you attended (project) restaurant advertisement	filling in missing information; making a shopping list; ordering food; complaining about food Pronunciation: sounds often confused	ordering food & drink
US Cross-Continent Tours	opinion article (project) animal factfiles	listening for lexical items; comparing town & countryside Pronunciation: contrastive stress	ordering flowers; booking a flight
The World's Great Rainforests	a letter giving advice (project) traffic signs	giving advice; talking about house rules; identifying specific information Pronunciation: letters not pronounced	asking, giving or accepting advice
A Peking Paradise	narrative article about a visit to a famous building/landmark (project) short descriptions of landmarks	talking about places; giving details; listening for specific information Pronunciation: linked sounds	asking about currency & language
Famous Faces	letter of recommendation (project) a friendly letter describing a person	describing people; talking about films you like/dislike; multiple matching; listening for gist Pronunciation: stressed syllables	expressing preferences

Published by Express Publishing

Liberty House, New Greenham Park, Newbury,
Berkshire RG19 6HW
Tel.: (0044) 1635 817 363
Fax: (0044) 1635 817 463
e-mail: inquiries@expresspublishing.co.uk
http://www.expresspublishing.co.uk

First published March 2001
Fifth impression 2007

Made in EU

ISBN 978-1-84216-702-1

Acknowledgements

Authors' Acknowledgements

We would like to thank all the staff at Express Publishing who have contributed their skills to producing this book. Thanks
are due in particular to: Megan Lawton (Editor in Chief), Stephanie Smith and Sean Todd (senior editors), Michael Sadler
and Andrew Wright (editorial assistants), Richard White (senior production controller), the Express design team, Onyx
(recording producer) and Rachel Robbins, Kevin Harris, David Smith, Erica Thompson, Kimberly Baker, Timothy Forster,
Steven Gibbs, Eric Simmons, Christine Little and Eric Taylor for their support and patience. We would also like to thank
those institutions and teachers who piloted the manuscript, and whose comments and feedback were invaluable in the
production of the book.

The authors and publishers wish to thank the following, who have kindly given permission for the use of copyright material:

© Alain Pepin for the article on p. 11; © LEGOLAND for the article on p. 31

Photograph Acknowledgements

© Alain Pepin for pictures on p. 11; Brotherton Collection University of Leeds for pictures of Frances & the Leaping Fairy
and Fairy offering flower to Elsie on p. 19; © SeaWorld All rights reserved for pictures on p. 27, © LEGOLAND for
picture of The Dragon Ride on p. 31; NMEC for picture on p. 89; AUDIO VISUAL for pictures of Mel Gibson on p. 103
(WARNER); Jodie Foster on p. 103 (© 1997 BY WARNER BROS.); Julia Roberts on (COPYRIGHT © 20TH CENTURY
FOX FILM CORPORATION. ALL RIGHTS RESERVED.) on p. 103; Nicholas Cage, Meg Ryan and Antonio Banderas on
p. 103; Photo File section, Unit 4 for pictures of Roger; Armao for pictures of jewellery on p. 28.

Colour Illustrations: Nathan, Chris

Music Compositions & Arrangement by Ted and Taz

While every effort has been made to trace all the copyright holders, if any have been inadvertently overlooked the publishers
will be pleased to make the necessary arrangements at the first opportunity.

Introduction to the Teacher

Click on 2 is a complete course for learners studying English at Elementary level. It allows for flexibility of approach which makes it suitable for classes of all kinds, including large or mixed ability classes.

The coursebook consists of five modules of two units each. Each unit is designed to be taught in four 50-minute lessons. The corresponding unit in the Workbook provides the option of an additional lesson. The coursebook also contains five Self-Assessment sections and an adventure story in seven episodes with accompanying language exercises. *Click on 2* and its components may be covered in a total of about 65 teaching hours.

Course Components

Student's Book

The Student's Book is the main component of the course. Each unit is based on a single theme and the topics covered are of general interest. All units follow the same basic structure (see **Elements of the Coursebook**).

Teacher's Book

This Teacher's Book contains Teacher's Notes, fully interleaved with the Student's Book. These provide step-by-step lesson plans and suggestions about how to present the material. Also included is a full Key to the exercises in the S's Book and tapescripts of the listening material.

Workbook

The Workbook is divided into two parts. The first part consists of ten units corresponding to those in the S's Book. It contains exercises to revise, consolidate and extend Ss' learning through a variety of tasks. The second part, called **Click on Grammar**, summarises and revises the specific grammar items dealt with in each unit of the course and offers additional exercises. At the end of the book there are ten **Progress Tests** one for each unit. A separate **Teacher's Key** reproduces the pages of the Workbook, overprinted with full answers to all exercises.

Test Booklet

The Test Booklet contains five tests, each in two equivalent versions to ensure result reliability, especially with larger classes. Ss sitting next to each other work on different tests, but are tested in the same language areas. The tests facilitate the assessment of Ss' progress and enable the teacher to pinpoint Ss' specific weaknesses. There is also an Exit Test which covers all the material learnt at this level and can be used as an effective assessment test for those planning to move on to the next level.

Class Audio CDs

The Class Audio CDs contain all the recorded material which accompanies the course. This includes the dialogues and texts in the Listening and Reading sections, as well as model dialogues, Pronunciation and the material for all listening tasks.

Student's Audio CD

The S's Audio CD contains the recorded dialogues and the main texts in the Listening and Reading sections of the S's Book for the purposes of homework and preparation, as well as the seven episodes of the story.

Elements of the Coursebook

Each unit contains the following sections:

Lead-in

- Assisted by pictures, Ss are introduced to the **vocabulary** and **grammar** of the unit.
- A **listen and repeat** drill presents everyday phrases and sentences which will be encountered in the dialogues that follow.

Listening and Reading

Each unit comprises two Listening and Reading texts.
- The first **Listening and Reading** text presents situational dialogues in a variety of everyday contexts. Students are made familiar with natural, everyday language.
- The second **Listening and Reading** text presents meaningful articles on cross-cultural topics.

In this way, Ss practise simple everyday communication. Skills like reading for gist or for specific information are also practised, and vocabulary is seen in a functional and meaningful context.

Vocabulary

Vocabulary is practised through various types of exercises. A particular feature of the book is the teaching of **collocations**, which helps Ss to remember vocabulary items as parts of set expressions.

Grammar

- The grammar items of each unit are presented by means of clear and concise theory boxes.
- **Grammar exercises and activities** reinforce Ss' understanding of these items.

Listening tasks and Speaking practice

- Ss can develop their **listening skills** through a variety of tasks. These tasks employ the vocabulary and grammar practised in each unit, in this way reinforcing understanding of the language taught in the unit.
- **Controlled speaking activities** have been carefully designed to allow Ss guided practice before leading them to **less structured speaking activities**.

Photo File

These sections provide visual and linguistic input for closely controlled **Writing Practice**. Ss are referred to the Photo File section at the back of the book by **Projects** which feature in each unit. These should be discussed in class before being assigned as written homework.

Pronunciation

Pronunciation activities help Ss to recognise sounds and reproduce them correctly.

Communication

These sections provide practice in real-life communication. Standard expressions and language structures associated with realistic situations are extensively practised.

Vocabulary Revision Games

These sections use the format of a team competition to consolidate learning of vocabulary and phrases presented in the unit.

Reading texts

These texts practise specific reading skills (e.g. paragraphing, working with cloze texts, etc), while at the same time providing a model text for the writing tasks which follow them.

Writing

The writing sections have been carefully designed to ensure that Ss systematically develop their writing skills.

- A **model text** is presented and thoroughly analysed, followed by guided practice of the language to be used.
- The final task is based on the model text and follows the detailed **plan** provided.
- All writing activities are based on realistic types and styles of writing such as letters, descriptions, stories and articles.

'Do you know ...?'

At the end of each unit, interesting trivia boxes provide a short reading task.

Module Self-Assessment sections

These follow every second unit, and reinforce Ss' understanding of the topics, vocabulary and structures that have been presented.

- The material has been designed to help Ss learn new language in the context of what they have already mastered, rather than in isolation.
- Each section concludes with an entertaining song which practises the language items presented in the preceding units.
- A marking scheme allows Ss to evaluate their progress and identify their weaknesses.

Grammar Reference section

- This section offers full explanations and revision of the grammar structures presented throughout the book.
- It can be used both in class and at home to reinforce the grammar being taught. The "Rules for Punctuation" section at the back of the book includes a full explanation of the rules in a clear and concise manner.

The Guide to UK & USA Culture and the American English – British English Guide

- These sections offer an insight into the cultural similarities and differences between the two major English-speaking nations.
- Interesting and informative, they provide the student with cultural information, not usually taught in the classroom.

Adventure story

The story of *The Hound of the Baskervilles* is presented in comic strip format in seven episodes.

- Ss are invited to read for enjoyment.
- Each episode is followed by a variety of tasks, offering the opportunity for extra practice and consolidation.

SUGGESTED TEACHING TECHNIQUES

A. Presenting new vocabulary

Much of the new vocabulary in *Click on 2* is presented through pictures. Ss are asked to **match the pictures to listed words** *(see Ss' Book Unit 2, p. 14, Ex. 1a)*.
Vocabulary is always presented in context, and emphasis is placed on **collocations**, since memorising new words is easier if they are presented in lexical sets. *(see S's Book Unit 2, p. 20, Ex. 24)*
Further techniques that you may use to introduce new vocabulary include:

- **Miming.** Mime the word you want to introduce. For instance, to present the verb **sing**, pretend you are singing and ask Ss to guess the meaning of the word.
- **Synonyms, opposites, paraphrasing and giving definitions.** Examples:
  - present the word **store** by giving a synonym: "Store; shop."
  - present the word **sad** by giving its opposite: "Sad; not happy."
  - present the word **weekend** by paraphrasing it: "Weekend; Saturday and Sunday."

- present the word **garage** by giving its definition: "Garage; the place next to the house where we put our car."
- **Example.** Examples place vocabulary into context and consequently make understanding easier. For instance, introduce the words **city** and **town** by referring to a city and a town in the Ss' country: "Rome is a city, but Parma is a town."
- **Visual prompts:** Show pictures, photographs or drawings to make understanding easier.
- **Use of dictionary:** Encourage Ss to try to explain the word, then check if they are correct using their dictionaries.
- **Sketching.** Draw on the board a simple sketch of the word or words you want to explain. For instance:

tall   short

- **Flashcards.** Flashcards made out of magazine or newspaper pictures, photographs, ready-made drawings and any other visual material may also serve as vocabulary teaching tools.
- **Use of L1.** In a monolingual class, you may explain vocabulary in the Ss' mother tongue, although this method should be employed in moderation.
- **Use of dictionary.** In a multilingual class, Ss may occasionally refer to a bilingual dictionary.

The choice of technique depends on the type of word or expression. For example, you may find it easier to describe an action verb through miming, and not through a synonym or definition.

B. Choral and individual repetition

Repetition will ensure that Ss are confident with the sound and pronunciation of the lexical items and structures being taught.

- Always ask Ss to repeat chorally before you ask them to repeat individually. Repeating chorally will help Ss feel confident enough to then perform the task on their own.

C. Listening and Reading

You may ask Ss to read and listen for a variety of purposes:

- **Listening and reading for gist.** Ask Ss to read or listen to get the gist of the dialogue or text being dealt with. *See S's Book, Unit 2, p. 15, Ex. 4. Tell Ss that in order to complete this task successfully, they need not understand every single detail in the three dialogues that follow. They need only tell you which dialogue is about life in the 17th century, which is about free-time activities in the past and which is a person's lifestyle then and now.*

- **Listening and reading for detail.** Ask Ss to read or listen for specific information. *See S's Book, Unit 2, p. 19, Ex. 20. Ss will have to read or listen to the text for a second time in order to put the sentences in the correct order and then use the sentences to talk about Elsie and the fairies. They are looking for specific details in the text and not for general information.*

D. Speaking

- Speaking activities are initially **controlled**, allowing for guided practice. *See S's Book, Unit 2, p. 18, Ex. 16a where Ss use the same structure to talk about Sandra's lifestyle then and now.*
- Ss are then led to **less structured** speaking activities. *See S's Book, Unit 2, p. 18, Ex. 16b where Ss are invited to talk about their lifestyle when they were five after having been provided with the necessary lexical items and structures.*

E. Writing

All writing tasks in *Click on 2* have been carefully designed to closely guide Ss to produce a successful piece of writing.

- Always read the **model text** provided and deal with the tasks that follow in detail. Ss will then have acquired the necessary language to deal with the final writing task. *See S's Book, Unit 2, p. 21, Exs 29, 30, 31.*
- Make sure that Ss understand that they are writing for a **purpose**. Go through the writing task in detail so that Ss are fully aware of **why** they are writing and **who** they are writing to. *See S's Book, Unit 2, p. 21, Ex. 32. Ss are asked to write a short biography of Jules Verne for their school magazine.*
- Make sure Ss follow the detailed **plan** they are provided with. *See S's Book, Unit 2, p. 21, Ex. 32.*
- It would be well-advised to actually complete the task orally in class before assigning it as written homework. Ss will then feel more confident to produce a complete piece of writing on their own.

F. Projects

- When dealing with project work, Ss can find visual and linguistic input in the **Photo File** section at the back of the S's Book.
- It is necessary to prepare Ss well in class before they attempt the writing task at home.

G. Assigning homework

It is strongly recommended that homework is regularly assigned and routinely checked. Independently from the **suggested homework** sections in the Teacher's Notes, you should feel free to assign tasks which will serve the specific needs of your class.

When assigning writing tasks, prepare Ss as well as possible in advance. This will help them to avoid errors and get maximum benefit from the task.

Commonly assigned tasks include:

Copy - Ss copy an assigned extract;
Dictation - Ss learn the spelling of particular words without memorising the text in which they appear;
Vocabulary - memorisation of the meaning of words and phrases;
Reading Aloud - assisted by the S's cassettes or CDs, Ss practise at home in preparation for reading aloud in class;
Project - after they have been prepared in class, Ss complete the writing task in the Photo File section; and
Writing - after thorough preparation in class, Ss are asked to produce a complete piece of writing.

H. Correcting students' work

All learners make errors - they are part of the process of learning. The way you deal with errors depends on what the Ss are doing.

- **Oral accuracy work:**
  Correct Ss on the spot, either by providing the correct answer and allowing them to repeat it, or by indicating the error but allowing Ss to correct it. Alternatively, indicate the error and ask other Ss to provide the answer.
- **Oral fluency work:**
  Allow Ss to finish the task without interrupting, but make a note of the errors made and correct them afterwards.
- **Written work:**
  Do not over-correct; focus on errors that are directly relevant to the point of the exercise. When giving feedback you may write the most common errors on the board and get the class to attempt to correct them.

Remember that rewarding work and praising Ss is of great importance. Post good written work on a noticeboard in your classroom or school, or give 'reward' stickers. Praise effort as well as success.

I. Class organisation

- **Open pairs**
  The class focuses its attention on two Ss doing the set task together. Use this technique when you want your Ss to offer an example of how a task is done. *(See Unit 2, Ex. 12, p. 17 in the book.)*
- **Closed pairs**
  Pairs of Ss work together on a task or activity, while you move around offering assistance and suggestions. Set out the task clearly before beginning closed pairwork.

- **Stages of pairwork**
  - Set Ss in pairs.
  - Set the task and time limit.
  - Rehearse the task in open pairs.
  - In closed pairs, ask Ss to do the task.
  - Go round the class and help Ss.
  - Open pairs report back to the class.
- **Group work**
  Groups of three or more Ss work together on a task or activity. Class projects or role play are most easily done in groups. Again, give Ss a solid understanding of the task in advance.
- **Rolling questions**
  Ss one after the other ask and answer questions assisted by prompts. *(See Unit 2, Ex. 11b, p. 17 in the book.)*

J. Using the Student's Cassettes or Audio CDs

- Dialogues and texts are recorded on the S's cassettes or audio CDs. Ss have the chance to listen to these recordings at home as many times as they want to improve their pronunciation and intonation.

  - S listens to the recording and follows the lines.
  - S listens to the recording with pauses after every sentence/exchange. S repeats as many times as needed, trying to imitate the speaker's pronunciation and intonation.
  - S listens to the recording again. S reads aloud.

K. Using L1 in class

- Use L1 in moderation and only when necessary.

Abbreviations

Abbreviations used in the Student's Book and Teacher's Notes are as shown below:

T	Teacher
S(s)	Student(s)
HW	Homework
L1	Students' mother tongue
Ex.	Exercise
p(p).	Page(s)
e.g.	For example
i.e.	That is
etc	Etcetera
sb	Somebody
sth	Something

Lifestyles

◆ **Before you start...**

What's your name?
How old are you?
Where are you from?
How many members are there in your family?
Do you like English?

◆ **Listen, read and talk about...**

What
do you do?

UNIT 1

- people's daily routines
- everyday & free-time activities
- jobs
- sports & hobbies
- countries & nationalities

Module 1
Units 1-2

◆ Learn how to ...

- give personal information
- tell the time
- talk about routines and free-time activities
- talk about past activities
- talk about possessions
- say dates

◆ Practise ...

- present simple
- present continuous
- adverbs of frequency
- present continuous with a future meaning
- past simple
- used to
- prepositions of place (at, in, on,)
- the possessive case
- possessive adjectives

◆ Write ...

- a letter to a friend telling your news
- an article about a person's daily routine
- a diary entry
- a biography

Then & Now

UNIT 2

- family members
- days of the week
- possessions
- past routines/habits/activities

1 What do you do?

Lead-in

1 🎧 Listen to the sounds and tick (✓) the sentences which match. Use the sentences to describe the picture.

1 The birds are singing. ....
2 The children are swimming. ....
3 The ducks are quacking. ....
4 A boy is crying. ....
5 A helicopter is flying over the camp. ....
6 Someone is riding a horse. ....
7 The radio is playing. ....
8 The wind is blowing. ....
9 A dog is barking. ....
10 Children are laughing. ....

It's summer time at Kendal Camp. The birds are singing.

2 Match the people to their jobs, then use the prompts to ask and answer, as in the example.

1	Dave	a	Art teacher
2	Marek	b	Drama teacher
3	Anita	c	driver
4	Bill	d	horse riding coach

1 Dave - drive the camp coach - talk to a girl
   A: What does Dave do?
   B: He drives the camp coach.
   A: What is he doing now?
   B: He's talking to a girl.
2 Bill - teach Art - drink cola
3 Anita - teach Drama - eat a sandwich
4 Marek - teach horse riding - read a magazine

Objectives

Vocabulary: daily routines; everyday and free-time activities; jobs; sports and hobbies; the time; countries and nationalities
Reading: reading for detailed understanding
Listening: listening for specific information; listening to complete a table
Speaking: expressing likes - dislikes; agreeing - disagreeing; talking about jobs/daily routines; talking about everyday and free-time activities
Communication: giving personal information
Pronunciation: word stress
Grammar: present simple; adverbs of frequency; present continuous; present continuous with a future meaning; prepositions of time
Project: an article about a secretary's daily routine
Writing: a letter to a friend giving news

Lesson 1 (pp. 6 - 7)

1 • Read aloud the title of the unit. Ask Ss to say when we ask this question (*to find out about a person's job.*) Ask Ss to look at the picture. Ask Ss questions to set the scene e.g. *Where are these people — at a summer camp or in the garden? (At a summer camp.) How many people work there? (4) How do you know that? (They are wearing uniforms.) What are their names?* etc

• Ask Ss to read sentences 1 to 10 aloud one at a time. Play the cassette. Ss listen and tick (✔) the sentences which match the sounds. Check Ss' answers by asking individual Ss to read the appropriate sentences aloud. Then, explain/elicit the meaning of any new words by using Ss' L1. Individual Ss use the sentences to describe the picture.

ANSWER KEY

Sentences to be ticked: 1, 3, 5, 6, 7, 9, 10

Suggested answer: It's summer time at Kendal camp. The ducks are quacking and a dog is barking. Someone is riding a horse. A helicopter is flying over the camp. The radio is playing and children are laughing.

• Ask Ss to quickly scan sentences 1 to 10, underline the verb form and identify the tense (*present continuous*). Elicit from Ss the form of this tense (**personal pronoun + be + verb -ing**), and its use. Ask: *When are these actions happening? (Now, at the time of speaking.)*

2 • Ask Ss to look at the picture and match the people to their jobs.

ANSWER KEY

1 c	2 d	3 b	4 a

• Read item 1, then invite two Ss to read out the example. Ask Ss to underline **does Dave do, drives**. Ss identify the tense (present simple). Ask: *Do we use the present simple to describe an action which is happening now or an action which happens every day? (Every day)*
Choose two Ss and do item 2 orally in class. Do the same with the remaining items.

ANSWER KEY

2 A: *What does Bill do?*
   B: *He teaches Art.*
   A: *What is he doing now?*
   B: *He's drinking cola.*
3 A: *What does Anita do?*
   B: *She teaches Drama.*
   A: *What is she doing now?*
   B: *She's eating a sandwich.*
4 A: *What does Marek do?*
   B: *He teaches horse riding.*
   A: *What's he doing now?*
   B: *He's reading a magazine.*

3 • Play the cassette. Ss listen and repeat either chorally or individually.
   • Present these phrases/sentences by giving examples or by miming.
      e.g. **Who's that man?** (Point to Dave in the picture and say: *Who's that man? He's Dave.*)
      Come on! (Pretend you are leaving the classroom. Look at the Ss and waving your arm say: *Come on! Let's go to the playground.*) etc

4 Read sentences 1 to 3 aloud. Play the cassette. Ss listen and write the correct letter next to each sentence.

> *ANSWER KEY*
>
> *1 B   2 L   3 A*

5 a) Read sentences 1 to 3 aloud. Allow Ss three minutes to read the dialogues silently and circle the correct answer. Check Ss' answers by asking individual Ss to read out the correct answer.

> *ANSWER KEY*
>
> *1 B   2 A   3 C*

   b) Play the cassette for Ex. 4 again. Ss listen and follow the lines, then Ss take roles and read the dialogues aloud.

   c) Ss look at the phrases/sentences in Ex. 3, then read and say who said each one.

> *ANSWER KEY*
>
> *Sue asked, "Who's that man?"*
> *Sue asked, "What does she do?"*
> *Mary said, "Come on!"*
> *Mary said, "Let's introduce ourselves."*
> *Sue said, "After you."*
> *Dave asked, "How can I help you?"*
> *Dave said, "It's this way."*
> *Dave asked, "Don't you mind working on Saturdays?"*
> *Steve asked, "Fancy joining us?"*
> *Kate said, "Sorry, I can't."*
> *Steve asked, "Why not?"*
> *Kate said, "See you then."*

Memory Game

Ask Ss to look at the sentences in Ex. 3 for two minutes. Ss then close their books and, in teams, try to remember as many phrases/sentences as possible. Each correct phrase/sentence gets 1 point. The team with the most points is the winner.
e.g. Team A S1: Come on!
     Team B S1: After you.   etc

3 🔊 **Listen and repeat.**

- Who's that man?
- What does she do?
- Come on!
- Let's introduce ourselves.
- After you.
- How can I help you?
- It's this way.
- Don't you mind working on Saturdays?
- Fancy joining us?
- Sorry, I can't.
- Why not?
- See you then.

Listening and Reading

4 🔊 **Listen and match the sentences to the people. Write L (for Laura), B (for Bill) or A (for Alan).**

1 He's drinking cola. ☐
2 She's looking for the Art room. ☐
3 He's flying the camp helicopter. ☐

5 a) Read the dialogues (A, B and C) and circle the correct answer A, B or C.

1 Anita is from Poland.
   A Right.   B Wrong.   C Doesn't say.

2 It's Laura's first visit to the camp.
   A Right.   B Wrong.   C Doesn't say.

3 Kate likes horse riding.
   A Right.   B Wrong.   C Doesn't say.

A
Sue: Who's that man?
Mary: Which one?
Sue: The one who is drinking cola.
Mary: That's Bill. He's the Art teacher.
Sue: Oh, and who's that woman with him?
Mary: That's Anita.
Sue: What does she do?
Mary: She's the Drama teacher.
Sue: Where is she from?
Mary: Brazil. Come on! Let's introduce ourselves.
Sue: Okay. After you.

B
Laura: Hello. I'm Laura. Laura Newton.
Dave: Hi, Laura. My name's Dave. How can I help you?
Laura: I'm looking for the Art room.
Dave: It's this way. Come on.
Laura: Thanks.
Dave: Is it your first time here?
Laura: Yes, it is.
Dave: Are you a student at St George's?
Laura: Yes, I am, but I have a part-time job at weekends.
Dave: Really? What do you do?
Laura: I work in a supermarket.
Dave: Don't you mind working on Saturdays?
Laura: Not really.

C
Steve: Hey, Kate! We're going sailing. Fancy joining us?
Kate: Sorry, I can't.
Steve: Why not?
Kate: I'm waiting for Alan.
Steve: Where is he?
Kate: He's flying the camp helicopter at the moment.
Steve: Oh, right. Are you going horse riding later?
Kate: Yes. See you then.
Steve: OK. Bye.

b) In pairs, read out the dialogues.

c) Read the dialogues and underline the phrases/sentences used in Ex. 3. Who said each phrase/sentence?

7

Vocabulary

• The time

6 **a)** Complete the sentences with the time phrases.

• o'clock • half past • (a) quarter to • (a) quarter past • twenty past • twenty to

It's .... It's six ....

six. or It's six twenty. ....

It's .... It's ....

.... eight. .... seven.

or It's seven forty. or It's seven thirty.

It's .... It's ....

.... eight. .... ten. or It's

or It's seven forty-five. ten fifteen.

Listening

b) Listen and fill in the missing times.

Kendal Camp – Monday

in the morning

.... - 10:15

10:45 - ....

in the afternoon

4:05 - ....

.... - 7:00

Speaking

c) In pairs, ask and answer, as in the example.

A: *What time does the **sailing lesson** start?*

B: *It starts at **nine ten/ten past nine** in the **morning**.*

A: *What time does it finish?*

B: *It finishes at **ten fifteen/(a) quarter past ten**.*

• Everyday & Free-Time Activities

Speaking

7 Use the prompts to say what you do/don't do during the week: in the morning/afternoon/evening; on Saturday mornings; on Sunday evenings; on Friday afternoons.

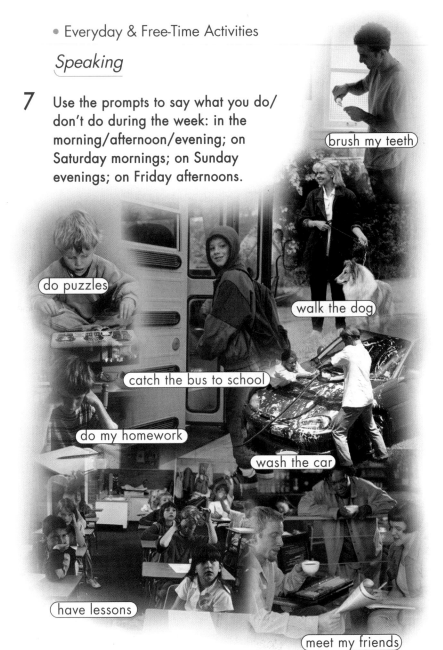

brush my teeth

walk the dog

do puzzles

catch the bus to school

do my homework

wash the car

have lessons

meet my friends

I catch the bus to school in the morning.
I don't walk the dog on Saturday mornings.

• Jobs

8 Match the definitions to the words, then make sentences, as in the example.

☐ 1	look after sick people	A shop assistant
☐ 2	type letters and answer the phone	B journalist
A 3	serve customers	C nurse
☐ 4	make wooden furniture	D carpenter
☐ 5	report the news	E DJ
☐ 6	design clothes	F secretary
☐ 7	play records on the radio	G hairdresser
☐ 8	cut hair	H fashion designer
☐ 9	design buildings	I accountant
☐ 10	keep financial accounts	J architect

A - 3 A shop assistant is someone who serves customers.

Lesson 2 (pp. 8 - 9)

* • Check Ss' HW (10').
  • Play the Memory Game as described in Lesson 1 Ex. 5c p. 7(T).

6 a) • Ss close their books. Draw a clock face on the board and label it as shown below.

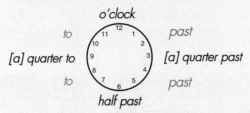

o'clock
to   past
[a] quarter to   [a] quarter past
to   past
half past

  • Draw hands on the clock face. Ss say, chorally and individually, what time is shown.
  • Explain that we can tell the time in two ways — e.g. *twenty past nine* or *nine twenty*. Write several times in numerals on the board. Ss use both ways to say what time is shown.
    e.g. [write 12:15 on the board.]
        Ss: It's twelve fifteen. It's (a) quarter past twelve.
  • Ss' books open. Allow Ss two minutes to do the exercise. Check Ss' answers around the class.

ANSWER KEY

It's **twenty past** six.   It's six **o'clock**.
It's **twenty to** eight.   It's **half past** seven.
It's **(a) quarter to** eight.   It's **(a) quarter past** ten.

b) Ask Ss to read Monday's timetable at Kendal Camp. Play the cassette. Ss listen and fill in the missing times. Check Ss' answers around the class.

ANSWER KEY

in the morning	in the afternoon
9:10 - *10:15*	4:05 - *5:30*
10:45 - *11:50*	6:00 - *7:00*

TAPESCRIPT

Sally: Good morning, James!
James: Ugh! Sally. You're up early.
Sally: I know! I'm going sailing. Are you coming?
James: Oh yes - the sailing lesson. What time does it start?
Sally: At ten past nine, so hurry up.
James: Sorry? Did you say ten to nine?
Sally: No, silly, ten **past** nine.
James: Hm. And what time does it finish?
Sally: At a quarter past ten.
James: Oh, right. OK, I'll come with you, but I'm going back to bed afterwards.
Sally: No, you're not! We've got a Drama lesson at ten forty-five.
James: And what time does the Drama lesson finish?
Sally: At ten to twelve.
James: Ten to ... what?
Sally: Ten **to twelve**. What's wrong with you this morning?
James: I'm tired. I need to sleep.
Sally: Well you can have a nap at noon. Then we're going horse riding.
James: Horse riding? What time does that start?
Sally: At five past four. The lesson finishes at half past five.
James: Five past five?
Sally: James! I said **half** past five. Then there's an Art lesson at six o'clock.
James: Art at six o'clock.
Sally: That's right. The lesson finishes at 7 o'clock. It's a very busy day.
James: Oh, alright. I'll be ready in a minute.
Sally: Well, make sure you wash out your ears. You're driving me mad!

c) Choose two Ss to read out the example. Ss, in closed pairs, act out similar dialogues. Check Ss' answers around the class, then ask some pairs to report back to the class.

SUGGESTED ANSWER KEY

A: What time does the Drama lesson start?
B: It starts at ten forty-five/a quarter to eleven.
A: What time does it finish?
B: It finishes at eleven fifty/ten to twelve.   etc.

  As an extension, ask Ss questions about their daily routine, as in the example.
  e.g. Teacher: What time do you usually get up?
        S1: I usually get up at seven o'clock.
        Teacher: What time do you usually have lunch?
        S2: I usually have lunch at about half past one.   etc.
        Teacher: What time do you usually leave school/work?   etc.

7 • Ss look at the pictures. Read the prompts aloud. Explain that these activities are part of a person's daily routine. Elicit from Ss other phrases which are used to describe a person's daily routine and write them on the board. **Suggested routine:** get up, get dressed, have breakfast, go to school/work, ride my bicycle to school/work, stop for lunch, finish school/work, do shopping, do homework, have dinner, watch TV etc. Ss, one after the other, make sentences using the prompts in the book as well as the phrases listed on the board.

SUGGESTED ANSWER KEY

I brush my teeth every morning and every evening.
I have lessons every day during the week.
I walk the dog every afternoon.
I don't wash the car on Saturday mornings.
I do my homework every evening.
I meet my friends every Friday afternoon.
I don't meet my friends on Sunday evenings.
I do puzzles every evening.
I don't go to school on Sunday evenings.   etc

  • As an extension, Ss can talk about their daily routines using phrases of their own.

8 Read aloud the jobs listed (A - J). Present these words: **sick, serve, customers, wooden, report, design, records, financial accounts** by giving examples or by asking Ss to look up the meaning of each word in their dictionaries.
e.g. **sick:** ill, not feeling well
   customers: people who buy things in a shop
Allow Ss two minutes to match the jobs to the appropriate definitions, then make sentences. Check Ss' answers around the class.

ANSWER KEY

B	5	A journalist is someone who reports the news.
C	1	A nurse is someone who looks after sick people.
D	4	A carpenter is someone who makes wooden furniture.
E	7	A DJ is someone who plays records on the radio.
F	2	A secretary is someone who types letters and answers the phone.
G	8	A hairdresser is someone who cuts hair.
H	6	A fashion designer is someone who designs clothes.
I	10	An accountant is someone who keeps financial accounts.
J	9	An architect is someone who designs buildings.

9 Ask Ss to look at the pictures. Read the picture prompts aloud. Then, read the phrases in the list and ask Ss to say which are positive (*I like/enjoy, I'm good at*), negative (*I hate, I can't stand*) or neutral (*I don't mind*). Choose two Ss to read the examples aloud. Point out that we use **so + auxiliary verb + personal pronoun** to agree with affirmative statements and **neither + auxiliary verb + personal pronoun** to agree with negative statements. Write on the board:

	Agree	Disagree
I like fishing.	So do I.	Really? I don't.
I hate fishing.	So do I.	Really? I like it.
I don't like fishing.	Neither do I.	Oh, I don't mind it.
I can't stand fishing.	Neither can I.	Well, I like it.

Ss copy this into their notebooks. Then Ss, in pairs, talk as in the example.

> **SUGGESTED ANSWER KEY**
>
> - A: I like shopping.   • A: I hate cooking.
>   B: So do I.   B: Oh, I don't mind it.
>
> - A: I'm good at climbing. • A: I enjoy gardening.
>   B: So am I.   B: Really? I don't.   etc

Project (p. 9)

Ss look at the Photo File section. Explain that the pictures show Julie's daily routine and free-time activities. Ask questions to check Ss' understanding.

e.g. What time does she get up? (7:30)
What time does she catch the bus to work? (8:30)
What time does she start work? (9:00)
What does she do at work? (She types letters.)
What does she do at 1:00? (She has a break for lunch.)
What time does she finish work? (5:00)
What does she do in the evenings? (She reads a book or watches TV.)
What does she do at weekends? (She rides her bike or she has lunch/dinner with her friends.)

Point out that Ss can use any other phrases which describe a person's daily routine as well as the picture prompts to talk about Julie's daily routine and free-time activities. Do the exercise orally in class, then assign it as written HW. See Photo File section Unit 1 for the Answer Key.

10 • Ss' books closed. Present the present simple. Say, then write on the board: *I work as a teacher.* Underline **work** and explain that this verb is in the present simple. Present the other persons in the same way. Elicit from Ss how the third person singular is formed. Write on the board: *I work, I play, I fly, I wash, I catch, I press, I box, I go,* and elicit the third person singular. Write these on the board underlining the endings (*he works, he plays, he flies, he washes, he catches, he presses, he boxes, he goes*).

• Drill your Ss. Say verbs in the 1st person singular. Ss say the verb in the third person. Check spelling on the board.
  e.g. T: I live   T: I try
        S1: he lives   S2: he tries   etc.

• Elicit from Ss the negative/interrogative forms. Say a sentence in the affirmative. Ss say the sentence in the negative and interrogative. Write Ss' answers on the board and underline **does, doesn't**. Drill your Ss.
  e.g. T: John likes fishing.
        S1: **Does** John like fishing?
        S2: John **doesn't like** fishing.

• Present the present continuous the same way as with the present simple. Write the following on the board:
  1 Sarah **lives** in London.
  2 Sarah **is cooking** now.
  3 Sarah **is seeing** her friends tonight.
Underline the verb forms. Ss identify the tenses. Explain that we use the present simple for permanent states (Example 1) and present continuous for an action happening at the moment of speaking (Example 2), or for fixed future arrangements (Example 3). Ask Ss to make true sentences about themselves using these two tenses.

a) Ss' books open. Allow Ss two minutes to read the text and identify the tenses, then say the time expressions used with each tense.

> **ANSWER KEY**
>
> **Present Simple** - work, talk, work, love
> **Present Continuous** - 'm typing, 'm going, 'm looking forward to (future meaning)
> **Time expressions:** • now, at the moment, these days (present continuous) • every day/month/etc, always, sometimes, usually, never, etc (present simple) • next month/week/etc, tonight, tomorrow etc (present continuous with future meaning)

b) • Allow Ss two minutes to match the verbs in bold to their use. Check Ss' answers orally in class. Refer Ss to the Grammar Reference section for details.

> **ANSWER KEY**
>
> 2 (pres. simple) love   4 (pres. cont.) 'm going
> 3 (pres. cont.) 'm typing 5 (pres. cont.) 'm looking
>   forward to

• As an extension, Ss talk about their fixed arrangements for tonight.
  e.g. S1: I'm going out tonight.
        S2: We're having dinner with friends tonight.
        S3: I'm playing tennis tonight.   etc

11 Explain the key, then read the prompts. Present any unknown words in Ss' L1 or by giving an example. Choose two Ss to read out the example. Ss, in open pairs, use the prompts to act out similar dialogues.

> **ANSWER KEY**
>
> 2 A: Where does Ann come from?
>   B: She comes from England.
>   A: What's her job?
>   B: She's a nanny.
>   A: What does she do at work?
>   B: She looks after children.
>   A: Does she like her job?
>   B: Yes, she loves it.   etc

> ┌─── Suggested Homework ───┐
>
> 1 **Copy:** Ex. 10a (p. 9)
> 2 **Vocabulary:** Exs 6 & 8 (p. 8), Ex. 9 (p. 9)
> 3 **Reading aloud:** Ex. 10a (p. 9)
> 4 **Dictation:** Exs. 6a & 8 (p. 8)
> 5 **Act out:** Ex. 6c (p. 8), Exs 9 & 11 (p. 9)
> 6 **Project:** (p. 9)

climbing

shopping

scuba diving

fishing

cutting the grass

rollerblading

eating out

cycling

canoeing

surfing the net

gardening

ice-skating

snorkelling

water-skiing

cooking

reading books

- Agreeing - Disagreeing

Speaking

9 Look at the pictures, then use the prompts to talk, as in the examples.

- I like/enjoy ... • I hate ... • I don't mind ...
- I'm good at ... • I can't stand ...

- A: I like rollerblading.
  B: So do I. / Really? I don't.

- A: I can't stand fishing.
  B: Neither can I. / Oh, I don't mind it.

- Project

Look at the Photo File section and complete the article about Julie's daily routine.

Grammar

- Present Simple or Continuous

10 a) Read what Sandra says and identify the tenses in bold. Which time expressions go with each tense?

Hi! I'm Sandra and I'm a secretary. I **work** for an Insurance company. Every day from 9.00 am to 5.00 pm I **talk** to customers or **work** on the computer.
I **love** my job. At the moment, I'm **typing** a letter for my boss. Next week I'm **going** on holiday to the Caribbean. I'm **looking forward to** it.

b) Which tense does Sandra use to describe:

1 a daily routine? *present simple (work/talk)*
2 a permanent state? ....
3 an action happening at the moment of speaking? ....
4 a fixed arrangement in the near future? ....
5 an action happening around the moment of speaking? ....

Speaking

11 In pairs, use the prompts to ask and answer, as in the example.

1 Paula – Brazil – gardener – look after plants (♥)
2 Ann – England – nanny – look after children (♥♥)
3 Costas – Greece – security guard – protect buildings (✗)
4 Juan & Rosa – Spain – flight attendants – serve passengers (O)
5 Jacek – Poland – stockbroker – buy and sell stocks and shares (♥♥)

A: Where does Paula come from?
B: She comes from Brazil.
A: What's her job?
B: She's a gardener.
A: What does she do at work?
B: She looks after plants.
A: Does she like her job?
B: Yes, she does.

Key
♥♥ love
♥ like
O not mind
✗ hate

9

• Adverbs of frequency

12 Put the adverbs of frequency in order, then study the examples. Use adverbs of frequency to talk about your daily routine.

100% ┬ always
75% ┼ ....
50% ┼ ....
25% ┼ ....
10% ┼ ....
0% ┴ ....

usually
never
often
always
sometimes
seldom

I **always get up** at 7 o'clock in the morning.
I **am sometimes** late for school.

Listening

13 a) What is each person doing? Listen and write letters in the boxes, as in the example.

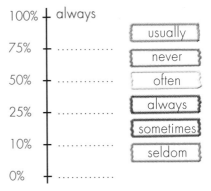

Tony ☐
Bill ☐
Becky ☐
Kate ☐
Matt ☐ C
Laura ☐

b) Ask and answer, as in the example.

A: Is Matt reading a newspaper?
B: No, he isn't. He's ...

c) What are you doing now? What are your friends doing now?

14 Ask and answer, as in the example.

Irene – hairdresser (talk on the phone)
Ron & Alice – journalists (do a crossword)
Sheila – accountant (make a salad)
Bob – vet (do the shopping)

A: What does Irene do at work?
B: She cuts hair.
A: Is she cutting hair now?
B: No, she isn't. She's ...

15 Look at the Browns' notes, then in pairs, ask and answer questions, as in the example.

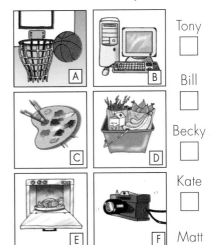

Sunday — 2nd have barbecue
Monday — 3rd see a play
Tuesday — 4th visit parents
Wednesday — 5th play tennis
Thusrday — 6th take dog to the vet
Friday — 7th take children to circus
Saturday — 8th go to a garage sale

S1: Are the Browns having a barbecue on Tuesday?
S2: No, they aren't. They're visiting their parents. Are the Browns ...

16 Put the verbs in brackets into the present simple or the present continuous. Which verbs refer to the present/future?

1 We usually .... (go) to school on foot.
2 Look at David. He .... (make) lunch.
3 Josh .... (play) tennis this afternoon.
4 They .... (fly) to Madrid next Friday.
5 I .... (go) sailing. Fancy joining me?
6 .... (you/want) to try rock climbing while you're here?
7 He .... (not/like) fishing.
8 Jane .... (look for) a new flat at the moment.

Lesson 3 (pp. 10 - 11)

* • Check Ss' HW (10').
  • Ss, in pairs, act out the dialogues in Exs 6c, 9 and 11.

12 • Read the list of adverbs, then help Ss put them in order. Read the examples aloud. Ask Ss to underline the adverbs of frequency. Point out that we use adverbs of frequency to say how often something happens. Ask Ss to underline the verbs in the examples. Explain that adverbs of frequency are put before the main verb (*I always get up early*) but after an auxiliary or modal verb (*I am always getting into trouble*).

ANSWER KEY

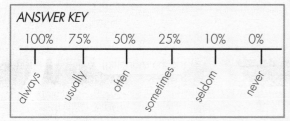

| 100% | 75% | 50% | 25% | 10% | 0% |

always usually often sometimes seldom never

• Ask Ss to think of daily routine activities (*get up, get dressed, have a shower, have breakfast/lunch/dinner etc*). Write them on the board. Allow Ss two minutes to think of their daily routine. Various Ss report back to the class. Point out that Ss should use adverbs of frequency.

SUGGESTED ANSWER KEY

*I **always** get up at 7 o'clock in the morning. I get dressed, have breakfast then I catch the 7:30 bus to school. We **usually** arrive at 7:50. Lessons start at 8:10. We **usually** have a break for lunch at 12:00. We **always** eat at the school canteen. Lessons start again at 1:00. I leave school at about 3:30. Mum **usually** picks me up from school. When we get home, I **often** have a snack, then I do my homework. We **usually** have dinner at 7:30, then I **sometimes** read a book or watch TV. I **never** go out on weekdays. I usually go to bed at about 8:30 in the evening.*

13 a) Ask Ss to look at the pictures and identify the action shown in each (*play basketball, play computer games, paint a picture etc*). Explain the task, then play the cassette twice. Ss listen and match the people to the activities. Check Ss' answers orally in class.

ANSWER KEY

| Tony | D | Becky | G | Matt | C |
| Bill | H | Kate | B | Laura | A |

TAPESCRIPT

• Tony is having a party tonight, so he needs to buy lots of food. He's in the supermarket now doing some shopping.
• Bill loves football. His favourite team is Leeds United. He's watching them now, in a match on TV.
• Becky is interested in the news. She is reading a newspaper. She reads one every day.
• Kate is playing on her computer. She has to fight all the aliens and find the magic stone to win the game.
• Matt is an artist. He is painting a beautiful picture of a lake. He wants to give the picture to his mum.
• Laura enjoys playing sports. Right now, she is playing basketball in the park with her friends.

b) Read out the example. Ss, in pairs, act out similar dialogues. Check Ss' performance, then choose some pairs to report back to the class.

SUGGESTED ANSWER KEY

B: .... painting a picture.
A: Is Kate taking photographs?
B: No, she isn't. She's playing on her computer.
A: Is Bill reading a newspaper?
B: No, he isn't. He's watching TV.
A: Is Laura doing some shopping?
B: No, she isn't. She's playing basketball.
A: Is Becky painting a picture?
B: No, she isn't. She's reading a newspaper.
A: Is Tony cooking dinner?
B: No, he isn't. He's doing some shopping.

c) *SUGGESTED ANSWER KEY*

I'm having an English lesson now.
My friends are doing an exercise.   etc.

14 • Read out the prompts. Ask Ss: *What does Irene do?* (*She's a hairdresser.*) Ask: *What does she do at work?* (*She cuts hair.*) Refer Ss to Ex.8 p.8 in the Student's Book if they have difficulty describing each person's job. Choose two Ss to read out the example.
• Ss, in pairs, act out similar dialogues. Check Ss' answers round the class, then have some pairs report back to the class.

ANSWER KEY

B: ... talking on the phone.
A: What do Ron and Alice do at work?
B: They report the news.
A: Are they reporting the news now?
B: No. they aren't. They are doing a crossword.
A: What does Sheila do at work?
B: She keeps financial accounts.
A: Is she keeping financial accounts now?
B: No, she isn't. She's making a salad.
A: What does Bob do at work?
B: He looks after sick animals.
A: Is he looking after sick animals now?
B: No, he isn't. He's doing the shopping.

15 • Explain that the notes show the Browns' fixed arrangements for next week. Read out the notes and explain any unknown words.
• Read the example, then Ss, one after the other continue the exercise.

SUGGESTED ANSWER KEY

S2:   ... seeing a play on Monday?
S3:   Yes, they are. Are the Browns having a barbecue on Wednesday?
S4:   No, they aren't. They're playing tennis. Are the Browns taking the dog to the vet on Thursday? etc.

16 Allow Ss two minutes to do the exercise. Check Ss' answers on the board.

ANSWER KEY

1 go (P)	4 are flying (F)	7 doesn't like (P)
2 is making (P)	5 'm going (F)	8 is looking for (P)
3 is playing (F)	6 Do you want (F)	

17 • Ask Ss to look at the pictures and try to guess what job the person in the pictures does *(a diver, an underwater stuntman)*.
  • Ss look at the pictures more closely and in pairs identify what each picture shows. Check Ss' answers.

> *ANSWER KEY*
>
> someone swimming underwater   pict. 1
> diving equipment   pict. 3
> kayaking   pict. 2
> someone wearing a wetsuit and a helmet   pict. 1

18 • Allow Ss two minutes to read sentences 1 to 5.
  • Play the cassette. Ss listen and underline the correct word.
  • Check Ss' answers.

> *ANSWER KEY*
>
> 1 surveying   3 computer   5 boring
> 2 7 am   4 long

19 • Read aloud statements 1 - 5. Allow Ss about four minutes to read the text silently and correct the statements. Check Ss' answers around the class.

> *ANSWER KEY*
>
> 2 Wrong! He doesn't drive to work. He rides his bike to work.
> 3 Wrong! He doesn't leave the office at 12 am. He leaves the office at 1 pm.
> 4 Wrong! Alain doesn't enjoy going skiing in his spare time. He enjoys going water-skiing, kayaking and snorkelling.
> 5 Wrong! Alain doesn't hate working underwater. He loves it.

  • Help Ss to explain the highlighted words, by giving examples, synonyms or in Ss' L1.
    e.g. **typical**: ordinary
  • Play the cassette again. Ss listen and follow the lines, then individual Ss read aloud from the article.

20 Write the headings on the board and elicit answers from Ss to complete the table *(What time does Alain wake up? How does he get to work? What times does he start work? etc)*. Ss copy the completed table into their notebooks, then use their notes to talk about Alain Pepin.

> *SUGGESTED ANSWER KEY*
>
> **daily routine:**
> get up at 7am; have breakfast; ride his bike to work; start work at 8am; spend all morning in front of his computer; leave office at 1pm; have lunch; pack his equipment and set off; set up the equipment; get into the water
>
> **free-time activities:**
> water-skiing; kayaking; snorkelling; spend time planning/practising/training for his stunts

feelings about working underwater:
loves it; enjoys it; feels full of energy; has a great sense of achievement.

> *... he rides his bike to work. Alain starts work at 8am. He spends all morning in front of his computer. He leaves the office at 1pm. He has lunch, then he packs his equipment and sets off to the location of the stunt. He sets up the equipment and gets into the water.*
> *In his free time Alain goes water-skiing, kayaking and snorkelling. He also spends time planning, practising and training for his stunts.*
> *Alain loves working underwater. He feels full of energy and has a great sense of achievement.*

> **Suggested Homework**
>
> 1 **Copy:** any of the paragraphs in Ex. 19 (p. 11)
> 2 **Vocabulary:** highlighted words Ex. 19 (p. 11)
> 3 **Reading aloud:** Ex. 19 (p. 11)
> 4 **Dictation:** highlighted words Ex. 19 (p. 11)
> 5 **Act out:** Ex. 14 (p. 10)
> 6 **Speaking:** Ss should be able to talk about Alain Pepin by looking at their notes (Ex. 20, p. 11)

Listening & Reading

17 Look at the pictures. Which shows: someone swimming underwater ......; diving equipment ......; kayaking ......; someone wearing a wetsuit and a helmet ......;

18 🎧 Listen and underline the correct word.

1 In the morning, he works in a **surveying/surfing** office.
2 A typical summer day for Alain starts around **8 am/7am**.
3 Alain spends all morning in front of his **equipment/computer**.
4 A photo shoot usually takes a **long/short** time to complete.
5 Working underwater can be a bit **funny/boring** in the winter.

19 Read the interview and correct the statements 1 to 5, as in the example. Then, explain the highlighted words.

1 Alain leads a normal life. *Wrong! Alain doesn't lead a normal life. He leads a double life.*
2 He drives to work.
3 He leaves the office at 12 am.
4 Alain enjoys going skiing in his spare time.
5 Alain hates working underwater.

Speaking

20 Read the article again and make notes under the following headings, then talk about Alain Pepin.

- daily routine - free-time activities
- feelings about working underwater

Alain gets up at 7 am. He has breakfast, then ...

a real-life PERSON

You could say that Alain Pepin leads a double life. In the morning he works in a surveying office, doing clerical work, but in the afternoons and at weekends he does something much more exciting — he is an *underwater stuntman*. In this week's article he tells us what a *typical* summer day in his life is like.

What time do you get up?
A *typical* summer day for me starts around 7 am. I have breakfast and ride my bike to work. I start work at 8 am. I spend all morning in front of my computer working until *lunchtime*.

What do you do after work?
Well, I leave the office at 1 pm and have lunch. If the weather is fine, I pack my equipment and set off to the location of the stunt. When I get there, I set up the equipment and get into the water. This is when the fun starts. I move about in and under the water in a wetsuit and helmet performing tricks. It's quite tiring though, because each stunt is different and takes a different length of time. A photo shoot usually takes a long time to complete because everything has to be perfect.

What do you do when you are not diving?
I enjoy going water-skiing, kayaking and snorkelling, I spend most of my spare time, however, planning, practising and training for my stunts.

How do you like working underwater?
I love it. It can be a bit boring in the winter, though, when the weather is cold. It is difficult to get a swimming pool all to myself so I can practise. But when I'm diving, I really enjoy it. Every time I come home after work, I feel full of energy and I have a great sense of achievement.

Vocabulary Practice

21 Fill in the correct word from the list, then make sentences using the completed collocations.

- financial • photo • spare • underwater
- report • sense • lead • sit • clerical
- perform • part-time

1 to .... a double life
2 a(n) .... stuntman
3 a(n) .... shoot
4 to .... in front of a computer
5 .... work
6 .... time
7 to .... tricks
8 a(n) .... job
9 a great .... of achievement
10 .... accounts
11 to .... the news

22 Fill in: *about, in, from, at, to, of, for, after.*

1 to work .... an office; 2 .... weekends; 3 he's .... Brazil; 4 to think .... something; 5 a lot .... fun; 6 a typical day .... his life; 7 to work .... nine .... five; 8 to stay .... home; 9 to be full .... energy; 10 to look .... sb (= search); 11 to wait .... sb; 12 to look .... sick people

23 Fill in the correct word.

1 What is a t _ _ _ _ _ _ _ day like in the life of a secretary? (ordinary)
2 She works from 9am to m _ _ _ _ _ _, then she has a break for lunch. (noon)
3 Stella l _ _ _ _ _ a normal life. (has)
4 It takes a long time to c _ _ _ _ _ _ _ _ a photo shoot. (finish)
5 Let me i _ _ _ _ _ _ _ _ _ myself. I'm Ralph Barren. (present)
6 Nurses l _ _ _ a _ _ _ _ _ sick people. (take care of)

24 Vocabulary Revision Game: In teams, make sentences with the words/phrases in the list.

- seldom • introduce ourselves
- don't you mind • going sailing
- start work • a break
- full of energy • spare time
- fancy • this way
- where ... from
- meet friends • is barking
- the fun starts
- go horse riding
- quacking • wooden furniture
- I'm good at • set off

Communication

• Giving personal information

25 Listen and fill in the missing words, then use the prompts to act out similar dialogues.

A: What's your 1) ....?
B: Ricky.
A: And your 2) ....?
B: Connors.
A: Can you 3) .... that, please?
B: C - O - double N - O - R - S.
A: What 4) .... are you, Ricky?
B: I'm **American**.
A: Where are you 5) .... in **America**?
B: I'm from **California**.

- Anita Eder - Austria - Vienna
- Pierre Durall - France - Dieppe
- Keiko Miaggi - Japan - Tokyo
- Velia Rabal - Spain - Barcelona
- Rosa Ferès - Brazil - Brasilia
- Fernado Lopez - Chile - Santiago

Pronunciation (word stress)

26 Listen and underline the syllable of each word where the stress is. Listen again and repeat.

teacher - doctor - assistant - secretary - carpenter - journalist - hairdresser - accountant - designer - architect - stuntman - footballer - receptionist

Game

Choose one student to be the leader. He/She chooses one of the places: at school/work/the seaside, in the bedroom/kitchen/garden/living room etc. The class, in teams, try to guess what he/she is doing now. The team which guesses correctly gets one point. Choose another student and continue the game. The team with the most points is the winner.

e.g. *Leader: I'm in the park. What am I doing? Guess.*
Team A S1: Are you riding your bike?
Leader: No, I'm not. etc

Lesson 4 (pp. 12 - 13)

* Check Ss' HW (10').

21 • Allow Ss three minutes to fill in the correct word. Check Ss' answers round the class.

> **ANSWER KEY**
>
> | | | | |
> |---|---|---|---|
> | 1 lead | 5 clerical | 9 sense |
> | 2 underwater | 6 spare | 10 financial |
> | 3 photo | 7 perform | 11 report |
> | 4 sit | 8 part-time | |

• Ss make sentences using the completed collocations as they appear in the list.
  e.g. S1: Alain Pepin **leads a double life.**
       S2: He is an **underwater stuntman.** etc.

22 • Allow Ss two to three minutes to fill in the correct preposition. Check Ss' answers round the class.

> **ANSWER KEY**
>
> | | | | |
> |---|---|---|---|
> | 1 in | 4 about/of | 7 from, to | 10 for |
> | 2 at | 5 of | 8 at | 11 for |
> | 3 from | 6 in | 9 of | 12 after |

• As an extension Ss make sentences using the phrases as they appear in the list.
  e.g. S1: Alain Pepin works **in an office** in the mornings.
       S2: **At weekends,** he likes going water-skiing. etc.

23 • Allow Ss two to three minutes to fill in the correct word. Check Ss' answers round the class.

> **ANSWER KEY**
>
> | | | |
> |---|---|---|
> | 1 typical | 3 leads | 5 introduce |
> | 2 midday | 4 complete | 6 look after |

24 Ss, in teams, make sentences using the words/phrases in the order they appear in the list. Each correct sentence gets 1 point. The team with the most points is the winner.
e.g. Team A S1: He **seldom** goes water-skiing.
     Team B S1: Let us **introduce ourselves.** etc

25 Allow Ss two minutes to read the dialogue. Play the cassette. Ss listen and fill in the missing words. Check Ss' answers by asking them to read out from the dialogue.

> **ANSWER KEY**
>
> 1 name 2 surname 3 spell 4 nationality 5 from

• Play the cassette again. Ss listen and follow the lines, then Ss read the dialogue aloud in pairs.
• Read out the prompts and elicit from Ss the nationalities that match the countries mentioned in the prompts. Write them on the board: *(Austria - Austrian; France - French; Japan - Japanese; Spain - Spanish; Brazil - Brazilian; Chile - Chilean).*
• Ss, in pairs, act out similar dialogues using the prompts. Check Ss' performance around the class.

e.g. A: What's your name?
     B: Anita.
     A: And your surname?
     B: Eder.
     A: Can you spell that, please?
     B: E - D - E - R.
     A: What nationality are you, Anita?
     B: I'm Austrian.
     A: Where are you from in Austria?
     B: I'm from Vienna. etc

Competition Revision Game

• Revise the following nationality adjectives, checking spelling on the board: *Poland - Polish; China - Chinese; Turkey - Turkish; America - American; Portugal - Portuguese; Greece - Greek; England - English; Scotland - Scottish; Ireland - Irish; Italy - Italian; Mexico - Mexican; India - Indian; Canada - Canadian; Argentina - Argentinian; Egypt - Egyptian;* etc. Ss copy these into their notebooks. Ss close their books. Divide the class into two teams. Say the name of a country. Ss, in teams, say the matching nationality. Each correct answer gets 1 point. The team with the most points is the winner.
  e.g. Teacher: Poland   Teacher: China
       Team A S1: Polish   Team B S1: Chinese etc.

26 • Play the cassette. Ss listen and underline the stressed syllable in each word. Check Ss' answers.
• Play the cassette again. Ss listen and repeat individually.

> **ANSWER KEY**
>
> *doc*tor – *assis*tant – *sec*retary – *car*penter – *jour*nalist – *hair*dresser – ac*coun*tant – de*sign*er – *arch*itect – *stunt*man – *foot*baller – re*cep*tionist

Game (p. 12)

Ss play the game as described in the Student's Book. Ss can also play the game in teams.
e.g. Leader: I'm in the kitchen. What am I doing? Guess.
     Team A S1: Are you reading a newspaper?
     Leader: No, I'm not.
     Team B S1: Are you eating a sandwich?
     Leader: No, I'm not.
     Team A S2: Are you cooking?
     Leader: Yes, I am.

Possible verbs for each place:

at school:	have a lesson, do an exercise, write on the board, read out a text etc.
at work:	type a letter, make coffee, answer the phone, talk on the phone, make photocopies, etc.
at the seaside:	lie on the beach, swim, play with a ball, make a sandcastle etc
in the bedroom:	sleep, lie on my bed, listen to music, watch TV, tidy, make my bed, do my homework etc
in the kitchen:	cook, make a salad, lay the table, wash the dishes, drink water, make an omelette etc
in the garden:	plant flowers, play with the dog, sit on the grass, play football, cut the grass etc
in the living room:	watch TV, talk on the phone, listen to the radio, sit on the sofa, drink tea etc
in the park:	walk, play football, play basketball, feed the ducks, fly a kite, walk the dog, ride my bike, etc

27 • Explain to Ss that they are going to read a letter someone sent to his friend giving news. Ask Ss: *What kind of news might he give? (About his new house; school exams; what he was doing while on holiday.)* etc

• Explain to Ss that they are going to read a letter from which four sentences have been removed. Point out that these sentences are topic sentences i.e. sentences which introduce each paragraph. Allow Ss three minutes to read the letter and fill in the correct sentence. Point out that one sentence does not fit the letter. Check Ss' answers by asking individual Ss to read from the letter.

ANSWER KEY

1 C   2 A   3 E   4 B

---

28 a) Read the questions aloud and help Ss answer them. Before Ss do item 5, explain what opening/closing remarks are, i.e. sentences we use to start (opening) or end (closing) a letter.

SUGGESTED ANSWER KEY

1 The letter is from Ryan to Angie.
2 It starts with: Dear Angie, and it ends with: Love, Ryan. Point out that a friendly letter starts with **Dear + your friend's first name,** and it ends with **Love,/Yours,/Best wishes, your first name**.
3 Phrases to be ticked: Yours; Best wishes; Lots of love
4 Paragraph two is about Ryan's daily routine. He uses the present simple. Paragraph three is about Ryan's fixed arrangements. He uses the present continuous with a future meaning.
5 Paragraph one includes Ryan's opening remarks. Paragraph four includes Ryan's closing remarks.

---

b) Explain to Ss what a topic sentence is, then help Ss identify them in Ryan's letter. Help Ss suggest other appropriate ones.

ANSWER KEY

Topic sentences in Ryan's letter.

1 Hi, how are you?
2 There's so much to do here that I don't know where to begin.
3 We're all looking forward to this weekend.
4 Well, that's all for now.

Suggested alternative topic sentences

1 How's it going?
2 We have lots of activities throughout the day.
3 I can't wait until this weekend.
4 That's all my news.

---

29 Explain that the advertisement is for a summer camp. Allow Ss two minutes to read the advertisement silently, then Ss answer the questions.

ANSWER KEY

1 In the morning we go sailing, we have Drama classes and we go water-skiing.
In the afternoon we go swimming and play water sports. In the evening we play games around the campfire or go to the theatre.
2 This weekend we are visiting a ranch on Saturday and on Sunday we are having a big party.

---

30 Explain the task to Ss, pointing out that they should use the text in Ex. 27 as a model as well as their answers to Ex. 29. Read out the plan. Help individual Ss complete the task orally, then assign it as written HW.

SUGGESTED ANSWER KEY

Dear Roberta,

How's it going? I'm having an exciting time at summer camp. The place is quiet and the weather is fantastic.

Every day we have lots of activities. In the mornings I go sailing. I also have Drama classes, then I go water-skiing. At noon we have a delicious lunch. In the afternoon we go swimming or play water sports. In the evening we play games around the campfire. Sometimes we go to the theatre.

This weekend is really special. We are visiting a ranch on Saturday and spending the whole day there. On Sunday we're having a big party with lots to eat and drink.

Well, that's all for now. See you soon.
Yours,
Susie

---

31 Read the sentences aloud and help Ss fill in the correct number.

ANSWER KEY

• 800   • 18,000   • 70,000

(Suggested Homework)

1 **Copy:** dialogue in Ex. 25 (p. 12)
2 **Vocabulary:** Exs 21, 22, 24 (p. 12)
3 **Reading aloud:** Ex. 25 (p. 12)
4 **Dictation:** Exs 21, 22, 24 (p. 12)
5 **Act out:** Ex. 25 (p. 12)
6 **Writing:** Ex. 30 (p. 13)

(Lesson 5)

Check Ss' HW.
Workbook: Unit 1
              Click on Grammar 1

Writing (a letter to a friend giving news)

27 Read the letter and fill in the appropriate topic sentences. There is one sentence you do not need.

A There's so much to do here that I don't know where to begin.
B Well, that's all for now.
C Hi, how are you?
D It's the end of my first week here.
E We're all looking forward to this weekend.

Dear Angie,

[1] I'm having a great time here at summer camp. The place is lovely and the weather is good.

[2] In the mornings we have Art lessons or we go swimming. In the afternoons we go canoeing or horse riding. Everyone looks forward to the evenings, when we all sit together around the campfire. We usually have a barbecue, sing songs or tell stories. It's just great.

[3] We've got lots of exciting plans. On Saturday we're going rafting. We're spending the whole day on the river and having a picnic lunch. Then on Sunday we're having a big party with live music and lots of food and drink. I can't wait!

[4] See you in a couple of weeks.

Love,
Ryan

28 a) Read the letter again and answer the questions.

1 Who is the letter from? Who is the letter to?
2 How does the letter start/finish?
3 Which of the phrases can you use instead of *Love*? Tick (✔) Yours ...., Thanks again ...., Best wishes ...., Lots of love ...., Fine ....
4 Which paragraphs are about Ryan's daily routine/ fixed arrangements? What tenses does Ryan use in these paragraphs?
5 Which paragraphs include Ryan's opening/ closing remarks?

b) *A topic sentence starts a paragraph. It is the summary of the paragraph or an introduction to the topic of the paragraph.* **Replace the topic sentences in the letter with other appropriate ones.**

29 Imagine you are at Sunrise summer camp. Read the advertisement, then choose activities from the advertisement to answer the questions.

SUNRISE SUMMER CAMP
California - America

morning activities: sailing, Drama classes, water-skiing

afternoon activities: swimming, playing water sports

evening activities: play games around campfire, go to theatre

This weekend: Sat: visit a ranch
Sun: have a big party

1 What do you do at the camp: in the morning? in the afternoon? in the evening?
2 What are you doing this weekend?

30 Use your answers from Ex. 29 and the plan below to write a letter to a friend of yours telling him/her your news. (80 words) Use the letter in Ex. 27 as a model.

Plan

Dear (friend's first name),
Introduction
(Para 1) *opening remarks - what the place/ weather is like*
Main Body
(Para 2) *what you do every day*
(Para 3) *what you are doing this weekend*
Conclusion
(Para 4) *closing remarks*
Yours,
(your first name)

31 Fill in the correct number: *18,000, 70,000, 800.*

do you know...?

• In Britain there is one doctor for every .... people.
• In Afghanistan there is only one doctor for every .... people.
• In Ethiopia there is one doctor for every .... people.

2 Then and Now!

Lead-in

1 **a)** Which picture shows: fields; someone jet-skiing; people foxhunting; a car park; huge buildings; people travelling by coach; a woman wearing a long dress; a polluted lake; a clean river?

b) Make sentences, as in the examples.

- travelled by **coach / car**
- lived in **houses / blocks of flats**
- rivers were **clean / dirty**
- went **foxhunting / jet-skiing**
- women wore **long dresses / jeans**

People travelled by coach 300 years ago.
People didn't travel by car 300 years ago.

2 What is life like nowadays?
How do people travel?
Where do they live?
What do they wear?
What are their favourite free-time activities?

3 🎧 Listen and repeat.

- Yes, but not only that.
- That sounds quite boring, though.
- I'm glad I wasn't around then.
- Did you have a happy childhood?
- But I love every minute of it.
- It's not an original, though.
- Can you imagine living in those days?
- That's true.

1

2

3

4

5

- Read out the examples. Explain that *didn't travel* is the negative form of *travelled* and write it on the board next to *travelled*. Ask Ss to say the negative form of the rest of the verbs which are on the board, and write them on the board, too. Elicit how the negative is formed (**didn't + infinitive of the verb**).
- Point out that *were* does not follow this pattern to form its negative *(weren't)*.
- Elicit the interrogative forms of these verbs the same way as you did with the negative and write them on the board. *(Did they travel? Did they live? Were they? Did they go? Did they wear?)*
- Ask Ss to read the examples and underline the past time adverbial *(300 years ago)*. Say various time adverbials. Ss say which are used in the present and which in the past.
  Suggested list: now, every day, at the moment, yesterday, last week
- Ss use the prompts to make sentences, as in the example.

ANSWER KEY

- *People lived in houses 300 years ago.*
- *People didn't live in blocks of flats 300 years ago.*
- *The rivers were clean 300 years ago.*
- *The rivers weren't dirty 300 years ago.*
- *People went foxhunting 300 years ago.*
- *People didn't go jet-skiing 300 years ago.*
- *Women wore long dresses 300 years ago.*
- *Women didn't wear jeans 300 years ago.*

2 Read the questions. Ss answer.

SUGGESTED ANSWER KEY

Life is very modern, fast etc nowadays.
People travel by car, aeroplane, bus or ship.
People live in blocks of flats, villas, cottages etc.
People wear jeans, T-shirts, shirts etc.
Their favourite free-time activities are jet-skiing, surfing the net, jogging, scuba diving etc.

3 Play the cassette. Ss listen and repeat, chorally or individually. Present each phrase/sentence by giving examples.
e.g. **But I love every minute of it.** (Say to Ss: *I love jet-skiing. I often go in the summer with my friends. It's quite dangerous, but I love every minute of it.*)

Objectives

Vocabulary: family members; lifestyles; days of the week; possessions; past routines/habits/activities; dates
Reading: reading for specific information
Listening: listening for gist; listening for lexical items & verb phrases; listening for specific information
Speaking: talking about past habits/routines
Communication: talking about past activities
Pronunciation: /e/ pronounced or silent
Grammar: past simple (regular & irregular verbs); used to; prepositions of place (at, on, in); possessive case; possessive adjectives
Project: a diary entry
Writing: a biography

Lesson 1 (pp. 14 - 15)

1 a) • Ask Ss to look at the pictures on pp. 14 – 15 and say which show life in the past and which show life in the present. Ask Ss to guess what time period in the past the pictures depict (17th – 18th century).
- Read out the words/phrases in the list one at a time. Ss match them to the pictures.

ANSWER KEY

fields – pict. 2
someone jet-skiing – pict. 5
people foxhunting – pict. 2
a car park – pict. 8
huge buildings – pict. 4
people travelling by coach – pict. 6
a woman wearing a long dress – picts 1, 6
a polluted lake – pict. 7
a clean river – pict. 3

b) • Read out the prompts. Ask Ss to highlight, using their text markers, the verb forms which are in the past. Write them on the board. Ask: *When did all these things happen? Now? (In the past.)*
- Ask Ss which verbs are regular past forms i.e. verb + ed *(travelled, lived)* and which are irregular *(were, went, wore)*. Ss then say the relevant verbs in the present simple form. If Ss have difficulty, ask them to look at the Irregular Verbs section in the Student's Book.
- As an extension ask Ss to look at the Irregular Verbs section for two to three minutes, then close their books. Divide the class into two teams. Say verbs in the infinitive form. Teams, in turn, say the corresponding past form. Each correct answer gets 1 point. The team with the most points is the winner.
  e.g. Teacher: drive
  Team A S1: drove
  Teacher: go
  Team B S1: went   etc

4 Explain the task, then play the cassette. Ss listen to the dialogues and match them to the topics. Check Ss' answers.

> **ANSWER KEY**
>
> 1 C   2 A   3 B

5 a) Read sentences 1 to 3 aloud. Allow Ss three to four minutes to read the dialogues silently and mark the sentences *Yes* or *No*. Check Ss' answers, then elicit the meaning of the words/phrases in bold, asking Ss to give examples or explanations in their L1.
  e.g. **childhood:** early years of life
      times: experiences   etc

> **ANSWER KEY**
>
> 1 Yes   2 Yes   3 No

b) Play the cassette for Ex. 4 again. Ss listen and follow the lines, then Ss take roles and read the dialogues aloud.

c) Allow Ss two minutes to quickly scan the dialogues and highlight the phrases/sentences using their text markers, then say who said each one.

> **ANSWER KEY**
>
> Ted said, "Yes, but not only that."
> Ann said, "That sounds quite boring, though."
> Ann said, "I'm glad I wasn't around then."
> Linda said, "Did you have a happy childhood?"
> Danny said, "But I love every minute of it."
> Tim said, "It's not an original, though!"
> Bill said, "Can you imagine living in those days?"
> Tim said, "That's true."

Memory Game
Ask Ss to look at the phrases/sentences in Ex. 3 for two minutes. Ss then close their books and, in teams, try to remember as many of them as possible. Each correct phrase/sentence gets 1 point. The team with the most points is the winner.

> **Suggested Homework**
>
> 1 **Copy:** dialogue C (p. 15)
> 2 **Vocabulary:** Ex. 3 (p. 14) and words in bold in Ex. 5a (p. 15)
> 3 **Reading aloud:** any dialogues A - C (p. 15).
>   (Point out that Ss practise *reading aloud* at home using the S's cassette/audio CD.)
> 4 **Dictation:** phrases/sentences from Ex. 3 (p. 14)
> 5 **Speaking:** a) Ss should be able to make sentences about life then & now by looking at the pictures on pp. 14 - 15
>   b) Ss memorise any five sentences from Ex. 3 (p. 14)

Listening and Reading

4 🎧 Listen and match the dialogues to the topics.

1 life in the 17th century ☐
2 free-time activities in the past ☐
3 a person's lifestyle then and now ☐

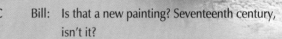

5 a) Read the dialogues and mark the sentences 1 to 3 Yes or No, then explain the words in bold.

1 People used to go hunting in the past. ☐
2 Danny had a great time as a child. ☐
3 People travelled by train in the 17th century. ☐

A

Ann: Why are the people in this painting wearing red jackets?

Ted: Oh, in those days, people used to go hunting and those are the clothes they wore.

Ann: What did they hunt?

Ted: Foxes. In the past foxhunting was a popular sport, but the hunts themselves were **social occasions**, too.

Ann: Really? You **mean** that's what people did **for fun**?

Ted: Yes, but not only that. They used to go for walks and had picnics by the rivers.

Ann: That sounds quite boring, though.

Ted: Perhaps to you, because you're **used to** playing on your computer or rollerblading in the park.

Ann: Yeah. I'm glad I wasn't around then.

B

Linda: So, Danny, could you tell me a little about yourself? Were you born in London?

Danny: No, **I was born** in Cumbria, but we moved to London when I was twelve years old.

Linda: Did you have a happy **childhood**?

Danny: Oh yes! We didn't have much money then, but we had some great **times**. We lived in a small village and every weekend we went **camping** by the **lake**.

Linda: How do you spend your weekends now?

Danny: Working in the studio. When I have some free time, though, I go jet-skiing. I really enjoy it.

Linda: Isn't it **dangerous**?

Danny: Yes it is. But I love every minute of it.

C

Bill: Is that a new painting? Seventeenth century, isn't it?

Tim: Yes, I bought it last week. It's not an **original**, though!

Bill: Can you imagine living in those days?

Tim: Yes, I'm sure life was **tough** without electricity, telephones, washing machines ...

Bill: And I bet it used to take days just to travel from one place to another.

Tim: Yeah, imagine – no cars, trains or planes, just coaches.

Bill: At least there was no **pollution** in those days.

Tim: That's true. Rivers were clean, and the air was **pure**.

Bill: You know, maybe life wasn't so bad back then, **after all**!

b) Read out the dialogues in pairs.

c) Read the dialogues again and highlight the phrases/sentences used in Ex. 3. Who said each phrase/sentence?

Vocabulary

- **Family Members & Dates**

6 a) Fill in: *son, husband, mother, cousin, aunt, nephew.*

grandfather (grandad) father	grandmother (grandma) ....
....	daughter
uncle	....
....	wife
cousin	....
....	niece

b) Look at this part of the royal family tree. Now choose five people from the family tree and say when each person was born and when they died.

Queen Victoria was born in 1819. She died in 1901.

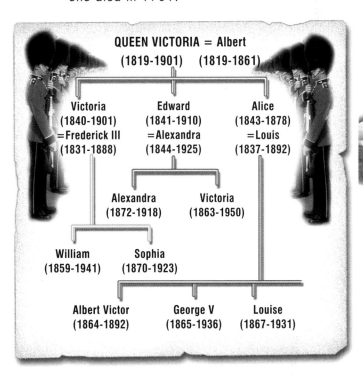

QUEEN VICTORIA = Albert
(1819-1901)   (1819-1861)

Victoria
(1840-1901)
=Frederick III
(1831-1888)

Edward
(1841-1910)
=Alexandra
(1844-1925)

Alice
(1843-1878)
=Louis
(1837-1892)

Alexandra
(1872-1918)

Victoria
(1863-1950)

William
(1859-1941)

Sophia
(1870-1923)

Albert Victor
(1864-1892)

George V
(1865-1936)

Louise
(1867-1931)

c) Look at the royal family tree again and ask and answer questions, as in the example.

A: *When was Queen Victoria born?*
B: *She was born in 1819.*
A: *When did she die?*
B: *She died in 1901.*
A: *How was she related to Sophia?*
B: *She was her grandmother.*   *etc*

Game

Choose a leader. The leader says a name which belongs to a member of his/her family. Students, in teams, try to guess how this person is related to the leader. The team who guesses correctly gets 1 point. Choose another leader and continue the game. The team with most points is the winner.

Leader: Peter.
Team A S1: Is Peter your brother?
Leader: No, he isn't. etc

Grammar

- **Past Simple**

7 a) Read the texts. Which refers to the present? Which refers to the past?

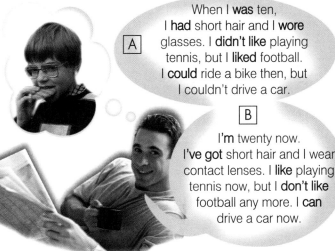

A When I **was** ten, I **had** short hair and I **wore** glasses. I **didn't like** playing tennis, but I **liked** football. I **could** ride a bike then, but I couldn't drive a car.

B I'm twenty now. I**'ve got** short hair and I **wear** contact lenses. I **like** playing tennis now, but I **don't like** football any more. I **can** drive a car now.

b) Use the verbs in bold to complete the table.

PRESENT	PAST
am	....
....	had
wear	....
....	liked
don't like	....
can	....

We use the past simple for actions which happened at a definite time in the past. *He went to the Bahamas last year. (When? Last year.)*
Time expressions used with the past simple: *yesterday, ago, last Monday/week/month/year/ etc, in 1989, etc, a week/month ago etc*

Lesson 2 (pp. 16 - 17)

* • Check Ss' HW (10').
  • Play the Memory Game as described in Lesson 1 Ex. 5c p. 15(T).

6 a) • Allow Ss two minutes to complete the table. Check Ss' answers.

> **ANSWER KEY**
>
> | | |
> |---|---|
> | father | mother |
> | son | daughter |
> | uncle | aunt |
> | husband | wife |
> | cousin | cousin |
> | nephew | niece |

• As an extension ask Ss to make sentences about their family members. Write on the board: *My grandad's name is John.* Underline *grandad's* and explain that *'s* is used to show possession. Ss make sentences about their families.

b) • Read the table. Quickly revise how we read dates. Write the following dates on the board, and next to them write in words.
  e.g. 1819: eighteen nineteen
       1901: nineteen oh one
       2002: two thousand and two
• Read aloud the example, then Ss do the exercise orally in class.

> **SUGGESTED ANSWER KEY**
>
> • Albert was born in 1819. He died in 1861.
> • Edward was born in 1841. He died in 1910.
> • Alexandra was born in 1872. She died in 1918.
> • William was born in 1859. He died in 1941.
> • Louise was born in 1867. She died in 1931. *etc*

• As an extension Ss practise the dates, as in the example.
  e.g. S1: This person died in 1878.
       S2: Alice. This person was born in 1867.
       S3: Louise. This person was born in 1872. etc

c) • Two Ss read out the example. Quickly revise possessive adjectives. Say, then write on the board: *I am John. Ann is my sister.* Underline **I** and **my**. Explain that **my** is a possessive adjective. Say various subject pronouns. Ss say the corresponding possessive adjective.
  e.g. T: you
       S1: your
       T: we
       S2: our   etc

• Present **was related to** in Ss' L1, then Ss, in open pairs, act out similar dialogues.

> **SUGGESTED ANSWER KEY**
>
> A: When was Albert born?
> B: He was born in 1819.
> A: When did he die?
> B: He died in 1861.
> A: How was he related to Queen Victoria?
> B: He was her husband.   etc

Game (p. 16)
Play the game as described in the Student's Book.

7 a) Ss read the two short texts and answer the questions.

> **ANSWER KEY**
>
> A refers to the past   B refers to the present

b) • Focus Ss' attention on the verbs in bold. Help Ss complete the table.

> **ANSWER KEY**
>
> | PRESENT | PAST |
> |---|---|
> | am | was |
> | have | had |
> | wear | wore |
> | like | liked |
> | don't like | didn't like |
> | can | could |

• Point out that *had/could* are the same in all persons.
• Remind Ss that *he/she/it* have a different form in the present simple from the other persons, (*I play, he plays*) but that all past simple forms are the same (*I played, he played*). Refer Ss to the Grammar Reference section for more details.
• Using prompts on the board, elicit from Ss questions and answers about what they do every day.
  Suggested list: wash dishes, do homework, play football, sleep late, brush teeth, walk the dog
  e.g. S1: Do you wash the dishes every day?
       S2: No, I don't. Do you do your homework every day?
       S3: Yes, I do. Do you play football every day?   etc
  Now, ask Ss to do the same using *yesterday* instead of *every day.*
  e.g. S1: Did you wash the dishes yesterday?
       S2: Yes, I did. Did you do your homework yesterday?
       S3: No, I didn't. Did you play football yesterday?   etc
• Read out the theory box. As an extension Ss make true sentences about themselves using the time expressions listed in the box.

8 Read out the prompts and explain the task. Focus Ss' attention on the prepositions of place box (*at, on, in*) and ask them to memorise them. Ask Ss to read the example aloud, then Ss ask and answer rolling questions.

> **SUGGESTED ANSWER KEY**
>
> S3: ...were your parents yesterday morning?
> S4: They were at the shops. Where was your brother last summer?
> S5: He was in the mountains. Where was your uncle last weekend?
> S6: He was at the seaside. Where was your cousin last November?
> S7: She was on holiday. Where were your neighbours last night?
> S8: They were at the sports centre etc.

9 a) Explain the task. Read out the prompts, then play the cassette. Ss listen and put a tick or a cross accordingly. Check Ss' answers, then Ss ask and answer rolling questions.

> **ANSWER KEY**
>
> Items to be ticked: 1, 2, 5, 7
>
> S2: ... a guitar?
> S1: Yes, she did. Did she have a mobile phone?
> S2: No, she didn't. Did she have an alarm clock?
> S1: No, she didn't. Did she have a television?
> S2: Yes, she did. Did she have a computer?
> S1: No, she didn't. Did she have a dog?
> S2: Yes, she did.

TAPESCRIPT
A: Oh, Claire. Look at this old teddy bear. Is this yours?
B: Yes. It's very old. I had it when I was seven.
A: Ah. Did you have this alarm clock when you were seven? It looks old, too.
B: It **is** old, but I didn't have it when I was seven. I didn't have an alarm clock, then.
A: Oh. What did you have when you were seven? Did you have this computer?
B: No, of course not. That's new. I couldn't use a computer when I was seven.
A: Oh. Right. Well, did you have this television?
B: Not **that** one, no. But I did have a television when I was seven. I used to watch my favourite cartoons in my bedroom.
A: Hmm. What about this mobile phone?
B: Don't be silly! I didn't have a mobile phone when I was seven. I had a guitar though.
A: Really? Could you play the guitar when you were seven?
B: No, but my mum wanted me to learn to play a musical instrument so I chose the guitar.
A: What **did** you have when you were seven?
B: Alright, if you really want to know —
A: I do, I do.
B: I had Bones when I was seven.
A: Bones?
B: Yes, Bones. My dog. He's very old, now.

b) Ss, one after the other make true sentences about themselves.

> **SUGGESTED ANSWER KEY**
>
> When I was seven I had a bicycle/a bike/a doll's house etc.
> When I was seven I didn't have a CD player/a video recorder/a computer etc.

10 Present these words: **draw, play chess, hide-and-seek, hopscotch** by miming the actions or giving an example. Ss, then, make true sentences about themselves.

11 a) Read the verbs in the list. Ss say the relevant past tense form. Write them on the board. Ss identify which are regular and which are irregular.

> **ANSWER KEY**
>
> **Regular:** study - studied, travel - travelled, play - played, visit - visited, tidy - tidied, rent - rented
>
> **Irregular:** take - took, go - went, give - gave, write - wrote, lose - lost, break - broke, drink - drank, eat - ate, see - saw

b) Choose two Ss to read out the example, then Ss, one after the other, ask and answer questions.

> **SUGGESTED ANSWER KEY**
>
> S2: ... last go on holiday?
> S3: I went on holiday two years ago. When did you last study English?
> S4: I studied English yesterday. When did you last travel by coach?
> S5: I travelled by coach last month.   etc

12 • Explain the task, then ask Ss to make full questions for items 1 to 7. Then, allow them about two minutes to match the questions to the answers. Check Ss' answers orally in class.

> **ANSWER KEY**
>
> 1 C   3 A   5 D   7 E
> 2 F   4 G   6 B

• Now Ss, in pairs, ask and answer questions using the prompts.

> **ANSWER KEY**
>
> A: When did she leave?
> B: She left on the 2nd of July.
> A: How did she get there?
> B: She got there by plane.
> A: How long did she spend there?
> B: She spent two weeks there.
> A: Where did she stay?
> B: She stayed in a five-star hotel.
> A: How much did she pay?
> B: She paid £500.
> A: What did she take with her?
> B: She took light clothes and a camera.

Suggested Homework

1 **Copy:** texts in Ex. 7a (p. 16)
2 **Vocabulary:** prompts in Exs 10 and 11 (p. 17)
3 **Reading aloud:** Ex. 12 (p. 17)
4 **Dictation:** irregular verbs
5 **Speaking:** Ex. 6c (p. 16), Exs 10 and 11b (p. 17)

Note: Ask Ss to memorise ten irregular past forms every lesson from the Irregular Verbs section.

Speaking

8 Use the prompts to ask and answer questions, as in the example.

Where was/were ...

you	last Sunday
your best friend	two weeks ago
your parents	yesterday morning
your brother/sister	last summer
your uncle/aunt	last weekend
your cousin(s)	last November
your neighbours etc	last night etc

at: school, work, the cinema, the shops, home, a hotel, the sports centre, the seaside, etc
on: holiday, an island, the beach, a farm, etc
in: the mountains, the living room, the classroom, the garden, etc

S1: Where were you last Sunday?
S2: I was at home. Where was your best friend two weeks ago?
S3: He was on holiday. Where ... etc

Listening

9 a) Listen and tick (✓) what Claire had, or cross out (✗) what she didn't have when she was seven. Then, ask and answer questions, as in the example.

1 ✓ teddy bear   2 □ guitar
3 □ mobile phone   4 □ alarm clock
5 □ TV   6 □ computer   7 □ dog

S1: Did Claire have a teddy bear when she was seven?
S2: Yes, she did. Did she have ... etc

Speaking

b) What did/didn't you have when you were seven?

10 What could you/couldn't you do when you were six?

- ride a horse • fly a plane • read • write
- play cricket • dive • swim • count • draw
- play chess • use a computer • use a camera
- cook • play hide-and-seek • play the guitar
- speak English • play football • play hopscotch

I couldn't ride a horse when I was six.
I could write when I was six.

Speaking

11 a) Which of the verbs in the list have regular past forms? Which have irregular past forms?

When did you last ... ?

- take a photo
- go on holiday
- study English
- travel by coach
- play snakes and ladders
- give sb a present
- visit your friend
- play video games

- write a letter
- lose something
- go out with friends
- break something
- drink lemonade
- eat at a restaurant
- see your grandparents
- tidy your room
- rent a video

b) Ask and answer questions, as in the example.

S1: When did you last take a photo?
S2: I took a photo a week ago. When did you ... etc

12 Meg went on holiday last summer. Match the questions to the answers. In pairs, ask and answer questions, as in the example.

1 □ Where/go?	A By plane.
2 □ When/leave?	B £500.
3 □ How/get there?	C Japan.
4 □ How long/spend there?	D In a five-star hotel.
5 □ Where/stay?	E Light clothes and a camera.
6 □ How much/pay?	F 2nd July.
7 □ What/take with her?	G Two weeks.

A: Where did Meg go?
B: She went to Japan.

Listening

13 Listen and write the correct day under each picture, then say what Pat did last week.

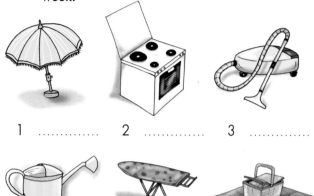

1 .... 2 .... 3 ....

4 .... 5 .... 6 ....

14 a) Read the text and put the verbs into the past simple.

Tom Stevens 1) .... (live) in the country on a big farm. He 2) .... (have) a happy childhood, but he 3) .... (want) to see the world. When Tom 4) .... (leave) school, he 5) .... (decide) to join the navy. He 6) .... (spend) the next ten years sailing around the world. He 7) .... (travel) to lots of places and 8) .... (meet) lots of people. Tom 9) .... (save) his money and one day he 10) .... (say) goodbye to the navy. He 11) .... (go) back to his village, 12) .... (buy) a farm of his own, and 13) .... (start) work. A year later he 14) .... (marry) Carla, his schoolfriend, and they 15) .... (have) three children. Tom and Carla 16) .... (live) happily on their farm and 17) .... (be) lucky enough to have lots of grandchildren.

b) Now complete the questions.

1 "Where .... Tom .... as a boy?" "On a farm."
2 "What .... he .... to do?" "To see the world."
3 "What .... Tom .... to join?" "The navy."
4 How many years .... he .... at sea?" "Ten years."
5 "Where .... he .... when he left the navy?" "Back to his village."
6 "What .... he .... ? "A farm."

7 "Who .... he ....?" "Carla."
8 "How many children .... they ....?" "Three."

- **Project**

Look at the Photo File section and complete Lisa's diary.

- **Used to**

15 Study the examples, then answer the questions.

- Laura **used to have/had** short hair. (state) - She has long hair now.
- Laura **used to walk/walked** to work. (past habit) - She drives to work now.
- Laura **went** to Italy last month. (NOT: Laura ~~used to go~~ to Italy last month.)

1 What do we use to describe an action which happened at a specific time in the past?
2 What can we use to describe past habits/states?

16 a) Sandra was very poor until the day she won £100,000 in a competition. Look at the prompts and ask and answer questions, as in the example.

THEN
- buy second-hand clothes
- live in a small flat
- work long hours
- not go out
- eat in fast-food restaurants

NOW
- buy designer clothes
- live in a huge flat
- have lots of free time
- go to parties
- eat in expensive restaurants

A: *Did Sandra use to buy designer clothes?*
B: *No, she didn't. She used to buy second-hand clothes. etc*

Speaking

b) What about you when you were five?
Did you use to have a nickname?
Where did you use to spend your holidays?
Did you use to have a hobby?
What games did you use to play?
Did you use to have a pet?
What was your favourite toy?
What did you like/hate doing?

18

Lesson 3 (pp. 18 - 19)

* • Check Ss' HW (10').
  • While practising Ex. 6c, Ss have their books open, but they cover the examples.

13 • Ask Ss to look at the pictures and identify the activities each picture suggests.
  (1 go to the beach; 2 cook; 3 clean the house/hoover the carpets; 4 water the plants; 5 do the ironing; 6 go on a picnic)
  • Explain the task. Play the cassette. Ss listen and write the correct day. Check Ss' answers, then individual Ss make sentences about Pat. As an extension, Ss talk about what they did last week.

ANSWER KEY

1 Friday   3 Monday   5 Tuesday
2 Thursday   4 Wednesday   6 Sunday

1 On Monday Pat cleaned the house/hoovered every room.
2 On Tuesday Pat did the ironing.
3 On Wednesday Pat watered the plants/spent the whole afternoon in the garden.
4 On Thursday Pat cooked/spent the whole morning cooking.
5 On Friday Pat went to the beach/took the children to the beach.
6 On Sunday Pat went on a picnic (with her friends).

TAPESCRIPT
A: Hello, Pat. I haven't seen you all week.
B: Well, I've been really busy. I'm very tired now.
A: Oh dear. Tell me all about it.
B: Well, on Monday I had to clean the house. It took hours.
A: Oh, dear.
B: I had to hoover every room. It was exhausting!
A: And what about Tuesday?
B: Oh, on Tuesday I had a pile of ironing to do.
A: Oh, I hate ironing.
B: Me too. Then, on Wednesday I spent the whole afternoon in the garden.
A: Did you water the plants?
B: Yes, it took ages.
A: What about Thursday?
B: Well, on Thursday I spent the whole morning in the kitchen cooking.
A: Why?
B: We had Tom's boss and his wife for dinner.
A: I see. And Friday?
B: Well, on Friday I took the children to the beach. We spent the whole day there.
A: Oh, I bet that was nice.
B: Yes, we had a great time, I spent Saturday at home, but on Sunday we went on a picnic with our friends.
A: Sounds exciting.
B: Yes, it was really nice.

14 a) Present these words: **navy, save, schoolfriend** by giving examples or in Ss' L1. Allow Ss two to three minutes to do the exercise. Check Ss' answers by asking individual Ss to read from the text.

ANSWER KEY

1 lived   7 travelled   13 started
2 had   8 met   14 married
3 wanted   9 saved   15 had
4 left   10 said   16 lived
5 decided   11 went   17 were
6 spent   12 bought

b) Do item 1 with Ss, then Ss do the rest of the exercise. Check Ss' answers while they read out the completed questions.

ANSWER KEY

1 did, live   5 did, go
2 did, want   6 did, buy
3 did, decide   7 did, marry
4 did, spend   8 did, have

Project (p. 18)

Ask Ss to look at the Photo File section and explain what a diary is. Help Ss identify the picture prompts, then Ss complete Lisa's diary orally. Assign this as written HW.
See Photo File section Unit 2 for the Answer Key.

15 • Ss' books closed. Write on the board: *When I was twelve years old I **used to have** long hair. I **didn't use to have** short hair. I have short hair now.*
  Underline *used to*. Explain that we use this structure to talk about past habits or states. Explain that the negative form is *didn't use to* and the interrogative is *Did I use to ...?*
  • Ss' books open. Ask Ss to read the examples, and answer questions 1 and 2.

ANSWER KEY

1 We use the past simple to describe an action which happened at a specific time in the past.
2 We can use 'used to' or the past simple to describe past habits/states.

Write on the board: *I used to wake up early while on holiday last summer. I'm used to waking up early.* Underline **used to wake up** and **'m used to waking up**. Point out that **used to** takes an **infinitive** and refers to the **past**, whereas **'m used to** takes an **-ing form** and refers to the **present**.

16 a) Read out the situation, then go through the prompts and present any unknown words by giving examples or in Ss' L1. Ask two Ss to read out the examples. Then Ss act out similar dialogues in open pairs.

ANSWER KEY

A: Did Sandra use to live in a huge flat?
B: No, she didn't. She used to live in a small flat.
A: Did Sandra use to have lots of free time?
B: No, she didn't. She used to work long hours.
A: Did Sandra use to go to parties?
B: No, she didn't. She didn't use to go out.
A: Did Sandra use to eat in expensive restaurants?
B: No, she didn't. She used to eat in fast-food restaurants.

b) Read the questions, one at a time. Ss answer.

SUGGESTED ANSWER KEY

Yes, I did. My nickname was "Mouse". I spent my holidays on my grandparents' farm. I used to collect shells. I used to play snakes & ladders, hide-and-seek and hopscotch. I had a cat called Molly. My favourite toy was my teddy bear. I liked playing in the park and watching cartoons on TV. I hated eating spaghetti.

17 a) Explain what a fairy tale is. Say: *Peter Pan, Cinderella, Snow White and the Seven Dwarfs* are *fairy tales*. Ask Ss to name any other fairy tales they've heard of or read. Then, Ss answer the questions.

> **SUGGESTED ANSWER KEY**
>
> *I do like reading fairy tales. My favourite one is Peter Pan.*

b) Explain what a fairy is, then Ss do the exercise.

> **ANSWER KEY**
>
> *A   shows a dancing fairy.*
> *B   shows a fairy offering a flower.*
>
> *Ss' own answers. (No, I don't believe in fairies. I used to believe in them when I was little.)*

18 Explain that Ss are going to listen to extracts from Elsie's diary. Read the question, then Ss listen and find the answers. Check Ss' answers.

> **ANSWER KEY**
>
> *Frances - A*
> *Elsie - B*

19 • Allow Ss three to four minutes to read the extracts silently and correct sentences 1 to 5. Check Ss' answers, then help Ss explain the meaning of the words in bold by giving examples, paraphrasing or by giving synonyms/opposites. Ask Ss to check their answers in their dictionaries.
  e.g. **miss:** If you miss sth, you feel sad because you no longer have it or experience it.

> **ANSWER KEY**
>
> *1 Elsie spent every day **by the stream**.*
> *2 Elsie fell into the **stream**.*
> *3 Sir Conan Doyle wrote an article about **the fairies/Elsie and Frances**.*
> *4 Frances and Elsie **weren't** happy about being famous.*
> *5 Elsie **didn't** draw the fairies in the photograph.*

• Play the cassette for Ex. 18 again. Ss listen and follow the lines. Individual Ss read out the extracts.

20 a) Allow Ss two minutes to do the exercise. Check Ss' answers.

> **ANSWER KEY**
>
> | | | |
> |---|---|---|
> | 2 D | 4 C | 6 E |
> | 3 F | 5 A | 7 G |

b) Individual Ss use the sentences to talk about Elsie and the fairies.

> **SUGGESTED ANSWER KEY**
>
> *Elsie moved from Africa to Cottingley, a small village in England. She stayed with her aunt and uncle. Every day she went to the woods with her cousin, Frances. They liked the woods a lot because there were fairies there. One day Uncle Arthur lent them his camera and they took photos of the fairies. Uncle Arthur couldn't believe his eyes. He said that the girls were playing tricks. A famous author, Sir Arthur Conan Doyle, saw the pictures. He wanted to write an article about the girls and the fairies. The article was a great success and the girls became famous. The girls weren't happy though, because every day reporters came to the village to take pictures and interview them.*

(Suggested Homework)

1 **Copy:** any of the extracts from Ex. 19 (p. 19)
2 **Reading aloud:** any three extracts from Ex. 19 (p. 19)
3 **Dictation:** any of the extracts from Ex. 19 (p. 19)
4 **Speaking:** Ex. 20b (p. 19) [Ss should be able to talk with books closed]
5 **Writing:** Project (p. 18)

Reading & Listening

17 a) Do you like reading fairy tales? Which is your favourite? A

b) Look at the pictures. Which shows a dancing fairy? Which shows a fairy offering a flower? Do you believe in fairies? B

18th June, 1917

Dear Diary,
England is very cold. I **miss** the **sunshine** of Africa. Cottingley is a very small village. There isn't much to do here. I'm glad I'm **staying** with Aunt Polly and Uncle Arthur because they're very kind to me, and I have my cousin Frances to play with. We spend every day by the **stream** in the woods watching the fairies.

15th July

Frances and I went down to the stream again today to play, but I **fell** in and got my shoes and **socks wet**. Mother was very **angry** with me and said I mustn't go there again, but I can't **stay away**. I tried to tell her about the fairies but she doesn't **believe** me.

17th July

Good news! Uncle Arthur **lent** us his camera to take photos of the fairies. He couldn't believe his eyes when he saw a photo of me with a fairy offering me a flower! He says Frances and I are **playing tricks** and we can't use his camera again, but I think Mother and Aunt Polly believe us!

12th August

Guess what! A very famous **author** called Sir Arthur Conan Doyle saw our pictures and wants to write an **article** about Frances and me. He wants us to take more pictures of the fairies, too. He's sending a **reporter** to **interview** Frances and me.

30th November

Sir Arthur's article was a **big hit** . It made Frances, me and 'The Cottingley Fairies' famous. I know I should be happy, but I'm not. Every day reporters come to Cottingley to take photos of the village and the **stream**. They always want to ask a lot of questions. I can't **stand** them.

25th December

Frances doesn't like being famous. She wants to tell everyone we never saw the fairies and that it was all a big **joke**. She wants me to say I drew the fairies in the photograph and that they aren't **real**. Everyone knows that I draw and paint very well; but I can't say that — my mother told me it's **wrong** to tell **lies**!

---

18 🔁 Listen and find which picture shows Elsie, and which picture shows Frances.

19 Read the extracts from Elsie's diary, then read the sentences 1 to 5 and correct them. Read again and explain the words in bold.

1 Elsie spent every day on the beach.
2 Elsie fell into the sea.
3 Sir Conan Doyle wrote an article about ghosts.
4 Frances and Elsie were happy about being famous.
5 Elsie drew the fairies in the photograph.

A	Sir Arthur Conan Doyle saw the pictures.
B	1	Elsie moved to Cottingley.
C		They took pictures of the fairies.
D		Elsie and Frances saw fairies in the woods.
E		Sir Conan Doyle wrote an article about the fairies.
F		Elsie and Frances borrowed Uncle Arthur's camera.
G		The girls became famous.

Speaking

20 a) Read the extracts again, and put the sentences in the correct order.

b) Use the sentences above to talk about Elsie and the fairies.

Vocabulary Practice

21 Replace the adjectives in bold with their correct opposite from the list.

• miserable • big • dirty • horrible • small

1 **clean** rivers ≠ ....
2 **huge** buildings ≠ ....
3 **happy** childhood ≠ ....
4 **fantastic** time ≠ ....
5 **small** village ≠ ....

22 Fill in: *to, in, with, by, about, on, at.*

1 to travel .... coach; 2 to be .... holiday; 3 to move .... London; 4 to live .... a house; 5 to be kind .... someone; 6 to work .... the studio; 7 to go camping .... the lake; 8 to be .... home; 9 to be angry .... someone; 10 to write an article ...... someone; 11 to live ...... a farm

23 Fill in the correct word. For each pair of sentences, use the same word twice.

1 a Do you believe in fairies?
   b She couldn't believe her eyes when she opened the door.
2 a She likes .... tennis.
   b Stop .... tricks.
3 a Can you please .... up? I can't see you.
   b Your jokes are horrible. I can't .... them.
4 a I often sleep late and .... the bus to work.
   b I like working here, but I .... my old job.
5 a Josh .... off the ladder and broke his leg.
   b Sharon .... in love with her husband the very moment she saw him.
6 a Can you tell me the .... to the bus station, please?
   b I don't like the .... he talks to me.

24 Fill in the correct word from the list, then make sentences using the collocations.

• great • big • block • five-star • fairy
• popular • famous • play • social • tell

1 .... of flats   6 a .... author
2 .... sport   7 a .... hit
3 .... occasions   8 to .... tricks
4 .... times   9 to .... lies
5 .... hotel   10 .... tales

25 Vocabulary Revision Game: In teams, make sentences using the phrases/sentences below.

• went foxhunting • original • imagine living • sounds boring • was born • moved • pure • great times • pollution • stream • interview • miss • in the woods • lent • can't stand • article • big joke • fairies • much to do

Communication
(past activities)

26 Fill in the missing words, then listen and check. In pairs, use the prompts to act out similar dialogues.

A: 1) .... did you go **on holiday**?
B: I went to **the beach.**
A: 2) .... did you do there?
B: I swam in the sea.
A: Did you enjoy it?
B: 3) ...., I loved it.

• on your birthday – restaurant – eat/pizza
• like/it – no/hate it
• last Saturday – park – feed ducks – enjoy it – yes/like it

Speaking

27 Answer the questions about yourself.

Where were you born?
Where did you grow up?
When did you start school?
When did you learn to write?
When did you learn to read?
What was your favourite subject when you were seven?

Pronunciation
/e/ pronounced or silent

28 Listen and tick (✓). Listen again and repeat.

	pronounced	silent		pronounced	silent
liked			looked		
wanted			rested		
hated			moved		
walked			ended		

Lesson 4 (pp. 20 - 21)

* Check Ss' HW (10').

21 Allow Ss two minutes to do the exercise. Check Ss' answers orally. As an extension, Ss make sentences using the phrases.

ANSWER KEY

1 dirty   3 miserable   5 big
2 small   4 horrible
---

e.g. There used to be **clean rivers** 100 years ago.
There are **dirty rivers** nowadays.
There are **huge buildings** in the area.   etc

22 Allow Ss two minutes to fill in the prepositions. Check Ss' answers orally. Then, Ss make sentences using the phrases.

ANSWER KEY

1 by   5 to   9   with
2 on   6 in   10 about
3 to   7 by   11 on
4 in   8 at
---

e.g. Do you like travelling **by coach**?
John isn't here. He's **on holiday**.

23 Explain the task to Ss, then read out the examples. Ss, in closed pairs, try to find the missing words. Check Ss' answers.

ANSWER KEY

2 playing   5 fell
3 stand   6 way
4 miss
---

24 Allow Ss two minutes to do the exercise. Check Ss' answers, then Ss make sentences using the collocations.

ANSWER KEY

1 block   5 five-star   9   tell
2 popular   6 famous   10 fairy
3 social   7 big
4 great   8 play
---

e.g. I live in a **block of flats**.
Foxhunting was a **popular sport**.

25 Ss in teams make sentences using the words/phrases in the order they appear in the list. Each correct sentence gets one point. The team with the most points is the winner.
e.g. Team A S1: People **went foxhunting** 200 years ago.
Team B S1: This painting is an **original**.   etc.

26
- Allow Ss two minutes to complete the dialogue. Play the cassette. Ss listen and check. Choose two Ss to read out the completed dialogue.
- Ss, in closed pairs, use the prompts to act out similar dialogues. Check Ss' performance around the class.

ANSWER KEY

1 Where   2 What   3 Yes

A: What did you do on your birthday?
B: I went to a restaurant.
A: What did you eat there?
B: I ate pizza.
A: Did you like it?
B: No, I hated it.

A: Where did you go last Saturday?
B: I went to the park.
A: What did you do there?
B: I fed the ducks.
A: Did you enjoy it?
B: Yes, I liked it.
---

27 Allow Ss two minutes to read the questions and prepare their answers. Ss then answer the questions orally in class.

SUGGESTED ANSWER KEY

I was born in London.
I grew up in York.
I started school when I was five.
I learnt to write when I was six.
I learnt to read when I was five.
My favourite subject was Art.
---

28 Play the cassette. Ss listen and tick. Check Ss' answers, then play the cassette again. Ss listen and repeat individually.

ANSWER KEY

	pronounced	silent
liked		✓
wanted	✓	
hated	✓	
walked		✓
looked		✓
rested	✓	
moved		✓
ended	✓	
---

29 a) • Point to the picture and ask Ss to say who this person is (*a famous author who wrote about the Cottingley fairies*). Elicit from Ss what the article can be about (*about his life and his works*). Explain that this piece of writing is a biography and elicit where such pieces of writing can be found (*in an encyclopaedia, a school magazine etc*).

• Allow Ss three minutes to read the article silently and put the paragraphs into the correct order. Check Ss' answers while they read aloud from the article.

ANSWER KEY

1 B	2 D	3 A	4 C

• Elicit the meaning of these words: **poor health, talented, earned, knighthood, medicine, keen, interested in, ghosts** by asking Ss to give examples, opposites or explaining the word in Ss' L1.

e.g. **poor health:** often ill

talented: gifted; having a natural ability to do sth well   etc

b) Explain the task and read out the examples. Ss, one after the other, ask and answer rolling questions.

30 Help Ss match the paragraphs to the headings, then allow them two minutes to prepare their answers for questions 1 to 3. Check Ss' answers.

ANSWER KEY

early years	Para 2
person's name - famous for	Para 1
date of death - comments	Para 4
later years	Para 3

1 Past simple, because Sir Arthur Conan Doyle is no longer alive.
2 The writer begins by talking about Doyle's early years, then moves on to his later years.
3 **First paragraph** - full name of the author and what he is famous for.
   Last paragraph - date of death and age at time of death, final comments, achievements.
---

31 Allow Ss three minutes to read the information about Jules Verne as well as the questions 1 to 9. Play the cassette. Ss listen and underline the correct word. Check Ss' answers, then Ss talk about Jules Verne.

ANSWER KEY

1 Law	4 Michel	7 Intelligent
2 1857	5 Three	8 Science fiction
3 Stockbroker	6 Sailing	9 Seventy-seven

TAPESCRIPT

A: Good evening and welcome to "Famous Lives". Tonight, the famous life we are talking about is that of Jules Verne. With us in the studio is James Hargreaves, whose biography of the famous author is on sale in all good bookshops. Mr Hargreaves, welcome to the programme.
B: Thank you, Tony. And please, call me James.
A: Alright, James. Now, what can you tell us about Jules Verne?
B: Well, Jules Gabriel Verne, to give him his full name, was a great author. He was born in 1828 in Nantes, France, and his many wonderful books, including "A Journey to the Centre of the Earth", "Twenty Thousand Leagues Under the Sea", "Around the World in Eighty Days" and "From Earth to the Moon", are still famous today.
A: Yes, that's true. They're still very popular books. But what about Verne's earlier career?

B: Ah, well. He studied Law in Paris.
A: Law?
B: Yes. His parents wanted him to be a lawyer, you see. But Verne began writing instead, and in 1862 he published his first novel. "Five Weeks in a Balloon". It soon became very successful.
A: I see. That's interesting. Perhaps you could tell us a little about Verne's personal life.
B: Of course. He got married in 1857 to a very wealthy woman named Honorine de Viane. Verne became a stockbroker, but he kept writing. Four years later, he and Honorine had a son, Michel.
A: Hmm. Did Verne have any hobbies?
B: Oh yes. Jules Verne was a world traveller as well as an author. He had three boats and he loved sailing.
A: So he was quite an adventurer.
B: Yes, he was. But I think the most important thing about Jules Verne was that he was a very intelligent man. His fantastic stories predicted many future events and inventions. Verne is known as the grandfather of science fiction.
A: Yes, you're right. I suppose the sad thing is that he didn't live long enough to see all those predictions come true.
B: Hmm, yes. He died in 1905 in Amiens, France, but he was an old man — 77 years old — and he had a full and rewarding life.
A: James Hargreaves, thank you for joining us on "Famous Lives".
B: It was my pleasure.
A: We'll be back next week, when Josie Jordan will be here to tell us ...

32 Present the plan and remind Ss that they should use the article in Ex. 29 as a model. Ensure that Ss can complete the task orally, then assign it as written HW.

SUGGESTED ANSWER KEY

Jules Gabriel Verne was known as the grandfather of science fiction. He was a great writer and wrote many books including 'Journey to the Centre of the Earth', 'Twenty Thousand Leagues Under the Sea', 'From Earth to the Moon' and 'Around the World in Eighty Days' which are still famous today.

Verne was born in 1828 in Nantes, in France. He studied Law in Paris, but instead of becoming a lawyer, he began writing. He was a world traveller as well as an author. He had three boats and loved sailing.

Jules got married in 1857 to Honorine de Viane, a very wealthy woman. He became a stockbroker, but he kept writing. Four years later they had a son, Michel.

Jules Verne wrote excellent science-fiction stories that predicted many future events and inventions. He died in 1905 at the age of 77.
---

33 Present the words: **celebrated, arms, legs, brush, mouth** by giving examples or by asking Ss to look them up in their dictionaries. Ss read the sentences and fill in the correct words. Check Ss' answers.

ANSWER KEY

1 businessman   2 composer   3 painter

Suggested Homework

1 **Copy:** Ex. 26 (p. 20)
2 **Vocabulary:** Exs 21, 22, 24, 25 (p. 20)
3 **Reading aloud:** Ex. 29a (p. 21)
4 **Dictation:** Exs 24, 25 (p. 20)
5 **Act out:** Ex. 26 (p. 20)
6 **Writing:** Ex. 32 (p. 21)

Lesson 5

• Check Ss' HW.
• Workbook: Unit 2
          Click on Grammar 2

Writing (a biography)

29 **a) Read the article and put the paragraphs into the correct order.**

Arthur Conan Doyle

A [ ] It is surprising that with such a busy life Arthur had time for a family, but in 1885 he married Louise Hawkins and they had three children. They travelled all over the world until they returned to England because of Louise's poor health. She died in 1906. A year later, Doyle married Jean Leckie and moved to Sussex.

B [ ] Most people love the stories about the famous detective Sherlock Holmes, but not many people can tell you about the man who wrote them. His name was Arthur Conan Doyle.

C [ ] Sir Arthur Conan Doyle was a very talented man. His good work and his great books earned him a knighthood. He died in 1930 at the age of 81.

D [ ] He was born in Edinburgh on 22nd May, 1859 and was one of ten children. He did well at school, but didn't like it very much. He studied medicine and became a doctor. As well as a great writer, he was a good sportsman and a keen photographer. He was also interested in things like ghosts and fairies.

b) Ask and answer questions about Sir Arthur Conan Doyle.

S1: *What stories did Doyle write?*
S2: *The Sherlock Holmes stories. Where was he born?*
S3: *He was born ...*

30 **Look at the biography and match the paragraphs to the headings, then answer the questions.**

early years ....
person's name — famous for ....
date of death — comments ....
later years ....

1 Which tense does the writer use? Why?
2 In which order does the writer talk about the events in Doyle's life?
3 What information does the writer include in the first/last paragraphs?

31 Listen and underline the correct word. Use your answers and the information to talk about Jules Verne.

> Jules Gabriel Verne, author (known as the grandfather of science fiction)
> 1828, Nantes, France - 1905, Amiens, France
> Books: Five Weeks in a Balloon, A Journey to the Centre of The Earth, Twenty Thousand Leagues Under the Sea, Around the World in Eighty Days, From Earth to the Moon

1 What did he study? Law/Medicine
2 When did he marry Honorine de Viane? 1857/1862
3 What did he work as? Lawyer/Stockbroker
4 What was his son's name? Michel/Jean
5 How many boats did he have? Two/Three
6 What were his hobbies? Sailing/Flying
7 What kind of person was he? Nervous/Intelligent
8 What kind of stories did he write? Science fiction/Historical
9 How old was he when he died? Sixty-seven/Seventy-seven

32 Write a short biography of Jules Verne for your school magazine (120 - 150 words). Use the information in Ex. 31 as well as the plan below. You can use the article in Ex. 29 as a model.

Plan

Introduction
(Para 1) *name of person - what famous for*
Main Body
(Para 2) *early years (when/where born, education, etc)*
(Para 3) *later years (marriage, achievements, etc)*
Conclusion
(Para 4) *date of death, comments*

33 Fill in: *painter, businessman, composer.*

do you know...

- George Train, an American 1) ...., went around the world in 80 days in 1870.
- Wolfgang Amadeus Mozart, the famous 2) ...., wrote his first piece of music at the age of five.
- Sarah Biffin (1784-1850) from Liverpool became a celebrated 3) .... even though she was born without arms or legs. She used to hold her pen, pencil or brush in her mouth.

EPISODE 1

The Hound of the Baskervilles

A New Case for Sherlock Holmes

A man called Dr Mortimer comes to see Sherlock Holmes, the famous London detective.

1 Well ... do you know about the curse of the Baskerville family?

Dr Mortimer, you know my friend Dr Watson, don't you? Now, how can we help you?

Sit down by the fire and tell us about it.

2 Sir Hugo Baskerville was an evil man. In 1643, he kidnapped a neighbour's daughter and took her to Baskerville Hall.

3 The girl managed to escape, but Sir Hugo and his friends chased her across the moor.

The girl died of fear. Suddenly they saw a huge black hound with eyes of fire. It killed Sir Hugo. He was the first Baskerville to die that way — but not the last.

4

5 In June, Sir Charles Baskerville died. The hound killed him!

What a frightening story!

6

It's interesting, but it's only an old legend. What do you want me to do?

7 I want you to protect Sir Henry Baskerville. Sir Charles was a very rich man. Now his nephew, Sir Henry, will inherit all his money and property.

8 Sir Henry is the last of the Baskervilles. I don't want *him* to die, too.

I'll do what I can to help him. Bring him to see me tomorrow morning.

22

Pre-Reading Activities

1 **Look at the pictures. Which show(s):**

1 a fireplace?   1, 7
2 a black hound with eyes of fire?   4
3 men chasing a girl across the moor?   3
4 Sherlock Holmes, the famous detective? 1, 6, 8

Listening and Reading Activities

2 🎧 **Listen and write *Yes* or *No*.**

1 Dr Watson is Holmes' friend.   Yes
2 Sir Hugo was a good man.   No
3 The hound killed Sir Hugo.   Yes
4 Sir Charles was a very poor man.   No

3 **Read the episode on p. 22 and answer the questions using one to three words.**

1 Who came to see Holmes?
Dr Mortimer.
2 Who kidnapped a girl?
Sir Hugo Baskerville.
3 What did the girl die of?
Fear.
4 Who killed Sir Charles?
The hound.
5 Who is Sir Charles' nephew?
Sir Henry.

4 **Read the episode and underline all past forms. Which are regular? Which are irregular?**

was (I), kidnapped (R), took (I), managed (R), chased (R), died (R), saw (I), killed (R)

5 **Who is in need of Holmes' protection? Do the crossword and find out. Use words from the episode.**

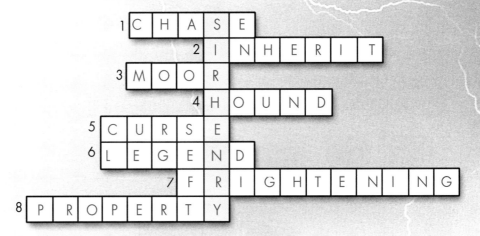

1 C H A S E
2 I N H E R I T
3 M O O R
4 H O U N D
5 C U R S E
6 L E G E N D
7 F R I G H T E N I N G
8 P R O P E R T Y

1 to run after sb in order to catch them
2 to receive money and property from sb who is dead
3 large area of open grassland
4 dog used for hunting
5 supernatural power causing unpleasant things to happen to sb
6 famous old story
7 causing fear; scary
8 land and buildings

Grammar

• **Pronouns & Possessive Adjectives**

Subject pronouns:	I, you, he , she, it, we, you, they
Object Pronouns:	me, you, him, her, it , us, you, them
Possessive adjectives:	my, your, his, her, its, our, your, their
Possessive pronouns:	mine, yours, his, hers, —, ours, yours, theirs

6 **Read the summary and replace the words in bold with words from the table above, then identify the words.**

Dr Mortimer visits Holmes in 1) **Holmes'** [his] house. Holmes introduces 2) **Dr Mortimer** [him] to 3) **Holmes'** [his] friend, Dr Watson. Dr Mortimer tells 4) **Holmes and Dr Watson** [them] that Sir Hugo Baskerville kidnapped a girl and took 5) **the girl** [her] to Baskerville Hall. 6) **The girl** [She] escaped, but Sir Hugo and 7) **Sir Hugo's** [his] friends chased 8) **the girl** [her]. The girl died of fear. 9) **Sir Hugo and his friends** [They] saw a huge black hound. 10) **The huge black hound** [It] killed Sir Hugo. Then, in June, Sir Charles Baskerville died. The hound killed 11) **Sir Charles** [him]. Dr Mortimer asks Holmes to help. He wants 12) **Holmes** [him] to protect Sir Henry Baskerville. 13) **Sir Henry Baskerville** [He] will inherit all Sir Charles' money and property. Dr Mortimer doesn't want 14) **Sir Henry** [him] to die. Holmes says that 15) **Holmes** [he] will help Sir Henry.

1 *his (poss. adj)*

7 🎧 **Listen to the episode again and follow the lines. Take roles and act out the episode.**

Units 1 - 2

Vocabulary

1 **What's the time? Say it in two ways.**

(See Suggested Answers section)   *(8 marks)*

2 **a) Fill in:** *have, get, go, talk, do, catch, meet, brush, surf, walk, wash, visit.* **Use the phrases to talk about what you do on Mondays.**

get up; have breakfast; have lessons; do homework; go to work; have a break; talk on the phone; meet friends; do crosswords; brush teeth; wash the car; catch the bus; surf the net; do the shopping; walk/wash the dog; visit relatives; go to bed

(10 marks)

b) What do you do in your free time? at weekends?

(See Suggested Answers section)   *(7 marks)*

3 **Fill in the correct verb.**

1 An architect d e s i g n s buildings.
2 A secretary t y p e s letters.
3 A journalist r e p o r t s the news.
4 A shop assistant s e r v e s customers.
5 A nurse l o o k s after sick people.

(5 marks)

4 **Fill in:** *borrow, spend, stand, alone, pocket, believe, typical, moved.*

1 Can you please leave me alone?
2 How do you spend your free time?
3 What is a typical day like for a nurse?
4 Tom can't stand football. He likes cricket instead.
5 How much pocket money do you get each week?
6 Our flat was too small so we moved to another.
7 Dad couldn't believe his eyes when he saw my exam results.
8 Can I borrow your camera to take some photos?

(8 marks)

Grammar

5 **Put the verbs in brackets into the** *present simple* **or the** *present continuous.*

1 Jenny doesn't wash **(not/wash)** her hair every day.
2 Mr and Mrs Brown drive **(drive)** to work together in the mornings.
3 Jane is going **(go)** to Spain on holiday this year.
4 Is she using **(she/use)** the computer at the moment?
5 He walks **(walk)** to school most days.
6 Brian isn't working **(not/work)** today. It's his day off.
7 What are you wearing **(you/wear)** to the party tonight, Sharon?
8 Do you fancy **(you/fancy)** playing tennis?

(8 marks)

6 **Use the prompts to say what Winnipeg used to be like and what it is like today.**

• very few cars • nice houses • huge blocks of flats • trees • gardens • clean air • polluted air

There used to be very few cars in the streets.
Today, there are a lot of cars in the streets.
(See Suggested Answers section)

(10 marks)

7 **Put the verbs in brackets into the past simple.**

1 A: How was **(be)** the party last night?
  B: Great. We had **(have)** a fantastic time, thanks.
2 A: Tony called **(call)** while you were out.
  B: Oh. Did you take **(you/take)** a message?
3 A: Rob travelled **(travel)** all over Europe last year.
  B: Did he have **(he/have)** a good time?

24(T)

4 A: Did you see **(you/see)** that film on TV last night?

B: No, I didn't watch **(not/watch)** TV yesterday.

(8 marks)

Communication

8 Fill in the missing sentences. Then, in pairs, read out the dialogues.

> • What do you do • What time does the lesson start
> • What did you do yesterday • Have you got the time

- A: 1) Have you got the time, please?
  B: It's a quarter past ten.
- A: 2) What did you do yesterday, Steve?
  B: I went fishing.
- A: 3) What do you do?
  B: I'm an architect.
- A: 4) What time does the lesson start?
  B: At 4 o'clock.

(8 marks)

Reading

9 Read the article and put the paragraphs into the correct order, then answer the questions.

Always in the News

A 3 At 4pm she's back in the office, racing to finish her article. Then her editor reads it and she makes the final changes before the newspaper goes to print. She usually finishes work at 6:30pm.

B 5 Ann has some advice to give to young people who want to get a job like hers. "You can do anything you want to! The only thing you need is determination."

C 2 The work is quite tough. At 8:30 every day she's in the office writing articles. Each one takes a lot of work. She makes hundreds of phone calls to find out information and most days she goes out to interview people or attend a big event.

D 1 Ann Reynolds is a journalist. She works for a daily newspaper called the San Francisco Chronicle.

E 4 In her free time Ann writes her own poems and books. Sometimes, she drives to the countryside.

1 What does Ann do? **She's a journalist.**
2 What time does she start/finish work? **She starts work as 8:30 and finishes at 6:30 pm.**

3 What does she do in her free time? She writes poems and books. Sometimes she drives to the countryside.
4 What advice does she give? "You can do ... determination."

(8 marks)

Writing (a short article)

10 Use the notes to write a short article about Lynn Smith (100-120 words). Use the text in Ex. 9 as a model.

Plan

(See Suggested Answers section)
(20 marks)

Introduction
(Para 1) *Lynn Smith – DJ – Chicago Radio*
Main Body
(Para 2) *gets up 3:30 am – has a shower – goes to the studio – starts work 5:30 am – on air until 10 am – plays records – talks to listeners*
(Para 3) *finishes work 12 am – afternoons are free – usually spends time with her family – goes to parties in the evening*
(Para 4) *likes driving her car – being with her family – playing tennis*
Conclusion
(Para 5) *Lynn loves her job – "I love radio – I have fun while I work."*

(Total = 100 marks)

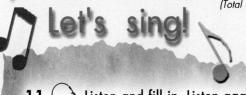

11 Listen and fill in. Listen again and sing.

Fairies in the Wood

Many years ago, when I was very 1) **young**
And there was lots of magic around
I went out for a 2) **walk** in the wood
And this is what I found.

On a stone by a 3) **stream** in the heart of the wood
Danced a beautiful shining light
Dancing there on a stone in the 4) **wood**
A truly wonderful sight.

I looked at the light and soon I saw
It was a 5) **fairy** with golden wings
She spoke to me right there in the wood
And 6) **told** me magical things.

I 7) **believed** in fairies right there and then
And I knew that they were good
And I knew that I could 8) **never** forget
My magical walk in the wood.

Reminiscences & Tales

◆ **Before you start...**

What do you do every day?
What do you do in your spare time?
What did/didn't you have when you were five?
What was life like 300 years ago?

◆ **Listen, read and talk about...**

Have you ever ...?

- theme parks
- injuries
- lost property
- favourite possessions
- jewellery

What a day!

Module 2
Units 3-4

◆ **Learn how to ...**

- describe objects
- talk about activities you have/haven't taken part in
- talk about colours, materials and shapes
- talk about household chores
- talk about yourself and your feelings
- talk about injuries
- talk about past experiences
- talk about different means of transport

◆ **Practise ...**

- present perfect
- just/yet/already/since/for/never/ever
- past continuous
- adjectives & adverbs
- linkers (while, as, so, because)

◆ **Write ...**

- an article about your favourite possession
- a letter to a lost property office
- a beginning and ending to a story
- a story

3 Have you ever ... ?

Lead-in

1 What can you see in the pictures? Tick (✓) then make sentences, as in the example.

a parade	☐	a sea turtle	☐
a train	☐	a handbag	☐
a theme park	☐	a haunted house	☐
a museum	☐	a firework display	☐
a ticket	☐	a rollercoaster	☐
a wallet	☐	a pool	☐
a watch	☐	a fish	☐

I can't see a parade but I can see a sea turtle.

2 Ask and answer, as in the examples.

- to a wedding/parade/firework display/ theme park
- on a rollercoaster/train/plane
- in a haunted house

- A: Have you ever been to a wedding?
  B: Yes, I have.
  A: When was it?
  B: **Last Sunday.**

- A: Have you ever been on a **train**?
  B: No, I haven't.

3 🎧 Listen and repeat.

- Very funny!
- Here's your chance.
- What's the matter?
- Has anyone seen my handbag?
- What does it look like?
- What's in it? Anything important?
- I've already checked.
- Let's have a better look.
- What a relief!
- How was your trip?
- We had a great time.
- What was it like?
- It was out of this world.
- Here! Take a look.

Listening and Reading

4 🎧 Listen to the dialogues. Which of the three people has lost something? Tick (✓).

Alice .... Judy .... Josh ....;

5 a) Read the dialogues (A-C) and match them to the pictures, then answer the questions. Who ...

1 ... is looking at some pictures?
2 ... wants to take some pictures?
3 ... has been on a rollercoaster recently?
4 ... has got a problem with an animal?
5 ... hasn't had a holiday for a long time?

1

26

Vocabulary: objects; shapes; jewellery; injuries; colours; materials
Reading: reading for specific information
Listening: listening for specific information; picture-prompted multiple choice
Speaking: talking about theme parks; talking about activities you have (not) done
Communication: describing lost property
Pronunciation: /e/–/eə/, /ɪe/–/eə/
Grammar: present perfect; just, yet, already, since, for, never, ever
Project: a letter to the lost property office
Writing: an article describing your favourite possession

Lesson 1 (pp. 26 - 27)

1 • Ask Ss to look at the pictures on pp 26 - 27. Explain that they have been taken at a theme park. Read out the prompts, one at a time. Ss tick what they can see. Explain/Elicit any unknown vocabulary in Ss' L1.

ANSWER KEY

items to be ticked:
a theme park, a sea turtle, a firework display, a rollercoaster, a pool

---

• After Ss have completed the task, individual Ss make sentences, as in the example.

SUGGESTED ANSWER KEY

I can't see a museum, but I can see a sea turtle.
I can't see a handbag, but I can see a firework display.

---

2 • Read out the phrases in the list and explain any unknown words. Say, then write on the board: *I have been to a parade*. Underline **have been**. Ask Ss: *When did I go?* (We don't know.) Explain that this tense is the present perfect and is used for actions which happened some time in the past, but we do not know when. Elicit how the present perfect is formed (**have/has + past participle**). Refer Ss to the Irregular Verbs section to see the past participles of the irregular verbs. Drill your Ss. Say words and Ss, one after the other, make sentences.
Suggested list: the cinema; the park; the supermarket; the theatre; the florist's etc.
e.g. S1: I have been to the cinema.
 S2: I have been to the park. etc.

• Say, then write on the board: *I went to a parade last week*. Underline **went** and **last week**. Elicit from Ss the tense form (past simple).
Ask: *When did I go to a parade? (Last week.)* Explain that we use the past simple for actions which happened at a definite time in the past.

• Write on the board: *I haven't been to a parade*. Underline **haven't been** and explain that this is the negative form of the present perfect. Drill your Ss. Use the suggested list above. Ss make sentences.
e.g. S1: I haven't been to the cinema.
 S2: I haven't been to the park. etc.

• Say, then write on the board: *Have you ever been to a parade?* Underline **Have you ever been**. Explain that this is the interrogative form of the present perfect. Write on the board: *Yes, I have./No, I haven't*. Explain that these are the short answers for the present perfect. Use the suggested list and drill with Ss.
e.g. T: Have you ever been to a parade?
 S1: Yes, I have.
Ss, in open pairs, act out similar dialogues. Refer Ss to the Grammar Reference section for more details.

• Choose two Ss to read out the examples, then Ss act out similar dialogues in open pairs.

SUGGESTED ANSWER KEY

• A: Have you ever been to a parade?
 B: Yes, I have.
 A: When was it?
 B: Last Saturday. etc.
• A: Have you ever been to a theme park?
 B: No, I haven't. etc.

---

3 Play the cassette. Ss listen and repeat either chorally or individually. Present these phrases/sentences by giving examples, or in Ss' L1 if necessary
e.g. **Has anyone seen my handbag?** (Show your handbag to Ss, then hide it under your desk. Say: *I can't find my handbag. Has anyone seen my handbag?*)
How was your trip? (Choose a S and ask: *Where did you go last summer?* (e.g. *I went to France.*) Ask: *How was your trip?* etc.)

4 Explain the task then play the cassette, twice if necessary. Ss tick accordingly. Check Ss' answers.

ANSWER KEY

Judy

---

5 a) Allow Ss three or four minutes to read the dialogues silently and match them to the pictures, then answer questions 1 to 5. Check Ss' answers.

ANSWER KEY

• dialogue A - picture 2
 dialogue B - picture 1
 dialogue C - picture 3
• 1 Dave 3 Alice 5 Dave
 2 Judy 4 Josh

---

b) • Help Ss explain the words in bold by giving examples, miming or in Ss' L1.

     e.g. **finger**: (Point to one of your fingers and say: *This is my finger.*)

     leather: (Show Ss your e.g. wallet and say: *This is my wallet. It's a leather wallet not a plastic one.*) etc.

• Play the cassette for Ex. 4 again. Ss listen and follow the lines, then take roles and read the dialogues aloud.

c) Allow Ss two minutes to quickly read the dialogues and highlight the phrases/sentences used in Ex. 3 with their text markers, then say who said each one.

ANSWER KEY

Josh said, "Very funny."
Alice said, "Here's your chance."
Pat and Bill asked, "What's the matter?"
Judy asked, "Has anyone seen my handbag?"
Bill asked, "What does it look like?"
Bill asked, "What's in it? Anything important?"
Judy said, "I've already checked."
Bill said, "Let's have a better look."
Judy said, "What a relief!"
Dave asked, "How was your trip?"
Alice said, "We had a great time."
Dave asked, "What was it like?"
Alice said, "It was out of this world."
Alice said, "Here! Take a look."

Memory Game

Ask Ss to look at the phrases/sentences in Ex. 3 for 1 minute. Then, Ss close their books and in teams try to remember as many phrases/sentences as possible. Each correct phrase/sentence gets 1 point. The team with the most points is the winner.

e.g. Team A S1: What a relief!
Team B S2: Here! Take a look. etc

Suggested Homework

1 **Copy:** dialogue A or C Ex. 5a (p. 27)
2 **Vocabulary:** Ex. 1 (p. 26), Ex. 3 (p. 26)
3 **Reading aloud:** dialogues A - C Ex. 5a (p. 27) (Point out that Ss practise *reading aloud* using the S's cassette/audio CD.)
4 **Dictation:** words in Ex 1(p. 26)
5 **Act out:** a) Ex. 2 (p. 26)
     b) Ss memorise any six sentences from Ex. 3 (p. 26)

b) Explain the words in bold, then in pairs, read out the dialogues.

c) Read the dialogues and highlight the phrases/sentences used in Ex. 3. Who said each phrase/sentence?

A

Pat: Have you ever seen sea turtles, Josh?

Josh: Yes, but I've never seen such a big one.

Pat: Hey! What are you doing?

Josh: I want to **touch** it.

Pat: Be careful. You're wearing your watch.

Josh: It's OK. Look! The turtle is coming. (SPLASH!) Oh no!

Pat: What's the matter?

Josh: It tried to eat my **finger**.

Pat: It probably thought you were a fish.

Josh: Very funny!

B

Bill: Judy, look! The Sea World firework display has just started.

Judy: It's **marvellous**. Let's take some pictures. Oh no!

Bill: What's the matter, Judy?

Judy: Has anyone seen my handbag? I can't find it.

Bill: What does it look like?

Judy: You know — it's blue **canvas** with **leather straps**.

Bill: What's in it? Anything important?

Judy: Yes, my camera and my leather wallet.

Bill: Have you looked under the table?

Judy: Yes, I've already **checked**. It's not there.

Bill: Let's have a better look ... What is **hanging** on the back of the chair under your coat?

Judy: My handbag! What a relief!

C

Dave: How was your trip to the USA, Alice?

Alice: It was fantastic. We had a great time, thanks.

Dave: What was it like?

Alice: It was out of this world. Here! Take a look at the photos.

Dave: Wow! Did you really go on the rollercoaster?

Alice: Yes, it was great. Haven't you ever been on a rollercoaster?

Dave: Yes, but that was years ago. I haven't been on one **since then**.

Alice: You know what you **should** do?

Dave: What?

Alice: Get a ticket to Sea World as soon as you can.

Dave: I think you are **right**. I haven't been on holiday for years.

Alice: Well! Here's your chance.

2

3

Vocabulary

• Describing Objects

6 **a)** Look around your class and make true sentences using the colours on the right.

The desks are brown.

b) Look at the pictures. Use the prompts to make sentences, as in the example.

1 It's a blue plastic frame with glass stones on it.

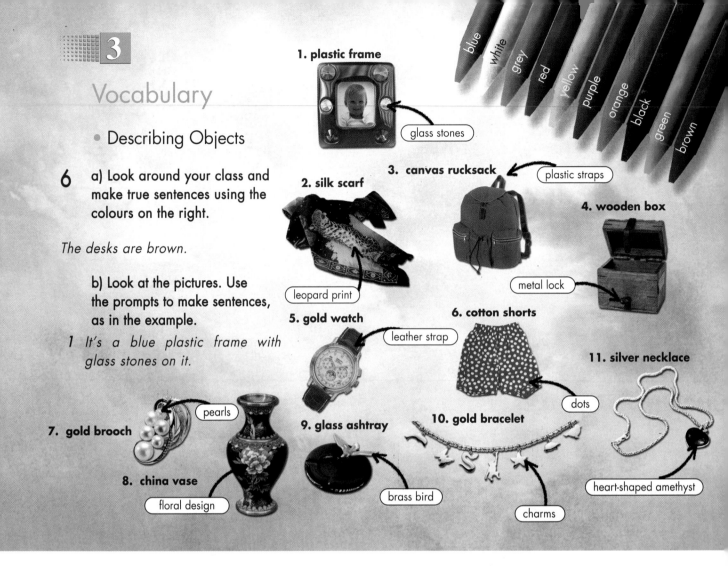

blue white grey red yellow purple orange black green brown

1. plastic frame — glass stones

2. silk scarf — leopard print

3. canvas rucksack — plastic straps

4. wooden box — metal lock

5. gold watch — leather strap

6. cotton shorts — dots

7. gold brooch — pearls

8. china vase — floral design

9. glass ashtray — brass bird

10. gold bracelet — charms

11. silver necklace — heart-shaped amethyst

• Shapes

7 When Mrs Adams came home last night she found out that some of her jewellery was missing. Look at the pictures, then use the prompts to describe Mrs Adams' jewellery, as in the example.

round   triangular   oval   rectangular   square

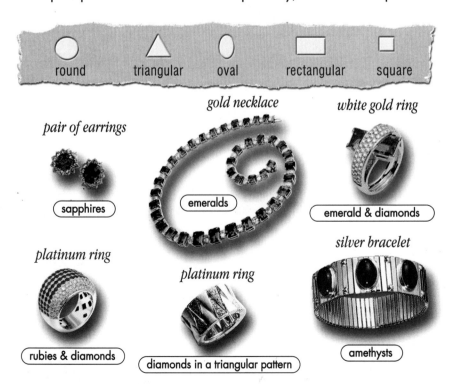

pair of earrings — sapphires

gold necklace — emeralds

white gold ring — emerald & diamonds

platinum ring — rubies & diamonds

platinum ring — diamonds in a triangular pattern

silver bracelet — amethysts

*Mrs Adams had a pair of **earrings** with oval **sapphires**.*

Game

Divide the class into two teams. Choose a picture from Exs. 6 or 7. Ss, in teams, ask questions until they find the picture. Each correct guess gets one point. The team with the most points is the winner.

Teacher: *(picture showing watch)*
Team AS1: *Is it made of plastic?*
Teacher: *No, it isn't. etc.*

• Project

Mrs Mills was at the Hilton Hotel in London last week for two days. When she got home she realised she didn't have her handbag. Complete the letter she sent to the hotel.

Lesson 2 (pp. 28 - 29)

* • Check Ss' HW (10').
 • Play the Memory Game as described in Ex. 5c p. 27(T).

6 a) Revise colours. Read out each colour, then Ss do the exercise.

SUGGESTED ANSWER KEY

The table is grey.
The walls are white.
Mary's jacket is red.
Tony's rucksack is blue.
The chairs are black.   etc.

---

b) • Read out the prompts. Ask Ss to say which of the words describe materials (*plastic, glass, silk, canvas, wooden, metal, gold, leather, cotton, china, silver, brass*) and write them on the board.
 • Read out the example, then Ss make sentences.

ANSWER KEY

 2 It's a silk scarf with a leopard print on it.
 3 It's a red canvas rucksack with black plastic straps.
 4 It's a wooden box with a metal lock.
 5 It's a gold watch with a leather strap.
 6 They're red cotton shorts with white dots on them.
 7 It's a gold brooch with pearls.
 8 It's a blue china vase with a floral design.
 9 It's a blue glass ashtray with a brass bird on it.
 10 It's a gold bracelet with charms on it.
 11 It's a silver necklace with a heart-shaped amethyst.

 • As an extension, Ss describe objects in the classroom.
  e.g. John has got a blue bag with white straps.
    Mary has got a silver watch with a blue plastic strap.

7 • Read out the shapes, then present each piece of jewellery and the stones in them.
 • Read out the example, then Ss make sentences.

ANSWER KEY

 • Mrs Adams had a gold necklace with square emeralds.
 • Mrs Adams had a white gold ring with a rectangular emerald and small round diamonds.
 • Mrs Adams had a platinum ring with small round rubies and diamonds.
 • Mrs Adams had a platinum ring with diamonds in a triangular pattern.
 • Mrs Adams had a silver bracelet with oval amethysts.

Game (p. 28)
Ss, in teams, play the game as described in the Student's Book.
e.g. Team B S1: Is it made of gold?
  Teacher: Yes, it is.
 Team A S2: Has it got charms on it?
  Teacher: No, it hasn't.
 Team B S2: Has it got a leather strap?
  Teacher: Yes, it has.
 Team B S3: It's the gold watch.

Project (p. 28)
Explain the situation, then refer Ss to the Photo File section. Ask Ss to describe the objects in the pictures. Explain that the letter Mrs Mills wrote is a formal letter. Focus Ss' attention on the beginning and ending of the letter, and explain that Mrs Mills signs off using *Yours faithfully* + *her full name* because she does not know the name of the person she is writing the letter to.
After Ss have completed the task orally in class, assign it as written HW.
See Photo File section Unit 3 for the Answer Key.

8 Ask Ss to identify the objects in the pictures. Play the cassette. Ss listen and tick the correct answer. Check Ss' answers, then Ss make full sentences. As an extension, Ss can describe each object.

> **ANSWER KEY**
>
> 1 A   2 A   3 B   4 A

TAPESCRIPT

1 What has John bought?

> **John:** What do you think of this?
> **Lee:** It's great. What is it made of?
> **John:** It's made of leather and it's got a pocket on the front.
> **Lee:** I like its colour, too.
> **John:** Yes, brown is my favourite colour.

2 What has Sally bought?

> **Sally:** Do you like my new hat?
> **Lucy:** The straw one?
> **Sally:** No, this is for my sister. Mine is this one.
> **Lucy:** The striped one?
> **Sally:** Yes, I wanted to buy a plain blue one, but then I saw this one and I couldn't resist it.
> **Lucy:** It's definitely you.

3 What has Ken bought for Linda?

> **Linda:** Oh Ken, it's beautiful. Thank you.
> **Ken:** Oh I'm glad you like it. I was about to buy you a watch when I saw it.
> **Linda:** It's fabulous. I've always wanted a ring like this.
> **Ken:** Well, I couldn't decide between a round or a square design, but then I remembered your favourite colour is blue.
> **Linda:** You chose well. I love it.

4 What hasn't Tony got in his bedroom?

> **Robin:** Wow, Tony, what a great room!
> **Tony:** Thanks. I spend a lot of time in here.
> **Robin:** I'm not surprised. I've only got a TV in my room.
> **Tony:** I don't like watching TV. I prefer playing games on my computer, or talking to my friends on the phone.

9 • Read out the examples. Ask Ss to identify the tenses in bold, then help Ss answer questions 1 to 5.

> **ANSWER KEY**
>
> 1 the present perfect (has finished)
> 2 the past simple (finished)
> 3 the present perfect (has fallen)
> 4 We form the present perfect with have/has + past participle.
> 5 We form the past participle of regular verbs with the main verb + ed.

• Read out the table. Also explain the meaning of the time expressions. Refer Ss to the Grammar Reference section for further details. Help Ss where necessary.

10 Explain that the pictures show people who have got a problem. Read out the prompts, then choose two Ss to read out the example. Ss, in open pairs, act out similar dialogues.

> **ANSWER KEY**
>
> 2 A: What's wrong with him?
>   B: He has caught a cold.
> 3 A: What's wrong with him?
>   B: He has hurt his ankle.
> 4 A: What's wrong with him?
>   B: He has lost a tooth.
> 5 A: What's wrong with her?
>   B: She has bruised her knee.
> 6 A: What's wrong with him?
>   B: He has hit his head.

(Suggested Homework)

> 1 **Copy:** grammar table of the present perfect (p. 29)
> 2 **Vocabulary:** Exs 6, 7 (p. 28)
> 3 **Reading aloud:** sentences in Ex 7 (p. 28)
> 4 **Dictation:** eight to ten words from Ex. 6 (p. 28)
> 5 **Speaking:** describe the objects in Ex. 6 (p. 28)
> 6 **Project:** (p. 28)

Listening

8 Listen and tick (✓) the correct answer.

1 What has John bought?

A ☐   B ☐   C ☐

2 What has Sally bought?

A ☐   B ☐   C ☐

3 What has Ken bought for Linda?

A ☐   B ☐   C ☐

4 What hasn't Tony got in his bedroom?

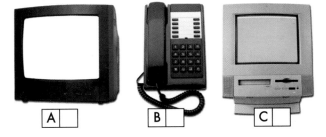

A ☐   B ☐   C ☐

Grammar

- **Present Perfect (have/has+past participle)**

9 Study the examples and answer the questions.

*He **has fallen** asleep.*

*He **has finished** his homework.*
*He **finished** it half an hour ago.*

1 Which verb describes an action which happened at an **unstated time in the past**?
2 Which verb describes an action which happened at a **specific time in the past**?
3 Which verb describes an action whose **result is visible in the present**?
4 How do we form the present perfect?
5 How do we form the past participle of regular verbs?

Affirmative:	I/you/we/they **have** called. he/she/it **has** called.
Negative:	I/you/we/they **haven't** called. he/she/it **hasn't** called.
Interrogative:	**Have** I/you/we/they called? **Has** he/she/it called?
Short answers:	Yes, { I/you/we/they **have**. he/she/it **has**. No, { I/you/we/they **haven't**. he/she/it **hasn't**.

Time expressions used with the present perfect: *yet, just, already, never, ever,* etc

10 What has happened to each person? Write questions and answers, as in the example.

A: *What's wrong with him?*
B: *He has broken his arm.*

1 break/arm   2 catch/cold   3 hurt/ankle

4 lose/tooth   5 bruise/knee   6 hit/head

11 In pairs, use the prompts to ask and answer questions, as in the example.

1 see / lion? yes / last year
   A: *Have you ever seen a lion?*
   B: *Yes, I have.*
   A: *Really? When did you see one?*
   B: *Last year.*
2 drive / car? yes / last week
3 eat / mango? yes / last summer
4 fly / in a plane? yes / last April
5 visit / theme park? yes / last weekend
6 play / computer game? yes / last night

• yet / already / just

12 Study the examples and complete the rules.

Have you watered the plants **yet?**

Sorry, I haven't done it **yet.**

Have you cooked the dinner **yet?**

Yes, I've **already** done it.

Have you walked the dog **yet?**

Yes, I've **just** done it.

We use .... in questions and negations. We use .... or .... in affirmative sentences.

13 What has just happened? Listen and tick the correct answer, then write sentences, as in the example.

1 Judy - break/vase ☑ close/window ☐
   Judy has just broken a vase.
2 Sam - have/bath ☐ jump into/river ☐
   ....
3 Kim - hoover/carpet ☐ wash/dishes ☐
   ....
4 Sarah - turn on/TV ☐ knock on/door ☐
   ....
5 Dan - crash/car ☐ cut/grass ☐
   ....

Listening

14 The Smiths are on holiday in Edinburgh. Listen and tick (✓) what they have done or cross out (✗) what they haven't done yet. Then make sentences, as in the examples.

☑ visit the castle
☒ go to the zoo
☐ go shopping at Waverley Shopping Centre
☐ walk around the Old Town
☐ see a play at the Edinburgh Playhouse
☐ go on a ferry cruise

They have already visited the castle.
They haven't been to the zoo yet.

Speaking

15 What routine activities have you already done today? What haven't you done yet? Make sentences, as in the examples, using prompts from the list and/or your own ideas.

• tidy/room
• eat/dinner
• do/homework
• water/plants
• wash/dishes
• walk/dog
• watch/TV
• hoover/carpet
• comb/hair
• make/bed
• brush/teeth
• dust/furniture

I've already tidied my room.
I haven't had dinner yet.

16 Complete the prompts in bold, using the *present perfect* and *just* or *never*, as in the examples.

1 I can't sleep in here.   I/not sleep/tent
   I've never slept in a tent before.
2 They are very happy.   they/have/baby
   They've just had a baby.
3 Who is that woman?   I/not see her/before
   ....
4 This is my new dress.   I /buy it
   ....
5 I'm not hungry.   I/have/lunch
   ....
6 Mum is angry with John.   he/break/window
   ....

Lesson 3 (pp. 30 - 31)

* Check Ss' HW (10').

11 • Explain the task. Read out the prompts. Choose two Ss to read out the example, then Ss, in closed pairs, act out similar dialogues. Check Ss' performance, then choose some pairs to act out the dialogues.

ANSWER KEY

2 A: Have you ever driven a car?
B: Yes, I have.
A: Really? When did you drive one?
B: Last week.

3 A: Have you ever eaten a mango?
B: Yes, I have.
A: Really? When did you eat one?
B: Last summer.

4 A: Have you ever flown in a plane?
B: Yes, I have.
A: Really? When did you fly in one?
B: Last April.

5 A: Have you ever visited a theme park?
B: Yes, I have.
A: Really? When did you visit one?
B: Last weekend.

6 A: Have you ever played a computer game?
B: Yes, I have.
A: Really? When did you play one?
B: Last night.

12 Read out the examples and help Ss complete the rules.

ANSWER KEY

We use **yet** in questions and negations.
We use **already** or **just** in affirmative sentences.

Drill your Ss. Give prompts and one of the three time expressions. Ss make sentences.

Suggested prompts: tidy/room, make/bed, do/homework, cook/dinner, wash/dishes, clean/windows
e.g. Teacher: tidy/room – yet
     S1: Have you tidied your room yet?
Teacher: make/bed – already
     S2: I've already made the bed.   etc

13 • Read out the prompts and present any unknown words in Ss' L1.
• Explain the task, then play the cassette. Ss listen and tick accordingly. Check Ss' answers, then Ss make sentences, as in the example.

ANSWER KEY

• 2 jump into/river   4 knock on/door
  3 hoover/carpet   5 crash/car
• 2 Sam has just jumped into the river.
  3 Kim has just hoovered the carpet.
  4 Sarah has just knocked on the door.
  5 Dan has just crashed the car.

14 • Explain that Edinburgh is the capital city of Scotland. Read out the prompts and present any unknown words in Ss' L1.
• Explain the task then play the cassette. Ss listen and tick or cross out accordingly.
• Check Ss' answers. Read out the examples, then individual Ss make sentences. After Ss have completed the exercise orally you can assign it as written HW.

ANSWER KEY

✓ go shopping at Waverley Shopping Centre
✓ walk around the Old Town
✗ see a play at the Edinburgh Playhouse
✗ go on a ferry cruise

They have already been shopping at Waverley Shopping Centre.
They haven't seen a play at the Edinburgh Playhouse yet.
They have already walked around the Old Town.
They haven't been on a ferry cruise yet.

TAPESCRIPT

Mrs Smith: Oh! I'm exhausted and there's still so much to see and do.
Mr Smith: Yes. Edinburgh really is a fascinating place. What do you think, Alison?
Alison: Oh, it's brilliant! I loved the castle. It was beautiful. I wanted to stay there all day!
Ben: No way! I was bored. I want to go to the zoo.
Mr Smith: Well, we'll go to the zoo tomorrow. We can't do everything at once, you know.
Mrs Smith: Well, I know you'll laugh, but my favourite place so far has been the Waverley Shopping Centre. There were so many lovely shops.
Mr Smith: Oh, I noticed. You spent a fortune yesterday.
Mrs Smith: Well, what shall we do this evening? Fancy walking around the Old Town?
Ben: Not again! We walked around the Old Town yesterday!
Alison: Well, how about seeing a play at the Edinburgh Playhouse? We haven't been there yet.
Mrs Smith: That's a good idea.
Mr Smith: Sorry, but I'm not in the mood for that.
Alison: Why don't we go on a ferry cruise?
Ben: That's a good idea. Let's go!

15 • Read out the prompts and present any unknown words in Ss' L1, by giving examples or by miming.
• Allow Ss two minutes to write two true sentences about themselves. Ss then read out their sentences.

SUGGESTED ANSWER KEY

I've already done my homework.
I haven't watered the plants yet.
I've already washed the dishes.
I haven't walked the dog yet.   etc

16 • Read out the examples. Point out that we use *never* with the present perfect instead of the negative form of the present perfect (haven't done).
• Allow Ss two minutes to complete the exercise. Check Ss' answers while they read out their sentences.

ANSWER KEY

3 I've never seen her before.
4 I've just bought it.
5 I've just had lunch.
6 He's just broken the window.

3

17 a) Read out the questions and elicit answers from Ss.

> *SUGGESTED ANSWER KEY*
>
> *Yes, I've been to a theme park. I went there last summer. It was very big with rides, rollercoasters and haunted houses.*

b) Ask Ss to look at the pictures and tick the items they can see. Help Ss where necessary.

Items to be ticked: famous cartoon characters, rides, a castle, an old-fashioned riverboat, an aquarium

18 Explain that Legoland, Disneyland Paris and Asterix Park are huge theme parks in Europe. Ask Ss to look at the pictures 1 to 5. Explain the task, then play the cassette. Ss listen and mark accordingly. Check Ss' answers.

> *ANSWER KEY*
>
> picture 1   L (Legoland)
> pictures 2, 4   A (Asterix Park)
> pictures 3, 5   D (Disneyland Paris)

19 a) Read out questions 1 to 5, then allow Ss two to three minutes to read the advertisements silently and answer the questions. Check Ss' answers.

> *ANSWER KEY*
>
> 1 Legoland   4 Asterix Park
> 2 Disneyland Paris   5 Legoland
> 3 Asterix Park, Disneyland Paris

b) • Allow Ss two minutes to quickly scan the texts. Ss then explain the words in bold by giving examples or miming or in Ss' L1 if necessary. Help Ss where necessary.
> • Ss underline the sentences/phrases which best describe each picture. Check Ss' answers.

> *ANSWER KEY*
>
> 1 the amazing Dragon Ride
> 2 the entertaining Dolphin Theatre
> 3 an old-fashioned riverboat
> 4 the famous cartoon character, Asterix
> 5 Sleeping Beauty's elegant castle

c) • Play the cassette for Ex. 18 again. Ss listen and follow the lines, then individual Ss read out from the texts.
> • Ss, in closed pairs, make notes under the headings. Write the headings on the board while Ss do the activity. Elicit answers from Ss to complete the table. Ss compare their notes to what you have written on the board and correct accordingly. Individual Ss talk about the theme parks.

> *SUGGESTED ANSWER KEY*
>
> | Name | Location/Size | What to do/see there |
> |---|---|---|
> | Legoland | Windsor 150 acres | seven themed activity areas; fifty rides; live shows; Castleland; Dragon Ride; Duplo Gardens; My Town; Wild Wood; Miniland |
> | Asterix Park | north of Paris 400 acres | six themed areas; rides; shows; Dolphin Theatre; rollercoasters |
> | Disneyland Paris | Paris 5,000 acres | five themed areas; rides; attractions; Fantasyland; Sleeping Beauty's castle; Frontierland; old-fashioned riverboat |

> *SUGGESTED ANSWER KEY*
>
> *Legoland is in Windsor. It is set in 150 acres of countryside. There are seven themed activity areas. You can visit Castleland and try the Dragon Ride or take a trip to Duplo Gardens where younger children can have a great time.*
>
> *Asterix Park is 35 km north of Paris. It is set in 400 acres of land and it is based on the famous cartoon character Asterix. It has six themed areas, so you can travel back in time through twenty centuries. There is the Dolphin Theatre and exciting rollercoasters. It is the perfect place for all the family.*
>
> *Disneyland Paris is set in almost 5,000 acres and there are five fantastic themed areas. You can enter a fairy-tale kingdom in Fantasyland or visit Frontierland and ride on an old-fashioned riverboat.*

> (Suggested Homework)
>
> 1 **Copy:** any of the texts Ex. 19a (p. 31)
> 2 **Vocabulary:** words in bold in the texts Ex. 19a (p. 31)
> 3 **Reading aloud:** any of the texts Ex. 19a (p. 31)
> 4 **Dictation:** any ten of the words in bold in the texts (p. 31)
> 5 **Speaking:** Ss look at their notes in their notebooks and talk about the three themed parks (Ex. 19c, p. 31)

Listening & Reading

17 **a)** Have you ever been to a theme park? What was it like?

b) What can you see in the pictures? Tick (✓).

famous cartoon characters ...; jewellery ...; rides ...;
live shows and attractions ...; a castle ...; a hospital ...;
an old-fashioned riverboat ...; a theatre ...;
an aquarium ...; a rollercoaster ...; blocks of flats ...

18 🎧 Look at the pictures, then listen and mark the pictures. Write L (for Legoland), D (for Disneyland Paris) or A (for Asterix Park).

19 **a)** Read the advertisements and answer the questions 1 to 5.

Which theme park(s)...
1 isn't in the same country as the other two?
2 is the biggest of all?
3 have themes based on cartoon characters?
4 has themes from 2,000 years ago?
5 has the most themed activity areas?

b) Read the advertisements again and explain the words in bold. Then, underline the sentence/ phrase which best describes each picture.

Speaking

c) Read the advertisements and make notes under the headings, then talk about each theme park.

• name • location/size • what to do/see there

Legoland is in Windsor. It is set in 150 acres of countryside ...

LEGOLAND

For **fun** and **adventure**, come to Legoland, Windsor. Set in 150 **acres** of beautiful countryside, there is something for all the family. At Legoland, Windsor, there are seven **themed** activity areas with over fifty rides, live shows and **attractions**. Visit Castleland and try the amazing Dragon Ride, or take a trip to the Duplo Gardens, where younger children can have a wonderful time. Don't forget My Town, Wild Wood or Miniland. There's just so much to see! Come to Legoland, Windsor for more fun than you've ever **dreamed of**. It's a great way to spend a day!

ASTERIX PARK

35km north of Paris, the Asterix amusement park, set in about 400 acres, is waiting to **thrill** and entertain you. **Based on** the famous cartoon character, Asterix, the park has six themed areas **allowing** you to **travel back in time** through twenty **centuries**. There is plenty to do at Asterix park, with rides and shows to **suit** all ages and **tastes**, from the entertaining Dolphin Theatre to the most exciting rollercoasters you've ever been on. Asterix park is the perfect place for all the family to enjoy a fabulous day out. Come and share the fun!

DISNEYLAND PARIS

Whatever your age, you're sure to have the trip of a **lifetime** when you visit the **magical** world of Disneyland Paris set in almost 5,000 acres. There are five fantastic themed areas, each with its own fabulous rides and attractions. Enter a fairy-tale **kingdom** in Fantasyland, where Sleeping Beauty's **elegant** castle will take your **breath** away. Have you ever wanted to **experience** the wild, wild west? Visit Frontierland and ride on an old-fashioned riverboat. There's a world of fun and **adventure** waiting for you at Disneyland, Paris. Come and visit the wonderful world of Disney today!

• Since / For

20 Study the examples. Which do we use to state: the moment an action started? the duration of an action?

*He has been in Paris **for three days**.*
*He has been in Paris **since Monday**.*

Speaking

21 Use the prompts to make sentences, as in the examples.

- • not/see him
- • live here
- • not/work
- • be in England
- • not/travel abroad
- • not/tidy my room
- • know John
- • not/watch TV
- • not/sleep
- • not/eat
- • have this bike

- • January
- • a long time
- • two years
- • three months
- • 1985
- • Friday
- • ten years
- • yesterday evening
- • last Monday
- • lunchtime
- • last year

S1: I haven't seen him since January.
S2: I have lived here for a long time.

22 Put the verbs in brackets into the *present perfect* or *past simple*.

1 A: 1) .... (you/study) for tomorrow's test?
   B: Yes, I have. I 2) ....
      .... (spend) all yesterday afternoon studying.
   A: So, 3) ....
      (you/learn) everything?
   B: I think so, but I'm a bit nervous.
   A: Why are you nervous? You 4) ....
      .... (always/be) good at History.
   B: History? But I 5) ....
      (think) it was a *Physics* test!!

2 A: John, 1) .... (you/see) my old Spice Girls CD?
   B: No. Why — 2) ....
      (you/lose) it?
   A: Yes. It 3) .... (disappear).
   B: Well, I 4) .... (hear) Lucy listening to music an hour ago. Maybe she 5) .... (borrow) it.

3 A: Sam! Look at this mess! I 1) ....
      (ask) you to tidy it up.
   B: I know! I 2) ....
      (start) tidying up an hour ago, but I 3) ....
      .... (not/finish) yet.
   A: I can see that! Why 4) ....
      .... (you/not/put) these clothes away?
   B: I'm sorry. I 5) ....
      (not/do) it yet. But I 6) ....
      .... (find) this ring.
   A: My diamond ring! I 7) ....
      (lose) it weeks ago! Thank you, Sam.

Vocabulary Practice

23 **Vocabulary Revision Game: In teams, make sentences with words/phrases from the list.**

- • thrill • attractions • lifetime • look like
- • ever • chance • riverboat • strap • woollen
- • gold • entertain • adventure • already checked
- • matter • is hanging • rollercoaster
- • spend a day • relief

24 **Fill in the correct word from the list, then make sentences.**

- • lost • wild • cartoon • live • fairy-tale
- • leather • old-fashioned • themed

1 .... shows   5 .... character
2 .... areas   6 .... kingdom
3 .... west   7 ...... property office
4 .... riverboat   8 .... strap

25 **Fill in:** *of, for, in, on, at, out.*

1 set .... 150 acres; 2 to dream .... sth; 3 to wait .... sb; 4 based .... a character; 5 to take a look .... some pictures; 6 to ride .... a riverboat; 7 ...... fun; 8 to be .... holiday; 9 to be .... of this world; 10 to travel back .... time

26 **Underline the correct word.**

1 You don't look well. What's the **wrong/matter**?
2 We're going on a two-day **trip/travel** to London this weekend.
3 Wait a **time/minute**. I've never met him before.
4 Did you **spend/pass** the day in the countryside?
5 The beauty of the place is sure to take your **life/breath** away.
6 The place **suits/fits** all ages and tastes.

Lesson 4 (pp. 32 - 33)

* Check Ss' HW (10').

20 • Read out the examples and help Ss to answer the questions.

ANSWER KEY

We use **since** to state the moment an action started.
We use **for** to state the duration of an action.

• Drill your Ss. Say various time expressions, Ss in teams add **since** or **for**. Each correct completed phrase gets 1 point. The team with the most points is the winner.

Suggested list: 1991, three o'clock, two days, Monday, August, six hours, a long time, yesterday etc.

e.g.　Teacher: 1991
　　　Team A S1: since 1991
　　　Teacher: two days
　　　Team B S1: for two days　　etc.

21 Read out the prompts and present any unknown words in Ss' L1, then read out the examples to explain the task. Ss, one after the other, make sentences using the prompts.

SUGGESTED ANSWER KEY

S3: I haven't worked for two years.
S4: I've been in England for three months.
S5: I haven't travelled abroad since 1985.
S6: I haven't tidied my room since Friday.
S7: I've known John for ten years.
S8: I haven't watched TV since yesterday evening.
S9: I haven't slept since last Monday.
S10: I haven't eaten since lunchtime.
S11: I've had this bike since last year.　　etc

---

22 Explain the task, then Ss, in closed pairs, do the exercise. Check Ss' answers by asking Ss to read out their answers.

ANSWER KEY

1　1　Have you studied
　　2　spent
　　3　have you learnt
　　4　have always been
　　5　thought

2　1　have you seen
　　2　have you lost
　　3　has disappeared
　　4　heard
　　5　has borrowed

3　1　asked
　　2　started
　　3　haven't finished
　　4　haven't you put
　　5　haven't done
　　6　have found
　　7　lost

---

23 Ss, in teams, make sentences using the words/phrases in the order they appear in the list. Each correct sentence gets one point. The team with the most points is the winner.

e.g.　Team A S1: Asterix Park is waiting to **thrill** you.
　　　Team B S1: There are a lot of **attractions** in Legoland.

24 Allow Ss two minutes to fill in the missing words. Check Ss' answers, then ask Ss to make sentences using the completed phrases.

e.g.　S1: There are many **live shows** to see in Legoland.
　　　S2: There are six **themed areas** in Asterix Park.

ANSWER KEY

1　live　　　　　　5　cartoon
2　themed　　　　6　fairy-tale
3　wild　　　　　7　lost
4　old-fashioned　8　leather

---

25 Allow Ss two minutes to fill in the missing prepositions. Check Ss' answers, then ask Ss to make sentences using the completed phrases.

e.g.　S1: The park is **set in 150 acres**.
　　　S2: Have you ever **dreamt of** visiting Legoland? etc

ANSWER KEY

1　in　　　　5　at　　　　9　out
2　of　　　　6　on　　　　10　in
3　for　　　7　for
4　on　　　　8　on

---

26 Explain the task, then allow Ss two minutes to underline the correct word. Check Ss' answers while Ss read out the sentences.

ANSWER KEY

1　matter　　3　minute　　5　breath
2　trip　　　4　spend　　　6　suits

---

27 a) • Ask Ss to look at the pictures and identify the objects, then describe them.

e.g. a blue pen with a silver lid, a brown leather wallet, a blue bag with white handles, a black camera, a pair of brown plastic sunglasses

• Play the cassette. Ss listen and tick the pictures. Check Ss' answers

ANSWER KEY

pictures to be ticked: B, C, D

b) • Play the cassette for Ex. 27a again. Ss listen and follow the lines. Then, Ss read out the dialogue in pairs.

• Read out the prompts and explain any unknown words. Ss, in closed pairs, use the prompts to act out similar dialogues.

ANSWER KEY

• *A: Has anyone seen my **purse**?*
B: What does it look like?
*A: It's **black** with **silver letters**.*
B: What's in it?
*A: My **credit cards** and some **money**.*
• *A: Has anyone seen my **briefcase**?*
B: What does it look like?
*A: It's **brown** with a **gold lock**.*
B: What's in it?
*A: My **car keys** and **papers**.*
• *A: Has anyone seen my **handbag**?*
B: What does it look like?
*A: It's **orange** with a **yellow strap**.*
B: What's in it?
*A: My **purse** and **watch**.*

28 a) Explain the task. Play the cassette. Ss listen and tick accordingly. Check Ss' answers. Ss repeat either chorally or individually.

ANSWER KEY

	/e/	/eə/		/ɪe/	/eə/
ferry	✓		fare		✓
fairy		✓	fear	✓	
Mary		✓	hair		✓
merry	✓		here	✓	

b) Play the cassette. Ss listen and follow the lines. Play the cassette again with pauses for Ss to repeat.

29 a) • Explain what *favourite possession* means, then elicit from Ss what their favourite possession is. (e.g. a ball, a doll, a camera, a teddy bear etc)

• Explain the task, then read aloud the first sentence and help Ss correct the mistake, justifying their answer. Allow Ss two or three minutes to complete the task. Check Ss' answers, then Ss check the meaning of any unknown words in their dictionaries.

ANSWER KEY

1 gave   2 of   3 my   4 reminds   5 bring
Picture to be ticked: B

b) Individual Ss read out from the text. Help Ss answer the questions.

ANSWER KEY

• *The **first paragraph** says **what** the writer's favourite possession is, **who** gave it to him, **when** he was given it and **the reason why** he was given it.*
*The **second paragraph** includes the **description** of the object.*
*The **third paragraph** includes the writer's **feelings** about the object.*
• *The writer uses mainly the past simple because the object was given to him when he was eleven years old (i.e. an action which happened at a stated time in the past).*

30 Discuss the questions in class. Help Ss where necessary.

SUGGESTED ANSWER KEY

My favourite possession is a silver watch. My grandfather gave it to me on my first day at secondary school. It had a blue face with silver hands and a navy blue leather strap. It's my favourite watch and always reminds of my grandfather.

31 Explain the task, then read out the plan. Ask Ss to use their answers from Ex. 30 to describe their favourite possession using the article in Ex. 29 as a model. After Ss have done the task orally in class, assign it as written HW.

SUGGESTED ANSWER KEY

On my first day at secondary school, my grandfather gave me a beautiful silver watch.

It had a blue face with silver hands and a navy blue leather strap. I never took it off and I was really happy when somebody asked me the time. It was my favourite possession and I was very proud to wear it.

After a few years, it was too small for me, but I bought a bigger strap and every time I wear it I remember my grandfather and the happiness it brought me.

32 Allow Ss two minutes to complete the task. Check Ss' answers while they read them out.

ANSWER KEY

• *$ 400 million*
• *2,285 m – 5 mins 50 secs*
• *1843*

Suggested Homework

1 Copy: dialogue Ex. 27b (p. 33)
2 Vocabulary: Exs 23, 24, 25 (p. 32)
3 Reading aloud: Exs 27b, 29a (p. 33)
4 Dictation: Para 2 – article Ex. 29a (p. 33)
5 Act out: Ex. 27b (p. 33)
6 Writing: Ex. 31 (p. 33)

Lesson 5

• Check Ss' HW.
• Workbook: Unit 3
Click on Grammar 3

Communication

Describing Lost Property

27 a) Listen and tick (✓) the correct pictures.

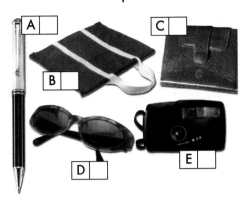

b) Read out the dialogue, then in pairs, use the prompts to act out similar dialogues.

A: Has anyone seen my **bag**?
B: What does it look like?
A: It's **blue** with **white handles**.
B: What's in it?
A: My **wallet** and **sunglasses**.

- purse - black/silver letters - credit cards/some money
- briefcase - brown/gold lock - car keys/papers
- handbag - orange/yellow strap - purse/watch

Pronunciation

28 a) Listen and tick (✓). Listen again and repeat.

	/e/	/eə/		/ɪə/	/eə/
ferry			fare		
fairy			fear		
Mary			hair		
merry			here		

b) Listen and repeat.

It's not **fair** to **stare** at **Mary**.
Come **here** and fix my **hair**.
I've paid the **fare** for the **ferry**.
Jerry shared his **pear** with **Claire**.

Writing (an article describing your favourite possession)

29 a) Read the article and correct the mistakes in bold. Which of the two objects does the writer describe? Tick (✓).

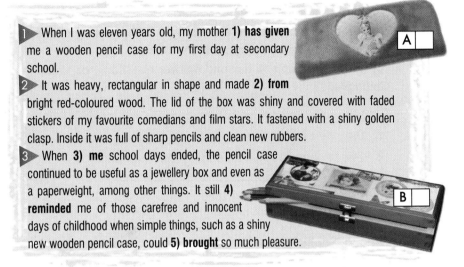

1 ▶ When I was eleven years old, my mother **1) has given** me a wooden pencil case for my first day at secondary school.

2 ▶ It was heavy, rectangular in shape and made **2) from** bright red-coloured wood. The lid of the box was shiny and covered with faded stickers of my favourite comedians and film stars. It fastened with a shiny golden clasp. Inside it was full of sharp pencils and clean new rubbers.

3 ▶ When **3) me** school days ended, the pencil case continued to be useful as a jewellery box and even as a paperweight, among other things. It still **4) reminded** me of those carefree and innocent days of childhood when simple things, such as a shiny new wooden pencil case, could **5) brought** so much pleasure.

b) Read the article again. What information is there in each paragraph? Why does the writer mainly use the past simple?

30 What is your favourite possession? Who gave it to you? When/Why? What is it like? How do you feel about it?

31 Your teacher has asked you to write an article describing your favourite possession explaining how you feel about it (80-100 words). Use your answers from Ex. 30, as well as the plan below, to write your composition. You can use the article in Ex. 29 as a model.

> **Plan**
> Introduction
> (Para 1) *what it is; who gave it to you; when; why*
> Main Body
> (Para 2) *description of object*
> Conclusion
> (Para 3) *how you feel about the object*

32 Read and fill in the correct facts from the box below.

| 11.6 km / 2,285 m | $400 million / $187,000 |
| 1843 / 1913 | 4 hrs 36 mins / 5 mins 50 secs |

do you know...

- Disneyland Florida cost .... to build.
- The rollercoaster at Lightwater Valley, England, is .... long. The ride lasts for ....
- Tivoli Gardens in Copenhagen, Denmark, is the world's oldest amusement park. It opened in ....

4 What a day!

Lead-in

1 **a) These photographs were taken at 2 o'clock yesterday afternoon. Who was/were: running a bath; grating cheese; having a snack; hanging out the washing?**
b) Use the prompts to ask and answer questions, as in the example.

1 Paul / fish?
A: Was Paul fishing at 2 o'clock yesterday afternoon?
B: No, he wasn't. He was reading a newspaper.
2 Mary / read a newspaper?
3 Adam and David / run a bath?
4 Sarah / hang out the washing?
5 Billy and Tony / have a snack?
6 Tom and Steve /grate cheese?
7 Lyn / read a book?
8 Ben / talk on the phone?

Listening

2 🎧 **Listen and repeat.**

- I'm so sorry!
- How did it start?
- A normal afternoon, then?
- I think I can guess what happened.
- How shocking!
- I have no idea.
- They talked for ages.
- What a silly thing to do!
- You're soaking wet!

3 🎧 **Listen to the dialogues and correct the words in bold in sentences 1 to 3.**

1 Paul's **car** has burnt down.
....
2 Sarah was running a bath when the **doorbell** rang.
....
3 Adam slipped again and fell into the **lake**. ....

Reading

4 **a) Read the dialogues and answer the questions, then explain the words in bold.**

1 What were Paul and his family doing when Tom came home?
2 Who did Tom come home with?
3 What happened when Paul's son plugged in his electric guitar?
4 Who was on the phone when Sarah answered it?
5 What happened to Sarah?
6 What happened to Adam when he slipped the first time?
7 How did Adam fall into the river?

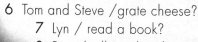
Adam & David

Sarah

Paul

Lyn

3 A: *Were Adam and David running a bath at 2 o'clock yesterday afternoon?*
   B: *No, they weren't. They were fishing.*
4 A: *Was Sarah hanging out the washing at 2 o'clock yesterday afternoon?*
   B: *No, she wasn't. She was running a bath.*
5 A: *Were Billy and Tony having a snack at 2 o'clock yesterday afternoon?*
   B: *No, they weren't. They were reading a book.*
6 A: *Were Tom and Steve grating cheese at 2 o'clock yesterday afternoon?*
   B: *No, they weren't. They were having a snack.*
7 A: *Was Lyn reading a book at 2 o'clock yesterday afternoon?*
   B: *No, she wasn't. She was talking on the phone.*
8 A: *Was Ben talking on the phone at 2 o'clock yesterday afternoon?*
   B: *No, he wasn't. He was grating cheese.*

2 • Play the cassette. Ss listen and repeat either chorally or individually.
• Present the phrases/sentences by giving examples or by miming.
   e.g. *I'm so sorry!* (Walk by a S. Pretend to slip and push some of his books onto the floor. Say *I'm so sorry! I didn't mean to.*) etc.

3 • Read out sentences 1 to 3 and explain the task.
• Play the cassette. Ss listen and correct the words in bold. Check Ss' answers.

ANSWER KEY

1 house   2 phone   3 river

4 a) • Read out questions 1 to 7. Allow Ss three to four minutes to read the dialogues silently and answer the questions. Check Ss' answers.

ANSWER KEY

1 *Paul was reading a newspaper, his wife was doing the hoovering and their daughter, Lyn, was talking on the phone*
2 *He came home with his pop group friends.*
3 *When Paul's son plugged in his electric guitar the fire started.*
4 *It was her sister.*
5 *She forgot she was running a bath so she flooded her bathroom.*
6 *When Adam slipped the first time, he landed in the mud.*
7 *As he was getting out of the mud, he slipped again.*

• Help Ss explain the words in bold by giving examples or synonyms.
   e.g. **burnt down:** destroyed by fire
        hoovering: cleaning the carpets, floors etc using a vacuum cleaner etc.

Vocabulary: misfortunes and accidents; feelings; means of transport; notices; past activities; parts of the body
Reading: a story
Listening: listening for lexical items and verb phrases; listening for specific information; prioritising
Speaking: talking about yourself; speaking from notes
Communication: at the doctor's
Pronunciation: silent /t/
Grammar: past continuous; adjectives; adverbs; linkers (while, and, when, but, as, so, because)
Project: a beginning and an ending of a story
Writing: a story

Lesson 1 (pp. 34 - 35)

1 a) • Present the past continuous. Write on the board: *I was having lunch at 2 o'clock yesterday afternoon.* Underline *was having*. Explain that this tense form is the past continuous and elicit form: **(personal pronoun + was + verb -ing)**. Ask Ss: *When was I having lunch? (At 2 o'clock yesterday afternoon.)* Explain that we use the past continuous to describe activities going on for a period of time in the past. Drill your Ss. Give prompts. Ss make sentences modelling the structure.
Suggested prompts: read a comic, watch TV, sleep, have a bath, tidy my room, water the plants etc.
   e.g.   T: read a comic - Bob
      Bob: *I was reading a comic at 2 o'clock yesterday afternoon.*
         T: watch TV - Sally
      Sally: *I was watching TV at 2 o'clock yesterday afternoon.* etc.
• Ask, then write on the board: *Were you having lunch at 2 o'clock yesterday afternoon?* Underline *Were you having*. Explain that this is the interrogative form of the past continuous. Elicit/Give answer: *(Yes, I was/No, I wasn't.)*
• Ask Ss to look at the pictures. Explain that these pictures were taken at 2 o'clock yesterday afternoon. Ss answer the questions.

b) • Read out item 1 and explain the task. Ss, in open pairs, complete the exercise orally in class.

ANSWER KEY

• 1 *Who was running a bath? (Sarah)*
  2 *Who was grating cheese? (Ben)*
  3 *Who was having a snack? (Tom and Steve)*
  4 *Who was hanging out the washing? (Mary)*

• 2 A: *Was Mary reading a newspaper at 2 o'clock yesterday afternoon?*
     B: *No, she wasn't. She was hanging out the washing.*

4

b) Play the cassette for Ex. 3 again. Ss listen and follow the lines, then take roles and read out the dialogues.

c) Allow Ss two minutes to look at the phrases/ sentences in Ex. 2 again, then read the dialogues (A - C) and underline them. Ss then say who said each phrase/sentence.

ANSWER KEY

Helen said, "I'm so sorry!"
Helen said, "How did it start?"
Helen asked, "A normal afternoon, then?"
Helen said, "I think I can guess what happened."
Helen said, "How shocking!"
Don said, "I have no idea."
Kaye said, "They talked for ages."
Don said, "What a silly thing to do!'
Jessie said, "You're soaking wet!"

Memory Game

Ask Ss to look at the phrases/sentences in Ex. 2 for 1 minute. Then, Ss close their books and in teams try to remember as many phrases/sentences as possible. Each correct phrase/ sentence gets 1 point. The team with the most points is the winner.

e.g. Team A S1: I'm so sorry.
　　　Team B S2: I have no idea.　　　etc.

Suggested Homework

1 **Copy:** dialogue A or C (p. 35)
2 **Vocabulary:** Ex. 1 (p. 34) words in bold in dialogues A - C (p. 35)
3 **Reading aloud:** dialogues Ex. 4a (p. 35) (Point out that Ss practise *reading aloud* at home using the S's cassette/audio CD.)
4 **Dictation:** Ex. 2 (p. 34)
5 **Speaking:** a) Ex. 1 (p. 34)
　　　　　　　　b) Ss memorise any five sentences from Ex. 2 (p. 34)

A

Helen: Paul, I heard your house **burnt down**. I'm so sorry! How did it start?

Paul: Well, I was reading a newspaper, my wife was doing the **hoovering** and Lyn was talking on the phone.

Helen: A normal afternoon, then?

Paul: Yes. Then my son Tom came home with his pop group friends, and they wanted to **practise**.

Helen: I think I can **guess** what happened.

Paul: Yes. He **plugged in** his electric guitar and ... bang! – the fire started.

Helen: How shocking!

B

Kaye: Do you know what Sarah did yesterday?

Don: I have no idea.

Kaye: Well, she was getting ready to bath her little daughter. She was running the bath when the phone rang, so she went to answer it.

Don: Yes, and ... ?

Kaye: And it was her sister. So, they talked **for ages**.

Don: Mm-hmm ...

Kaye: But Sarah didn't **realise** that the water was still running in the bathroom.

Don: Oh, no!

Kaye: Oh, yes! She **flooded** her bathroom!

Don: What a silly thing to do!

C

Jessie: Adam! Look at you! You're **soaking wet**! What happened?

Adam: David and I were fishing when I slipped on a rock.

Jessie: Oh, no! And you fell into the water?

Adam: No, I **landed** in the **mud**.

Jessie: But how did you get wet?

Adam: Well, as I was getting out of the mud, I slipped again.

Jessie: Ah, so then you fell into the river.

Adam: Yes, but **at least** I'm not **muddy** now.

b) Take roles and read the dialogues aloud.

c) Read the dialogues again and underline the phrases/sentences used in Ex. 2. Who said each phrase/sentence?

Mary

Tom & Steve

Ben

Billy & Tony

Vocabulary

• Misfortunes & accidents

5 **a)** What happened to each of these people yesterday? Match the pictures (A-F) to the prompts (1-6), then make sentences, as in the example.

A 1 Jill

D ☐ Greg

B ☐ Claire

E ☐ Mike

C ☐ Tom

F ☐ Tony

1 crash/tree	3 burn/hand
Jill crashed	4 break/tooth
into a tree.	5 hurt/leg
2 sprain/ankle	6 cut/finger

b) Complete these sentences, using the prompts above.

1 Jill was driving home from work yesterday when she crashed into a tree.
2 Tom was slicing some bread yesterday when ...
3 Claire was jogging in the park yesterday when ...
4 Mike was playing football yesterday when ...
5 Tony was eating sweets yesterday when ...
6 Greg was cooking yesterday when ...

• Feelings

6 How does each person feel? Match the prompts in the list to the pictures (1-5), then make sentences, as in the example.

1 lonely and miserable
... bored and annoyed
... exhausted but pleased
... surprised and excited
... relieved and happy

Jo feels **lonely and miserable** *because she hasn't got any friends.*

• Means of Transport

7 **a)** Where can you see these notices? Circle the correct answer.

PLEASE DON'T TALK TO THE DRIVER
(bus) / ferryboat

FASTEN YOUR SEAT BELT
ambulance / aeroplane

EMERGENCY STOP ONLY
£500 FINE FOR IMPROPER USE
train / taxi

LIFE JACKET UNDER SEAT
fire engine / hovercraft

PLEASE HAVE EXACT CHANGE READY
bus / helicopter

b) How many means of transport can you think of which we:
- drive? *(e.g. car, lorry)* - fly? *(e.g. aeroplane)*
- ride? *(e.g. scooter)* - travel in/on? *(e.g. ship, train)*

c) How do you travel to school/work?
Which means of transport do you use the most?
Which is your favourite means of transport?

Lesson 2 (pp. 36 - 37)

* • Check Ss' HW (10').
  • Play the Memory Game as described in Lesson 1 Ex. 4c p. 35(T).

5 a) Ask Ss to look at the pictures. Read out the prompts one at a time. Ss match the pictures to the prompts. Check Ss' answers, then Ss make full sentences.

ANSWER KEY

2 – B, Claire sprained her ankle.
3 – D, Greg burnt his hand.
4 – F, Tony broke his tooth.
5 – E, Mike hurt his leg.
6 – C, Tom cut his finger.

b) Read out the example. Point out that we use **when** to link two clauses – a past continuous clause (longer action) and a past simple clause (shorter action). Allow Ss 1 minute to complete the sentences. Check Ss' answers.

ANSWER KEY

2 ... he cut his finger.
3 ... she sprained her ankle.
4 ... he hurt his leg.
5 ... he broke his tooth.
6 ... he burnt his hand.

6 • Read out the prompts and explain any unknown words in Ss' L1.
  • Explain the task. Read out what Jo is thinking, then read out the example. Allow Ss two minutes to do the exercise. Check Ss' answers.

ANSWER KEY

• 5 bored and annoyed
  4 exhausted but pleased
  3 surprised and excited
  2 relieved and happy

• 2 Karen feels relieved and happy because her son is going to get well.
  3 Kim feels surprised and excited because she has won first prize.
  4 Dennis feels exhausted but pleased because (he had to work all night but) he has finished his report.
  5 Jenny feels bored and annoyed because she has been there for an hour.

7 a) Explain the task. Read out the notices one at a time and help Ss circle the correct answer. While Ss do the exercise present/elicit the meaning of any unknown words by asking Ss to give a synonym or an example.

ANSWER KEY

FASTEN YOUR SEAT BELT – aeroplane
EMERGENCY STOP ONLY ... – train
LIFE JACKET UNDER SEAT – hovercraft
PLEASE HAVE EXACT CHANGE READY – bus

b) Write the verbs on the board in a table. Elicit answers from Ss and complete it. Ss copy it into their notebooks.

SUGGESTED ANSWER KEY

drive:	truck, bus, taxi, car, ambulance, train, fire engine etc
ride:	bike, horse, motorbike etc
fly:	helicopter etc
travel in:	a car, a helicopter, a hot-air balloon etc
travel on:	a bus, a hovercraft, a train, a ship etc

c) Elicit appropriate answers from Ss.

SUGGESTED ANSWER KEY

I drive my car to work.
I usually take the bus to school.
I use the train the most.
My favourite means of transport is the plane.

8 • Ask Ss to look at the pictures. Read out the first example. Ask: *What was Tony doing at ten o'clock yesterday morning? (He was painting a picture.)*

• Read out the second example: *He was windsurfing when he lost his balance and fell into the water.* Ask: *How many actions are there? (3 – was windsurfing - he lost, fell into).* Ask: *Which action happened first? (was windsurfing).*

• Ask Ss to identify the tense forms. *(The first action is in the past continuous, the second action is in the past simple.)* Give prompts for Ss to model the structure. e.g. watch TV - phone ring, walk down street - see John, cook - lights go off   etc.

• Read out the third example. Explain that *was raining* and *were walking* set the scene, i.e. give background information to a story.

• Read out the fourth example. Focus Ss' attention on **while**, which is used to join two simultaneous actions.

• Help Ss answer questions 1 to 5, then read out the grammar table. Refer Ss to the Grammar Reference section for more details on the form and use of the past continuous.

ANSWER KEY

1 was talking –	*4 lost, fell (past simple)*
was reading	*5 was raining - were*
2 was painting	*walking*
3 was windsurfing	

9 a) • Ask Ss to look at the picture and say what each person was doing at 11 o'clock yesterday morning.
   e.g. A boy was flying a kite.
       Another boy was riding a bike.
       A girl was picking flowers.
       A woman was rowing a boat.
       A boy was making some sandwiches.
       A girl was skipping.

• Explain the task. Point out that one person in the picture is not mentioned. Play the cassette twice. Ss listen and draw lines. Check Ss' answers.

Sarah   Tom   David   Ella   Stephen

TAPESCRIPT

A: Where's David? I can't see him.
B: He's over there. He's flying his kite.
A: Yes, that's right. Where's Stephen?
B: Stephen is making some sandwiches. Oh no, sorry. Tom is making some sandwiches. Stephen is riding his bicycle.
A: Oh yes! I can see him now. He's wearing his brown sweater and jeans. Where is Ella? Is she having a picnic?
B: No, she isn't. Ella is picking flowers.
A: Oh yes! She's got a nice basketful.

B: Yes, and look, there's Sarah in a boat.
A: I thought she was picking flowers, too.
B: No, she isn't. She's rowing. She likes it a lot.
A: I like rowing, too.
B: I don't. I think it's too tiring.

b) Read out the examples. Ss make sentences. Check Ss' answers. You can assign this as written HW.

ANSWER KEY

Sarah was rowing a boat at eleven o'clock yesterday morning.
Tom was making sandwiches at eleven o'clock yesterday morning.
Ella was picking flowers at eleven o'clock yesterday morning.
Stephen was riding his bicycle at eleven o'clock yesterday morning.

10 Explain the task, then allow Ss two minutes to prepare their answers. Check Ss' answers.

SUGGESTED ANSWER KEY

At 8:30 am yesterday I was having breakfast.
At 8:30 am last Saturday I was shopping.
At 2:00 pm yesterday I was having lunch.
At 2:00 pm last Saturday I was riding my bicycle.
At 6:00 pm yesterday I was watching TV.
At 6:00 pm last Saturday I was reading a book. etc

11 Do item 1 with Ss. Allow Ss two to three minutes to do the exercise. Check Ss' answers by writing them on the board while Ss read the dialogue. Ask Ss to justify their answers.

ANSWER KEY

1	*played*	*8*	*fell*
2	*took*	*9*	*Did you break*
3	*had*	*10*	*scratched*
4	*were playing*	*11*	*was*
5	*were talking*	*12*	*ran after*
6	*was walking*	*13*	*tore*
7	*pushed*		

Justification:

items 1, 2, 3, 8, 9, 10, 11, 12, 13 - actions which happened at a stated time in the past and are finished.

items 4, 5, - actions which were happening at a certain time in the past.

item 6 - action which was happening when another action interrupted it.

item 7 - action which interrupted an action in progress.

Suggested Homework

1 Copy: grammar table - past continuous (p. 37)
2 Vocabulary: prompts in Exs 5, 6, 7 (p. 36)
3 Reading aloud: Ex. 11 (p. 37)
4 Dictation: any ten words from prompts in Exs. 5, 6, 7 (p. 36)
5 Act out: Ex. 10 (p. 37)

Grammar

- Past Continuous (was/were + -ing)

8 Read the examples, then answer the questions.

Tony **was painting** a picture at ten o'clock yesterday morning.

He **was windsurfing** when he **lost** his balance and **fell** into the water.

It **was raining** softly that Friday afternoon. Pete and Ann **were walking** by the river.

She **was talking** on her mobile while he **was reading** his newspaper.

1 Which verbs describe **two actions which were happening at the same time** in the past?
2 Which verb describes **an action happening at a certain time** in the past?
3 Which verb describes **an action happening when another action interrupted it**?
4 Which verb describes **an action that interrupted an action in progress**? Which tense is this?
5 Which verb **sets the scene** in the introduction to a story?

Affirmative:	I was working, you were working, he was working, etc
Negative:	I wasn't working, you weren't working, he wasn't working, etc
Interrogative:	Was I working? Were you working? Was he working? etc
Short answers:	Yes, I was. / Yes, you were. / Yes, he was. / etc
	No, I wasn't. / No, you weren't. / No, he wasn't. / etc

Time expressions used with the past continuous: *while, when, as, all day yesterday*, etc

Listening

9 a) Listen and draw lines, as in the example.

Sarah   Tom   David   Ella   Stephen

b) Say what each person was doing at eleven o'clock yesterday morning.

e.g. David was flying a kite at eleven o'clock yesterday morning.

Speaking

10 What were you doing at these times
- yesterday?   - last Saturday?

- 6:00 am   • 8:30 am   • 11:00 am
- 2:00 pm   • 6:00 pm   • 9:30 pm   • 11:30 pm

At 6:00 am yesterday, I was sleeping.
At 6:00 am last Saturday, I was flying to Rome.

11 Put the verbs into the *past simple* or the *past continuous*.

A: What did you do yesterday?
B: Well, I 1) .... (play) tennis with Andy in the morning.
A: That's nice.
B: Yes — then, in the afternoon, I 2) .... (take) my dog for a walk in the park. I 3) .... (have) a great time. Children 4) .... (play) football, and other people 5) .... (talk). Unfortunately, as I 6) .... (walk) home, a boy on his rollerblades 7) .... (push) me and I 8) .... (fall) over.
A: 9) .... (you/break) anything?
B: No, I only 10) .... (scratch) my knee. But Bernie, my dog, 11) .... (be) very angry at the boy. He 12) .... (run after) him and 13) .... (tear) his shorts.
A: Oh no!

4

12 Listen and underline the correct word in bold, then make full sentences, as in the example, to tell the story.

1 Laura / walk / along street / when it / start/ <u>raining</u>/ blowing.
Laura was walking along the street when it started raining.

2 As she / run / towards an old house/thunder / **rumble/flash** above.

3 Laura **knock/ring** on the door / but / there be / no answer.

4 She push / door which slowly **creak / crack** open.

5 As Laura / walk into the hall / she hear / someone **laughing/crying**.

6 Scared / she turn around / but / heavy door/ **close/slam** behind her.

13 Fill in: *and, when, while, as, so* or *because,* **as in the example.**

1 It was raining this morning so I took an umbrella to work.

2 I left London .... I was ten years old.

3 John put on his coat .... left the house.

4 She decided not to buy the bicycle .... it was too expensive.

5 Mary cooked lunch .... I was tired.

6 I saw Bill driving a new car .... I was waiting for the bus.

7 Steve was hoovering the carpets .... Mary was dusting the furniture.

8 It was very dark .... he didn't see the man crossing the road.

Game

Choose a leader. He/She says where he/she was last Saturday at 11 o'clock in the morning. The class, in teams, try to guess what he/she was doing. Each correct guess gets 1 point. The team with the most points is the winner.

Leader: Last Saturday at 11 o'clock in the morning I was at home. What was I doing? Guess.
Team A S1: *Were you sleeping?*
Leader: No, I wasn't.
Team B S1: *Were you doing your homework?*
Leader: No, I wasn't. ... etc

• Adjectives/Adverbs

14 Study the examples and complete the rules.

He is a very **careful** driver. (adjective)

He drives very **carefully**. (adverb)

- Adjectives describe n.......... . They have the same form in the singular and the plural. *He is a **clever** boy. They are **clever** boys.*
- Adverbs describe v........... . Most adverbs usually add -....... to the adjective. (*careful - carefully*)
  Adjectives ending in -le drop the e and take y (*terrible - terribly*)
  Adjectives ending in a **consonant + y** drop y and take -ily (*happy - happily*)
  Irregular forms: good → well, hard → hard, fast → fast, early → early, late → late

15 Fill in the spaces with the correct form — adjective or adverb — of these words, then answer the questions.

• cold • dark • fast • strong • heavy • patient • nervous • quick • sudden

It was a 1) cold (adj) winter's night. There was a 2) strong (adj) wind blowing and it was raining 3) .... Jenny Mason was standing at the bus stop in a 4) .... street, waiting 5) .... for the last bus home. 6) ...., she heard footsteps coming 7) .... towards her. Her heart was beating 8) .... as she looked 9) .... into the darkness.

1 When was it?
2 What was the weather like?
3 Who is the main character?
4 Where was she?
5 What was she doing?
6 What happened?

• Project

Look at the Photo File section. Use the prompts to say, then write, a beginning and an ending to the story.

Lesson 3 (pp. 38 - 39)

* Check Ss' HW (10').

12 • Explain the task. Read out the sentences and present new words in Ss' L1 or by giving examples.
   • Play the cassette twice if necessary. Ss underline the correct word. Check Ss' answers, then Ss make full sentences. After Ss have completed the exercise you can assign it as written HW.

ANSWER KEY

• 2 rumble   4 creak   6 slam
  3 knock   5 laughing

• 2 As she was running towards an old house thunder rumbled above.
  3 Laura knocked on the door, but there was no answer.
  4 She pushed the door which slowly creaked open.
  5 As Laura was walking into the hall she heard someone laughing.
  6 Scared, she turned around, but the heavy door slammed behind her.

13 Explain the task. Read out the example, then allow Ss two minutes to complete the exercise in closed pairs. Check Ss' answers on the board while individual Ss read out their sentences.

ANSWER KEY

2 when   6 while
3 and   7 while
4 as/because   8 so
5 because/as

Game (p. 38)

Ss, in teams, play the game as described in the Student's Book. Before the game starts the leader writes on a piece of paper what he was doing.
e.g. Team A S2: Were you planting flowers?
     Leader: No, I wasn't.
     Team B S2: Were you watching TV?
     Leader: Yes, I was.
     Teacher: Team B gets 1 point. Now, *Steve* you are the leader.   etc.

14 • Ss close their books. Write on the board. *I am a careful driver.* Underline **careful**. Ask: *What kind of driver am I? (Careful).* Ask: *Which word does careful describe? (Driver).* Explain that **careful** is an adjective. Write on the board. *They are careful drivers.* Underline **careful**. Ask: *Which word does careful describe? (Drivers).* Elicit that adjectives are the same in the singular and plural.

• Write: *I drive carefully.* Underline **carefully**. Ask: *How do I drive? (Carefully).* Ask: *Which word does carefully describe? (drive)* Explain that **carefully** is an adverb.
• Ss open their books. Read out the examples, then help Ss complete the rules.

ANSWER KEY

Adjectives describe **nouns**. They have the same form in the singular and the plural.
Adverbs describe **verbs**. Most adverbs usually add *-ly* to the adjective.

• Drill your Ss. Say adjectives. Ss say the relevant adverb form. Check Ss' spelling on the board.
  Suggested adjective list: pretty, careless, sudden, soft, good, patient, nervous, fast, early   etc.
      e.g. T: pretty
           S1: prettily
            T: careless
           S2: carelessly   etc.

Refer Ss to the Grammar Reference section for more details.

15 Explain the task. Allow Ss two minutes to fill in the answers. Check Ss' answers on the board while Ss identify the form - adjective or adverb. Then, help Ss answer the questions.

ANSWER KEY

• 3 heavily (adv)   7 quickly (adv)
  4 dark (adj)   8 fast (adv)
  5 patiently (adv)   9 nervously (adv)
  6 Suddenly (adv)

• 1 A cold winter's night.
  2 It was cold, the wind was blowing and it was raining heavily.
  3 Jenny Mason.
  4 At a bus stop in a dark street.
  5 She was waiting for the last bus home.
  6 She heard footsteps coming towards her.

Project (p. 38)

Ask Ss to look at the Photo File section. Elicit what the story can be about *(an athlete taking part in a race).* Present new words by giving examples or in Ss' L1, then allow Ss two minutes to expand the prompts into full sentences. Check Ss' answers, then assign it as written HW.
See Photo File section Unit 4 for the Answer Key.

16 Ask Ss to look at the pictures. Explain that they are not in order. Read out the questions one at a time. Ss underline the correct answers. Present any unknown words by giving synonyms or examples.

ANSWER KEY

1	*in the desert*	*4*	*men on camels*
2	*two men*	*5*	*a tent*
3	*it exploded*	*6*	*grateful*

---

17 Explain the task, then play the cassette, twice if necessary. Ss do the exercise. Check Ss' answers.

ANSWER KEY

A - 5   B - 2   C - 3   D - 1   E - 4

---

18 a) Explain the task. Ss read out sentences A to D. Allow Ss two minutes to do the exercise. Check Ss' answers, then Ss explain the words in bold by giving examples or by looking up these words in their dictionaries.

e.g. **set off:** start a journey

bang: loud noise e.g. an explosion   etc.

ANSWER KEY

1 B   2 D   3 A

---

b) Allow Ss two minutes to read the story again and underline the appropriate sentences. Check Ss' answers.

ANSWER KEY

Para 1 – *...had no idea what would happen to him **when** he set off...*
– *The view was beautiful, **but** the sun was boiling hot **as** Frank...*

Para 2 – *Rick was taking pictures **when** he heard...*
– *Frank yelled, **as** the plane...*

Para 3 – *They checked the radio, **but** it wasn't working.*
– *Frank tried to stop him, **but** he wouldn't listen.*
– *"You stay here **and** try to fix..."*
– *He took a water bottle **and** started walking.*

Para 4 – *The sun was burning his skin **as** he went on...*
– *...of turning back **when** he saw...*
– *He tried to wave back, **but** he fell exhausted...*

Para 5 – *Rick smiled gratefully **and** said...*

---

19 • Play the cassette for Ex. 17 again. Ss listen and follow the lines, then individual Ss read out from the text.

• Read out sentences A to E. Ss, in closed pairs, put the sentences into the correct order. Check Ss' answers, then individual Ss use the pictures and the sentences to tell the story.

• Help Ss suggest another title.

ANSWER KEY

• *A 2   B 4   C 1   D 5   E 3*

• *Last month Rick Anderson set off for the Sahara Desert in a small plane. He wanted to take some pictures. As he and Frank, the pilot, were flying over the Sahara, they heard a loud bang and the plane began to lose altitude. Frank managed to land the plane, but the radio wasn't working. Rick left Frank to fix the radio and decided to go for help. It was very hot in the desert. Soon Rick had no water left in the bottle. Suddenly, he saw some men on camels. He tried to wave to them, but he fell onto the sand. When Rick opened his eyes he saw he was in a tent with Frank and some Bedouin men. Frank told him how the men found them. Rick was very grateful to them.*

• *Suggested titles:*
  • *The Rescue*
  • *A Trip to Remember*
  • *A Terrifying Experience*

(Suggested Homework)

---

1 **Copy:** Ex. 12 (p. 38)
2 **Vocabulary:** words in bold in story Ex. 18a (p. 39)
3 **Reading aloud:** story Ex. 18a (p. 39)
4 **Dictation:** words in bold in story Ex. 18a (p. 39)
5 **Speaking:** Ex. 19 (p. 39)
6 **Project:** (p. 38)

Listening & Reading

16 Look at the pictures and underline the correct answer to questions 1-6.

1 Where did the story take place? **at sea/in the desert**
2 Who were the main characters? **two men/Bedouins**
3 What happened to the plane's engine as they were flying? **it exploded/it crashed**
4 Who saved them? **men on camels/friends**
5 Where did they take them to? **their plane/a tent**
6 How did the two men feel? **grateful/annoyed**

17 🎧 Listen to the story and put the pictures (A-E) into the correct order.

18 a) Read the story and fill in the sentences below. One sentence does not match. Then, explain the words in bold.

A Frank was there, too.
B A few minutes later, Frank managed to land the plane safely in the desert.
C All he could do was try to find someone to help.
D His head ached and his lips were dry and cracked.

b) Read the story again and underline the sentences which are linked with *when*, *and*, *but*, *as*.

Speaking

19 Read the story again and put the sentences A - E into the correct order. Use the sentences and the pictures to tell the story. Can you give another title to the story?

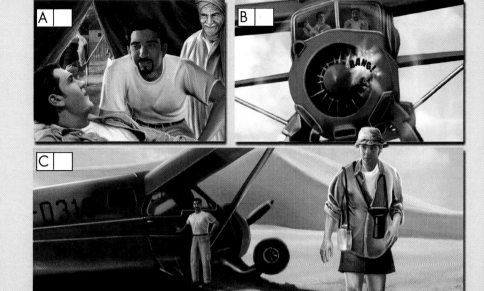

A ☐

B ☐

C ☐

D ☐

E ☐

LOST IN THE DESERT

Rick Anderson, a magazine photographer, had no idea what would happen to him when he **set off** over the Sahara Desert in a small plane last month. The view was beautiful, but the sun was boiling hot as Frank, the pilot, **flew** slowly over the desert.

Rick was taking pictures when he heard a loud **bang**. "What's that noise?" he asked Frank. "Something's wrong with the **engine**!" Frank **yelled**, as the plane began to **lose altitude**.

☐1☐ They checked the **radio**, but it wasn't working. Rick decided to go for help. Frank tried to stop him, but he wouldn't listen. "You stay here and try to fix the radio," Rick said. He took a water bottle and started walking.

The sun was burning his **skin** as he went on, **hour after hour**, through the hot desert. ☐2☐ There was no water left in the bottle. He was thinking of turning back when he saw some people on camels in the distance. One of them was **waving** to him. Rick couldn't believe his eyes. He tried to wave back, but he fell exhausted onto the sand.

When Rick opened his eyes he was inside a **tent**. ☐3☐ "Some Bedouin men on camels found me at the plane," Frank said softly. "Then we followed your **footprints** in the sand. Everything's fine now." Rick smiled **gratefully** and said, "Thanks to the Bedouins. Oh — maybe we can take some photos of them for the magazine!"

A ☐	There was a loud bang and the plane began to lose altitude.
B ☐	Rick saw some men on camels before he fell onto the sand.
C ☐	Rick and Frank were flying over the Sahara desert.
D ☐	Some Bedouins rescued them.
E ☐	The radio wasn't working, so Rick decided to go for help.

Communication

• At the doctor's

20 Listen and fill in the missing words. Then, in pairs, use the prompts to act out similar dialogues.

A: Good afternoon, Mr Brown. What's the 1) ....?

B: I sprained my 2) .... while I was jogging.

A: I see. Can I have a 3) .... at it?

B: Yes, of course.

A: Does it 4) .... ?

B: Yes, it does.

A: You should keep this bandage on and rest your ankle for the next few 5) ....

- Mrs Barker / cut finger / slice vegetables / keep it clean / change the dressing every day
- Mr Peters / burn hand / light fire / rub this cream on / put a bandage on it
- John / scrape knee / skateboard in the park / wash it carefully / put a plaster on it

Vocabulary Practice

21 **Vocabulary Revision Game: In teams, make sentences with words/phrases from the list.**

- set off • plugged in • muddy • relieved
- land the plane • fell exhausted • view
- followed footprints • head ached • yelled
- realise • flooded • was waving • for ages
- said softly • smiled • gratefully • realise
- was hoovering • was getting ready

22 **Fill in:** *in, into, on, over, at.*

1 to talk .... the phone; 2 to fall .... the water; 3 to land .... the mud; 4 to slip .... a rock; 5 to crash .... a tree; 6 to fly .... the desert; 7 lost .... the desert; 8 .... the distance; 9 people .... camels; 10 footprints .... the sand; 11 .... least

23 **Underline the correct word.**

1 "I think there's something **mistaken/wrong** with the car," John said.

2 I haven't seen Ann for **time/ages**.

3 Josh **lost/missed** his way to York and stopped to ask for directions.

4 The pilot managed to **bring/land** the plane safely on the ground.

5 What would you like for **desert/dessert**: apple pie or ice cream?

6 Can you please **fasten/tie** your seat belt?

7 His head **hurt/ached** because of the strong sun.

8 The sun was boiling **warm/hot** as we reached Egypt.

24 **Fill in the correct words from the list, then make sentences.**

- to hang out • soaking • to lose • to run
- a loud • electric • cracked • boiling

1 .... guitar   5 .... altitude
2 .... a bath   6 .... bang
3 .... wet   7 .... lips
4 .... hot   8 .... the washing

Pronunciation (silent /t/)

25 Listen and circle each *t* in bold which is not pronounced. Listen again and repeat.

Listen to the tiny birds in their nest.

Look at the castle! It's beautiful, isn't it?

Fasten your seat belts and stop whistling.

Writing (a story)

To write a story, we start by **setting the scene**: we write **when** and **where** the event happened, **who** the people in the story were, **what** the weather was like and what happened first.

In the **main body paragraphs** we describe the *events in the order they happened*. We can use *and, also, but*, etc to join sentences or ideas.

In the **last paragraph** we write **what happened in the end** and **how the people felt**. We can use **adjectives** or **adverbs** to make our story more interesting. We normally use **past tenses** in stories.

ANSWER KEY

1 on   4 on   7 in   10 in
2 into   5 into   8 in   11 at
3 in   6 over   9 on

Lesson 4 (pp. 40 - 41)

* Check Ss' HW (10').

20 • Set the scene (a patient is seeing his doctor). Explain the task. Play the cassette. Ss listen and fill in the missing words. Check Ss' answers on the board while Ss, in pairs, read out the dialogue.
• Read out the prompts. Present these words: **slice, dressing, bandage, scrape, knee, plaster** by giving examples. Then, Ss in closed pairs, use the prompts to act out similar dialogues. Check Ss' answers round the class, then ask some pairs to act out their dialogues.

ANSWER KEY

• 1 problem   3 look   5 days
  2 ankle   4 hurt

• - A: Good afternoon, Mrs Barker. What's the problem?
    B: I cut my finger while I was slicing vegetables.
    A: I see. Can I have a look at it?
    B: Yes, of course.
    A: Does it hurt?
    B: Yes, it does.
    A: You should keep it clean and change the dressing every day.

  - A: Good afternoon, Mr Peters. What's the problem?
    B: I burnt my hand while I was lighting the fire.
    A: I see. Can I have a look at it?
    B: Yes, of course.
    A: Does it hurt?
    B: Yes, it does.
    A: You should rub this cream on and put a bandage on it.

  - A: Good afternoon, John. What's the problem?
    B: I scraped my knee while I was skateboarding in the park.
    A: I see. Can I have a look at it?
    B: Yes, of course.
    A: Does it hurt?
    B: Yes, it does.
    A: You should wash it carefully and put a plaster on it.

21 Ss, in teams, make sentences using the words/phrases in the order they appear in the list. Each correct answer gets one point. The team with the most points is the winner.
e.g. Team A S1: We **set off** for New York early in the morning.
Team B S1: He **plugged in** his guitar and started playing.   etc.

22 Allow Ss two minutes to fill in the prepositions. Check Ss' answers, then ask Ss to make sentences using the completed phrases.
e.g. S1: She spent all morning **talking on the phone**.
S2: Be careful not **to fall into the water**. etc.

23 Explain the task, then allow Ss two minutes to do the exercise. Check Ss' answers while Ss read out their sentences. As an extension, ask Ss to make sentences using the words which were not underlined. Help Ss where necessary.
e.g. S1: You have **mistaken** me for my brother.
S2: What's the **time**?   etc.

ANSWER KEY

1 wrong   3 lost   5 dessert   7 ached
2 ages   4 land   6 fasten   8 hot

24 Allow Ss two minutes to fill in the words. Check Ss' answers, then ask Ss to make sentences using the completed phrases. Each correct sentence gets one point.
e.g. Team A S1: Tom got an **electric guitar** for his birthday.
Team B S1: She was **running a bath** when the phone rang.   etc.

ANSWER KEY

1 electric   4 boiling   7 cracked
2 to run   5 to lose   8 to hang out
3 soaking   6 a loud

25 • Explain the task, then play the cassette. Ss listen and circle. Check Ss' answers.
• Play the cassette again pausing between sentences for Ss to repeat either chorally or individually.

ANSWER KEY

Listen to the tiny birds in their nest.
Look at the castle. It's beautiful, isn't it?
Fasten your seat belts and stop whistling.

Writing (a story)
Read out the theory box. Refer Ss to the story on p. 39 and ask questions to check that Ss understand the theory.
e.g. T: Where did the story happen?
S1: In the Sahara Desert.
T: When did the story happen?
S2: Last month.
T: Who were the people in the story?
S3: Rick and Frank.
T: What was the weather like?
S4: It was boiling hot.   etc

26 a) Explain the task. Ss look at the pictures. Discuss with Ss which of the phrases in the list are possible in this story.

> **SUGGESTED ANSWER KEY**
>
> *sprained her ankle, orange flames, start the car, thick smoke, leave immediately, flashing light, relieved, be alive, run fast, watching TV*

b) Read out the sentences A to F. Ss match them to the pictures. Do item A with Ss, then, Ss in closed pairs, complete the sentences. Check Ss' answers while they read out the completed sentences.

> **ANSWER KEY**
>
> A 2 ...orange flames ...   D 1 ...watching TV ...
> B 5 ...flashing light ...   E 6 ...be alive ...
> C 3 ...start the car ...   F 4 ...sprained her ankle ...

c) Ask Ss to look at the pictures, then elicit answers from Ss. Help Ss where necessary by setting the scene.
> e.g.   T: Look at picture 1. What was Ray doing?
>   S1: He was watching TV.
>   T: What was on TV?
>   S2: News about a huge fire.
>   T: How do you think Ray felt?
>   S3: Scared/Shocked/Surprised.   etc

> **SUGGESTED ANSWER KEY**
>
> Pict. 1 scared/surprised/   Pict. 5 exhausted but
>   shocked   relieved
> Pict. 2 worried   Pict. 6 relieved and
> Pict. 3 desperate   happy
> Pict. 4 afraid

27 a) Ask Ss to read the sentences 1 to 6 silently. Play the cassette. Ss listen and correct the words. Check Ss' answers while Ss read out the corrected sentences.

> **ANSWER KEY**
>
> 2 mother   4 street   6 policemen
> 3 black   5 trees

TAPESCRIPT

It was a hot, sunny morning in southern California last summer. Ray Dakin was watching TV in his room. Suddenly, the TV station announced that there was a huge fire in the area where Ray lived.

He got up immediately and called his mother, Maggie. "Mum!" he shouted. "We have to leave the house — NOW!" As Ray was going downstairs, he looked out of the window and saw orange flames about a mile away.

The air was very hot and the wind was blowing black smoke towards the house. Ray and his mother hurried outside and got into the car. Maggie desperately tried to start the car, but nothing happened.

They both jumped out of the car and ran as fast as they could down the street. The fire was close behind them. While they were running, Maggie fell and sprained her ankle.

The nearby trees were now on fire, and there was thick smoke all around them. "Go on without me!" Maggie said. Ray shook his head and picked Maggie up. He carried her as fast as he could, without looking back. At last he saw the flashing light of a police car through the smoke. They were saved!

Two policemen ran towards them and helped them into the car. "You're lucky to be alive," one of the policemen said. Ray was exhausted but relieved and happy. He looked at his mother and smiled.

b) Individual Ss tell the story. Then, allow Ss two to three minutes to work in closed pairs and suggest another ending. Ss read out their answers.

> **SUGGESTED ANSWER KEY**
>
> *Ray stumbled towards the police car, but the two policemen didn't see him. They got into the car and drove away. Ray and his mother were very tired and scared. They were helpless and stranded.*

28 • Explain the task and the plan, then ask questions to make sure Ss can do the exercise.
> e.g. T: Where did the story take place?
>   S1: In southern California.
>   T: When did it happen?
>   S2: Last summer.
>   T: Who were the main characters in the story?
>   S3: Ray and his mum, Maggie.
>   T: What happened in the beginning?
>   S4: Ray was watching TV when he heard an announcement that there was a huge fire in the area.
>   T: What did Ray do?
>   S5: He shouted to his mum to leave the house.
>   T: How did Ray feel?
>   S6: Scared.
>   T: What happened when Maggie tried to start the car?
>   S7: She couldn't start it.
>   T: What did they do?
>   S8: They jumped out of the car and started running.
>   T: What happened to Maggie?
>   S9: She fell and sprained her ankle.
>   T: What did Ray do?
>   S10: He picked Maggie up and carried her as fast as he could.
>   T: Who saved them?
>   S11: Two policemen.
>   T: How did they feel?
>   S12: Happy and relieved.

• Ss, one after the other, look at the pictures in Ex. 26 and the sentences in Exs. 26b and 27a and tell the story. After Ss have completed the task orally, assign it as written HW.

29 Present the words: **sank, crossing, passengers, survived** by giving examples. Ss read and complete the survivor's name.

> **ANSWER KEY**
>
> *Hugh Williams*

(Suggested Homework)

> 1 **Copy:** Ex. 26b (p. 41)
> 2 **Vocabulary:** Exs 21, 22, 23 (p. 40)
> 3 **Reading aloud:** Ex. 27a (p. 41)
> 4 **Dictation:** Ex. 20 (p. 40)
> 5 **Act out:** Ex. 20 (p. 40)
> 6 **Writing:** Ex. 28 (p. 41)

(Lesson 5)

• Check Ss' HW.
• Workbook: Unit 4
              Click on Grammar 4

26 a) The pictures show what happened to Ray Dakin last summer in southern California. Which of these phrases can you use to say what happened?

- sprained her ankle • orange flames
- swimming • start the car • fog
- catch a train • thick smoke
- leave immediately • flashing light • relieved
- be alive • cut finger • run fast • watching TV

Mum! We have to leave the house NOW!

b) Match the sentences (A-F) to the pictures (1-6). Then, use phrases from a) above to complete the sentences.

A ☐ As Ray was going downstairs, he looked out of the window and saw .... about a mile away.

B ☐ At last he saw the .... of a police car through the smoke.

C ☐ Maggie desperately tried to .... , but nothing happened.

D ☐ Ray Dakin was .... in his bedroom.

E ☐ "You're lucky to .... ," one of the policemen said.

F ☐ While they were running, Maggie fell and ....

c) How did Ray feel in each picture?

27 a) Listen to the story and correct the mistake in bold in each topic sentence.

1 It was a ~~cold~~, sunny morning in southern California last summer.   hot

2 He got up immediately and called his **sister**, Maggie.   ....

3 The air was very hot and the wind was blowing **white** smoke towards the house. ....

4 They both jumped out of the car and ran as fast as they could down the **mountain**.   ....

5 The nearby **houses** were now on fire, and there was thick smoke all around them.   ....

6 Two **firefighters** ran towards them and helped them into the car.   ....

b) Use the sentences above, together with the pictures and sentences in Ex. 26, to tell the story. Can you give another ending to the story?

28 A teen magazine is running a competition for the best short story with the title "Up in Flames" (120-150 words). Write your story for the competition. You can use the plan below, as well as the information in Exs. 26-27.

Plan

Introduction
(Para 1)   *set the scene (who, where, when, what)*

Main Body
(Paras 2-3)   *develop the story (events in the order they happened)*

Conclusion
(Para 4)   *end the story; people's feelings*

29 Read the information. Can you guess the survivor's name?

do you know...

On 5 December 1664, a boat sank while crossing the Menai Strait, off North Wales. Only one of the 81 passengers survived. His name was Hugh Williams.

On 5 December 1785, another boat sank in the same place. There was only one survivor. His name was Hugh Williams.

On 24 August 1820, another ship sank there. The only survivor's name was ....

41

The Hound of the Baskervilles

Strange Happenings

Dr Mortimer brings Sir Henry Baskerville to meet Sherlock Holmes and Dr Watson.

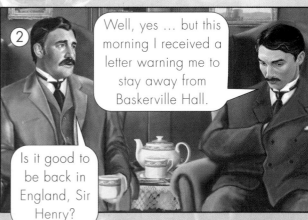

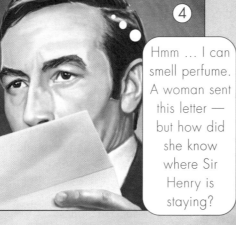

Pre-Reading Activities

1
- Who are the two men on the left in pic. 1? (Dr Mortimer, Sherlock Holmes) **Who is the man on the right?** (Sir Henry Baskerville)
- **What is strange about the letter in pic. 3?** (It is not handwritten. It is made up of newspaper cuttings.)
- **Which pictures show a cab?** (pictures 7 & 8)

Listening and Reading Activities

2 🎧 **Listen and underline the correct word.**

1 This morning Sir Henry received a note/**letter**.
2 A **man/woman** sent the letter.
3 Somebody took one of Sir Henry's **boots**/bags.
4 **Dr Watson**/Dr Mortimer must go to Baskerville Hall.

3 **Read the episode on p. 42, then read the answers and write appropriate questions to match them.**

1 Where **did** Sir Henry live?
In Canada.
2 What **could** Holmes smell?
Perfume.
3 What **was** stolen?
One of Sir Henry's boots.
4 Who **was** following Sir Henry?
The man in the cab.
5 What **did** Holmes ask Watson to write?
A report.

4 **Read the episode again and find the words which mean**

1 reach	arrive
2 get (a letter)	receive
3 go after	follow
4 go back	return

Grammar

- May / Can (asking for permission)

5 a) **Study the examples. Which of the sentences can we use when we do not know the other person very well?** (A)

> A May I see the letter, please?   B Can I see the letter?

b) **Match the answers to the questions above.**

Yes, of course.	A		Okay.	B
Sure.	B		No problem.	B
By all means.	A			

6 **Look at the pictures, then use the prompts below and the sentences in Ex. 5b to complete the speech bubbles.**

make a photocopy, have a look at the photos, see your credit card, sit with you (Suggested answers)

May I see your credit card?
Yes, of course.

Can I sit with you?
Sure.

May I make a photocopy?
By all means.

Can I have a look at the photos?
Sure.

7 🎧 a) **Listen to the episode again, then take roles and act out the episode.**

b) **Put the events in the correct order, then give a summary of the episode.**

4 Holmes saw a man in a cab following Sir Henry.
2 Sir Henry showed Holmes the letter.
5 The man went to Waterloo Station.
3 Holmes asked Sir Henry to return to his hotel.
1 Holmes met Sir Henry.
6 Holmes asked Watson to go to Baskerville Hall with Sir Henry.

Vocabulary

1 **Fill in:** *yelled, soaking, bruised, leather, plastic, hoovered, lose, ankle, experience, suit.*

1 My suitcase has got brown leather straps.
2 The plane began to lose altitude when the engine failed.
3 She put the photo in a red plastic frame.
4 He fell down the steps and sprained his ankle.
5 Sam tidied the room and hoovered the carpet.
6 He fell off his bike and bruised his knee.
7 The theme park has rides to suit all ages.
8 I've always wanted to experience life in the jungle.
9 Look at John! He is soaking wet!
10 "Quick! Lock all the doors!" Dave yelled.

(10 marks)

2 **Underline the correct word.**

1 It is freezing/**boiling** hot outside.
2 As they were flying the engine **exploded**/landed.
3 Eat at least two **slices**/bowls of bread daily.
4 Let's drive/**ride** our bikes to the park.
5 We watched the firework **display**/attraction with excitement.
6 How was your **trip**/travel to France?
7 We had the holiday of a **lifetime**/ages in Spain.
8 There were a lot of rides to enjoy/**suit** everyone.

(8 marks)

3 **Use the words in the list to describe each object, as in the example.**

• straps • face • stones • glass • plastic • blue
• red • gold • silver • pearl • black • leather

suitcase   watch   necklace

            ring

e.g. It's a blue plastic suitcase with black plastic straps. (See Suggested Answers section)

(10 marks)

4 **Fill in:** *in, for, at, into, to, over.*

1 The farm is set in 100 acres.
2 John was waiting for Mary when it started raining.
3 Tim slipped and fell into the water.
4 Can't you at least help me with the dishes?
5 It was exciting to fly over the desert.
6 Sally waved goodbye to Peter and left.
7 He could see a light in the distance.
8 Look! There are footprints in the sand.

(8 marks)

Grammar

5 **Fill in:** *yet, just, already, never, ever, since, for.*

1 I've just made a cake. Would you like some?
2 She has never travelled abroad before.
3 We have lived in this village for ten years.
4 Hasn't Jane finished her homework yet?
5 This is the worst meal I've ever had.
6 He hasn't played tennis since last week.
7 You needn't do the washing up. I've already done it.

(7 marks)

6 **Write three things you have already done; haven't done yet; have never done, as in the examples.** (See Suggested Answers section)

I have already done my homework.
I haven't tidied my room yet.
I have never been to America.

(8 marks)

7 **Put the verbs in brackets into the** *past simple* **or the** *past continuous.*

1 Susan wrote **(write)** a long letter yesterday.
2 Mark was cooking **(cook)** dinner when the phone rang **(ring)**.
3 Paul didn't go **(not/go)** out yesterday.
4 He was eating **(eat)** breakfast when he heard **(hear)** a knock on the window.
5 The children were playing **(play)** in the park when it started to rain.
6 What were you doing **(you/do)** when he called **(call)** you last night?

7 Did you have (you/have) a good time at the party?

8 John didn't type (not/type) all the letters yesterday.

9 A: Did she break (she/break) her arm while she was skiing (ski)?
B: Yes.

10 First she cleaned (clean) the house, then she washed (wash) the dishes. After that, she went (go) shopping.   *(10 marks)*

Communication

8 Fill in the missing sentences. Then, in pairs, read out the dialogues.

• What's wrong with you? • My purse and my watch. • What does your watch look like?

1 A: What does your watch look like?
B: It's gold with a leather strap.

2 A: What's in your handbag?
B: My purse and my watch?

3 A: What's wrong with you?
B: I cut my finger while I was cooking.
(6 marks)

Reading

9 Put the verbs in brackets into the correct tense, then ask and answer questions, as in the example.

Dear Louise,

We 1) are having (have) a wonderful time here in Rome. The weather is quite good. We 2) are staying (stay) in a nice hotel near the train station.

So far we 3) have visited (visit) the Colosseum, the Fontana di Trevi and Piazza d'España. We 4) haven't visited (not/visit) the Vatican yet. Yesterday we 5) ate (eat) at a wonderful restaurant by the river. While we 6) were having (have) lunch though, it 7) started (start) raining so we 8) left (leave). Tomorrow we 9) are going (go) shopping in the famous Via Veneto.

I hope you 10) are having (have) a nice time. I 11) 'm looking forward to (look forward to) seeing you soon.

Love,

Francesca

S1: Where is Francesca?
S2: She's in Italy. What's the weather like?   etc.
(See Suggested Answers section)   *(13 marks)*

Writing (a letter to a friend giving news)

10 Bill has been in New York for a week. Expand the prompts into full sentences, then write the letter Bill sent to Tom (100-120 words). Use the letter in Ex. 9 as a model.

Plan

(See Suggested   *(20 marks)*
Answers section)

Dear Tom,
(Para 1) have/great time/New York - stay with/friend
(Para 2) so far/been to Manhattan/do some shopping on 5th Avenue/unfortunately/I shop/I lose/camera/not visit Liberty Island yet/tomorrow/we go/see a concert/ Carnegie Hall
(Para 3) come back next Monday/hope you/be OK.
See you,
Bill

(Total = 100 marks)

Let's sing!

11 Listen and fill in. Listen again and sing.

On a Rollercoaster

Higher than high
up in the 1) sky
on a rollercoaster.
Round and 2) round
on the ground
fast, faster and faster.

Still in the 3) park
but it's very dark.
And this place is very scary.
The haunted 4) house
is quiet as a mouse.
Then out jumps
something hairy!

Outside it's bright.
And very light.
Let's go to the dolphin
5) pool
buy ice cream,
sit and dream,
where it's 6) nice
and cool.

There's the parade.
The music's played
but it's 7) time to say goodbye.
It's been a great day
I wish I could 8) stay.
But it's time for home —
oh my!

Food & Entertainment

◆ **Before you start...**

Have you ever been to a theme park?
How are you feeling today?
What's your favourite possession?
Have you ever had an accident?
How do you go to school/work?

◆ **Listen, read and talk about...**

I'm going to be ...

UNIT 5

- clothes and fashion
- the weather
- plans & intentions
- shops & shopping

Module 3
Units 5-6

Food & Festivities

UNIT 6

- food & drink
- festivals
- cooking methods & equipment
- healthy eating

◆ Learn how to ...

- talk about measurements and sizes
- describe clothes
- talk about the weather and the forecast
- talk about your future plans
- prioritise your tasks
- talk about what clothes you like to wear
- make predictions
- express likes/dislikes
- justify your preferences
- make a complaint
- describe a celebration
- make a shopping list

◆ Practise ...

- future tenses (going to - will)
- present continuous (future meaning)
- countable & uncountable nouns
- plurals
- a/an/any/some/a lot of/ much/many/a few/a little

◆ Write ...

- a letter of complaint
- a letter to a friend about your plans
- an advertisement for a restaurant
- an article about a festival you attended

5 I'm going to be...

Lead-in

1 a) Jan and Tony are going to spend their summer holidays at a seaside hotel in Mexico. Look at the pictures on p. 46 and say what they are/aren't going to take with them.

They are going to take their goggles with them. They aren't going to take their gloves.

b) What do you think they will do there? Use the prompts to make sentences, as in the example. You can add to the list.

- go swimming every day
- lie on the beach all morning
- try traditional food
- take lots of pictures
- go sightseeing
- buy souvenirs

I think they'll go swimming every day.

2 What is/isn't Gina going to do when she grows up? Look at the pictures on p. 47 and the prompts and say, as in the example.

- be a famous singer
- live in a big house with a swimming pool
- make a lot of money
- work as a Maths teacher
- drive a sports car
- have two pet dogs
- wear expensive clothes
- make lots of records

I'm going to be a famous singer.

jacket — tent — shorts — goggles — binoculars — camera — goldfish — T-shirt — flippers — PASSPORT — boots — skis — umbrella — gloves — trainers — sunglasses — sandals

3 🎧 **Listen and repeat.**

- There's no point.
- I see. I expect you'll make a lot of money.
- I'm not sure, probably the end of next week.
- How long are you going to be away?
- Well, have a good trip then.
- It'll be a great experience, though.
- What's up?
- You haven't changed your mind, have you?
- What's the weather like over there?
- No way!

Jan   Tony

Objectives

Vocabulary: clothes; the weather; plans; intentions; fashion; measurements; shops; sizes
Reading: reading for gist
Listening: listening for specific information
Speaking: talking about your plans; prioritising
Communication: buying clothes
Pronunciation: homophones
Grammar: going to; will; present continuous (future meaning)
Project: a letter of complaint
Writing: a letter to a friend about your plans

Lesson 1 (pp. 46 - 47)

1 a) • Ask Ss to look at the pictures on p. 46. Explain that Jan & Tony are planning a holiday to Mexico and they are thinking about what they are going to take with them.
   • Explain the task. Read out the picture prompts, then the example. Explain that we use **going to** to talk about plans. Ss do the exercise.

ANSWER KEY

They are going to take their: binoculars, camera, shorts, flippers, T-shirts, passports, sandals, trainers, sunglasses.
They aren't going to take their: jackets, tent, goldfish, skis, boots, umbrellas.

b) • Explain the task. Read out the prompts, then the example. Ask Ss to underline 'll. Explain that this is the short form of **will**. Point out that we use **will** to say what we think/guess will happen. Give more examples for Ss to understand the use of will.
   e.g. Tomorrow will be cold.
        I think they will win on Sunday.
   Point out that **will** is the same in all persons.
   • Read out the prompts. Ss make sentences.

SUGGESTED ANSWER KEY

I think they'll lie on the beach all morning.
I think they'll try traditional food.
I think they'll take lots of pictures.
I think they'll go sightseeing.
I think they'll buy souvenirs.
I think they'll go dancing every night.
I think they'll visit museums.
I think they'll go to bed late.   etc.

2 • Ask Ss to look at the pictures on p. 47. Explain that Gina is thinking about what she is going to do when she grows up. Read out the prompts, then the example. Ss make sentences.

ANSWER KEY

I'm going to live in a big house with a swimming pool.
I'm going to make a lot of money.
I'm not going to work as a Maths teacher.
I'm going to drive a sports car.
I'm going to have two pet dogs.
I'm going to wear expensive clothes.
I'm going to make lots of records.

• As an extension ask Ss to tell the class what they are going to do when they grow up.
   e.g. I'm going to be a Drama teacher.
        I'm going to live in a nice cottage in the countryside.
        I'm going to have a big family.   etc.

3 • Play the cassette. Ss listen and follow the lines. Play the cassette again. Ss listen and repeat.
   • Present the phrases/sentences by giving examples, miming or using Ss' L1 if necessary.
   e.g. **No way!** (Ask Ss: *Can we eat in class?* Answer: *No way! We can't eat in class.*)

4 a) Explain the task, then read out the prompts. Play the cassette. Ss listen and match. Check Ss' answers.

ANSWER KEY

Gina - be a famous singer
Les - go to Africa on a business trip
Jan - go on holiday

---

b) • Read questions 1 to 5 aloud. Allow Ss four minutes to read the dialogues and answer the questions. Check Ss' answers, then help Ss explain the words in bold by giving a synonym or in Ss' L1 if necessary.

ANSWER KEY

1 *She's going to be a famous singer.*
2 *He's going to be away for about three and a half weeks.*
3 *His sister is going to look after his cat.*
4 *It's going to get hot soon.*
5 *She is going to take T-shirts, shorts and a couple of jumpers.*

• Play the cassette for Ex. 4a again. Ss listen and follow the lines, then take roles and read out the dialogues.

c) Allow Ss three minutes to read the dialogues again and underline the phrases/sentences. Ss then say who said each one.

ANSWER KEY

Gina said, "There's no point."
Gina's mum said, "I see. I expect you'll make a lot of money."
Les said, "I'm not sure, probably the end of next week."
John asked, "How long are you going to be away?"
John said, "Well, have a good trip then."
John said, "It'll be a great experience, though."
Franco asked, "What's up?"
Franco asked, "You haven't changed your mind, have you?"
Jan asked, "What's the weather like over there?"
Jan said, "No way!"

Memory Game

Ask Ss to look at the phrases/sentences in Ex. 3 for a minute, then close their books and, in teams, try to remember as many as possible. Each correct phrase/sentence gets 1 point. The team with the most points is the winner.
e.g. Team A S1: No way!
    Team B S1: What's up?   etc.

Suggested Homework

1 **Copy:** dialogue C in Ex. 4b (p. 47)
2 **Vocabulary:** picture prompts Ex 1a (p. 46)
3 **Reading aloud:** dialogues in Ex. 4b (p. 47) (Point out that Ss practise *reading aloud* at home using the S's cassette/audio CD.)
4 **Dictation:** words in bold in dialogues A - C (p. 47)
5 **Speaking:** a) the first four exchanges from dialogue B (p. 47)
          b) Ss memorise any five sentences from Ex. 3 (p. 46)

Listening and Reading

4 a) Listen and match the people to what they are going to do.

1 Gina   go to Africa on a business trip
2 Les   go on holiday
3 Jan   be a famous singer

b) Read dialogues A to C and answer the questions (1 - 5), then explain the words in bold. In pairs, read out the dialogues.

1 What is Gina going to do when she grows up?
2 How long is Les going to be away?
3 Who is going to look after Les's cat?
4 What does Franco say the weather is going to be like?
5 What will Jan take with her?

A
Mum: Gina, are you going to do your Maths **homework**?
Gina: No, Mum. There's no point.
Mum: Yes, there is. You will **need** Maths when you grow up.
Gina: No, I won't. I'm going to be a famous singer, so I won't need to know about Maths.
Mum: A famous singer?
Gina: Yes. I'm going to make lots of **records** and I'm going to do a **world tour** every year, so I'll see lots of different countries.
Mum: I see. I **expect** you'll make a lot of money.
Gina: Of course. I'm going to drive a real sports car, wear expensive clothes and have two pet dogs. I'm going to be very rich.
Mum: **In that case**, you'll need to know about Maths to look after all that money. Now do your homework!
Gina: Oh, Mum!

B
John: So, Les, when are you going to Africa?
Les: I'm not sure, probably the end of next week.
John: How long are you going to **be away**?
Les: About three and a half weeks.
John: Oh! So who's going to **water your plants** and **feed** your cat?
Les: Well, my next-door neighbour is going to water my plants and **collect** my letters but my cat is going to stay with my sister.
John: Well, have a good **trip** then.
Les: I'm going **on business**, not to have a good time.
John: It'll be a great **experience**, though.
Les: Yes, I **suppose** so, but I'll miss my cat.

C
Jan: Franco? Hi — it's Jan here. I'm calling from England.
Franco: Hi, Jan! What's up? You haven't changed your **mind**, have you?
Jan: No way! It's just that we're packing at the moment, and we aren't sure what clothes to bring. What's the weather like over there?
Franco: Well, it's been **cloudy** for the last few days, but the **forecast** says it's going to get hot soon.
Jan: Okay — so I'll **pack** T-shirts and shorts.
Franco: Yeah ... but remember, it can get quite **chilly** in the evenings, so bring a couple of jumpers, too.
Jan: Okay. Thanks. See you soon!
Franco: Bye.

c) Read the dialogues again and underline the phrases/sentences used in Ex. 3. Who said each phrase/sentence?

Gina

47

Vocabulary

• Clothes

5 a) Look at the pictures. Which are:
   - menswear?   - ladieswear?
   - footwear?   - accessories?

b) Which of the clothes in the pictures are casual. Which are formal?

cotton T-shirt   denim dress   short-sleeved shirt   dinner jacket

V-neck pullover   spotted tie   fur coat   baggy trousers   long-sleeved cardigan

polo neck jumper   high-heeled shoes   plain trousers   checked skirt   leggings

evening dress   silk scarf   leather skirt   woollen jumper   plastic raincoat

straw hat   waistcoat   suede belt   striped shorts

Speaking

6 Do you prefer wearing formal clothes or casual clothes?
What do you wear when you go:
- to a wedding reception?   - on a trip?
- to a restaurant for a formal dinner?
- on a picnic?
What size are you: small, medium, large, extra large?

• The weather

KEY

boiling hot	35°C
hot	30°C
warm	25°C
cool	15°C
chilly	10°C
cold	5°C
freezing cold	-5°C

7 Look at the key and the map. What will the weather be like tomorrow in each city? Ask and answer, as in the example.

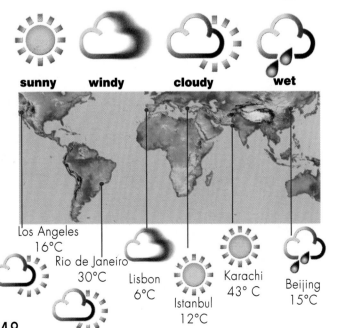

sunny   windy   cloudy   wet

Los Angeles 16°C
Rio de Janeiro 30°C
Lisbon 6°C
Istanbul 12°C
Karachi 43° C
Beijing 15°C

A: What will the weather be like in Los Angeles tomorrow?
B: It'll be cool and cloudy.

Listening

8 Read the sentences below, then listen to the weather forecast and mark each sentence as correct (✓) or incorrect (✗).

1 London will be warm and sunny tomorrow. .....
2 It will be cold and wet in Wales.   .....
3 Manchester will be warm tomorrow.   .....
4 It will be chilly in Scotland.   .....

Speaking

9 What's the weather like in your town today?
What's the forecast for tomorrow?
What's the weather like in your country in the spring/summer/autumn/winter?

10 In pairs, use words from Ex. 5 and Ex. 7 to ask and answer, as in the example.

A: What's the weather like today?
B: It's freezing cold.
A: I'll wear my fur coat, then.

Lesson 2 (pp. 48 - 49)

* • Check Ss' HW (10').
  • Play the Memory Game as described in Ex. 4c p. 47(T).

5 a) Read aloud the picture prompts. Ss repeat individually. Present any new words by giving examples, then Ss do the exercise.

SUGGESTED ANSWER KEY

menswear: cotton T-shirt, short-sleeved shirt, dinner jacket, V-neck pullover, baggy trousers, long-sleeved cardigan, waistcoat, striped shorts, polo neck jumper, plain trousers, woollen jumper

ladieswear: cotton T-shirt, denim dress, fur coat, baggy trousers, polo neck jumper, plain trousers, checked skirt, leggings, evening dress, leather skirt, plastic raincoat

footwear: high-heeled shoes

accessories: spotted tie, straw hat, suede belt, silk scarf

---

b) Present the words **casual** and **formal**. Then, Ss do the exericse.

SUGGESTED ANSWER KEY

casual clothes: cotton T-shirt, denim dress, short-sleeved shirt, V-neck pullover, baggy trousers, long-sleeved cardigan, striped shorts, polo neck jumper, plain trousers, checked skirt, leggings, leather skirt, woollen jumper, plastic raincoat

formal clothes: dinner jacket, spotted tie, fur coat, waistcoat, evening dress

---

6 Read out the questions, one at a time. Elicit answers from various Ss.

SUGGESTED ANSWER KEY

• I prefer wearing casual clothes.
• When I go to a wedding reception I wear an evening dress and my fur coat.
• When I go on a trip I wear a polo neck jumper and my baggy trousers.
• When I go to a restaurant for a formal dinner I wear my dinner jacket and tie.
• When I go on a picnic I wear my T-shirt and shorts.
• I'm medium.

---

7 Read out the key and present new words. Then, ask Ss to look at the map and read out the example. Ss, in open pairs, ask and answer questions.

ANSWER KEY

• A: What will the weather be like in Rio de Janeiro tomorrow?
  B: It'll be hot and cloudy.
• A: What will the weather be like in Lisbon tomorrow?
  B: It'll be cold and windy.
• A: What will the weather be like in Istanbul tomorrow?
  B: It'll be cool and sunny.

• A: What will the weather be like in Karachi tomorrow?
  B: It'll be boiling hot and sunny.
• A: What will the weather be like in Beijing tomorrow?
  B: It'll be cool and wet.

---

8 Explain the task. Read out sentences 1 to 4. Play the cassette. Ss listen and put a tick or a cross. Check Ss' answers, then play the cassette again for Ss to correct the incorrect sentences. Check Ss' answers.

ANSWER KEY

1 ✓   2 ✗   3 ✗   4 ✓

2 Wales will see sunshine in the morning, but it will be mostly cloudy for the rest of the day.
3 Manchester will see plenty of rain and it will be windy.

TAPESCRIPT

Good evening.

Well, those of you who live in the south of the country will see lots of sunshine tomorrow. In Brighton and London it will be warm and sunny with temperatures around 26°C. The east coast will be warm too, with light winds keeping the temperature at about 22°C. The west of England and Wales will see some sunshine in the morning, but it will be mostly cloudy for the rest of the day.

Moving further north, the temperatures will be lower and there will be a lot of wet weather about. Manchester, Preston and Liverpool will see plenty of rain and it'll be windy, too. The temperatures will stay at around 15°C so it will feel quite cool in these areas.

Scotland and Northern Ireland will have a bright start, but low temperatures will mean a chilly day for most people, so wrap up well to keep out the cold.

That's all from the National Weather Centre for today. Goodnight.

9 Ask questions, one at a time. Elicit appropriate answers from Ss.

SUGGESTED ANSWER KEY

• It's cool and cloudy.
• It'll be warm and sunny tomorrow.
• In the spring it is cool in the mornings and evenings, but warm during the day.
• In the summer it is hot and windy.
• In the autumn it is warm and windy.
• In the winter it is cold and wet.

---

10 Explain the task and read out the example. Then Ss, in closed pairs, act out similar dialogues. Check Ss' performance, then ask some pairs to act out their dialogues in class.

SUGGESTED ANSWER KEY

• A: What's the weather like today?
  B: It's chilly.
  A: I'll wear a woollen jumper and trousers, then.
• A: What's the weather like today?
  B: It's boiling hot and sunny.
  A: I'll wear a cotton T-shirt, shorts and a hat, then.
• A: What's the weather like today?
  B: It's cold and wet.
  A: I'll wear my plastic raincoat, then.   etc.

---

11 Explain the task, then read out the order form. Play the cassette. Ss listen and fill in the missing words. Check Ss' answers on the board.

Smart Choice

NAME :
Mrs J Johnson
CUSTOMER :
278-349 Z

Item	Material	Pattern/Colour	Size	Items
jumper	woollen	black	large	1
blouse	**cotton**	checked	**medium**	1
belt	leather	**brown**	small	1

TAPESCRIPT

A: Good morning. Thank you for calling Smart Choice. How may I help you?
B: Good morning... I'd· like to order some clothes from your January catalogue... My name is Jill Johnson...
A: May I have your customer number, please?
B: Yes, of course. It's 278-349 Z.
A: Thank you, Mrs Johnson. What would you like to order?
B: A jumper, please, the black woollen jumper on page 14... in a large, please.
A: One large black woollen jumper. Anything else?
B: Yes, the checked cotton blouse on page 39, please.
A: What size?
B: Medium, please.
A: One medium checked cotton blouse. Anything else?
B: The brown leather belt on page 42, size small and that's everything.
A: One small brown leather belt. Thank you. Wait just a moment please. *(pause)* Right, those items are all available and will be sent out to you today.
B: Thank you. Bye.
A: Thank you for your order. Goodbye.

Project (p. 49)

Ss look at the Photo File section. Explain that this is a letter of complaint that Mrs Johnson sent to Smart Choice because they sent her the wrong items. Explain the task. Point out that three sentences do not match. Ss do the exercise orally in class, then assign it as written HW. See Photo File section Unit 5 for the Answer Key.

12 Read out the examples and help Ss answer the questions.

> ### ANSWER KEY
>
> 1   'm going to buy (future intention)
> 2   'll buy (on-the-spot decision)

13 Read out the tables and elicit the rules from Ss. Refer Ss to the Grammar Reference section for more details.

14 Explain the task. Read out the picture prompts, then play the cassette, twice if necessary. Ss listen and mark accordingly. Check Ss' answers. Read out the example. Ss ask and answer rolling questions about Fiona's plans/intentions.

> ### ANSWER KEY
>
> - visit Egypt ✓
> - spend a week in a castle ✓
> - go on a cruise ✗
> - move to a big house ✓
> - open an animal rescue shelter ✓
>
> S3: ... Is she going to spend a week in a castle?
> S4: Yes, she is. Is she going to go on a cruise?
> S5: No, she isn't. Is she going to move to a big house?
> S6: Yes, she is. Is she going to open an animal rescue shelter?
> S7: Yes, she is.

TAPESCRIPT

A: So Fiona, what are you going to do with your money now that you're rich?
B: I'm not going to go out and buy diamonds and rubies or go on luxurious cruises, you know.
A: No, but you must have thought about what you'd like to do.
B: Well, I'd really like to see the Great Pyramids so I'm going to visit Egypt.
A: That's nice. What else are you going to do?
B: I'm going to spend a week in a castle. I've always wanted to do that.
A: Wow! But aren't you going to buy anything like a big house or a fancy sports car?
B: No, I don't need a car because I hate driving. I'm going to move to a big house and open an animal rescue shelter.
A: An animal rescue shelter! That's great.
B: I love animals. I don't want to see them suffer, so now this is my chance to help them.
A: That's fantastic.

15 Ss answer about themselves.

> ### SUGGESTED ANSWER KEY
>
> Next weekend I'm going (to go) on a picnic by the lake.
> This summer we're going to travel abroad.
> Next Friday morning I'm going to do the shopping.

16 Explain the task. Read out the prompts. Allow Ss three minutes to do the exercise. Check Ss' answers.

> ### ANSWER KEY
>
> 2   ... I'll take an aspirin.
> 3   ... I'll put my jacket on.
> 4   ... I'll have some orange juice.
> 5   ... I'll take an umbrella.
> 6   ... I'll open the window.

> (Suggested Homework)
>
> 1   Copy: Ex. 16 (p. 49)
> 2   Vocabulary: words in Exs 5 and 7 (p. 48)
> 3   Speaking: Ex. 14 (p. 49)
> 4   Dictation: any ten words from Exs 5 and 7 (p. 48)
> 5   Act out: Ex. 7 (p. 48)
> 6   Project: (p. 49)

Listening

11 Listen to Mrs Johnson ordering clothes by telephone, then fill in the order form below.

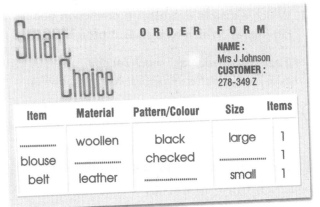

Smart Choice

ORDER FORM

NAME: Mrs J Johnson
CUSTOMER: 278-349 Z

Item	Material	Pattern/Colour	Size	Items
....	woollen	black checked	large	1
blouse	....			1
belt	leather	....	small	1

• Project

Look at the Photo File section and choose the best sentences to complete the letter Mrs Johnson sent to the Smart Choice company.

Grammar

• The Future

12 Read the examples and answer the questions.

We've run out of milk. Really? I'll buy some, then.

We've run out of milk. I know. I'm going to buy some on my way home.

1 Which verb form expresses a **future intention**?
2 Which expresses an **on-the-spot decision** (i.e. a decision taken at the moment of speaking)?

13 Study the tables, then say how we form the future with *going to* and *will*.

Affirmative:	I'm/you're/he's/etc going to buy
Negative:	I'm not/you aren't/he isn't/etc going to buy
Interrogative:	Am I going to buy? Are you going to buy? Is he going to buy? etc
Short answers:	Yes, I am/you are/he is. etc / No, I'm not/you aren't/he isn't. etc

Affirmative:	I/you/he/etc will buy
Negative:	I/you/he/etc won't buy
Interrogative:	Will I/you/he/etc buy?
Short answers:	Yes, I/you/he/etc will. / No, I/you/he/etc won't.

14 Fiona has won a lot of money. Listen and mark the pictures to show what she is going to do (✓) and isn't going to do (✗). Then, ask and answer, as in the example.

visit Egypt ☐
buy a diamond ring ✗
spend a week in a castle ☐
go on a cruise ☐
move to a big house ☐
open an animal rescue shelter ☐

S1: Is she going to buy a diamond ring?
S2: No, she isn't. Is she going to visit Egypt?
S3: Yes, she is. Is she ...?

Speaking

15 What are you going to do: - next weekend? - this summer? - next Friday morning?

• Will (on-the-spot decisions)

16 Complete the sentences using the prompts, as in the example.

• have an early night   • open the window
• take an aspirin   • put my jacket on
• have some orange juice   • take an umbrella

1 I'm tired. *I'll have an early night.*
2 I have a headache. ....
3 It's cold. ....
4 I'm thirsty. ....
5 It's raining today. ....
6 It's hot in here. ....

• Going to (predictions based on what we see)

17 **a) What is going to happen next? Match the pictures to the prompts, then write sentences, as in the example.**

a slip on a banana skin   d fall off the ladder
b fall into the hole   e wash the car
c answer the phone   f walk into the lamp post

(1-a) He's going to slip on a banana skin.

b) What is each person going to do? Make sentences, as in the example.

1 That looks very nice on you, Ann.
   Ann is going to buy a dress.
2 You get the racquets, Tom, and I'll get the balls.
3 Don't forget to buy milk and potatoes, Carla.
4 Hurry up, Kate! The film starts at 8 o'clock!
5 Oh, no! There goes the school bus, Kelly!

18 **Fill in *be going to* or *will*.**

1 A: Oh, no! I've missed the bus!
   B: Don't worry. I .... give you a lift.

2 A: Why is he wearing those old clothes?
   B: He .... paint the fence.

3 A: That dress looks very nice on you.
   B: Do you think so? I .... buy it, then.

4 A: Has she decided what to do about the job?
   B: Yes, she .... apply for it.

5 A: Your shirt is dirty.
   B: I know. I .... wash it.

• Will (predictions about the future/promises)

19 **Which example expresses a prediction about the future? Which expresses a promise?**

A: *I'll call you* as soon as I reach London.
B: I think *he'll be* rich and famous when he grows up.

20 **Match the pictures to the sentences. Which expresses: a prediction about the future; a promise; an on-the-spot decision; a prediction based on what we see; a future intention?**

1 I'll try on this one.
2 I'm going to lie on the beach all day.
3 Look out! You're going to fall!
4 She'll buy a new house next year if she has enough money.
5 I'll buy you a computer on your birthday.

Game

Look at the list of things Sam has got. Choose one of the things in the list. Ss, in teams, say what Sam is going to do. Each correct sentence gets one point. The team with the most points is the winner.

Suggested list: a toothbrush, a pen, a bottle of shampoo, a mobile phone, a brush, tea and sugar, a chicken and two kilos of potatoes, a vacuum cleaner, a bucket of water and a sponge, flippers, a camera, some CDs, etc

   T: Sam has got a toothbrush.
Team AS1: He's going to brush his teeth.   *etc*

*   Check Ss' HW (10').

17 a)
*   Ask Ss to look at the pictures. Explain that something is going to happen. Read out the example, and check the meaning. Ask: *Has he slipped on a banana skin yet? (No.) When? (Soon.) How do you know? (There's a banana skin in front of him. He hasn't seen it.)*
*   Read out the prompts one at a time. Ss match them to the pictures. Allow Ss two minutes to make sentences. Check Ss' answers, then assign it as written HW.

ANSWER KEY

(2 - e) He's going to wash the car.
(3 - f) He's going to walk into the lamp post.
(4 - c) She's going to answer the phone.
(5 - d) He's going to fall off the ladder.
(6 - b) She's going to fall into the hole.

b) Explain the task, then read out the example. Ss, in closed pairs, do the exercise. Check Ss' answers as various Ss read out their sentences. As an extension, you can assign the exercise as written HW.

SUGGESTED ANSWER KEY

2 They are going to play tennis.
3 She is going to do the shopping.
4 They are going to go to the cinema.
5 She is going to be late for school.

18 Explain the task, then allow Ss two minutes to complete the exercise. Check Ss' answers and ask Ss to justify them.

ANSWER KEY

1 will (on-the-spot decision)
2 is going to (future intention)
3 will (on-the-spot decision)
4 is going to (future intention)
5 am going to (future intention)

19 Read out the examples and help Ss match them to the meaning.

ANSWER KEY

A - promise
B - prediction about the future

20 Explain the task. Allow Ss two minutes to match the pictures to the sentences. Check Ss' answers as Ss say what each sentence expresses.

ANSWER KEY

A - 2 (future intention)
B - 3 (prediction based on what we see)
C - 5 (promise)
D - 4 (prediction about the future)
E - 1 (on-the-spot decision)

Game (p. 50)
Play the game as described in the Student's Book.

SUGGESTED ANSWER KEY

T: Sam has got a pen.
Team B S1: He's going to write a letter.
T: Sam has got a bottle of shampoo.
Team A S2: He's going to wash his hair.
T: Sam has got a mobile phone.
Team B S2: He's going to call his friend.
T: Sam has got a brush.
Team A S3: He's going to brush his hair.
T: Sam has got tea and sugar.
Team B S3: He's going to make some tea.
T: Sam has got a chicken and two kilos of potatoes.
Team A S4: He's going to cook lunch.
T: Sam has got a vacuum cleaner.
Team B S4: He's going to hoover the carpets.
T: Sam has got a bucket of water and a sponge.
Team A S5: He's going to wash the car.
T: Sam has got flippers.
Team B S5: He's going to go swimming.
T: Sam has got a camera.
Team A S6: He's going to take some pictures.

21 a) Read out the prompts, and help Ss match them to the pictures.

ANSWER KEY

5 - rubbish   1 - credit cards
4 - a mouse   6 - breathing masks
2 - brightly-coloured
    clothes

b) Read out the title and discuss it with Ss.

SUGGESTED ANSWER KEY

I think the article is about what clothes people will wear in the future.

22 Explain the task, then play the cassette. Ss underline the correct word. Check Ss' answers while individual Ss read out the sentences.

ANSWER KEY

1 electronic   2 water   3 platform

23 • Point out that we use *because* to express reason and *so that* to express result.
• Allow Ss three minutes to read the article. Help Ss explain the words in bold by giving an example or a synonym. Ss can also look up these words in their dictionaries.
• Ss, in closed pairs, match the two columns. Check Ss' answers, then Ss say complete sentences.

ANSWER KEY

(2 - d) We will go cybershopping **because** websites will sell things at lower prices than shops do.

(3 - b) People will wear light, cool clothes **so that** they can protect themselves from the sun.

(4 - e) When clothes get dirty, people will throw them away **because** there won't be much water.

(5 - a) Everyone will wear platform shoes **because** they won't want to walk in all the rubbish in the streets.

(6 - f) People will wear breathing masks **so that** they can protect themselves from air pollution.

24 a) Point out that Ss should link each point using: *also, in addition, furthermore, lastly, moreover* etc. Explain that these linkers are used to join similar ideas. Give an example, then allow Ss one to two minutes to get prepared to give a short summary of the article using the information in the columns.

SUGGESTED ANSWER KEY

... will wear clothes with microchips in them so that they can talk to their friends wherever they are. Furthermore, we will go cybershopping because websites will sell things at lower prices than shops do. In addition, people will wear light, cool clothes so that they can protect themselves from the sun. Also, when clothes get dirty people will throw them away because there won't be much water for people to wash them. What is more, everyone will wear platform shoes because they won't want to walk in all the rubbish in the streets. Lastly, people will wear breathing masks so that they can protect themselves from air pollution.

b) Ss' own answers.

SUGGESTED ANSWER KEY

• I think that people will wear spacesuits made of tinfoil and hats of rubber bands.
• I think that people will wear clothes like in the old films; suits for men and long dresses for women.
• I think that women will wear silver dresses covered in CDs.
• I think that boys will wear top hats with blue antennae, long-sleeved T-shirts and silver gloves.
• I think that we will all wear the same golden uniforms and boots.   etc

Suggested Homework

1 **Copy:** one of the texts in the article in Ex. 23 (p. 51)
2 **Vocabulary:** words in bold in article in Ex. 23 (p. 51)
3 **Reading aloud:** Ex. 23 (p. 51)
4 **Dictation:** words in bold in article in Ex. 23 (p. 51)
5 **Speaking:** Ex. 24 (p. 51)

Listening & Reading

21 **a) Look at the pictures. Which shows: somebody cybershopping? 3 rubbish? ... a mouse? ... brightly-coloured clothes? ... credit cards? ... breathing masks? ...**

b) **Look at the title of the article opposite. What do you think the article is about?**

22 **Listen and underline the correct word.**

1 In the year 2200 we will all wear **electronic/ electrical** clothes.
2 In the year 2200 there won't be much **air/water**.
3 In the future everyone will wear **flat/platform** shoes.

23 **Read the article and explain the words in bold, then match the prompts in the two columns using** *so that* **or** *because***, as in the example.**

1	Clothes/have microchips in them	a	they/not want to walk in all the rubbish in the streets.
2	We/go cybershopping	b	they/protect themselves from the sun.
3	People/wear light, cool clothes	c	we/talk to our friends wherever we are.
4	When clothes get dirty, people/throw them away	d	websites/sell things at ... lower prices than shops do.
5	Everyone/wear platform shoes	e	there/not be much water.
6	People/wear breathing masks	f	people/protect themselves from air pollution.

(1 - c) Clothes will have microchips in them so that we can talk to our friends wherever we are.

The World of Fashion in the Year 2200

Have you ever thought about what life will be like in the year 2200? Well, Class 2C at St John's School in Britain have thought about it, and here's what they wrote ...

1

In the year 2200 we will all wear electronic clothes with microchips in them so that we can talk to our friends wherever we are. Our clothes will be very **light** and **cool** to protect us from the strong sun. We will go cyber-shopping for clothes and visit different **websites** with a **click** of a mouse. We will be able to find whatever we want at lower prices than in the shops, so we won't have to go into the **city centre** to buy new clothes.

Charlene Lewis

2

I think that in the year 2200 there won't be much water so when clothes get dirty, people will **throw** them **away**. People will buy their clothes on the internet, not in shops. They will have a computer and a credit card and they will shop **online** in the **comfort** of their own home. It will be great because we won't have to stand in long **queues** or go from shop to shop. We will go from site to **site** instead!

Craig Miller

3

In the future everyone will wear platform shoes because they won't want to walk in all the **rubbish** in the streets. People will wear breathing masks to protect themselves from air pollution and special suits to protect themselves from the sun. They will buy everything on **the Net**, because there won't be any shops in the towns.

Barbara Shaw

Speaking

24 **a) Use the prompts in Ex. 23 to give a short summary of the article. Use,** *also, furthermore, in addition, moreover, lastly.* **Start like this:** *To start with, in 2200 people ...*

b) **What do** *you* **think people will wear in the year 2200?**

• Going to or Present Continuous?

25 Study the examples. Which tense form do we use for a fixed future arrangement? a future intention?

*They **are going to get married** soon.*
*They **are getting** married this Saturday.*

26 Fill in the correct form (*going to* or *present continuous*) of the verb in brackets.

1 Has Charlotte decided which dress she ....
.... (wear) to the party?
2 My friend .... (leave) for Brazil at 3:30 in the morning!
3 What time .... (she/arrive) tomorrow?
4 I .... (see) my dentist at 2 pm on Friday.
5 I .... (lie) on the beach all day while on holiday.

Communication

• Buying clothes

27 a) Fill in *match, fit, suit* or *look*. Then, listen and check.

Salesman: Good morning. Can I help you?
Mrs Jones: Good morning. I'd like to buy an outfit for my **daughter** — a nice **dress** with a **jacket** to 1) ....
Salesman: How about this?
Mrs Jones: Oh, that's nice! I think that will really 2) .... her.
Salesman: What size is **she**?
Mrs Jones: **Medium** will 3) .... her very well.
Salesman: Here you are — and here's the **jacket** to go with it.
Mrs Jones: I'm sure they'll 4) .... lovely on **her**.

b) In pairs, use the prompts to act out similar dialogues.

• son – pair of trousers – jumper – small
• mother – skirt – cardigan – extra large

Pronunciation (homophones)

28 Listen and mark if the words in each pair sound the same (✓) or slightly different (✗). Listen again and repeat.

1 whether weather ...
2 eats each ...
3 wear where ...
4 see sea ...
5 warm arm ...
6 buy by ...
7 chair share ...
8 no know ...

Vocabulary Practice

29 Vocabulary Revision Game: In teams, make sentences with words/phrases from the list.

• weather • forecast • great experience • trip
• lower prices • chilly • casual clothes • cloudy
• shop online • expensive clothes • pack • get dirty
• platform shoes • site • throw away • I expect

30 Fill in the correct word, then make sentences.

• baggy • world • V-neck • collect • strong
• freezing • change • boiling • credit • visit
• high-heeled • long

1 .... tours
2 to .... my letters
3 to .... my mind
4 .... trousers
5 .... pullover
6 .... cold
7 .... hot
8 .... shoes
9 .... sun
10 to .... a website
11 .... cards
12 .... queues

31 Fill in: *of, to, at, in, on, from.*

1 .... that case; 2 to go .... business; 3 .... lower prices; 4 to stand .... long queues; 5 .... the comfort ...... their own home; 6 ...... the Internet; 7 to go .... shop .... shop; 8 protection ...... the sun; 9 .... the streets; 10 click .... a mouse

32 Fill in *change, fit, matches, suit,* then explain how the meaning changes.

1 a) Do you have any small .... ? I only have a £10 note. b) Call me if you .... your mind.
2 a) He usually wears a .... and tie to work. b) I don't think you should wear those clothes. They don't really .... you.
3 a) This bag .... your shoes. They're the same colour. b) Young children shouldn't play with .... They might start a fire.
4 a) These shoes don't .... me. They're too small. b) He's very .... because he goes to the gym three times a week.

Lesson 4 (pp. 52 - 53)

* Check Ss' HW (10').

25 Read out the example. Ask: *Which of the two sentences is a future plan/intention? (They are going to get married soon.) Which sentence is a fixed arrangement; sth that they have already arranged to do? (They are getting married this Saturday.)* Check if Ss understand the meaning by giving further examples. Invite Ss to give examples of their own.

e.g. He **is going to spend** his summer holidays in Spain.

He **is leaving** for Spain tomorrow.   etc

> **ANSWER KEY**
>
> fixed future arrangement: are getting married
> future intention: are going to get married

26 Allow Ss two minutes to do the exercise. Check Ss' answers while individual Ss read out their sentences.

> **ANSWER KEY**
>
> 1 is going to wear   4 am seeing
> 2 is leaving   5 am going to lie
> 3 is she arriving

27 a) Allow Ss two minutes to do the exercise. Play the cassette. Ss listen and fill in. Check Ss' answers on the board, then Ss read out the dialogue. Make sure Ss understand the use of these words. Ask: *Which word do we use for size? (fit) Which word do we use for colours? (match)* etc

> **ANSWER KEY**
>
> 1 match   3 fit
> 2 suit   4 look

b) Ss, in open pairs, use the prompts to act out similar dialogues. Point out that Ss should replace the words in bold with the prompts.

> **ANSWER KEY**
>
> • Salesman: Good morning. Can I help you?
>   Mrs Jones: Good morning. I'd like to buy an outfit for my son – a nice pair of trousers with a jumper to match.
>   Salesman: How about this?
>   Mrs Jones: Oh, that's nice! I think that will really suit him.
>   Salesman: What size is he?
>   Mrs Jones: Small will fit him very well.
>   Salesman: Here you are – and here's the jumper to go with it.
>   Mrs Jones: I'm sure they'll look lovely on him.
> • Salesman: Good morning. Can I help you?
>   Mrs Jones: Good morning. I'd like to buy an outfit for my mother – a nice skirt with a cardigan to match.
>   Salesman: How about this?

> Mrs Jones: Oh, that's nice! I think that will really suit her.
> Salesman: What size is she?
> Mrs Jones: Extra large will fit her very well.
> Salesman: Here you are – and here's the cardigan to go with it.
> Mrs Jones: I'm sure they'll look lovely on her.

28 Explain the task. Play the cassette. Ss listen and tick or put a cross accordingly. Play the cassette again with pauses for Ss to listen and repeat.

> **ANSWER KEY**
>
> 1 ✔   3 ✔   5 ✘   7 ✘
> 2 ✘   4 ✔   6 ✔   8 ✔

29 Ss, in teams, make sentences using the words/phrases in the order they appear in the list. Each correct sentence gets one point. The team with the most points is the winner.

e.g. Team A S1: What's the **weather** like?
     Team B S1: The **forecast** says it's going to get hot soon.   etc

30 Allow Ss two minutes to do the exercise. Check Ss' answers, then Ss, in teams, make sentences.

e.g. S1: Singers go on **world tours** every year.
     S2: My sister is going to **collect my letters** while I'm away.   etc

> **ANSWER KEY**
>
> 1 world   5 V-neck   9 strong
> 2 collect   6 freezing   10 visit
> 3 change   7 boiling   11 credit
> 4 baggy   8 high-heeled 12 long

31 Allow Ss two minutes to do the exercise. Check Ss' answers, then Ss make sentences.

e.g. **In that case**, I'll take my coat with me.

> **ANSWER KEY**
>
> 1 in   5 in, of   8 from
> 2 on   6 on.   9 in/on
> 3 at   7 from, to   10 of
> 4 in

32 Allow Ss two minutes to do the exercise. Check Ss' answers by asking individual Ss to read out their completed sentences.

> **ANSWER KEY**
>
> 1 a change (n)   3 a matches (v)
>   b change (v)   b matches (n)
>
> 2 a suit (n)   4 a fit (v)
>   b suit (v)   b fit (adj)

33 a) Present these words/phrases: **have a look, bargains, top designers, what a pity, main shopping areas, dress up** by giving examples. Explain the task, then allow Ss two to three minutes to do the exercise. Check Ss' answers.

> *ANSWER KEY*
>
> *A 3*   *C 2*   *E 4*
> *B 5*   *D 1*

b) Help Ss do the exercise.

> *ANSWER KEY*
>
> **Para 1** – *opening remarks / reason for writing*
> **Para 3** – *plans for daytime*
> **Para 5** – *closing remarks*
> **Para 2** – *accommodation*
> **Para 4** – *plans for evening*

c) Explain the task giving examples, then allow Ss two minutes to quickly scan the letter and do the exercise. Check Ss' answers.

> *ANSWER KEY*
>
> *Para 1: I'm going to London. (fixed future arrangement)*
> *Para 2: We're staying at … (fixed future arrangement)*
> *Para 3: … we're going to go to Oxford Street … (future intention)*
> *I'm going to have a look … (future intention)*
> *Para 4: … Mum is going to take me … (future intention)*
> *Para 5: We're leaving on … (fixed future arrangement)*

34 a) Read out Sally's diary and help Ss make sentences. Ss can use the letter in Ex. 33a as a model.

> *ANSWER KEY*
>
> • *Sally's going to New York next weekend.*
> • *She's staying at the Holiday Inn, in downtown New York.*
> • *On Saturday morning she's going to go to Broadway in Soho. She's also going to visit the Canal Jean Company to find some bargains!*
> • *In the afternoon she's going to shop at Bloomingdales in Manhattan and see the latest fashion in designer clothes.*
> • *On Saturday night she's going to go to the Hard Rock Café. It will be a chance to wear her new clothes.*
> • *She's catching the 8 am flight home on Sunday.*

b) • Present the plan. Ask Ss questions to make sure they understand the task.
  e.g. T: Where is Sally going?
     S1: She's going to New York.
       T: Where is she staying?
     S2: At the Holiday Inn.
       T: What is she going to do on Saturday morning?

     S3: She's going to go to Broadway in Soho. She's also going to visit the Canal Jean Company to find some bargains.
       T: What is she going to do on Saturday afternoon?   etc

• Individual Ss talk about Sally's letter. After Ss have completed the task orally, assign it as written HW.

> *SUGGESTED ANSWER KEY*
>
> *Dear Nancy,*
>
> *How are you? I'm terribly excited because I'm going to New York next weekend.*
>
> *I'm staying at the Holiday Inn in downtown New York. There are plenty of shops all around, so it's convenient.*
>
> *On Saturday morning I'm going to go to Broadway in Soho. I'm also going to visit the Canal Jean Company to find some bargains. I'll probably stop at Bloomingdales in Manhattan in the afternoon. It's a bit expensive, but it'll be nice to see the latest fashion in designer clothes.*
>
> *On Saturday night I'm going to the Hard Rock Café. It's a trendy place, where they play great music and serve delicious food. It will be a chance to wear my new clothes.*
>
> *I'm catching the 8am flight home on Sunday – what a pity! Well, that's all for the moment. Write soon.*
>
> *Lots of love,*
> *Sally*

35 • Present these words: **store, occupies, storey, high, cover, square feet, stocks, total, labels** by giving examples. Allow Ss two minutes to do the exercise. Check Ss' answers while Ss read out the sentences.

• Revise cardinal/ordinal numbers. Say cardinal numbers. Ss, in teams say the appropriate ordinal numbers.
  e.g.   T: three
     Team A S1: third
          T: eleven
     Team B S1: eleventh

> *ANSWER KEY*
> • 11   • Fifth   • 5

(Suggested Homework)

1 **Copy:** Ex. 27a (p. 52)
2 **Vocabulary:** Exs 29, 30, 31 (p. 52)
3 **Reading aloud:** Ex. 27a (p. 53)
4 **Dictation:** any ten words from Vocabulary
5 **Act out:** first four exchanges from dialogue in Ex. 27a (p. 52)
6 **Writing:** Ex. 34 b(p. 53)

(Lesson 5)

• Check Ss' HW.
• Workbook: Unit 5
      Click on Grammar 5

Writing (a letter to a friend about your plans)

33 a) Read the letter and put the paragraphs in the correct order.

Dear Gillie,

A ☐ *On Saturday morning we're going to go to Oxford Street, in the West End. I'm going to have a look in Top Shop — they usually have some great bargains! In the afternoon we'll probably go to Knightsbridge to visit Harrods. It's a bit expensive, but it's nice to look at the latest fashion from the world's top designers.*

B ☐ *We're leaving on the 10 o'clock train to York the next morning — what a pity! Well, that's all for now. Write soon.*

C ☐ *We're staying at the White Rose Hotel in Paddington. It's near the city centre, so it will be easy for us to get to all the main shopping areas.*

D ☐ *Hi! How are you? Guess what — I'm going to London this weekend on a shopping trip with my mum! It's a special treat for my birthday, and I can't wait!*

E ☐ *On Saturday night, Mum is going to take me to Planet Hollywood in Piccadilly. It's a really popular place, with tasty food and great music. It'll be a chance to dress up in my new clothes.*

Lots of love,
Linda

b) Match the paragraphs to these topics.

☐ opening remarks/reason for writing
☐ plans for daytime   ☐ accommodation
☐ closing remarks   ☐ plans for evening

c) Read the letter again. Which of the actions are Linda's future fixed arrangements? Which are Linda's future intentions?

34 a) Look at Sally's diary for next weekend, then make sentences, using the *present continuous*, *going to* or *will*.

Friday 16
stay at Holiday Inn in downtown New York

Saturday 17
morning — Broadway in Soho — visit Canal Jean Company — find some bargains!
afternoon — shop at Bloomingdales in Manhattan (bit expensive) — nice to see latest fashion in designer clothes!
night — Hard Rock Café — trendy place — play great music — serve delicious food — chance to wear new clothes

Sunday 18
catch 8am flight home

b) Now use the information in Sally's diary, and the plan below, to write a letter from Sally to her friend Nancy (120-150 words). You can use the letter in Ex. 33 as a model.

Plan

Dear (+ your friend's first name)
Introduction
(Para 1)   *greeting/opening remarks and reason for writing*

Main Body
(Para 2)   *your accommodation*
(Para 3)   *your plans for the daytime*
(Para 4)   *your plans for the evening*
Conclusion
(Para 5)   *closing remarks*
Love/Lots of love/etc,
(your first name)

35 Read and underline the correct word.

do you know...

- Macy's department store occupies a whole block in Herald Square, New York City. It is **11/15** storeys high and covers an area of 2.15 million square feet.
- Saks department store on **Fifth/Sixth** Avenue, New York stocks a total of 1,252 designer labels – more than any other store in the world.
- Chanel No. **3/5** sells about 10 million bottles of perfume a year.

6 Food & Festivities

Lead-in

1 Look at the pictures and number the things in the list. Which of these are: - vegetables? - fruit? - drinks? - junk food? - pulses?

an apple ...	cornflakes ...	a peach ...
bagels ...	crisps/chips ...	a pear ...
bananas ...	a boiled egg ...	peppers ...
beans ...	fish ...	pizza ...
biscuits ...	grapes ...	rice ...
bread ...	lentils ...	soup ...
bread rolls ...	lettuce ...	spaghetti ...
broccoli ...	meat ...	spices ...
a burger ...	milk ...	spring onions ...
carrots ...	olives ...	a strawberry ...
cauliflower ...	an onion ...	sugar ...
cheese ...	an orange ...	tea ...
chicken ...	orange juice ...	tomatoes ...
coffee ...	pasta ...	

2 a) What is your favourite dish? What do you usually eat/drink: - at school/work? - on a special occasion (e.g. a birthday party)?

b) Do you like eating meat, or are you a vegetarian? Which of the things in Ex. 1 are not suitable for a vegetarian?

c) Which of the things in Ex. 1 are suitable for someone who wants a healthy diet?

3 Listen and repeat.

- Not much.
- It's all gone.
- There was a lot left over.
- He was starving!
- It'll just be bread and cheese for dinner now!
- Can I take your order?
- What about your diet?
- May I take your order?
- And for the main course?
- What's today's special?
- That sounds nice.

54

Objectives

Vocabulary: food & drink; food groups; kitchen equipment; cooking methods; festivals
Reading: reading for detailed understanding
Listening: listening for specific information
Speaking: expressing likes/dislikes; giving reasons; making a shopping list; describing celebrations
Communication: complaining about a meal
Pronunciation: words often confused
Grammar: countable & uncountable nouns; plurals; a/an/any/some; a lot of/much/many/a few/a little; nouns of quantity
Project: a restaurant advertisement
Writing: an article about a festival which you attended

Lesson 1 (pp. 54 - 55)

1 • Read out the title and ask Ss to guess what the unit is about (food related to celebrations). Ask Ss to name some foods or some celebrations. e.g. Thanksgiving etc
• Ask Ss to look at the pictures on pp 54 - 55. Read out the prompts in the list, one at a time. Ss say the corresponding number.

ANSWER KEY

an apple 21	cornflakes 19	a peach 38
bagels 15	crisps/chips 34	a pear 20
bananas 6	a boiled egg 28	peppers 1
beans 10	fish 14	pizza 36
biscuits 33	grapes 2	rice 18
bread 12	lentils 16	soup 40
bread rolls 30	lettuce 7	spaghetti 3
broccoli 9	meat 11	spices 41
a burger 35	milk 5	spring onions 26
carrots 25	olives 22	a strawberry 39
cauliflower 4	an onion 37	sugar 32
cheese 17	an orange 23	tea 31
chicken 8	orange juice 27	tomatoes 13
coffee 29	pasta 24	

• Write the five categories on the board. Elicit answers from Ss to complete the table. Ss copy it into their notebooks. Ss can add to the lists.

ANSWER KEY

vegetables: broccoli; carrots; cauliflower; lettuce; peppers; spring onions; an onion
fruit: an apple; bananas; grapes; olives; an orange; a peach; a pear; a strawberry; tomatoes
drinks: coffee; milk; orange juice; tea
junk food: a burger; crisps/chips; pizza
pulses: beans; lentils

• As an extension you can divide the class into two teams. Say one of the categories in Ex. 1 each time. Teams, in turn, say a matching word. Each correct answer gets one point. The team with the most points is the winner.

e.g. T: fruit
Team A S1: olives
T: Correct! One point for Team A – vegetable
Team B S1: carrots
T: Correct! One point for Team B – junk food
Team A S2: a burger   etc

2 a) Read out the questions one at a time. Ss answer them. Invite Ss to use the words listed in Ex. 1 as well as any others they can think of.

SUGGESTED ANSWER KEY

My favourite dish is chicken with rice. At school/At work I usually eat a sandwich and drink orange juice. On a special occasion like a birthday party I usually eat burgers or pizza and drink Coke.

b) Present the word **vegetarian** (sb who does not eat meat). Then, Ss answer the questions.

SUGGESTED ANSWER KEY

I like eating meat a lot. I think that burgers, chicken, fish and meat are not suitable for a vegetarian.

c) Ss prepare their answers in closed pairs. Check Ss' answers.

SUGGESTED ANSWER KEY

I think that apples, bananas, beans, broccoli, carrots, cauliflowers, chicken, cornflakes, boiled eggs, fish, grapes, lentils, lettuce, milk, olives, onions, oranges, orange juice, peaches, pears, peppers, rice, spring onions, strawberries, tomatoes etc are suitable for someone who wants a healthy diet.

3 • Play the cassette. Ss listen and repeat either chorally or individually.
• Present these phrases/sentences by giving examples or in Ss' L1 if necessary.
e.g. **Not much.** (Ask Ss to look at pict. No 31 (cup of tea). Ask: *How much tea is there?* Answer: ***Not much.*** *Just one cup.*)
It's all gone. (Pretend that you are drinking a cup of tea. When you have drunk all of it say: *There's nothing left.* ***It's all gone.***)   etc

4 Read out the prompts and explain any unknown words in Ss' L1. Explain the task. Play the cassette twice if necessary. Ss listen and tick accordingly. Check Ss' answers.

ANSWER KEY

Dial. A bread ✓ cheese ✓ rice ✓
Dial. B double cheeseburger ✓
large serving of fries ✓
side salad ✓ apple pie ✓ Diet Coke ✓
Dial. C vegetable soup ✓ grilled fish ✓
carrots ✓ mineral water ✓

---

5 a) Explain the task. Allow Ss two to three minutes to read the dialogues silently and do the task. Check Ss' answers, then help Ss explain the words in bold in Ss' L1 or by giving examples or synonyms.
e.g. **corner shop:** a small shop which sells flour, sugar, vegetables etc

---

ANSWER KEY

• *Dialogue A takes place in Sue and Bill's kitchen. Dialogue B takes place in a fast food restaurant. Dialogue C takes place in a restaurant.*

• *1 She's going to buy (a loaf of) bread, (some) cheese and (some) rice.*
2 A stray cat.
3 Les is on diet.
4 A large glass of mineral water.

---

b) Play the cassette for Ex. 4 again. Ss listen and follow the lines, then take roles and read out the dialogues.

c) Allow Ss two minutes to read the dialogues silently and underline the phrases/sentences from Ex. 3 in the dialogues, then Ss say who said each phrase/sentence.

ANSWER KEY

Bill said, "Not much."
Bill said, "It's all gone."
Sue said, "There was a lot left over."
Bill said, "He was starving!"
Sue said, "It'll just be bread and cheese for dinner now!"
The waitress asked, "Can I take your order?"
Ron asked, "What about your diet?"
The waiter asked, "May I take your order?"
The waiter asked, "And for the main course?"
Tim asked, "What's today's special?"
Tim said, "That sounds nice."

Memory Game

Ask Ss to look at the phrases/sentences in Ex. 3 for two minutes. Ss then close their books and, in teams, try to remember as many phrases/sentences as possible. Each correct phrase/sentence gets one point. The team with the most points is the winner.
e.g. Team A S1: Not much.
Team B S1: It's all gone. etc.

(Suggested Homework)

1 Copy: any of the dialogues A-C Ex. 5a (p. 55)
2 Vocabulary: words in Ex. 1 (p. 54)
3 Reading aloud: dialogues Ex. 5a (p. 55) (Point out that Ss practise *reading aloud* at home using the S's cassette/audio CD)
4 Dictation: any ten words from Ex. 1 (p. 54)
5 Act out: a) dialogue B Ex. 5a (p. 55)
b) Ss memorise five sentences from Ex. 3 (p. 54)

Listening and Reading

4 Listen to the dialogues and tick (✓) the food/drinks mentioned in each.

Dial. A bread …   fish …   cheese …   rice …

Dial. B double cheeseburger …   fried eggs …
large serving of fries …   pizza …
side salad …   fruit salad …   apple pie …
Diet Coke …

Dial. C pasta …   vegetable soup …   grilled chicken …
grilled fish …   carrots …   mineral water …

5 a) Read the dialogues and say where each one takes place, then answer the questions. Finally, explain the words in bold.

1 What is Sue going to buy from the corner shop?
2 Who ate the chicken left over from last night?
3 Who is on a diet?
4 What does Tim want to drink?

A Sue: I'm going to get some things from the **corner shop**, Bill. What do we need?

Bill: Let's see … Well, we need a **loaf** of bread and some cheese.

Sue: Is there any rice?

Bill: Not much. Perhaps you should get some more.

Sue: Okay. And there's plenty of chicken left from last night, so we can have that.

Bill: Um … it's all gone, actually.

Sue: All gone?! But there was a lot left over!

Bill: Er … I'm afraid I felt sorry for that **stray cat** again.

Sue: And you gave him all our chicken?

Bill: He was **starving**!

Sue: Well, I wanted to make chicken curry – but I think it'll just be bread and cheese for dinner now!

B Waitress: Can I take your order?

Les: Yes – I'd like a double cheeseburger with a large fries, a side salad and an apple pie, please.

Ron: But Les, what about your **diet**?

Les: Oh, yes, I **forgot**! Can I have a Diet Coke too, please?

C Waiter: Good evening, sir. May I take your **order**?

Tim: Yes, please. I'll have the vegetable soup to start with.

Waiter: And for the **main course**?

Tim: I'm not sure. What's today's **special**?

Waiter: It's grilled fish with carrots.

Tim: That sounds nice. I'll have that, please.

Waiter: Would you like anything to drink?

Tim: A **large** glass of **mineral water**, please.

Waiter: Thank you.

b) In pairs read out the dialogues.

c) Read the dialogues again and underline the phrases/sentences used in Ex. 3. Who said each phrase/sentence?

Vocabulary

• Food

6 a) Look at the food pyramid, then underline the odd word out in each of the groups below.

1 butter - oil - <u>bread</u> - chocolate
2 peanuts - grapes - eggs - cheese
3 chicken - broccoli - oranges - carrots
4 pasta - cornflakes - rice - cauliflower

b) Make sentences about each group.

Butter, oil and chocolate contain a lot of fat.

1 Fat

2 Protein

3 Vitamins

4 Carbohydrates

7 a) Label the pictures as *hot and spicy*, *sweet*, *sour* or *salty*, then try to add more things to each list.

1 ....
lemons, pickles, vinegar, ...
....

2 ....
cakes, ice cream, chocolates, ...

3 ....
pepper, ginger, chillies, ...
....

4 ....
popcorn, crisps, pretzels, ...
....

b) Now make sentences, as in the example.

*I don't like lemons, because they are too **sour**.*
*I prefer chocolates, because I love **sweet** things.*

8 a) Match the prompts to the pictures.

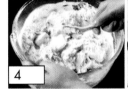

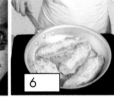

| 1 | 2 | 3 |
| 4 | 5 | 6 |

a fry fish
b grill meat
c bake bread
d mix ingredients
e chop tomatoes
f slice roast beef

b) What can you *chop, pour, bake, roast, boil, fry, mix, slice*?

c) Use the verbs in Ex. 8b and the prompts below, to make sentences, as in the example.

cooker

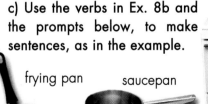

frying pan   saucepan

knife

wooden spoon

grill

We can grill fish on a grill.

Lesson 2 (pp. 56 - 57)

* • Check Ss' HW (10').
  • Play the Memory Game as described in Ex. 5c p. 55(T).

6 a) • Ask Ss to look at the food pyramid and identify the foods shown, then present the four categories.
  fat: cake, butter, chocolate, oil
  protein: meat, fish, peanuts, chicken, milk, beans
  vitamins: cauliflower, tomatoes, peppers, grapes, apples, oranges, bananas, carrots, melon
  carbohydrates: bread, bread rolls, cereal, pasta
  • Explain the task. Allow Ss two minutes to do the exercise. Check Ss' answers.

ANSWER KEY

2 grapes   3 chicken   4 cauliflower

b) Read out the example, then Ss make sentences.

ANSWER KEY

Peanuts, eggs and cheese contain a lot of protein.
Broccoli, oranges and carrots contain a lot of vitamins.
Pasta, cereal and rice contain a lot of carbohydrates.

7 a) • Present these words: **hot and spicy, sweet, sour, salty** by giving examples or in Ss' L1 if necessary.
  • Explain the task, then Ss do the exercise. Check Ss' answers.

ANSWER KEY

1 sour … grapefruit
2 sweet … jam, honey, melon, puddings etc
3 hot and spicy … curry, paprika etc
4 salty … crackers, peanuts

b) Read out the examples, then Ss do the exercise.

SUGGESTED ANSWER KEY

I don't like pickles, because they are too sour.
I prefer cakes, because I love sweet things.
I don't like pretzels, because they are too salty.
I prefer ginger, because I love spicy things.   etc

8 a) Read out the prompts one at a time and help Ss match them to the pictures.

ANSWER KEY

1 c   3 f   5 e
2 b   4 d   6 a

b) Present the words: **pour, boil, roast** by giving examples. Then, write all the words on the board in a table. Elicit answers from Ss and complete the table. Ss copy the completed table into their notebooks.

SUGGESTED ANSWER KEY

chop – onions, parsley etc
pour – oil, milk, water etc
bake – cakes, bread etc
roast – beef, chicken, potatoes etc
boil – vegetables, eggs, rice etc
fry   – chips, chicken, vegetables, rice etc
mix   – spices, sauces etc
slice – bread, onions, meat etc

c) Read out the prompts. Explain the task, then Ss make sentences, as in the example.

SUGGESTED ANSWER KEY

We can mix ingredients with a wooden spoon.
We can chop onions with a knife.
We can slice tomatoes with a knife.
We can fry meat in a frying pan.
We can boil rice in a saucepan.
We can roast chicken in a cooker.

9 • Explain that this is a restaurant advertisement. Ask questions: *What's the name of the restaurant? (The Lemon Tree.) What kind of restaurant is this? (Vegetarian.) Where is the restaurant? (At 2 Church Street.) What time does it open? (11am.) What time does it close? (No answer.)* etc.

• Play the cassette. Ss listen and fill in. Check Ss' answers on the board. Then ask Ss to explain these words: **stuffed peppers, blue cheese bake, cheesecake** by giving examples or by looking up these words in their dictionaries.

• Ss use the completed advertisement to talk about *The Lemon Tree* restaurant.

ANSWER KEY

• 1 midnight   3 cheese
   2 10   4 side

• *... is open from 11am until midnight daily. For lunch you can have a 3-course meal for only £10 per person. You can have tomato soup to start with. For your main course you can choose from stuffed peppers, vegetable pie or broccoli and blue cheese bake, all served with a side salad. For dessert you can choose from cheesecake or fruit salad.*

TAPESCRIPT

The Lemon Tree vegetarian restaurant on Church Street is now open from 11am until midnight every day. With a wide range of delicious dishes to choose from you won't notice that there's no meat on the menu. To introduce people to the delights of meat-free food we are offering a lunchtime special of a 3-course meal for only £10. This includes tomato soup to start and then a choice of main course. You can choose from sweet red peppers stuffed with a delicious mixture of rice and herbs, or a vegetable pie made with pastry and fresh garden vegetables, or broccoli and blue cheese bake. Each main course is served with a side salad. Then to round off your meal, choose from delicious cheesecakes or fruit salad. There's no need to book, but we do advise you to come early as tables are soon taken. See you soon!

Project (p. 57)

Ss look at the Photo File section. Explain that this is an advertisement for a restaurant. Ask Ss to identify the pictures then do the exercise orally in class. Assign it as written HW. See Photo File section Unit 6 for the Answer Key.

10 • Ss' books closed. Write on the board: *I've got a banana. I've got some cheese.* Underline **a banana, some cheese**. Explain that nouns like *banana* can be counted (countable nouns). Ask Ss to give examples (*an apple, a lemon, an onion* etc). Focus Ss' attention on *some cheese*. Explain that we cannot use *a/an* before the word *cheese*. We cannot say *one cheese, two cheeses,* etc. Explain that nouns like *cheese* cannot be counted (uncountable nouns). Elicit examples from Ss (*some bread, some milk, some sugar* etc).

• Ss' books open. Explain the task, then Ss do the exercise.

ANSWER KEY

banana C, cheese U, tea U, egg C, soup U, Coke U, sandwich C, pasta U, water U

• Ask two Ss to read out the example. Ss, in pairs, act out similar dialogues.

SUGGESTED ANSWER KEY

A: Is there anything to eat? I'm hungry.
B: How about an egg?
A: No, thanks. Can I have some soup, please?
B: Sure. Would you like some Coke, too?
A: Yes, please.   etc

---

11 • Read out the examples, then ask Ss questions to elicit the meaning.
   e.g. T: When do we use **a/an**?
         S1: With singular countable nouns in the affirmative, negative and interrogative.
         T: Do we use **a/an** with plural countable nouns in the affirmative?
         S2: No, we don't. We use **some**.
         T: Where else do we use **some**?
         S3: We use **some** with uncountable nouns in the affirmative.
         T: And what do we use with plural countable nouns in the negative and interrogative?
         S4: We use **any**.
         T: Where else do we use **any**?
         S5: We use **any** with uncountable nouns in the negative and interrogative.

ANSWER KEY

We use **a/an** in the affirmative, negative or interrogative with countable nouns in the singular.
We use **some** in the affirmative with countable nouns in the plural or uncountable nouns.
We use **any** in the negative and interrogative with countable nouns in the plural or uncountable nouns.

---

12 Explain the task, then allow Ss two minutes to do the exercise. Check Ss' answers while they read out the short exchanges in open pairs.

ANSWER KEY

1 a   4 a, some
2 an, any, a   5 an, any, a
3 any, some, some   6 some, any, some

---

13 Help Ss complete the table. Check Ss' spelling on the board, then Ss say the rules. Refer Ss to the Grammar Reference section in the Student's Book for more details.

ANSWER KEY

apple – **apples**, boy – **boys**, loaf – **loaves**,
bus – **buses**, peach – **peaches**, tomato – **tomatoes**,
berry – **berries**, knife – **knives**, glass – **glasses**,
box – **boxes**

man - **men**, woman - **women**, child - **children**,
person - **people**, mouse - **mice**, foot - **feet**,
tooth - **teeth**

Suggested Homework

1 **Copy:** dialogue in Ex. 10 (p. 57)
2 **Vocabulary:** new words in Exs 6, 7, 8 (p. 56)
3 **Reading aloud:** Ex. 12 (p. 57)
4 **Dictation:** any ten words from Exs 6, 7, 8 (p. 56)
5 **Act out:** Ex. 10 (p. 57)
6 **Project:** (p. 57)

Listening

Listening

9 Listen and fill in the missing information, then talk about *The Lemon Tree* restaurant.

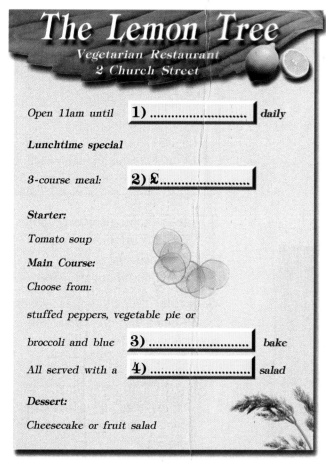

The Lemon Tree
Vegetarian Restaurant
2 Church Street

Open 11am until **1)** .... daily

Lunchtime special

3-course meal: **2) £**........................

Starter:
Tomato soup

Main Course:
Choose from:

stuffed peppers, vegetable pie or

broccoli and blue **3)** .... bake

All served with a **4)** .... salad

Dessert:
Cheesecake or fruit salad

*The Lemon Tree restaurant is a **vegetarian restaurant** at 2 Church Street. It ...*

• Project

Look at the Photo File section and complete the advertisement.

Grammar

• Countable/Uncountable Nouns

10 Look at the nouns in the list and write C (for countable) or U (for uncountable). In pairs, ask and answer, as in the example.

• banana ... • cheese ... • tea ... • egg ...
• soup ... • Coke ... • sandwich ... • pasta ...
• water ...

A: *Is there anything to eat? I'm hungry.*
B: *How about **a banana**?*
A: *No, thanks. Can I have **some cheese**, please?*
B: *Sure. Would you like **some tea**, too?*
A: *Yes, please.*

• a/an/any/some

11 Read the sentences and say when we use *a/an/some/any.*

COUNTABLE NOUNS	
Affirmative:	There is **a** sandwich.
	There are **some** bananas.
Negative:	There isn't **a** sandwich.
	There aren't **any** bananas.
Interrogative:	Is there **a** sandwich?
	Are there **any** bananas?

UNCOUNTABLE NOUNS	
Affirmative:	There is **some** tea.
Negative:	There isn't **any** tea.
Interrogative:	Is there **any** tea?

Would you like **an** egg / **some** Coke? (**offer**)
Can I have **a** burger / **some** olives, please? (**request**)

12 Fill in: *a, an, any, some.*

1 A: Is there any coffee?
  B: Sorry. There's .... packet of tea, though.
2 A: Can I have .... apple, please?
  B: Sorry, there aren't .... apples left. Would you like .... pear instead?
3 A: Have we got .... sugar?
  B: Yes, there's .... in the cupboard. Why?
  A: I want to make .... biscuits.
4 A: Would you like .... piece of cake?
  B: No, thanks. I'd rather have .... chocolate.
5 A: Could I have .... egg sandwich?
  B: Sorry, there aren't .... eggs left. Would you like .... cheese sandwich instead?
6 A: Would you like .... strawberries?
  B: Lovely. Is there .... ice cream left?
  A: Yes. I'll just get you ....

• Plurals

13 Fill in the plurals, then say how we form them.

apple –	tomato – .... *(but radio – radios)*
boy –	berry – ....
loaf –	knife – ....
bus –	glass – ....
peach –	box – ....
Irregular Plurals	person - ....
man -	mouse - ....
woman -	foot - ....
child -	tooth - ....

14 Choose the correct noun(s) of quantity for each sort of food/drink. Which other sorts of food/drink can we use each noun of quantity with?

• jar • bag • carton • glass • bowl • loaf • packet
• bar • piece • box • tin • cup • bottle • kilo • slice

a loaf/slice of bread
a .... of milk
a .... of chocolate
a .... of water
a .... of biscuits
a .... of Coke
a .... of cake

a .... of potatoes
a .... of sardines
a .... of cornflakes
a .... of jam
a .... of coffee
a .... of soup
a .... of sugar

• We use .... in the affirmative with countable and uncountable nouns.
• We use .... and .... in the negative and interrogative. We use .... with countable nouns, and .... with uncountable nouns.
• We use .... (= some, not many) in the affirmative with countable nouns.
We use .... (= some, not much) in the affirmative with uncountable nouns.

Speaking

15 In pairs, ask and answer, as in the examples.

A: How many **loaves of bread** do we need?
B: Two will be fine. How many ... etc

A: Would you like **a bowl of cornflakes**?
B: I've just had some cornflakes, thanks. Would you like ...

• a lot of — much/many — a few/a little

16 Study the examples, then complete the rules.

Countable Nouns		
Affirmative	There are **a lot of** bananas.	There are **a few** oranges.
Negative	There aren't **many** oranges.	
Interrogative	How **many** oranges are there?	

Uncountable Nouns		
Affirmative	There is **a lot of** bread.	There is **a little** butter.
Negative	There isn't **much** bread.	
Interrogative	How **much** bread is there?	

17 Look at the pictures on pp. 54 - 55 again, and make sentences using *a lot of, not much, not many* or *a few.*

There are a lot of grapes. There aren't many spring onions. There are a few oranges.

18 Fill in: *some, any, much, many, few, little.* **Listen and check, then read out the dialogue.**

A: Have you got enough to eat, David?

B: Yes, thanks. Oh — can I have a 1) .... more fried onions, please?

A: Of course. Here you are.

C: Is there 2) .... ketchup?

A: Isn't the food tasty enough already?

C: It's really delicious — but I would like a 3) .... ketchup for my chips.

A: Okay. I think there's 4) .... in the cupboard.

B: Can you pass the salt, please? I like a 5) .... salt on my food.

A: Here you are. Too 6) .... salt is bad for you, though.

C: I know. So 7) .... things I like are bad for me.

B: Would you like 8) .... of my chips? I can't eat 9) .... more. I'm full.

C: Okay. I'll take 10) .... off your plate.

Lesson 3 (pp. 58 - 59)

* Check Ss' HW (10').

14 • Read out the words in the list. Explain that these are nouns of quantity which can be used with countable and uncountable nouns. Present any unknown words Ss might have in Ss' L1.
   • Explain the task, then allow Ss two minutes to do the exercise. Check Ss' answers on the board, then Ss suggest other sorts of food/drink which can be used with these nouns.

SUGGESTED ANSWER KEY

a *carton/glass/bottle* of milk/juice etc
a *bar* of chocolate
a *bottle/glass* of water/orange juice/apple juice etc
a *packet/tin* of biscuits/sugar/spaghetti etc
a *bottle/glass* of Coke, milk etc
a *slice/piece* of cake/bread etc
a *kilo/bag* of potatoes/tomatoes etc
a *tin* of sardines/tuna/beans etc
a *bowl* of cornflakes/cereal/porridge/soup etc
a *jar* of jam/olives etc
a *cup/packet* of coffee/tea etc
a *packet/tin/bowl* of soup
a *kilo/packet/bowl* of sugar
a *box* of chocolates

---

15 • Ss identify the foods/drinks in the pictures [*tin of sardines, packet of spaghetti, piece of cheese, loaf of bread, jar of olives, carton of milk, bowl of popcorn, slice of pizza, cup of coffee, glass of water, bowl of cornflakes, slice of bread*].
   • Read out the examples. Ss, in closed pairs, practise using the picture prompts. Check Ss' performance, then ask some pairs to act out their dialogues in class.

SUGGESTED ANSWER KEY

   • A: *How many cartons of milk do we need?*
     B: *One will be fine. How many jars of olives do we need?*
     A: *Two will be fine. How many tins of sardines do we need? etc*
   • A: *Would you like a cup of coffee?*
     B: *I've just had some coffee, thanks. Would you like a slice of pizza?*
     A: *I've just had some pizza, thanks. Would you like a glass of water?*
     B: *I've just had some water, thanks. Would you … etc*

---

16 • Ss' books closed. Present the use of *a lot of* in the affirmative and *much/many* in the negative and interrogative with countable and uncountable nouns. Say, then write on the board: *I love milk. I drink **a lot of** milk. I also like oranges. I eat five oranges every day. I eat **a lot of** oranges.* Elicit from Ss that we use **a lot of** in the affirmative with countable and uncountable nouns.

• Draw on the board three oranges and half a glass of water. Say, then write on the board: *How many oranges are there? There aren't **many** oranges. There are **a few** oranges.* Elicit from Ss that we use **many** in the negative and interrogative with countable nouns. Point out that we use **a few** (=some, not many) in the affirmative with countable nouns.

• Say, then write on the board: *How much water is there? There isn't **much** water. There is **a little** water.* Elicit from Ss that we use **much** in the negative and interrogative with uncountable nouns. Point out that we use **a little** (=some, not much) in the affirmative with uncountable nouns. Ss' books open. Read out the examples, then Ss complete the rules.

ANSWER KEY

… a lot of …
… many … much … many … much
… a few …
… a little …

---

17 Explain the task, then read out the examples. Ss do the exercise orally in class.

SUGGESTED ANSWER KEY

There is a lot of spaghetti.   There aren't many biscuits.
There aren't many olives.   There isn't much tea.
There aren't many carrots.   There isn't much meat.
There isn't much milk.   There are a few bananas.
There are a few peppers.   There isn't much pasta. etc

---

18 • Explain the task, then present these words/phrases **fried, ketchup, cupboard, pass, salt, I'm full, plate** by giving examples. Allow Ss two minutes to do the exercise.
   • Play the cassette. Ss listen and check their answers, then in pairs, read out from the dialogue.

ANSWER KEY

1	few	6	much
2	any	7	many
3	little	8	some
4	some	9	any
5	little	10	some

---

19 • Ask Ss to look at the pictures and guess what the texts are about. [e.g. celebrations in the USA and China and food people have in each country] Ask: *What are the people in pict. 5 doing? (They are having a barbecue.)*

• Read out the prompts (a - f) one at a time. Ss match them to the pictures.

```
ANSWER KEY

a  1          c  3          e  4
b  6          d  5          f  2
```

20 Explain the task. Play the cassette twice if necessary. Ss do the exercise. Check Ss' answers.

```
ANSWER KEY

1  A          3  C          5  A
2  A          4  C          6  C
```

21 Read out the statements 1 to 6. Allow Ss two minutes to read the articles silently and do the exercise. Check Ss' answers.

```
ANSWER KEY

1  ✓          3  ✗          5  ✗
2  ✓          4  ✓          6  ✓
```

22 a) Play the cassette for Ex. 20 again. Ss listen and follow the lines, then read out from the articles. Help Ss explain the words in bold. Ss, then, in closed pairs complete the table. Check Ss' answers on the board. Individual Ss talk about the celebrations using the information in the table.

ANSWER KEY

Name of Festival	Chinese New Year	American Independence Day
Date	between 21 Jan. 20 Feb.	4 July
Reason for celebration	to welcome the new year and celebrate health, wealth & happiness	to celebrate being independent from Britain
Activities	street parades traditional meal with family	barbecues firework displays
Food	fish dishes, Chinese vegetables, sesame seed balls	burgers, chicken wings, potato salad

• *The Chinese celebrate New Year between 21 January and 20 February. They welcome the new year and celebrate health, wealth and happiness. There are street parades. People also have traditional meals with their families. They usually eat fish dishes and Chinese vegetables. They also eat sesame seed balls.*

• *The Americans celebrate Independence Day on the fourth of July. They celebrate their independence from Britain. Most people have barbecues and watch firework displays. They usually eat burgers, chicken wings and potato salad.*

b) Ss answer the questions.

```
SUGGESTED ANSWER KEY

We usually celebrate Mardi Gras to mark the end of a
season of festivities before of Lent. Jazz bands play
music while people watch street parades or dance the
samba. We usually eat traditional Cajun and creole
dishes like Gumbo, a thick spicy fish soup. We also
eat delicious dishes of chicken and chillies which are
hot and spicy.
```

```
( Suggested Homework )

1  Copy: one of the articles in Ex. 21 (p. 59)
2  Vocabulary: words in Ex. 18 (p. 58)
3  Reading aloud: articles in Ex. 21 (p. 59)
4  Dictation: words in Ex. 14 (p. 58)
5  Speaking: a) Ex. 22 (p. 59)
              b) Ex. 15 (p. 58)
```

Listening and Reading

19 Match the pictures (1-6) to the descriptions (a-f).

a burgers
b a street parade
c a Chinese fish dish
d a barbecue
e sesame seed balls
f a firework display

20 🎧 Listen to the articles and match the pictures to the celebrations. Write *C* (for Chinese New Year) or *A* (for American Independence Day).

21 Look at the statements below, then read the articles and mark each statement as *True* (✓), *False* (✗) or *Doesn't Say* (?).

1 Chinese New Year is an annual celebration. ....
2 People have parties at home to celebrate the Chinese New Year. ....
3 Sesame seed balls bring bad luck. ....
4 American Independence Day is a national celebration. ....
5 On the Fourth of July, people have fireworks at home. ....
6 People always have a barbecue on Independence Day. ....

Speaking

22 a) Read the articles again and explain the words in bold, then complete the table on the right. Finally, use your notes to talk about each celebration.

b) Are there any similar celebrations in your country? What are they called? Why/How do you celebrate them?

Food, Fun and Celebration around the World

Every year, between 21 January and 20 February, **millions** of people around the world **celebrate** Chinese New Year. During this festival we **welcome** the new year and celebrate **health**, **wealth** and **happiness**. There are lots of **colourful** street parades. People wear dragon and lion costumes and dance through the streets. It's fantastic! After the parade, I always go to my uncle's house for a traditional Chinese New Year's meal. We have some delicious fish dishes and Chinese vegetables. We also have sesame seed balls called Gum Tzin. People say these bring luck for the year ahead. I've had a very good year, so I think that last year's celebrations really were lucky for me!

Zhong Yajuan (16)

One of my favourite celebrations is Fourth of July. This is American Independence Day, when we celebrate being **independent** from Britain. Last year's Fourth of July was fantastic. The weather was great and I helped Dad with the barbecue. We cooked lots of burgers and **chicken wings**. My sister Louise made a special **potato salad**. It was delicious! In the evening we went to a huge firework display at our **local** park. The colours were **amazing**. I really enjoyed myself. I think that **traditional** celebrations like this one are great. I can't wait for the next Fourth of July.

Ann Johnson (14)

Name of festival	Chinese New Year	American Independence Day
Date	....	....
Reason for celebration	....	....
Activities	....	....
Food	....	....

59

23 a) Fill in: *some, any, much, many.*

A: I'm hungry. Are there 1) .... crisps?
B: No, sorry. There aren't 2) .... crisps.
  Would you like 3) .... biscuits?
A: Yes, please. Can I have a glass of **milk**, too?
B: Yes. We have to buy 4) .... Coke
  though, because there isn't 5) .... left.
A: There aren't 6) .... **apples**, either. Just a few.
B: I think we should go shopping this afternoon.

Speaking

b) Use the prompts to act out similar dialogues.

- apples - grapes - orange juice - coffee
  - strawberries
- eggs - chips - Coke - tea - peaches

24 Correct the mistakes, as in the example.

1 How much eggs do you need?   *many*
2 Would you like a water?   ....
3 I need any apples to make a pie. ....
4 I don't take many sugar in my tea. ....
5 Can I have any ketchup, please?   ....
6 I would like a orange juice.   ....

Communication

- **Complaining about a meal**

25 Fill in the missing words. Listen and check. Then, in pairs, act out similar dialogues using the prompts.

A: 1) .... me.
B: Yes, madam? What seems to be the 2) ....?
A: I'm afraid I can't **eat** this **soup**. It's too **spicy**.
  3) .... you change it for me, please?
B: Yes, certainly. I'm 4) .... about that.

- drink - milkshake - sweet
- eat - fish - salty
- drink - orange juice - sour

Pronunciation

26 Listen and number the words in the order you hear them. Listen again and repeat.

A ☐ eats   ☐ each   ☐ it's
B ☐ cheese ☐ she's   ☐ sees
C ☐ peach   ☐ peas   ☐ piece
D ☐ juice   ☐ choose ☐ shoes
E ☐ chop   ☐ shop   ☐ soap

Vocabulary Practice

27 Vocabulary Revision Game: In teams, make sentences with words/phrases from the list.

- vegetables • slices • bake bread • sour
- vitamins • side salad • bowl • loaf
- celebrate • frying pan • diet • vegetarian
- carton • spicy • left over • was starving
- mineral water • need • plenty of • delicious

28 Fill in the correct word from the list, then make sentences.

- sesame • cheese • corner • roast • fruit
- healthy • main • mineral • special • street

1 .... course   6 .... chicken
2 .... water   7 .... shop
3 .... occasion   8 .... sandwich
4 .... salad   9 .... seed balls
5 .... diet   10 .... parades

29 Fill in: *about, for, from, on, with, of.*

1 to be .... a diet; 2 to have sth ....
dinner; 3 to put salt .... your food; 4 to help
sb .... sth; 5 to have plenty .... sth; 6 to feel
sorry ...... sb; 7 to be sorry .... sth you did
wrong; 8 bad .... you; 9 to start ....;
10 to get sth .... the shop

30 Fill in the gaps with a word from the list.

- fried • chopped • roast • fresh • raw
- burnt • baked • boiled

1 My favourite meal is steak with ....
  onions.
2 Sushi is a type of Japanese food made with rice
  and .... fish.
3 I need some .... tomatoes to make a
  sauce for the pasta.
4 The traditional dish for Sunday lunch in England
  is .... beef and Yorkshire pudding.
5 I don't like chips, because they're full of oil, but
  I love .... potatoes.
6 A healthy diet should include a lot of ....
  .... fruit and vegetables.
7 I'm not very hungry — I think I'll just have a
  .... egg for breakfast.
8 Oh, no! I forgot about the food I was cooking,
  and now it's .... !

* Check Ss' HW (10').

23 a) Explain the task. Allow Ss two minutes to do the exercise. Check Ss' answers while they read out the dialogue.

ANSWER KEY

1 any	3 some	5 much/any
2 any	4 some	6 many

b) Ss act out similar dialogues in pairs.

SUGGESTED ANSWER KEY

- A: I'm hungry. Are there any apples?
  B: No, sorry. There aren't any apples. Would you like some grapes?
  A: Yes, please. Can I have a glass of orange juice, too?
  B: Yes. We have to buy some coffee though, because there isn't much left.
  A: There aren't many strawberries, either. Just a few
  B: I think we should go shopping this afternoon.

- A: I'm hungry. Are there any eggs?
  B: No, sorry. There aren't any eggs. Would you like some chips?
  A: Yes, please. Can I have a glass of Coke, too?
  B: Yes. We have to buy some tea though, because there isn't much left.
  A: There aren't many peaches, either. Just a few.
  B: I think we should go shopping this afternoon.

24 Explain the task, then Ss do the exercise. Check Ss' answers while they justify their answers.

ANSWER KEY

2 Would you like **some** water? (water is an uncountable noun)
3 I need **some** apples to make a pie. (affirmative sentence)
4 I don't take **much** sugar in my tea. (sugar is an uncountable noun)
5 Can I have **some** ketchup, please? (ketchup is an uncountable noun)
6 I would like **some** orange juice. (orange juice is an uncountable noun)

25 Allow Ss two minutes to do the exercise. Play the cassette for Ss to check their answers. Ss, in pairs, read out the completed dialogue, then in open pairs, use the prompts to act out similar dialogues.

ANSWER KEY

1 Excuse   2 problem   3 Could   4 sorry

SUGGESTED ANSWER KEY

- A: Excuse me.
  B: Yes, madam? What seems to be the problem?
  A: I'm afraid I can't drink this milkshake. It's too sweet. Could you change it for me, please?
  B: Yes, certainly. I'm sorry about that.

- A: Excuse me.
  B: Yes, madam? What seems to be the problem?
  A: I'm afraid I can't eat this fish. It's too salty. Could you change it for me, please?
  B: Yes, certainly. I'm sorry about that.

- A: Excuse me.
  B: Yes, madam? What seems to be the problem?
  A: I'm afraid I can't drink this orange juice. It's too sour. Could you change it for me, please?
  B: Yes, certainly. I'm sorry about that.

26 Explain the task. Play the cassette twice. Ss listen and number the words. Check Ss' answers, then play the cassette again with pauses for Ss to repeat chorally or individually.

ANSWER KEY

A	2 eats	1 each	3 it's
B	3 cheese	2 she's	1 sees
C	1 peach	3 peas	2 piece
D	3 juice	1 choose	2 shoes
E	2 chop	3 shop	1 soap

27 Ss, in teams, make sentences using the words/phrases in the order they appear in the list. Each correct sentence gets 1 point. The team with the most points is the winner.
e.g. Team A S1: Cauliflowers, spring onions and tomatoes are **vegetables**.
Team B S1: Can I have two **slices** of bread, please?   etc

28 Allow Ss two minutes to do the exercise. Check Ss' answers, then Ss make sentences using the completed phrases.
e.g. S1: You can have grilled fish and rice for the **main course**.
S2: Can I please have a glass of **mineral water**? etc

ANSWER KEY

1 main	5 healthy	8 cheese
2 mineral	6 roast	9 sesame
3 special	7 corner	10 street
4 fruit		

29 Allow Ss two minutes to do the exercise. Check Ss' answers around the class.

ANSWER KEY

1 on	3 on	5 of	7 about	9 with
2 for	4 with	6 for	8 for	10 from

30 Explain the task. Allow Ss two minutes to do the exercise. Check Ss' answers while Ss read out the completed sentences.

ANSWER KEY

1 fried	4 roast	7 boiled
2 raw	5 baked	8 burnt
3 chopped	6 fresh	

Game :

Play the game as described in the Student's Book. If Ss have difficulty they can play the game with their books open.

e.g. Team A S2: There is a lot of bread.
Team B S2: There is a cup of coffee.
Team A S3: There's a bowl of cornflakes.
Team B S3: There are some carrots.   etc

31 a) • Explain that the article describes a festival the writer attended. Ask Ss where they could find such a piece of writing (e.g. newspapers, school magazine etc).

• Present these words: **memories, May Day, maypole dance, covered, ribbons, buffet, hall, party games,** by giving examples or showing pictures.

e.g. **May Day:** 1st May
maypole dance: (Point to the picture and say: *The people in the picture are dancing round a maypole. This is a maypole dance.*) etc

• Explain the task, then allow Ss two minutes to do the exercise. Check Ss' answers.

ANSWER KEY

activities 2   feelings 4   food 3

---

b) • Allow Ss two to three minutes to scan the article and then answer the questions.

ANSWER KEY

1 The past simple because she describes a festival she attended when she was a girl.
2 Para 1: *I'll never forget … little girl.*
Para 2: *One of the … dance.*
Para 3: *After the dancing … delicious food.*
Para 4: *Today … used to.*
3 She feels happy because she has great memories.

• As an extension you can ask Ss to replace the topic sentences with other appropriate ones.

e.g. Para 1: How could I forget the way we celebrated May Day?
Para 2: What I liked most was the maypole dance.
Para 3: Food was one of the best parts of the festival.
Para 4: Unfortunately people don't celebrate May Day as they used to.

32 Read out the rubric, then elicit answers from Ss. Write Ss' answers on the board. Ss copy them into their notebooks. (Note: Decide on a certain festival to discuss that all Ss know about.)

SUGGESTED ANSWER KEY

1 California Strawberry Festival
2 15-17 May /Strawberry Meadows, California
3 To celebrate the harvest & to raise money for charity

---

4 – decorating trees and stalls with strawberries
– making special strawberry T-shirts, jewellery and hats
– rides in mini theme park
– strawberry shortcake eating contest
– visiting baby farm animals in the zoo
– shopping at stalls selling interesting arts and crafts
5 – strawberry tarts
– strawberry shortcake
– strawberries covered in chocolate
– strawberry pizza
– strawberry kebabs
6 excited about next year's festival

---

33 Explain the plan, then Ss use their answers in Ex. 32 follow the plan and talk about the festival as if they had attended it. Assign it as written HW.

SUGGESTED ANSWER KEY

A Berry Good Day Out

Last year I went to the California Strawberry Festival in a park called Strawberry Meadows in California. It started on 15 May and lasted for two days. It is held every year to celebrate the strawberry harvest and to raise money for charity.

People decorated trees and stalls with strawberries and made special strawberry T-shirts, jewellery and hats which we wore at the event. I went for a ride in the mini theme park and I visited baby farm animals in the zoo. My brother took part in a strawberry shortcake eating contest and won a prize. We also took a look at the many stalls which sold interesting arts and crafts.

For strawberry lovers there was a feast of strawberry tarts, strawberries covered in chocolate and everyone's favourite – strawberry pizza. Also popular were strawberry kebabs — strawberries on a stick with sugar on top!

The Strawberry Festival is perfect for a fun day out for the family. I had a great time and I am really excited about next year's festival.

---

34 Explain the task, then Ss do the exercise.

ANSWER KEY

1 T   2 F   3 T   4 T

Suggested Homework

1 **Copy:** Ex. 25 (p. 60)
2 **Vocabulary:** words in Exs 27, 28, 29, 30 (p. 60)
3 **Reading aloud:** article in Ex. 31a (p. 61)
4 **Dictation:** words in Exs 27, 28, 29, 30 (p. 60)
5 **Act out:** Ex. 25 (p. 60)
6 **Writing:** Ex. 33 (p. 61)

Lesson 5

• Check Ss' HW.
• Workbook: Unit 6
Click on Grammar 6

Game

Memory Game:
Ask Ss to look at the pictures on pp 54 & 55 for 1 minute. Ss close their books and in teams, try to remember what is in the pictures.

Team A S1: There are some spring onions.
Team B S1: There is a bottle of milk.   etc

Writing (an article about a festival which you attended)

31 **a) Read the article and match the paragraphs to the headings.**

• activities ... • name/date/place/reason 1 • feelings ... • food ...

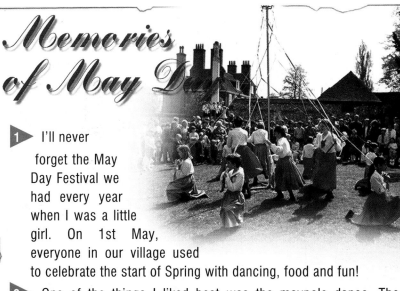

Memories of May Day

1 ▶ I'll never forget the May Day Festival we had every year when I was a little girl. On 1st May, everyone in our village used to celebrate the start of Spring with dancing, food and fun!

2 ▶ One of the things I liked best was the maypole dance. The children from my school made a circle around the maypole, and we covered the pole with pretty ribbons as we danced around it.

3 ▶ After the dancing we always had delicious food. There was a huge buffet in the village hall, with mountains of sandwiches, cakes and biscuits. At the end of the day, there was never any food or drink left, because we were so hungry after all the dancing and party games.

4 ▶ Today, not many English villages celebrate May Day in the traditional way we used to. I always had a great time though, and I feel happy when I remember that.

b) Read the article again and answer the questions.

1 Which tense does the writer use most often? Why?
2 Which is the topic sentence in each paragraph?
3 How does the writer feel about this festival?

32 **Read the rubric and answer the questions.**

Your teacher has asked you to write an article about a festival you attended. Write your article for your teacher (120-150 words).

1 Which festival are you going to write about?
2 When/Where did it take place?
3 What was the reason for celebrating the festival?
4 What activities did you/other people take part in?
5 What food did people make?
6 How do you feel about that festival?

33 **Use your answers in Ex. 32, as well as the plan below, to write your article for your teacher. You can use the article in Ex. 31a as a model.**

Plan

Introduction
(Para 1) *name/date/place/ reason*
Main Body
(Para 2) *activities*
(Para 3) *food*
Conclusion
(Para 4) *feelings about festival*

34 **Read the sentences and guess which one is *not* true.**

do you know...?

1 A giant burger weighing 2.5 tons was made in Wisconsin, USA, on August 5th, 1989.
2 Dublin restaurant manager Leslie Cooke paid $906 for one strawberry in 1977.
3 Louis XVI was the first French king to use a knife and fork.
4 Saffron is the most expensive spice in the world. A pound of saffron costs more than a pound of gold!

The Hound of the Baskervilles

Danger on Dartmoor

Dr Mortimer and Dr Watson travel to Dartmoor with Sir Henry. Baskerville Hall is not far from the station.

1 Sergeant, why are there so many policemen here?

A murderer called Seldon has escaped from Dartmoor Prison, sir. Don't worry, though — we'll catch him!

2 These are the Barrymores, your uncle's servants.

Welcome to Baskerville Hall, Sir Henry.

In the middle of the night …

3 What is Barrymore doing? Was *he* the man in the cab?

A few days later …

4 I think I'll walk to the village and post my report to Holmes, Sir Henry. Please don't leave the house alone — it may not be safe.

5

6 Good morning. You're Dr Watson, aren't you? I'm Jack Stapleton. That's my house, and there's my wife Beryl.

Pleased to meet you. Would you like to join me for a walk?

7 Shall we go this way?

Oh, no! That's the Grimpen Mire. There's quicksand everywhere! I know a safe way through, but for a stranger like you it's very dangerous.

8 AA-OO-OUH! WOO-OU-AHH!

What's that awful noise?

People say it's the Baskerville hound … a stupid old legend … Please excuse me, I must go …

9 Sir Henry, you must leave here at once! You are in terrible danger!

I'm not Sir Henry, I'm his friend. Are you Beryl Stapleton?

Pre-Reading Activities

1 **Look at the pictures and underline the correct word or phrase.**

1 Dr Watson travelled to Dartmoor in a coach/<u>on a train</u>.
2 He met <u>Sir Baskervilles' servants</u>/ a sergeant at Sir Henry's house.
3 Watson saw a man breaking a window/<u>signalling with a light</u> from his window.

2 **Look at picture 2. Who is wearing …**

- a coat Sir Henry/Dr Mortimer
- a tie Dr Watson/Dr Mortimer
- a bow tie Mr Barrymore
- an apron Mrs Barrymore
- a bowler hat Dr Watson
- a top hat Sir Henry/Dr Mortimer
- gloves Mr Barrymore
- a tuxedo Mr Barrymore

Listening and Reading Activities

3 **Listen and correct the words in bold.**

1 There are a lot of **murderers** at the station. *policemen*
2 The Barrymores are **policemen**. *servants*
3 Watson will walk to the village to post his **letter** to Holmes. *report*
4 The Baskerville hound is a stupid old **noise**. *legend*

4 **Read the episode. Which people did Dr Watson meet while in Dartmoor?** A policeman, The Barrymores and Jack & Beryl Stapleton

5 **Read the episode again and find the words which mean the opposite of the following.**

1 e s c a p e ≠ capture
2 c a t c h ≠ let go, release
3 a l o n e ≠ accompanied

4 s a f e ≠ dangerous
5 s t u p i d ≠ clever
6 a w f u l ≠ lovely
7 f a r f r o m ≠ close to

Grammar

• **Making Suggestions**

6 **a) Study the tables, then find two sentences in the episode which are suggestions.** Would you like to join me for a walk? Shall we go this way?

making suggestions	responding
Let's/We could go for a walk. Shall we/ Why don't we/ } go for a walk? Would you like to How about } going for a walk? What about	positively That's a good idea. That sounds great. negatively I don't think it's a good idea. That doesn't sound like a good idea.

b) In pairs, use the table to make and respond to suggestions, as in the example.

play	chess, darts, backgammon, hockey, football, video games
go	shopping, horse riding, for a walk, fishing, swimming
make	a cake, dinner, the bed
watch	a film, TV, the 8 o'clock news, a play, a football match
listen to	the radio, some CDs, music
do	the washing-up, the ironing, our homework, our hair

A: *What about playing chess?*
B: *That's a good idea.*

(Ss' own answers)

7 **Listen to the episode again and follow the lines, then take roles and act out the episode.**

8 **Expand the notes into full sentences.**

1 Dr Mortimer and Dr Watson travelled to Dartmoor with Sir Henry.
2 There were a lot of policemen at the station. They were looking for a murderer.
3 Sir Henry and Watson met the Barrymores at Baskerville Hall. They were his uncle's servants.
4 One night Watson saw Barrymore signalling with a light from a window and wondered if Barrymore was the man in the cab.
5 A few days later Watson went for a walk and met Jack and Beryl Stapleton.
6 Jack Stapleton told Watson that Grimpen Mire was very dangerous for a stranger.
7 Suddenly Watson heard an awful noise. Jack Stapleton said (that) it was the Baskerville hound.
8 Beryl Stapleton thought Watson was Sir Henry and told him to leave at once because he was in terrible danger.

Vocabulary

1 Circle the odd one out.

junk food: chips, pizza, (spices), burger
vegetables: cauliflower, broccoli, lettuce, (olives)
casual clothes: shorts, T-shirt, (evening dress), trainers
snacks: (spring onions), biscuits, soup, sandwich
fruit: pears, (peppers), grapes, peaches
utensils: saucepan, frying pan, grill, (carton)
material: (spotted), leather, wool, cotton

(7 marks)

2 Fill in: *corner shop, mineral, spicy, chopped, tins, annual, starving, windy, polo neck, high-heeled, credit, cybershopping.*

1 I don't like curry, it's too **spicy**.
2 The forecast says it's going to be **windy** tomorrow.
3 Can I have two **tins** of sardines, please?
4 I'm **starving**! Is there anything to eat?
5 Can you get me some milk from the **corner shop**?
6 It's our school's **annual** sports day next Saturday.
7 To give more flavour to this dish, just add a tin of **chopped** tomatoes.
8 Do they accept **credit** cards in this shop?
9 This evening dress looks best with **high-heeled** shoes.
10 Can I have a glass of **mineral** water, please?
11 With the increasing use of personal computers **cybershopping** will soon become more popular than going into town to buy things.
12 John bought me a lovely **polo neck** jumper for my birthday.

(12 marks)

3 Fill in: *on, for, in, from, about.*

1 I hate standing **in** long queues.
2 I'm **on** a diet, so no ice cream for me.
3 How can people who live in big cities protect themselves **from** air pollution?
4 I can't wait **for** my birthday party.
5 There are some really good websites **on** the net.
6 Now, that she has found a job, she is independent **from** her parents.
7 I'm really sorry **about** what happened.

(7 marks)

4 What is each person wearing? Look and say. What are you wearing today?
trainers, dress, V-neck pullover, straw hat, suit, trousers, tie, shirt, T-shirt, striped shorts, flat shoes, socks **etc.**
(See Suggested Answers section)

(14 marks)

Ted   Jim   John   Kim

5 Underline the correct word.

A: <u>How much</u>/How many are those cakes?
B: 50p each. How much/<u>How many</u> do you want?
A: Oh, only <u>a few</u>/a little. Six should be enough.
B: Shall I put them in a **packet**/<u>box</u> for you?
A: Yes please. Have you got some/<u>any</u> bread rolls?
B: Yes, we have.
A: Oh, lovely! Six of those, please.
B: Will that be all?
A: No, I'll have a <u>bar</u>/slice of dark chocolate, too.
B: I'm sorry. We haven't got a/<u>any</u> left!

(7 marks)

Grammar

6 Fill in *are/is/am going to* **or** *will.*

1 A: What's the matter?
   B: Watch out! You **are going to** crash into that lamp-post.
2 A: Oh, no, my computer is broken.
   B: I know. Josh **is going to** fix it this afternoon.
3 A: You forgot Shelley's birthday.
   B: Oh no. I **will** phone her now.
4 A: Your skin is burning!
   B: Okay. I **will** put some sun cream on.
5 A: The car is filthy!
   B: I know. I **am going to** clean it this evening.
6 A: I can't find my umbrella.
   B: I **will** help you find it.
7 A: You've broken my favourite mug!
   B: Sorry. I **will** buy you a new one tomorrow.
8 A: The kids' room is a mess.
   B: They know. They **are going to** tidy it later.

(8 marks)

7 Complete the sentences using *will*.

(Suggested answers)

1 I like this dress a lot. I will buy it.
2 I'm thirsty. I will drink some water.
3 I'm hungry. I will eat a sandwich.
4 I'm tired. I will go to bed.
5 I'm cold.I will close the window.

(5 marks)

Communication

8 Fill in the missing sentences, then in pairs read out the dialogues.

About a month.   It's cold and wet.

- A: How long are you going to be away?
  B: **1)** About a month.
  A: What's the weather like there?
  B: **2)** It's cold and wet.

And for dessert?   May I take your order

- A: **1)** May I take your order, madam?
  B: Yes, I'd like the grilled fish please.
  A: **2)** And for dessert?
  B: Just coffee, please.

(8 marks)

Reading

9 Read the letter and answer the questions.

Dear Sir/Madam,

I'm writing to complain about the service, food and prices at your restaurant, *The Salmon's Leap*.

I took my friends out for a birthday treat to your restaurant on Friday 16th May and had an awful meal. The waiter showed us to a table next to the kitchen and we weren't able to change to another one. It was very noisy and waiters were pushing past us all the time. When the waiter brought the drinks, he spilled cola on my new dress and ruined it. My steak was burnt although I ordered it medium rare and the coffee at the end of the meal was cold. When I got the bill, it was much more than I expected.

I would like you to pay to clean the dress and apologise for spoiling my special day. I must say, I used to eat regularly at *The Salmon's Leap*. I hope that your standards will improve again.

Yours faithfully,

Louise Lewis

1 Why did Louise write the letter?
2 What five complaints does she make?
3 What does she expect the manager to do?
(See Suggested Answers section)   *(12 marks)*

Writing

10 You visited *The Rosebowl* restaurant last Monday evening, but you were not pleased with the service, the quality of food or the prices. Use the plan below to write your letter of complaint (100-120 words). You can use the letter in Ex. 9 as a model.

(20 marks)

Plan   (See Suggested Answers section)

Dear Sir/Madam,

(Para 1)   *I'm writing to... Monday evening.*
(Para 2)   *waiters very slow – wait/hour/meal*
           pasta/too spicy – pizza/cold
           get bill – surprised how much/cost
(Para 3)   *I expect/apology for spoiling/evening.*
           hope/improve service – reduce/prices
           or else you/lose/customers

Yours faithfully,

(Total = 100 marks)

Let's sing!

11 Listen and fill in. Listen again and sing.

What's the weather **1)** like today?
It's sunny. It's the first of May.
Put on my T-shirt and my **2)** shorts,
Find my friends – play some sports.

What's the weather like today?
It's **3)** raining and the sky is grey.
Put on my **4)** boots and plastic coat,
Splash in puddles, make things float.

What's the weather like today?
The wind is **5)** blowing the clouds away.
Put on my scarf and **6)** woollen hat,
and kick the leaves then squash them flat.

What's the weather like today?
It's **7)** snowing – I'll go out and play.
Build a snowman, ride on my sled,
Have my tea and go to **8)** bed.

Making Choices & Decisions

◆ **Before you start...**

What are you going to do this weekend?
What kind of clothes do you prefer to
 wear?
What is the weather like today?
What do you think will be the fashion in
100 years time?
What is your favourite food?
What do you usually eat for breakfast/lunch/dinner?
What is your favourite festival? How do you celebrate it?

◆ **Listen, read and talk about...**

You'd better ...

UNIT 7

- animals, pets
- the solar system
- parts of the body
- geography: places, rivers, oceans

Module 4
Units 7-8

What are
the rules?

◆ Learn how to ...

- make comparisons
- give/ask for advice
- give an opinion
- describe an animal
- talk about the solar system
- justify your opinion and give reasons
- give orders
- make requests
- talk about environmental issues

◆ Practise ...

- comparisons of adjectives/adverbs
- conditionals (type 0 & type 1)
- unless
- the imperative
- can/can't, must/mustn't, have to/ don't have to, could/couldn't, should/shouldn't

◆ Write ...

- an animal factfile
- an opinion article
- what traffic signs mean
- a letter giving advice

7 You'd better ...

Lead-in

1 a) Look at the pictures. What can you see?

b) Use the prompts to make sentences, as in the examples.

1 the Earth/the moon: bigger – smaller
2 trains/planes: faster – more comfortable
3 cats/dogs: quieter/more loyal
4 roses/tulips: prettier/more popular

The Earth is bigger than the moon.
The moon is smaller than the Earth.

2 Ask and answer, as in the example.

1 the hottest? the Earth, the sun or the moon?
   A: Which is the hottest? the Earth, the sun or the moon?
   B: The sun is the hottest of all.
2 the noisiest? cats/dogs/parrots?
3 the most popular? tulips/orchids/roses?
4 the fastest? trains/planes/boats?

3 Listen and repeat.

- Let's go somewhere warmer.
- So does this one.
- Let's have a look.
- Oh dear. Look at the price!
- What about Portugal?

- You're right.
- That's settled, then.
- What do you fancy?
- They repeat whatever they hear.
- Good point!

Listening and Reading

4 Listen and underline what each speaker chooses.

Dialogue A   the Caribbean – Portugal – Sweden
Dialogue B   car – boat – plane
Dialogue C   dog – cat – parrot

5 a) Read the dialogues and answer the questions using *if*, as in the example, then explain the words in bold.

1 Why does Jane want to buy a parrot?
   If she buys a parrot, she won't have to walk it.
2 Why doesn't Betty want to go to Jersey by car?
3 Why doesn't Jim want to go to Sweden?

A Kathy: What about going to Sweden for our holidays this year?
   Jim: No, let's go **somewhere** a bit warmer. If we go there, we'll **freeze to death**.
   Kathy: But the hotel looks nice.
   Jim: So does this one. **In fact**, this hotel in the Caribbean is the nicest I've ever seen. And the weather is much hotter there.
   Kathy: Let's have a look. **Oh dear**. Look at the price! It's much more expensive than we can **afford**.
   Jim: We'd better find somewhere cheaper.
   Kathy: What about Portugal? I've heard it's as beautiful as the Caribbean, but not as **crowded**.
   Jim: Here's a nice hotel. It's not too expensive and it has a big swimming pool for the kids.
   Kathy: The restaurant looks nice, too. Let's call the **travel agent's** and get some more **information**.

Objectives

Vocabulary: animals; pets; parts of their bodies; the solar system; places; means of transport
Reading: reading for specific information
Listening: listening for lexical items; listening for specified information
Speaking: comparing city/countryside
Communication: at the florist's, at the travel agent's
Pronunciation: sentence stress
Grammar: comparisons of adjectives/adverbs; conditionals Type 0 - Type 1; unless
Project: traffic signs
Writing: an article expressing your opinion

Lesson 1 (pp. 66 - 67)

1 a) • Ask Ss to look at the pictures on pp 66 - 67 and identify what they see. Help Ss where necessary. [e.g. an orchid, a cat, tulips, a dog, roses, a train, a ship, a parrot, the sun, the Earth, the moon, a plane.]

• Ask Ss to look at the pictures of the Earth and the moon. Ask: *Are the two the same? (No.)* Say, then write on the board: *The moon is **smaller than** the Earth.* Underline **smaller than**. Explain that we use **adjective + er** with shorter adjectives and **than** to compare two people, things, animals etc. Give the word **bigger**. Ask Ss to construct a similar sentence. (*The Earth is bigger than the moon.*)

• Ask Ss to look at the pictures of the train and the plane. Ask: *Which are more comfortable to travel on planes or trains? (Trains.)* Write on the board: *Trains are more comfortable to travel on than planes.* Underline **more comfortable than**. Explain that we use **more + adjective + than** with longer adjectives to compare two people, things, animals etc.

• Drill your Ss. Write adjectives on the board. Ss say the adjectives in the comparative form. Write Ss' answers on the board checking for spelling.
Suggested adjective list: tall, short, big, fast, comfortable, expensive, careful, pretty, noisy, cheap, warm, difficult etc.
e.g. T: tall   T: short
     S1: taller (than)   S2: shorter (than) etc

b) • Read out the first prompt and the example, then Ss do the exercise orally in class.

SUGGESTED ANSWER KEY

2   *Planes are faster than trains.*
    Trains are more comfortable than planes.
3   *Cats are quieter than dogs.*
    Dogs are more loyal than cats.
4   *Tulips are prettier than roses.*
    Roses are more popular than tulips.

---

2 • Ask Ss to look at the pictures of the Earth, the moon and the sun. Ask: *Which is the hottest? (The sun.)* Say, then write on the board: *The sun is the hottest of all.* Underline **the hottest of**. Explain that we use **the + adjective + est + of** with shorter adjectives to compare three or more people, animals, things etc. Give the word **biggest**. Ask Ss to construct a similar sentence. (*The sun is the biggest of all.*)

• Ask Ss to look at the pictures of the train, the plane and the boat. Ask: *Which is **the most comfortable of all**? (The boat.)* Write on the board: *Boats are the most comfortable of all.* Underline **the most comfortable of**. Explain that we use **the most + adjective + of** with longer adjectives to compare three or more people, things, animals etc.

• Drill your Ss. Use the same list of adjectives as before. Choose an adjective. Ss say the adjective in the superlative form. Write Ss' answers on the board checking for spelling. Refer Ss to the Grammar Reference section at the back of the Student's Book for further details.

• Read out the first prompt and the examples, then Ss, in open pairs, do the exercise.

SUGGESTED ANSWER KEY

2   A: *Which are the noisiest? Cats, dogs or parrots?*
    B: *Dogs are the noisiest of all.*
3   A: *Which are the most popular? Tulips, orchids or roses?*
    B: *Roses are the most popular of all.*
4   A: *Which are the fastest? Trains, planes or boats?*
    B: *Planes are the fastest of all.*

---

3 Play the cassette. Ss listen and repeat either chorally or individually. Present the phrases/sentences to Ss by giving examples, miming or in Ss' L1 if necessary.
e.g. **Let's go somewhere warmer.** (Say: *It's very cold in Sweden. Pretend that you feel cold. Say: Let's go **somewhere warmer**. Let's go to Portugal. It's hot and sunny there.*) etc

4 Explain the task. Play the cassette. Ss do the exercise. Check Ss' answers.

ANSWER KEY

A — *Portugal*   B — *boat*   C — *parrot*

---

5 a) • Explain the task. Read out the example. Ask Ss to highlight the words **if, buys, won't have to.** Explain that **if** introduces conditional clause, in this case Conditional Type 1, and takes a verb in the present simple whereas the main clause requires a verb in the future. Point out that when the conditional clause precedes the main clause a comma is required to separate the two clauses. Ask Ss to read out the answer to get used to the form and pronunciation/intonation.

• Read out questions 2 and 3. Allow Ss two minutes to read the dialogues silently and answer the questions in writing. Check Ss' answers on the board.

ANSWER KEY

2   *If they go to Jersey by car, it will take them two days.*
3   *If Jim goes to Sweden, he'll freeze to death.*

• Help Ss explain the words in bold by giving examples or synonyms.
e.g. **somewhere:** a place
     In fact: Actually   etc

b) Play the cassette for Ex. 4 again. Ss listen and follow the lines, then take roles and read out the dialogues.

c) Allow Ss two minutes to read the dialogues and highlight the phrases/sentences using their text markers, then say who said each one.

ANSWER KEY

Jim said, "Let's go somewhere warmer."
Jim said, "So does this one."
Kathy said, "Let's have a look."
Kathy said, "Oh dear. Look at the price!"
Kathy asked, "What about Portugal?"
Rory said, "You're right."
Betty said, "That's settled, then."
Brian asked, "What do you fancy?"
Brian said, "They repeat whatever they hear."
Jane said, "Good point!"

Memory Game

Ask Ss to look at the sentences in Ex. 3 for two minutes. Ss then close their books and, in teams, try to remember as many sentences as possible. Each correct sentence gets 1 point. The team with the most points is the winner.
e.g. Team A S1: So does this one.
    Team B S1: You're right.   etc.

(Suggested Homework)

1 **Copy:** any of the dialogues A - C Ex. 5a (p. 66 - 67)
2 **Vocabulary:** words in bold in the dialogues Ex. 5a (pp. 66 - 67)
3 **Reading aloud:** dialogues Ex. 5a (pp. 66 - 67) (Point out that Ss practise *reading aloud* at home using the S's cassette/audio CD)
4 **Dictation:** any ten words from Vocabulary
5 **Speaking:** a) Ss memorise any five sentences from Ex. 3 (p. 66);
        b) Ss should be able to look at the pictures and make comparisons (Ex. 2, p. 66)

B

Betty: Are we going to Jersey for Mark and Helen's wedding?

Rory: Yes, but I'm not sure about the best **way** to get there.

Betty: Well, if we go by car it will **take** us two days.

Rory: Yes, but it's cheaper than the plane.

Betty: We could go by boat. It's the most comfortable way to travel.

Rory: You're right. And if we **book** a **cabin**, we'll get a good night's sleep and we'll be as fresh as **daisies** when we get there.

Betty: That's settled, then.

C

Jane: I'm thinking about getting a pet.

Brian: Really? What do you fancy – a dog or a cat?

Jane: Neither – I want to buy a parrot!

Brian: Why? Cats are **less** noisy and dogs are the most loyal animals I can think of.

Jane: I know, but I don't have to walk a parrot! Also, if I buy one, I can teach him to say things!

Brian: Well, you'd better be **careful** what you say to it. They repeat **whatever** they hear.

Jane: Good point!

b) In pairs, read out the dialogues.

Speaking

c) Read the dialogues again and highlight the phrases/sentences used in Ex. 3. Who said each phrase/sentence?

Vocabulary

• The Animal Kingdom

6 a) Look at the pictures. Which are: - birds? - mammals? - reptiles? - insects? - carnivores? - herbivores? - endangered species? - wild? - tame? - farm animals?

An eagle is a bird.

b) Use the adjectives and nouns in the boxes to describe these animals.

Adjectives	Nouns
big, small, heavy, sharp, long, thin, thick, short, long etc	scales, body, ears, legs, claws, beak, teeth, antlers, fur, tail, wings, head, feathers etc.

A bear has got a heavy body.

c) Underline the correct words in bold.

1 Parrots can learn to do tricks. They are very **slow/intelligent**.
2 Rabbits don't make a lot of noise. They are very **quiet/noisy**.
3 Chimpanzees are **funny/friendly**. They often make you laugh.
4 Horses will do what their rider tells them to do. They are very **playful/obedient**.
5 Dogs are very **loyal/quiet**. They are faithful to their owners.

Grammar

• Comparatives/Superlatives

7 Complete the table, then say how we form the comparative/superlative degree of adjectives.

adjective	comparative	superlative
thin	thinner	the thinnest
tall	taller	....
pretty	....	the prettiest
safe	....	the safest
difficult	more difficult	....
good	better	....
bad	....	the worst
much/many	....	the most
little	less	....
far	.... /	the furthest/ the farthest

8 Look at the planets. Listen and repeat their names, then use the adjectives in the list to make sentences comparing the planets, as in the examples.

The Solar System

1 Mercury
4,879 km;
+180°C

2 Venus
12,100 km; +480°C

3 Earth
12,756 km; +22°C

4 Mars
6,780 km;
-60°C

5 Jupiter
143,000 km;
-120°C

6 Saturn
120,000 km;
-150°C

9 Pluto
2,300 km;
-230°C

7 Uranus
51,120 km; -214°C

8 Neptune
49,528 km; -210°C

• big - small • hot - cold • beautiful
• close to the sun - far from the sun

*Uranus is **bigger than** Neptune.*
*Neptune is **not as big as** Uranus.*
*Jupiter is **the biggest of** all the planets.*   *etc*

Lesson 2 (pp. 68 - 69)

* • Check Ss' HW (10').
  • Play the Memory Game as described in Ex. 5c
    p. 67(T).

6 **a)** • Ask Ss to look at the pictures and read out the
       name of each animal.
    • Write the categories mentioned in the instructions
      for Ex. 6a on the board. Present each word by
      giving examples. Explain the task, then elicit
      answers from Ss and write them on the board. Ss
      copy the completed tables into their notebooks.
      Ss are welcome to add to each category.

ANSWER KEY

birds (animals which have feathers and wings)
goose, peacock, eagle, (canary, pigeon etc)
mammals (animals which give birth to babies and
feed their young with milk) bear, rabbit, dog, zebra,
leopard, camel, donkey, deer, chimpanzee (cow,
cat etc)
reptiles (animals with scaly skins which lay eggs)
snake, alligator (lizard, crocodile etc)
insects (small animals which have six legs and, most of
them, wings) wasp, (bee, fly, ant, beetle, butterfly etc)
carnivores (animals which eat meat) bear, leopard,
snake, dog, wasp, eagle (lion, tiger etc)
herbivores (animals which eat only plants) camel,
donkey, rabbit, zebra, goose, deer (sheep etc)
endangered species (animals which are in danger of
extinction) bear, eagle, leopard, (panda, elephant etc)
wild (animals which live in natural surroundings)
leopard, deer, bear, alligator, zebra, snake, camel
chimpanzee, eagle, peacock, goose, rabbit, wasp
(lion, tiger etc)
tame (animals which live/work with humans) dog,
donkey, rabbit, goose (cat etc)
farm animals (animals which live on a farm), donkey,
goose (cow, chicken, hen etc)

  • Ss use the completed tables to make sentences, as
    in the example.
    e.g. A wasp is an insect.
          A bear is a mammal.   etc

b) • Present the words in the boxes using the pictures.
    e.g. T: Which animals have got a long tail?
          S1: The zebra. / The camel. / The leopard. /
               The alligator. / The peacock. / The donkey.
          T: Which animals have got small wings?
          S2: The goose. / The wasp.   etc
  • Ss then describe each animal.

SUGGESTED ANSWER KEY

  • It has got a big head with small ears, short legs
    and a small tail.
  • The snake has got a long thin body and scaly skin.
  • The rabbit has got a small body with white fur.
    It's got big ears, a small tail and short legs.
  • The dog has got a big body. It's got big ears,
    long legs and a long tail.

  • The leopard has got a heavy body, sharp
    claws and sharp teeth. It's also got a long tail
    and long legs.   etc

  • As an extension you can choose a S to be the leader.
    He/She writes the name of an animal from the pictures
    on a piece of paper. Ss, in teams try to guess which
    animal it is. The S who guesses the animal becomes
    the leader, his/her team wins a point and you continue
    the game. The team with the most points wins.
      e.g.   Leader: (camel)
              Team A S1: Is it an insect?
              Leader: No, it isn't.
              Team B S1: Has it got long legs?
              Leader: Yes, it has.   etc.

c) Explain the task then do the exercise with Ss,
     explaining any unknown words by giving examples.

ANSWER KEY

1 intelligent   3 funny   5 loyal
2 quiet   4 obedient

---

7 • Allow Ss two minutes to complete the table. Help Ss
      where necessary. Check Ss' answers on the board.
      Elicit the forms and refer Ss to the Grammar Reference
      section for more details.

ANSWER KEY

adjective	comparative	superlative
thin	thinner	the thinnest
tall	taller	**the tallest**
pretty	**prettier**	the prettiest
safe	**safer**	the safest
difficult	more difficult	**the most difficult**
good	better	**the best**
bad	**worse**	the worst
much/many	**more**	the most
little	less	**the least**
far	**further/farther**	the furthest/the farthest

  • As an extension ask Ss to make sentences using the
    adjectives in the list.
    e.g. T: thinner
          S1: Joyce is thinner than Melissa.
          T: the best
          S2: Mr Smith is the best teacher in the school. etc

8 • Explain that the pictures show the solar system. Play
      the cassette with pauses for Ss to repeat chorally, then
      individually. Present the prompts on the pictures, then
      read out the prompts in the list.
    • Read out the examples. Explain that we use **not as ...
      as** to compare two things/people/objects etc which
      are not equal.
    • Help Ss make sentences, first orally, then in writing.

SUGGESTED ANSWER KEY

Jupiter is not as close to the sun as Mercury.
Venus is smaller than Earth.
Pluto is the coldest of all the planets.
Saturn is more beautiful than Venus.   etc

---

9 • Present the adjectives. Ss, in closed pairs, decide which adjectives match each picture. Ask Ss to make comparisons using the adjectives for each picture.
e.g. The city is dirty. It isn't as clean as the countryside. The countryside is safe to live in. The city is dangerous to live in.   etc

> **ANSWER KEY**
>
> **City:** dirty, busy, noisy, dangerous, expensive, exciting
> **Countryside:** clean, peaceful, quiet, safe, cheap, boring

• Ask two Ss to read out the example. Explain that we use **I'd rather** to express preference. Ss, in open pairs, act out similar dialogues.

> **SUGGESTED ANSWER KEY**
>
> A: Would you rather live in the city or in the countryside?
> B: I'd rather live in the countryside because it's safer and more peaceful. How about you?
> A: I wouldn't like to live in the countryside because it's more boring and quieter. I'd rather live in the city.

10 Read out the table and the examples. Ss make sentences comparing the two means of transport first orally, then in writing.

> **ANSWER KEY**
>
> 2 Travelling by car is **more convenient** than travelling by plane.
>   Travelling by plane is not **as convenient as** travelling by car.
>   Travelling by plane is **less convenient** than travelling by car.
> 3 Travelling by plane is **safer** than travelling by car.
>   Travelling by car is not **as safe as** travelling by plane.
>   Travelling by car is **less safe** than travelling by plane.
> 4 Travelling by car is **more comfortable** than travelling by plane.
>   Travelling by plane is not **as comfortable as** travelling by car.
>   Travelling by plane is **less comfortable** than travelling by car.

11 Explain the task then allow Ss two minutes to do the exercise. Check Ss' answers on the board.

> **ANSWER KEY**
>
> 2 the most luxurious   5 the most beautiful
> 3 the quickest   6 the cleanest
> 4 the most comfortable

12 Explain the task, then Ss do the exercise. Check Ss' answers on the board.

> **ANSWER KEY**
>
> 2 quieter   4 more dangerous
> 3 more loyal   5 cleverer

13 Present any unknown animals from the pictures. Explain the task. Play the cassette. Ss listen and do the exercise. Check Ss' answers, then Ss make sentences about each person's favourite pet, then about themselves.
e.g.   Josh's favourite pet is the lizard.
        Bill's favourite pet is the tortoise.   etc

> **ANSWER KEY**
>
> Josh – B   Ann – E
> Bill – F   Claire – G
> Dave – C   Becky – D

TAPESCRIPT
• Josh always wanted something exotic, so when he saw a nice green lizard at the pet shop he couldn't resist the temptation.
• Bill doesn't like noisy animals like monkeys, so he's got a nice quiet tortoise.
• Dave kept asking his grandfather to buy him a pet so he couldn't believe his eyes when he found a nice goldfish on his desk last Saturday morning.
• Ann wanted a pet for her birthday, so her parents bought her a guinea pig.
• Claire's house has got a big garden. She keeps her dogs there. They often play together after she finishes her homework.
• Becky has got lots of pets, but her favourite is her monkey because it's so funny.

Project (p. 69)

Ss look at the Photo File section. Present these words: **cat family, stripes, swamps, hogs, tough, shallow, breathe** in Ss' L1 or by giving examples, opposites, synonyms or showing pictures.
Ask Ss to read out the prompts, then talk about each animal using the prompts in the order they are given. After Ss have completed the task orally in class, assign it as written HW.
See Photo File section Unit 7 for the Answer Key.

> ╭─ Suggested Homework ─╮
>
> 1 **Copy:** dialogue Ex. 9 (p. 69)
> 2 **Vocabulary:** words in Ex. 6a (p. 68) & names of planets Ex. 8 (p. 68)
> 3 **Reading aloud:** Ex. 8 (p. 68)
> 4 **Dictation:** any ten words from Vocabulary
> 5 **Act out:** Ex. 9 (p. 69)
> 6 **Project:** (p. 69)

9 Match the adjectives to the pictures, then compare the city and the countryside, as in the example.

- clean/dirty • peaceful/busy
- quiet/noisy • safe/dangerous
- cheap/expensive • exciting/boring

A: *Would you rather live in the city or in the countryside?*

B: *I'd rather live in the city, because it's busier and more exciting. How about you?*

A: *I wouldn't like to live in the city because it's noisier and dirtier. I'd rather live in the countryside.*

10 Look at the table and make sentences, as in the examples.

	expensive	convenient	safe	comfortable
car		✓		✓
plane	✓		✓	

1 *Travelling by plane is **more expensive than** travelling by car.*
2 *Travelling by car is **not as expensive as** travelling by plane.*
3 *Travelling by car is **less expensive than** travelling by plane.*

11 Use the adjectives in the superlative form to complete the sentences.

- luxurious • beautiful • clean • sunny
- comfortable • quick

1 Visit Rhodes for your summer holiday this year – It's the sunniest island in Greece.
2 Stay at the Three Crowns Hotel – it's .... hotel in the city!
3 Fly Atlantic Airlines – it's .... way to reach your destination.
4 Take a coach tour across Switzerland – it's .... way to enjoy the magnificent scenery.

5 Leeds Castle is one of .... castles in England. Don't miss it!
6 The Seychelles have some of .... beaches in the world!

12 Look at the adjectives, then make sentences, as in the example.

- noisy • clever • quiet • dangerous • loyal

1 Monkeys are noisier than kittens. They chatter all the time.
2 Guinea pigs are .... than dogs. They don't make a lot of noise.
3 Dogs are .... than mice. They are very fond of their owners.
4 Monkeys are .... than lizards. They sometimes bite people.
5 Monkeys are .... than donkeys. They can paint pictures and draw.

Listening

13 Which is each child's favourite pet? Listen and write the letters in the boxes.

Josh	B	Ann	☐
Bill	☐	Claire	☐
Dave	☐	Becky	☐

• Project

Look at the Photo File section and write fact files about tigers and crocodiles.

Speaking

14 In pairs, use adjectives from the list to ask and answer about books/films/TV programmes etc.

- scary • boring • funny • exciting • romantic
- sad • silly • enjoyable

A: *Scream is the* **scariest** *film I've ever seen. What about you?*
B: *I think Halloween is even* **scarier***. The* **most boring** *programme on TV is ...* etc

• Geography quiz

15 Fill in the superlatives, then guess the answers. Finally, listen and check.

1 Which is .... (large) island in the world?
 A Australia B Greenland C Iceland
2 Which is .... (long) river in the UK?
 A the Thames B the Avon C the Severn
3 Which is .... (deep) ocean in the world?
 A the Indian B the Atlantic C the Pacific
4 Where is .... (wet) place in the world?
 A in India B in England C in Brazil
5 Where is .... (sunny) place in the world?
 A in Texas B in Arizona C in Brazil

• Comparisons of adverbs

16 Complete the table.

Adverb	Comparative	Superlative
slowly	....	....
happily	....	....
beautifully	....	....
hard	....	....
well	....	....

17 Put each of the words in brackets into the correct adverb form.

1 Jenny speaks .... (soft) than any of my friends.
2 "I can't believe it!" she said .... (sad).
3 I'm sorry, but could you speak a little .... (slow), please?
4 Of all the violinists in the orchestra, Jan plays .... (well).
5 "You'll have to work much .... (hard)!" said our teacher, Mr White.

• Conditionals (Type 0 - Type 1)

18 a) Match the conditional clauses (1-6) to the results (a-f), then answer the questions.

1 If you put money in this machine,
2 If you don't hurry up,
3 If you don't study,
4 If you need anything,
5 If you want to go on holiday this summer,
6 If you want to go camping next week,

a you'll miss your flight.
b it gives you a ticket.
c you'll need the right equipment.
d you'll need to book in advance.
e you won't pass your exams.
f you can always ask me.

- Which sentence talks about something which always happens as a result of something else?
- Which sentences talk about a real or very probable occasion in the present/future?
- In which sentence can we replace *if* with **when**?

b) Complete the table.

Type 0 Conditional
If/When + present simple → ....

Type 1 Conditional
If + ... → *will/can/must/etc* + bare infinitive
If + ... → – imperative

19 Put each verb in brackets into the correct tense.

1 A: Brrrr! It's so cold in here!
 B: If you .... (wear) a jumper, you .... (feel) a bit warmer.
2 A: I wouldn't mind going to the cinema tonight.
 B: Great! If I .... (finish) work on time, I .... (come) with you.
3 A: My car's broken down. I can't get to work!
 B: If you .... (hurry), you .... (catch) the bus.
4 A: Ooh, that cake looks nice!
 B: Try some. If you .... (like) it, I .... (give) you the recipe.

20 Expand the prompts into full sentences.

1 heat water → boil *If you heat water, it boils.*
2 temperature fall below 0°C → water freeze
3 boil water → make steam
4 heat metal → expand
5 put salt on ice → melt

Lesson 3 (pp. 70 - 71)

* Check Ss' HW (10').

14 • Present the words in the list in Ss' L1 or by giving examples.
  e.g. **scary:** sth that frightens you etc.
  Explain the task. Ask two Ss to read out the example. Explain that we use the superlative with the present perfect.
  • Ss, in open pairs, act out similar dialogues.

SUGGESTED ANSWER KEY

B: ... 'A Day With Us'. What about you?
A: I think 'Problems' is even more boring. The funniest film I've ever seen is 'The Puppet'. What about you?
B: I think 'How to marry a Millionaire' is even funnier. The most romantic book I've ever read is ... etc.

---

15 • Explain the task. Ss do the exercise. Check Ss' spelling by writing the words on the board.
  • Play the cassette. Ss listen and check their answers.

ANSWER KEY

1	the largest	– B	4	the wettest	– A
2	the longest	– C	5	the sunniest	– B
3	the deepest	– C			

TAPESCRIPT

Teacher: ... Come on now, class, close your books, please. We're going to have a little quiz in today's Geography lesson.
(Ss chorally) Oh, no, Sir, not a test!
Teacher: Not a *test*, a *quiz*. It's much more fun and if you've done your homework, you've got nothing to worry about, have you?
(Ss chorally) No, Sir!
Teacher: Okay, then, let's begin – Question one to the blue team. Which is the largest island in the world? Marty?
Marty: I think it's Iceland, Sir.
Teacher: No, sorry Marty, close, but you're not quite right. Yes, er Inge?
Inge: It must be Greenland, then?
Teacher: That's correct. One point to the red team. Okay – second question. Which is the longest river in the United Kingdom?
Bryan: Sir, Sir!
Teacher: Go on, then, Bryan, tell me.
Bryan: It must be the Thames!
Teacher: Sorry, Bryan, it isn't. The Thames may be the most famous, but it isn't the longest. Yes, Lisa?
Lisa: Is it the Severn?
Teacher: Yes, Lisa, it is. Another point to the red team. Now, I expect all of you to know the answer to question three. Which is the deepest ocean in the world? Yes – Lesley?
Lesley: That's easy, Sir, it's the Pacific.
Teacher: Correct! At last, a point for the blue team!
(Ss chorally) Hurray!
Teacher: Quiet please and listen carefully to question four. It's a bit more difficult. Ready?
(Ss chorally) Yes, Sir!
Teacher: Where is the wettest place in the world? Yes – Terry?
Terry: It must be England, mustn't it?
Teacher: Well, I can understand why you think that, but no, it's not. Becky?
Becky: I've just remembered – it's somewhere in India, isn't it?
Teacher: Yes, that's right. Well done, Becky. Another point to the blue team. Now, each team has two points, so everything depends on this, the last question. Where is the *sunniest* place in the world?
(Ss chorally) Sir, Sir, ...
Teacher: Okay, Sharon – you had your hand up first.
Sharon: Is it in America, Sir?
Teacher: Yes, it is – but where exactly?
Sharon: Er – Arizona – no, no – Texas?
Teacher: Oh dear, Sharon, I'm so sorry. **Arizona** was correct.
(Ss chorally) Oh, Sharon!!
Teacher: Never mind – Sharon, it's still two points each. Let's have a final question to ... (fade)

---

16 Help Ss complete the table. Check Ss' answers on the board.

ANSWER KEY

Adverb	Comparative	Superlative
slowly	more slowly	the most slowly
happily	more happily	the most happily
beautifully	more beautifully	the most beautifully
hard	harder	the hardest
well	better	the best

---

17 Explain the task then allow Ss two minutes to do the exercise. Check Ss' answers on the board.

ANSWER KEY

1	more softly	3	more slowly	5	harder
2	sadly	4	the best		

---

18 a) • Ss' books closed. Write on the board: *If you heat water, it boils.* Underline *if*, **heats**, **boils**. Explain that this conditional clause expresses a general truth. Point out that this is Conditional Type 0. Explain that we use the present simple in both the conditional clause and the main clause.
  • Write on the board: *If you leave early, you won't miss the bus. If you need his help, ask him.* Underline **leave, won't miss, need, ask**. Elicit the tense form for each (**leave:** present simple, **won't miss:** future, **need:** present simple, **ask:** imperative). Elicit from Ss that these sentences are Conditional Type 1, then elicit which tenses we can use (*present simple in the if-clause, future/the imperative in the main clause*).
  • Ss open their books. Explain the task. Ss do the exercise.

ANSWER KEY

1	– b	3	– e	5	– d
2	– a	4	– f	6	– c
• 1		• 2, 3, 4, 5, 6.		• 1	

---

b) Help Ss complete the table. Refer Ss to the Grammar Reference section for more details.

ANSWER KEY

Type 0 Conditional **present simple**
Type 1 Conditional **present simple, present simple**

---

19 Allow Ss two minutes to do the exercise. Check Ss' answers while Ss, in pairs, read out the short exchanges.

ANSWER KEY

1	wear, will feel	3	hurry, will catch
2	finish, will come	4	like, will give

---

20 Explain the task, then read out the example. Explain that these sentences are general truths (laws of nature) which means we need to use a Conditional Clause Type 0. Ss do the exercise first orally, then in writing.

ANSWER KEY

2 If the temperature falls below 0°C, water freezes.
3 If you boil water, it makes steam.
4 If you heat metal, it expands.
5 If you put salt on ice, it melts.

---

21 • Ask Ss to look at the pictures. Elicit which country they are taken from *(the USA)* then check if Ss can tell which specific town each shows.
    • Explain the task. Play the cassette. Ss listen and match. Check Ss' answers.

ANSWER KEY

New York – Carnegie Hall
Washington DC – White House
Chicago – Sears Tower
Las Vegas – The Strip
San Francisco – Twin Peaks

22 a) Explain the task. Read out sentences 1 to 10. Allow Ss four to five minutes to read the advertisement silently and do the exercise. Check Ss' answers.

ANSWER KEY

1 F   3 T   5 T   7 F   9 F
2 F   4 F   6 T   8 F   10 T

    b) • Help Ss explain the words in bold by giving examples.
       • Play the cassette for Ex. 21 again. Ss listen and follow the lines, then read out from the advertisement. Elicit where Ss could read such a piece of writing *(tourist brochure)*.

23 Write the names of the five cities on the board. Elicit answers from Ss and complete the table. Ss copy the table into their notebooks, then use the completed table to talk about each city.

SUGGESTED ANSWER KEY

— Washington DC: White House – Georgetown – memorials and statues – museums
  In Washington DC you can tour the White House, visit Georgetown, see memorials and statues and visit museums.
— Chicago: Sears Tower – Lake Michigan – theatre, music, dance.
  In Chicago you can go to the Sears Tower and Lake Michigan, and you can sample theatre, music and dance.
— Las Vegas: The Strip – casinos – entertainment
  In Las Vegas you can visit The Strip and go to casinos for fantastic entertainment.
— San Francisco: San Francisco Bay – Twin Peaks, – Chinatown
  In San Francisco you can go to San Francisco Bay and the Twin Peaks and you can eat out in Chinatown.

Suggested Homework

1 **Copy:** any of the paragraphs in the advertisement in Ex. 22a (p. 71)
2 **Vocabulary:** words in bold in the advertisement in Ex. 22a (p. 71)
3 **Reading aloud:** advertisment in Ex. 22a (p. 71)
4 **Dictation:** any ten words from Vocabulary
5 **Speaking:** Ss look at their notes and talk about the tour. (Ex. 23, p. 71)

Listening and Reading

21 🎧 Listen and match the places to their attractions.

New York   Sears Tower
Washington DC   Carnegie Hall
Chicago   Twin Peaks
Las Vegas   White House
San Francisco   The Strip

22 **a) Read the advertisement, about a tour of the USA, then mark these sentences as T (true) or F (false).**

1 The company offers tours of America once a year.
2 Carnegie Hall is a famous museum in New York.
3 Washington DC is the capital of the USA.
4 Georgetown is a new neighbourhood.
5 There are beaches in Chicago.
6 Las Vegas is in the desert.
7 'The Strip' is a luxury hotel.
8 Mt Davidson is a small hill in San Francisco.
9 Chinatown is a large Chinese restaurant in San Francisco.
10 A tour in April costs £6,395 per person.

b) Read the advertisement again and explain the words in bold.

Speaking

23 Make a list of what you can see in each city, then use your notes to talk about each city, as in the example.

New York: *Statue of Liberty - museums - Carnegie Hall*

In New York you can see the Statue of Liberty, visit museums or go to Carnegie Hall.

US CROSS-CONTINENT TOURS

operate all year round, and offer you the opportunity of a lifetime to visit five of the greatest US cities, crossing nine states in our 15-day tour.

Itinerary

Days 1-4

The tour begins with three days in New York City, the largest and busiest city in the USA. You can see the Statue of Liberty, visit the city's museums and spend an evening at Carnegie Hall, one of the best **concert halls** in the world. The city has a rich and **varied culture**, so there is **plenty** to see and do.

Days 4-7

In Washington DC, capital of the USA, you will **tour** the White House, the most famous building in the city and **home** to the **President**. You will also visit Georgetown, the oldest neighbourhood in Washington DC. For **history lovers**, Washington DC has more than 300 **memorials** and **statues**, and there are several museums in the Federal Triangle, which is the largest **complex** of **public** buildings in the city.

Days 7-9

Our next stop is beautiful Chicago, which is the third largest US city. Its **skyline** contains one of the tallest buildings in the world, the Sears Tower. The **shore** of Lake Michigan offers beautiful **scenery**, with open parks and beaches. During our two-day stay, you can **sample** great theatre, music and dance.

Days 9-12

We will spend three days in the wonderful **desert resort** of Las Vegas, visiting the city's most famous attraction, 'The Strip' — a collection of luxury hotels and **casinos** for fantastic entertainment.

Days 12-15

The last stop on our tour is one of the country's most **cosmopolitan** cities. San Francisco is full of amazing sights, from San Francisco Bay, one of the world's finest natural **harbours**, to the Twin Peaks of Mt Davidson and Mt Sutro, the largest of the city's **hills**. You will also eat out in colourful Chinatown, the largest Chinese **community** outside Asia.

Departure dates and prices *(per person)*

1st June → 31st Aug.	£6,725
1st Sept. → 30th Nov.	£6,135
1st Dec. → 28th Feb.	£5,535
1st March → 31st May	£6,395

Prices include all flights, 14 nights' 5-star **accommodation**, all meals and **excursions**.

US CROSS-CONTINENT TOURS

Tel: 0975 362897
e-mail: USCCTOURS@netscape.com

• Unless = if not

24 **Study the example, then rewrite the sentences.**

1 If it doesn't rain tomorrow, we'll go for a picnic.
   Unless it rains tomorrow, we'll go for a picnic.
2 I won't go to the party if I'm not invited.
3 Unless he remembers to set the alarm clock, he will oversleep tomorrow.
4 You can come out with us unless you've got other plans.
5 If you don't hurry up, you will miss the concert.

Game

In teams, use phrases from the list to make *If -* or *Unless -* sentences. Each correct sentence gets one point. The team with the most points is the winner.

• he/earn/more money • she/play/well
• we/miss/the bus • they/be/late
• you/work/hard • weather/be/fine
• I/have/time • John/come/my party
• it/rain/tomorrow • you/help me/the dishes

Team A S1: *If he earns more money, he'll move to a bigger house.*
Team B S1: *If she plays well, she'll win.   etc*

Communication

• At the florist's/At the travel agent's

25 a) **Listen to the dialogues and say what each customer is ordering/booking.**

b) **Read the dialogues. Then, in pairs, use the prompts to act out similar dialogues.**

1 A: Good morning, sir.
   B: Good morning! How much are the red **roses**?
   A: They are £ 2.00 each.
   B: I'll take a dozen of them.
   A: Certainly sir. That will be **£24**.

2 A: Hello. I'd like to book a flight to **Milan** on **Tuesday 12th**, please.
   B: Certainly … Yes, there's a seat available, returning on **Tuesday 19th**.
   A: Yes, that will be fine. How much is it?
   B: **£189** for business class, or **£139** economy.
   A: Okay. I'll fly economy class, please.

1 tulips / £1.20 each / £14.40
   carnations / 80p each / £9.60
2 Rome - Saturday 10th / 17th / £169 - £129
   New York - Monday 6th / 13th / £199 - £149

Pronunciation - sentence stress

26 **The meaning of a sentence differs if we stress different words. Read the sentence below, then listen and number the meanings in the order you hear them. Listen again and repeat.**

•I think that dogs are better pets than cats are.

A ☐ I *think* so, but I'm not sure.
B ☐ Dogs are *better* pets, not worse pets.
C ☐ *I* think so, but perhaps you don't agree.
D ☐ *Dogs*, not cats, are better pets.

Vocabulary Practice

27 **Vocabulary Revision Game: In teams, make sentences with words/phrases from the list.**

• tour • freeze • unless • harbour • most popular
• capital • sample • carnivores • sharp teeth
• desert • obedient • bigger than • loyal
• a lot cheaper • afford • colourful • crowded

28 **Fill in the correct word from the list, then make sentences using the collocations.**

• book • concert • endangered • luxury
• natural • public • solar • two-day

1 .... species   5 .... hall
2 .... buildings   6 a.................. stay
3 to .... a cabin   7 .... hotel
4 .... system   8 .... harbour

29 **Match the pairs of words to the pairs of sentences, then fill in each gap with the correct word from the pair.**

• tour/trip • bank/shore • brochure/leaflet

1 a) The campsite is located on the ....
   of a pretty lake.   b) We had a great picnic on the .... of the river near our house.
2 a) Our hotel looked much nicer in the ....
   the travel agent gave us!   b) Have you read this .... about the dangers of smoking?
3 a) My father is going to London on a business .... next week.   b) Our ....
   of Italy included visits to Rome and Florence.

72

Lesson 4 (pp. 72 - 73)

* Check Ss' HW (10').

24 • Read out the example. Explain that we can use **unless** instead of **if not** in Conditional Type 1.
 • Ss make sentences, first orally, then in writing.

> **ANSWER KEY**
>
> 2 I won't go to the party unless I'm invited.
> 3 If he doesn't remember to set the alarm clock, he will oversleep tomorrow.
> 4 You can come out with us if you haven't got other plans.
> 5 Unless you hurry up, you will miss the concert.

Game

Play the game as described in the Ss' Book.

> **SUGGESTED ANSWER KEY**
>
> Team A S2: If we miss the bus, we'll be late for school.
> Team B S2: Unless they are late, the boss won't be angry.
> Team A S3: If you work hard, you'll get a promotion.
> Team B S3: Unless the weather is fine, we won't go on a picnic.
> Team A S4: If I have time, I'll do the shopping.
> Team B S4: If John comes to my party, he'll bring his sister with him.
> Team A S5: Unless it rains tomorrow, we'll go to the beach.
> Team B S5: If you help me with the dishes, we will finish sooner.

25 **a)** Present the words: **dozen, business class, economy class** by giving examples.
 e.g. **dozen**: 12
 Also remind Ss of how **£, p** are read. [£ = pound, p = pence] Explain the task. Play the cassette. Ss do the exercise. Check Ss' answers.

> **ANSWER KEY**
>
> 1: order – a dozen red roses
> 2: book – a flight to Milan

b) Play the cassette again. Ss listen and follow the lines, then read out the dialogues. Ss, in pairs, use the prompts to act out similar dialogues.

> **ANSWER KEY**
>
> 1 • A: Good morning, sir.
>   B: Good morning! How much are the red tulips?
>   A: They are £1.20 (one pound, twenty pence) each.
>   B: I'll take a dozen of them.
>   A: Certainly sir. That will be £14.40 (fourteen pounds, forty pence)

> • A: Good morning, sir.
>   B: Good morning! How much are the red carnations?
>   A: They are 80p (eighty pence) each.
>   B: I'll take a dozen of them.
>   A: Certainly sir. That will be £9.60 (nine pounds, sixty pence)

> 2 • A: Hello. I'd like to book a flight to Rome on Saturday 10th, please.
>   B: Certainly... Yes, there's a seat available, returning on Saturday 17th.
>   A: Yes, that will be fine. How much is it?
>   B: £169 for business class, or £129 economy.
>   A: Okay. I'll fly economy class, please.

> • A: Hello. I'd like to book a flight to New York on Monday 6th, please.
>   B: Certainly... Yes, there's a seat available, returning on Monday 13th.
>   A: Yes, that will be fine. How much is it?
>   B: £199 for business class, or £149 economy.
>   A: Okay. I'll fly economy class please.

26 Explain the task. Ss listen and number the sentences. Check Ss' answers, then play the cassette again with pauses for Ss to repeat individually.

> **ANSWER KEY**
>
> A 2   B 4   C 1   D 3

27 Ss, in teams, make sentences using the words/phrases in the order they appear in the list. Each correct answer gets 1 point. The team with the most points is the winner.
 e.g. Team A S1: We can **tour** America in 15 days.
   Team B S1: Close the window or I'll **freeze** to death.   etc

28 Allow Ss two minutes to do the exercise. Check Ss' answers, then Ss make sentences using the completed phrases.
 e.g. Elephants are an **endangered species**.   etc.

> **ANSWER KEY**
>
> 1 endangered   5 concert
> 2 public   6 two-day
> 3 book   7 luxury
> 4 solar   8 natural

29 Explain the task. Help Ss do the exercise explaining any unknown words by giving examples.

> **ANSWER KEY**
>
> 1 a shore   3 a trip
> b bank   b tour
>
> 2 a brochure
> b leaflet

30 Allow Ss two minutes to do the exercise. Check Ss' answers, then Ss make sentences using the completed phrases.
e.g. We can fish from the **shore of the lake**. etc.

> **ANSWER KEY**
>
> 1 of   3 to   5 to   7 of   9 by
> 2 in   4 in   6 from   8 of   10 in

31 a) Explain that Ss are going to read an article about a person's opinion about trains. Present these words/phrases: **take the strain, traffic jams, stare at, motorway, concerned, pay for, is worth, cost, cope with, difference it makes** in Ss' L1. Ss read out from the article. Help Ss underline then replace the words in bold with appropriate ones from the list. Explain that *On the other hand/However* introduce an opposing argument, *Firstly/To start with, Furthermore/What is more/In addition/Secondly* list similar ideas and *All in all/In conclusion* are used to introduce a concluding point.

> **ANSWER KEY**
>
> 1 Firstly - To start with
> 2 Furthermore - What is more/In addition
> 3 Secondly - What is more/Furthermore/In addition
> 4 On the other hand - However
> 5 All in all - In conclusion

b) • Allow Ss two minutes to do the exercise.

> **ANSWER KEY**
>
> • opposing viewpoint & reasons: para 4
> • viewpoints & reasons: paras 2, 3
> • introduce topic & state opinion: para 1
> • restate opinion: para 5

• Ask questions to highlight/underline the writer's viewpoints, then find the reasons for each.
  e.g. *trains are safe - no traffic jams/less chance of accidents*
  e.g. *trains are pleasant to travel on - fast, comfortable*

Point out that the fourth paragraph gives the opposing viewpoint. Ask Ss to underline this viewpoint, then find the reason *(train fares are expensive - tickets cost a lot of money)*.

32 • Present the writing tip. Explain the task, then Ss do the exercise. Help Ss if necessary.

> **ANSWER KEY**
>
> 1-b, positive viewpoint   4-c, negative viewpoint
> 2-d, positive viewpoint   5-a, positive viewpoint
> 3-e, negative viewpoint

• Ss make sentences, first orally, then in writing.

> **SUGGESTED ANSWER KEY**
>
> *Firstly, air travel is the safest way to travel. There are fewer accidents than with other means of transport. Furthermore, it is a quick way to travel. You can travel a great distance in a little time. Also, because you can enjoy a meal and a film on most flights, air travel is very relaxing, too. However, air travel is quite expensive because tickets usually cost a lot of money. In addition, because the seats are very close together, air travel is not very comfortable.*

33 Explain the task, then ask Ss to do the exercise orally in class, then assign it as written HW.

> **SUGGESTED ANSWER KEY**
>
> *Why do thousands of people all around the world choose air travel over other means of transport? Because, in my opinion, it is the best way to travel.*
> *Firstly, aeroplanes are the safest way to travel. There are fewer accidents when travelling by plane than with other means of transport.*
> *Secondly, air travel is far quicker than, for example travelling by train. With planes you can travel a great distance in a little time. In addition, planes can take you anywhere in the world while you can't travel by train from Europe to America, for example.*
> *On the other hand, although air travel is relaxing since you can enjoy a meal and a movie on most flights, it is not very comfortable because the seats in the planes are very close together. Furthermore, air travel is quite expensive since you usually pay a lot of money for the tickets. Always remember, though, that you pay for speed, convenience and safety!*
> *All in all, I think that although air travel is expensive, it is worth it. You reach your destination in no time, safe and relaxed. If you have already travelled by plane, then you know what I mean. If you haven't, take my advice: try it! It will be an experience you'll never forget.*

34 Present these words: **ostrich, ton, at birth, foot** by giving examples. You can also ask Ss to look up these words in their dictionaries. Then allow Ss one minute to do the task. Check Ss' answers while they read out their sentences.

> **ANSWER KEY**
>
> • blue whale   • ostrich

> **Suggested Homework**
>
> 1 **Copy:** Ex. 25.1 (p. 72)
> 2 **Vocabulary:** Exs. 27, 28, 29 (p. 72)
> 3 **Dictation:** Ex. 25.1 (p. 72)
> 4 **Act out:** Ex. 25.2 (p. 72)
> 5 **Writing:** Ex. 33 (p. 73)

> **Lesson 5**

• Check Ss' HW (10').
• Workbook: Unit 7
              Click on Grammar 7

30 Fill in: *by, of, from, in, to.*

1 the shore ...... a lake; 2 ...... fact; 3 home .... the President; 4 the best .... the world; 5 to freeze .... death; 6 to be far .... sth; 7 full .... sth; 8 a collection .... sth; 9 to travel .... boat/car/plane; 10 to live .... the countryside

Writing (an article expressing your opinion)

31 **a)** **Read the article and underline the correct words in bold, then replace them with synonyms from the list.**

- In addition • Furthermore • To start with
- However • What is more • In conclusion

Trains are the Best!

1 Why do thousands of people every day let the train take the strain? Because travelling by train is, in my opinion, the best way to travel.

2 **1) Also/Firstly**, travelling by train is safe, you don't have to worry about traffic jams or other problems that you find on the roads. **2) Furthermore/However**, because there is no other traffic there is less chance of having an accident.

3 **3) Secondly/In addition**, travelling by train is far more pleasant than, for example, travelling by bus. Trains are faster, and what is more the seats are far more comfortable. You can also sit back and enjoy watching the countryside, instead of having to stare at other cars and buses on the motorway.

4 **4) On the other hand/Furthermore**, although trains are fast and comfortable, some people say that train fares are too expensive. Tickets cost a lot of money. As far as I'm concerned, though, you get what you pay for, and the extra speed, convenience, safety and comfort of a train is worth a little extra cost.

5 **5) All in all/Despite**, I think that although rail travel can be expensive it is worth it. There are no traffic jams to cope with and you can relax and enjoy the scenery in comfort and safety. So, next time you have to make a journey, why not try travelling by train and see what a difference it makes?

b) Match the paragraphs to the headings.

- opposing viewpoint & reasons: ....
- viewpoints & reasons: ....
- introduce topic & state opinion: ....
- restate opinion: ....

To write an article expressing your opinion, first make a list of the points for and against the specific topic. **In the first paragraph** we introduce the topic and clearly state our opinion. **In the second and third paragraphs** we write our points for the topic with reasons. In the **fourth paragraph** we write our points against the topic with reasons. In the last paragraph we say our opinion again in other words. We use: *Also, Firstly, Secondly, In addition, Moreover, Furthermore* etc to link similar ideas. We use: *On the other hand, However* etc to introduce an opposing idea. We use: *In conclusion, All in all* etc to begin the last paragraph.

32 **Match the viewpoints (1-5) about air travel to the reasons (a-e). Which are positive? Which are negative? Make sentences using** *Firstly, Furthermore, Also, In addition* **and** *However.*

Viewpoints	Reasons
1 quick way to travel	a you can enjoy a meal and a film on most flights
2 safe way to travel	b you can travel a great distance in a little time
3 expensive	c the seats are very close together
4 not very comfortable	d there are fewer accidents than with other means of transport
5 relaxing	e tickets usually cost a lot of money

33 **You teacher has asked you to write a short article about air travel. Use the plan below and the notes in Ex. 32 to write your article (120-150 words). You can use the article in Ex. 31a as a model.**

Plan

Introduction
(Para 1) *introduce topic, state your opinion*
Main Body
(Paras 2-3) *viewpoints & reasons*
(Para 4) *opposing viewpoint(s) & reason(s)*
Conclusion
(Para 5) *summarise/restate your opinion*

34 Fill in: *ostrich, blue whale.*

do you know...

- The .... is the biggest mammal in the world. It weighs 3 tons at birth.
- The .... is the largest bird in the world. It can be as much as 9 foot tall.

The Hound of the Baskervilles

The Midnight Watcher

Watson has been at Baskerville Hall for a week. He writes a daily report to send to Sherlock Homes.

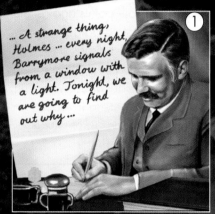

1 ... A strange thing, Holmes ... every night, Barrymore signals from a window with a light. Tonight, we are going to find out why ...

2 That night ...

Who are you signalling to, Barrymore?

3 Oh, it's my fault, sir! Seldon, the prisoner who escaped ... he's my brother, sir. We signal to tell him we're bringing food. I love him!

4 Look — there he is!

Poor Mrs Barrymore ... but we must catch Seldon. He's dangerous to society.

5 Are you all right?

Aaah!

6 He's escaped, Doctor. We'll never find him now.

Shh! Someone's watching us.

7 It isn't Seldon, and it isn't a policeman. I'm going to find out who it is.

Be careful, Watson!

At first light ...

8 Food and blankets ... this is someone's hiding place.

9

10 Footsteps! He's coming!

Good morning, Dr Watson. Please don't shoot me!

Pre-Reading Activities

1 **Look at the pictures. Read the sentences and underline the correct answers.**

a Who do you think Watson is writing to? Barrymore/<u>Holmes</u>

b What has Watson found in picture 9? <u>food and blankets</u>/trousers

c At what time of day does Watson find the hiding place? at night/<u>early in the morning</u>

d What is Watson holding in pictures 9 & 10? a camera/<u>a gun</u>

Listening and Reading Activities

2 🔊 **Listen to the episode and underline the correct word.**

1 The prisoner who escaped is Mrs Barrymore's father/<u>brother.</u>

2 Seldon is friendly/<u>dangerous</u> to society.

3 Watson finds someone's hiding <u>place</u>/blankets.

3 **Read the episode and answer the questions.**

1 Why do the Barrymores signal to Seldon?
To tell him they are bringing food.

2 Why is it important to catch Seldon?
Because he is dangerous to society.

3 Why is Sir Henry disappointed?
He thinks they won't find Seldon now.

4 What does Dr Watson hear?
He hears footsteps and then a voice.

Grammar
• Relatives

4 **Study the examples, then complete the rules.**

The prisoner **who** escaped is my brother.
Is that the dog **which/that** killed Baskerville?
The bicycle **which/that** he was riding belongs to his father.
That's the man **whose** house was on fire.

That's the place **where** Dr Watson found the blankets.

We use who for people, which for animals or things, whose to show possession and where for places.

5 **Make sentences, as in the example.**

post office/ place/buy stamps

postman/someone/ deliver letters

clock/something/ show the time

camels/animals live in the desert

circus/place/ see acrobats

vet/someone/look after sick animals

A post office is a place where you can buy stamps. A postman is someone who delivers letters. A clock is something which shows the time. Camels are animals which live in the desert. A circus is a place where you can see acrobats. A vet is someone who looks after sick animals.

6 **Fill in** *who's* **or** *whose***.**

1 Seldon is the man who's escaped from the police.

2 She's the girl whose brother got married yesterday.

3 Dave is the man whose dog was barking all night.

4 Mrs Barrymore is the woman whose brother escaped.

5 Dr Watson is the man who's got the gun.

7 **a) In which sentence do we use** *who:* **as a relative? as a question word?**

a He's the man who got the job. – relative

b Do you know who got the job? – question word

b) Read the episode and explain where 'who` is a relative and where it is a question word.
Pic. 2 – question word   Pic. 3 – relative   Pic. 7 – question word

8 🔊 **Listen to the episode again and follow the lines, then take roles and act out the episode.**

9 **a) Match the parts of the sentences, then use your answers to summarise the episode.**

1 Dr Watson wrote (d)
2 Dr Watson found the Barrymores (f)
3 Seldon, the prisoner who escaped (a)
4 Watson and Sir Henry (e)
5 Dr Watson found (b)
6 While Watson was waiting (c)

a was Mrs Barrymore's brother.
b someone's hiding place.
c he heard footsteps.
d a report to Holmes.
e followed Seldon.
f signalling to someone.

b) Who do you think the Midnight Watcher is?
Sherlock Holmes

8 What are the rules?

1 Look at the pictures. Which shows: rubbish ☐, litter on a beach ☐, unleaded petrol ☐, an endangered species ☐, sb recycling paper ☐, sb cutting down a tree in a rainforest ☐, factories polluting the air ☐, a polluted river ☐ ?

2 **a) Fill in *must* or *mustn't*.**

1 We .... pollute rivers.
2 We .... use only unleaded petrol.
3 We .... recycle paper, glass, etc.
4 We .... create so much rubbish.
5 We .... destroy rainforests.
6 We .... protect wildlife.
7 We .... drop litter on beaches.
8 We .... let factories pollute the air.

b) Use the rules above (1 - 8) and the prompts below to make sentences, as in the examples.

- fewer fish will die
- we will reduce air pollution
- we will save important resources
- the planet will be cleaner
- rare plants and animals will survive
- we will save endangered species
- beaches will be clean and safe
- the atmosphere will be cleaner

If we don't pollute rivers, fewer fish will die.
If we use only unleaded petrol, we will reduce air pollution.

3 **Listen and repeat.**

- Were you being naughty?
- I was only talking to the other children.
- How was I to know?
- You learn something new every day.
- Come with me, please.
- What are the rules?
- Don't worry.
- No problem.
- Do I have to share a bathroom?
- Oh, what a shame!
- I was looking forward to a day by the sea.
- If you're not a part of the solution, then you're part of the problem.

4 **Listen to the dialogues and match them to the rules the speakers talk about.**

1	environmental rules	dialogue ....
2	school rules	dialogue ....
3	house rules	dialogue ....

5 **a) Read the dialogues and highlight the rules in each, then tell the class. Finally explain the words in bold.**

A
Dad: How was your first day at school, Sally?
Sally: Horrible! The teacher **shouted** at me. I hate school!
Dad: Why did she shout at you? Were you being **naughty**?
Sally: I was only talking to the other children.
Dad: Oh, **I see**. Well you must be quiet and do your work.
Sally: But I didn't **understand** the exercise!
Dad: Well, if you don't understand something, you should ask your teacher.
Sally: **I tried**, but she told me to be quiet!
Dad: You should **put your hand up** first and **wait** until she speaks to you.
Sally: How was I to know? Nobody told me!
Dad: Well, you know now. School is like life, Sally. You learn something new every day!

A

76

Objectives

Vocabulary: the environment; signs; laws; rules
Reading: reading for specific information; understanding of global meaning
Listening: identifying specific information of a factual nature; understanding meaning
Speaking: giving advice; talking about house rules
Communication: asking for, giving & accepting advice
Pronunciation: letters not pronounced
Grammar: the imperative; can/can't, must/mustn't, have to/don't have to, could, should/shouldn't
Project: road signs
Writing: a letter giving advice

Lesson 1 (pp. 76 - 77)

1 Ask Ss to look at the pictures. Read out the prompts, one at a time. Ss match them to the pictures. Present any unknown words in Ss' L1.

ANSWER KEY

rubbish H, litter on a beach D, unleaded petrol G, an endangered species A, sb recycling paper C, sb cutting down a tree in a rainforest E, factories polluting the air B, a polluted river F

2 a) • Present **must/mustn't**. Write these sentences on the board: *We **must** protect wildlife. We **mustn't** pollute rivers.* Elicit the meaning of each sentence. (The first sentence expresses obligation and the second sentence expresses prohibition.)
  • Present these words in Ss' L1 or by giving examples: **create, destroy, protect, drop.**
  e.g. **create:** produce
  drop: let sth fall down
  Explain the task, then Ss do the exercise.

ANSWER KEY

1	mustn't	4	mustn't	7	mustn't
2	must	5	mustn't	8	mustn't
3	must	6	must		

b) • Read out the prompts, one at a time, presenting any unknown words in Ss' L1 or by giving examples.
  e.g. **rare:** sth which cannot be found easily.
  • Explain the task, then read out the examples. Ss make sentences, first orally, then in writing. Point out that we use a comma between the if - clause and the main clause.

ANSWER KEY

3 If we recycle paper, glass, etc, we will save important resources.
4 If we don't create so much rubbish, the planet will be cleaner.
5 If we don't destroy rainforests, rare plants and animals will survive.

6 If we protect wildlife, we will save endangered species.
7 If we don't drop litter on beaches, beaches will be clean and safe.
8 If we don't let factories pollute the air, the atmosphere will be cleaner.

3 • Play the cassette. Ss listen and repeat, either chorally or individually.
  • Present these phrases/sentences by giving examples.
  e.g. **Come with me, please.** (Go towards a S. Say to him/her miming the action: *I need some help.* **Come with me, please.** *Let's go to the teachers' room and bring some books.*)

4 Explain the task. Play the cassette. Ss do the exercise. Check Ss' answers.

ANSWER KEY

environmental rules - dialogue C
school rules - dialogue A
house rules - dialogue B

5 a) Explain the task. Give an example to Ss (e.g. dialogue A: You must be quiet and do your work), then allow Ss two minutes to highlight the rules using their text markers. Check Ss' answers. Then, help Ss explain the words in bold by giving a synonym or example.

ANSWER KEY

A You must be quiet and do your work.
You should ask your teacher if you don't understand something.
You should put your hand up first and wait until she speaks to you.

B You mustn't play loud music late at night.
You mustn't use the phone without asking.

C People shouldn't leave their rubbish behind.
They should take it home in a bag.
The council should provide bins.

b) Play the cassette for Ex. 4 again. Ss listen and follow the lines, then take roles and read out the dialogues.

c) Allow Ss two minutes to do the exercise. Check Ss' answers.

Sally's dad asked, "Were you being naughty?"
Sally said, "I was only talking to the other children."
Sally asked, "How was I to know?"
Sally's dad said, "You learn something new every day."
Mrs Smith said, "Come with me, please."
Jim asked, "What are the rules?"
Jim said, "Don't worry."
Jim said, "No problem."
Jim asked, "Do I have to share a bathroom?"
Mary said, "Oh, what a shame!"
Mary said, "I was looking forward to a day by the sea."
Mary said, "If you're not a part of the solution, then you're part of the problem."

Memory Game

Ask Ss to look at the phrases/sentences in Ex. 3 again for a minute. Ss then close their books and, in teams, try to remember as many sentences as possible. Each correct sentence gets 1 point. The team with the most points is the winner.

e.g. Team A S1: No problem.
      Team B S1: How was I to know?   etc

Suggested Homework

1 **Copy:** dialogue B Ex. 5a (p. 77)
2 **Vocabulary:** sentences in Ex. 2 (p. 76)
3 **Reading aloud:** dialogues A - C Ex. 5a (p. 76) (Point out that Ss practise *reading aloud* at home using the S's cassette/audio CD)
4 **Dictation:** same as for Vocabulary
5 **Speaking:** a) Ss memorise any five sentences in Ex. 3 (p. 76)
              b) Ss should be able to make rules with *must/mustn't* that match the pictures on pp. 76 - 77.

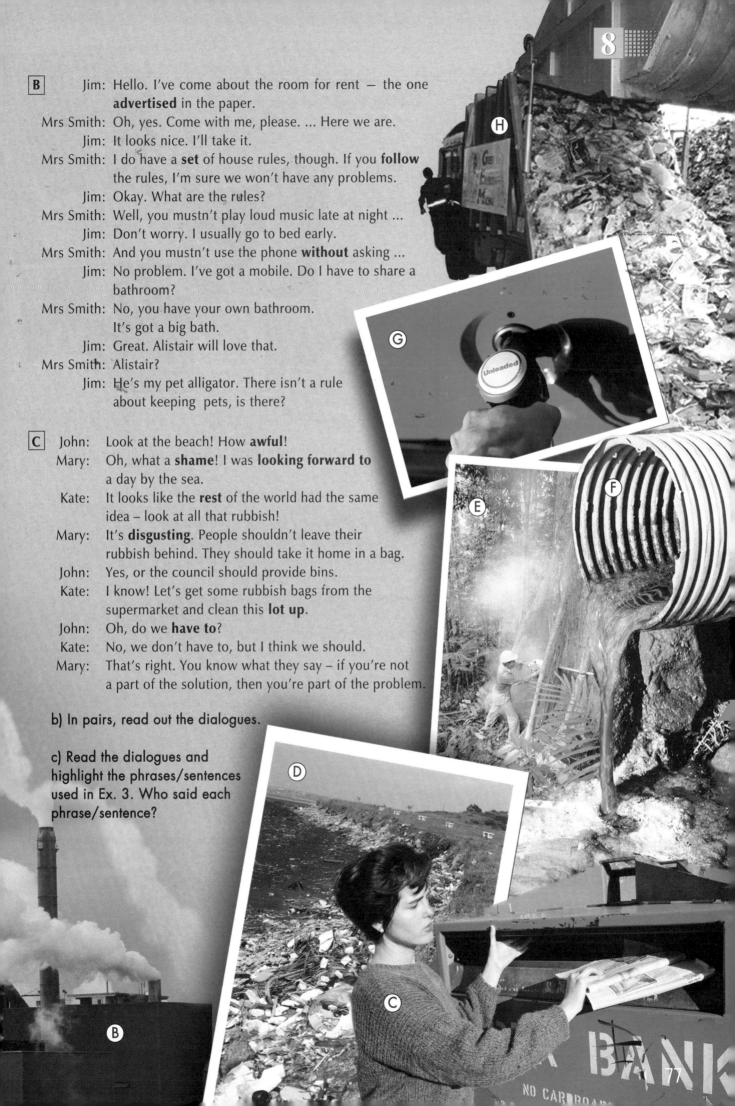

B

Jim: Hello. I've come about the room for rent — the one **advertised** in the paper.

Mrs Smith: Oh, yes. Come with me, please. ... Here we are.

Jim: It looks nice. I'll take it.

Mrs Smith: I do have a **set** of house rules, though. If you **follow** the rules, I'm sure we won't have any problems.

Jim: Okay. What are the rules?

Mrs Smith: Well, you mustn't play loud music late at night ...

Jim: Don't worry. I usually go to bed early.

Mrs Smith: And you mustn't use the phone **without** asking ...

Jim: No problem. I've got a mobile. Do I have to share a bathroom?

Mrs Smith: No, you have your own bathroom. It's got a big bath.

Jim: Great. Alistair will love that.

Mrs Smith: Alistair?

Jim: He's my pet alligator. There isn't a rule about keeping pets, is there?

C

John: Look at the beach! How **awful**!

Mary: Oh, what a **shame**! I was **looking forward to** a day by the sea.

Kate: It looks like the **rest** of the world had the same idea – look at all that rubbish!

Mary: It's **disgusting**. People shouldn't leave their rubbish behind. They should take it home in a bag.

John: Yes, or the council should provide bins.

Kate: I know! Let's get some rubbish bags from the supermarket and clean this **lot up**.

John: Oh, do we **have to**?

Kate: No, we don't have to, but I think we should.

Mary: That's right. You know what they say – if you're not a part of the solution, then you're part of the problem.

b) In pairs, read out the dialogues.

c) Read the dialogues and highlight the phrases/sentences used in Ex. 3. Who said each phrase/sentence?

77

Vocabulary

• Signs

6 **a) Where can you see these signs? Circle the correct answer.**

A in a library
B at a swimming pool

NO DIVING

A at a swimming pool
B at the theatre

PLEASE PAY HERE

A in a school
B in a shop

KEEP OFF THE GRASS

A in the jungle
B in a park

 **DO NOT TOUCH THE EXHIBITS**

A at a hospital
B in a museum

DO NOT FEED THE ANIMALS

A at a zoo
B in a museum

b) In pairs, ask and answer questions, as in the example.

A: *What does this sign mean?*
B: *It means you mustn't talk.*
A: *Where can you see a sign like this?*
B: *In a library. What does this sign mean? etc*

Grammar

• The imperative

We use the imperative to give orders.
Affirmative orders: **base form** of the verb — *Stop it!*
Negative orders: **don't + base form** of the verb — *Don't do it!*

7 **Look at the pictures and fill in the speech bubbles with orders from the list.**

• Eat your dinner!
• Don't touch the computer!
• Turn the page!
• Don't be naughty while I'm away!

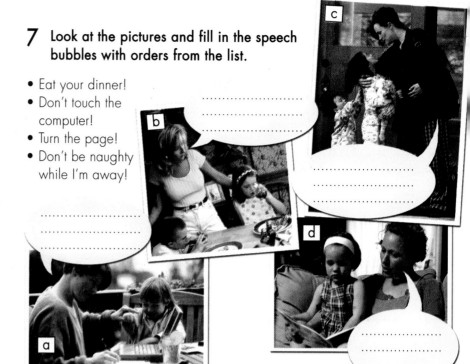

• can/can't – must/mustn't — have to/don't have to

8 **Study the examples and complete the rules.**

• *You **can** use the toilet. (You have permission.)*
• *You **can't** park here. (You don't have permission.)*
• *You **must** pay the rent on time. (That's the rule.)*
• *You **mustn't** smoke. (It's forbidden.)*
• *You **have to** clean your room. (It's necessary.)*
• *You **don't have to** make your bed. (It's not necessary, but you can if you want to.)*

1 We use .... to give permission.
2 We use .... to refuse permission.
3 We use .... to express obligation.
4 We use .... to express prohibition.
5 We use .... to express necessity.
6 We use .... to express absence of necessity.

• House Rules

9 **Listen and tick (✓) the correct box, then make full sentences, as in the example.**

	must	mustn't/ can't	can
cook food in your room			
invite friends to visit			
put posters on the walls			
stay out late			
play loud music at night			
pay the rent on time			
keep room clean and tidy			
keep pets			

You mustn't/can't cook food in your room.

Lesson 2 (pp. 78 - 79)

* • Check Ss' HW (10').
  • Play the Memory Game as described in Ex. 5c p. 77(T).

6 a) Explain that these are signs seen in various places. Explain the task, then Ss do the exercise. Check Ss' answers.

> *ANSWER KEY*
>
> *NO DIVING - A*
> *PLEASE PAY HERE - B*
> *KEEP OFF THE GRASS - B*
> *DO NOT TOUCH THE EXHIBITS - B*
> *DO NOT FEED THE ANIMALS - A*

b) Read out the example, then Ss do the exercise orally in class.

> *ANSWER KEY*
>
> *A: It means you mustn't dive.*
> *B: Where can you see a sign like this?*
> *A: At a swimming pool. What does this sign mean?*
> *B: It means you must pay here.*
> *A: Where can you see a sign like this?*
> *B: In a shop. What does this sign mean?*
> *A: It means you mustn't walk on the grass.*
> *B: Where can you see a sign like this?*
> *A: In a park. What does this sign mean?*
> *B: It means you mustn't touch the exhibits.*
> *A: Where can you see a sign like this?*
> *B: In a museum. What does this sign mean?*
> *A: It means you mustn't feed the animals.*
> *B: Where can you see a sign like this?*
> *A: At a zoo.*

7 • Present the imperative. Write on the board: *Stand up! Don't talk!* Elicit form. *(We use the base form of the verb for affirmative orders, we use don't and the base form of the verb for negative orders.)* Drill your Ss. Say affirmative orders, Ss say the relevant negative order.
  e.g. T: Talk!
        S1: Don't talk!
        T: Eat your food!
        S2: Don't eat your food!   etc
  Explain the task then Ss do the exercise. Check Ss' answers.

> *ANSWER KEY*
>
> *a) Don't touch the computer!*
> *b) Eat your dinner!*
> *c) Don't be naughty while I'm away!*
> *d) Turn the page!*

8 • Read out the examples explaining the meaning of each sentence. Check that Ss can distinguish the meaning of *don't have to (no obligation, no necessity)* from *mustn't (prohibition)*. Give various situations. Ss say whether they would use *don't have to* or *mustn't*.
  e.g. T: play loud music late at night
        S1: mustn't!
        T: make my bed at home
        S2: don't have to
        T: smoke in a hospital
        S3: mustn't
        T: wake up early on Sundays
        S4: don't have to   etc
  • Help Ss complete the rules.

> *ANSWER KEY*
>
> *1 can*   *4 mustn't*
> *2 can't*   *5 have to*
> *3 must*   *6 don't have to*

9 Read out the prompts. Play the cassette. Ss listen and tick. Check Ss' answers, then Ss make full sentences.

> *ANSWER KEY*
>
> | | must | mustn't/ can't | can |
> |---|:---:|:---:|:---:|
> | *cook food in your room* | | ✓ | |
> | *invite friends to visit* | | | ✓ |
> | *put posters on the walls* | | | ✓ |
> | *stay out late* | | | ✓ |
> | *play loud music at night* | | ✓ | |
> | *pay the rent on time* | ✓ | | |
> | *keep room clean and tidy* | ✓ | | |
> | *keep pets* | | ✓ | |
>
> *You can invite friends to visit.*
> *You can put posters on the walls.*
> *You can stay out late.*
> *You mustn't/can't play loud music at night.*
> *You must pay the rent on time.*
> *You must keep your room clean and tidy.*
> *You mustn't/can't keep (any) pets.*

TAPESCRIPT

Brian: So, Mrs Blake, are there any rules I should know about?
Mrs Blake: Only one or two. I don't allow guests to cook food in the rooms. It's a fire risk, you see. So you mustn't do that.
Brian: No, of course not. I'll use the kitchen.
Mrs Blake: I don't mind if your friends come round or if you put posters up on the walls.
Brian: Great! Can I stay out late at night?
Mrs Blake: Yes, that's not a problem. I'll give you a key.
Brian: What about playing music?
Mrs Blake: That's okay as long as you don't play loud music at night.
Brian: That's fair enough. Anything else?
Mrs Blake: Well, just pay the rent on time and keep your room clean and tidy and we'll get along fine. Oh, and of course, I don't allow pets.
Brian: That's okay. I don't have any. When can I move in?
Mrs Blake: Whenever you like.
Brian: How about tomorrow?
Mrs Blake: That will be fine.

8

10 • Ask Ss to say what they have/don't have to do as housework. Elicit answers. Give prompts if Ss can't think of any (e.g. wash the dog, water the plants, feed the cat, do the washing-up, tidy my room etc).
e.g. S1: I don't have to wash the dog.
S2: I have to water the plants.   etc
• Ss look at the pictures. Read out the examples, then Ss do the exercise.

SUGGESTED ANSWER KEY

S3: ... have to help with the cooking very often?
S4: Well, I don't have to help with the cooking every day, but I have to help sometimes. Do you have to water the plants very often?
S5: Yes, I have to water them every day. Do you have to hang out the washing very often?
S6: Well, I don't have to hang out the washing every day, but I have to do it sometimes. Do you have to do the shopping very often?
S7: Well, I don't have to do the shopping every day, but I have to do it sometimes.

---

11 Explain the task. Allow Ss two minutes to do the exercise. Check Ss' answers while Ss read out the completed sentences.

ANSWER KEY

1 A: ... have to ...
   B: ... don't have to, ... can ..., ...must ...
2 B: ... don't have to ...
3 A: ... don't have to ...
   B: ... mustn't ...
4 A: ... can't ..., ... have to ...
   B: Can ...

---

12 Explain the task, then read out the prompts and explain any unknown words. Read out the examples, then Ss make sentences, first orally, then in writing.

SUGGESTED ANSWER KEY

You mustn't/can't run in the corridors.
You mustn't/can't talk during lessons.
You must/have to be polite to teachers.
You must/have to do your homework.
You must/have to get to school on time.
You mustn't/can't leave the classroom during a lesson.
You can go out at lunchtime.
You can take a packed lunch with you.

---

13 Set the scene. Explain that Ss are going to listen to two teenagers talking about the laws in their countries. Explain that each country has got its own laws. Read out the prompts. Play the cassette. Ss listen and tick accordingly. Check Ss' answers. As an extension Ss can talk about the laws in their own country.

ANSWER KEY

1 Japan   4 UK
2 UK   5 Japan
3 Japan, UK

TAPESCRIPT

Gary: So, what do you think of England, Hiro?
Hiro: It's very different to Japan. I'd like to see the English countryside.
Gary: Come on then. I'll take you for a ride in my car.
Hiro: In your car? But you're only 17.
Gary: So? In England you can get a driving licence when you're 17.
Hiro: Really? In Japan you have to be 18.
Gary: Oh! How old do you have to be to ride a motorbike?
Hiro: 18. Isn't it the same in England?
Gary: No. You can ride a motorbike when you're 16 here.
Hiro: Wow! In Japan, the only thing you can do when you're 16 is leave school.
Gary: Oh yes. You can leave school at 16 here, too and you can even get married at 16 if your parents agree.
Hiro: Really? It's very different in Japan. You can't do anything without your parents' permission until you're 20.
Gary: What? Not even vote?
Hiro: No. How old do you have to be to vote here?
Gary: Here, you can vote when you're 18.
Hiro: You're really lucky. Anyway are we still going for a drive in your car?
Gary: Oh yes. Come on. Let's go.

Project (p. 79)

Ask Ss to look at the Photo File section. Explain that the pictures show road signs. Ss match the prompts to the pictures, then do the exercise orally in class. Assign it as written HW.
See Photo File section Unit 8 for the Answer Key.

Suggested Homework

1 **Copy:** sentences in Ex. 9 (p. 78)
2 **Reading aloud:** Ex. 12 (p. 79)
3 **Dictation:** sentences in Ex. 9 (p. 78)
4 **Speaking:** Ex. 6b (p. 78)
5 **Project:** (p. 79)
Note: Ss should be able to distinguish the use of modal verbs as described in Ex. 8 (p. 78).

Speaking

10 What housework/chores do you have to do, and how often? Look at the pictures and, in pairs, ask and answer, as in the example.

- do the washing-up
- walk the dog(s)
- help with the cooking

- water the plants
- hang out the washing
- do the shopping

S1: *Do you have to do the washing-up very often?*
S2: *Well, I don't have to do the washing-up every day, but I have to do it sometimes. Do you have to walk the dog(s) very often?*
S3: *Yes, I have to walk the dog(s) every day. Do you ...   etc.*

11 Fill in the gaps with *must, mustn't, have to, don't have to, can* or *can't*.

1 A: Do we .... finish this exercise in class?
   B: No, you .... You .... finish it at home if you like — but you .... finish it before the next lesson!

2 A: I hate waiting for the bus in the morning!
   B: Fortunately, I .... take the bus, because I go to school by bike.

3 A: You .... help me with the washing-up if you're busy, you know.
   B: No, I'm happy to help — but I .... forget to write my report for tomorrow.

4 A: I'm afraid I .... go out with you tonight — I .... visit my parents.
   B: .... I come with you, then?

12 Make sentences about school rules, using *must/have to, mustn't, don't have to, can* and *can't*. Use the prompts below, as well as your own ideas.

- wear a uniform
- eat in class
- run in the corridors
- talk during lessons
- be polite to teachers
- do your homework
- get to school on time
- leave the classroom during a lesson
- go out at lunchtime
- take a packed lunch with you

You don't have to wear a uniform.
You mustn't eat in class.

Listening

13 Read the laws below, then listen and tick (✓) the country/countries where each law applies.

	Japan	UK
1 You must be 18 to get a driving licence.	☐	☐
2 You can ride a motorbike at 16.	☐	☐
3 You can leave school at 16.	☐	☐
4 You can get married at 16.	☐	☐
5 You can't vote until you are 20.	☐	☐

● **Project**

Look at the Photo File section and write sentences using *must* or *mustn't* for each sign.

14 a) Study the examples. Which is more formal? When do we use these expressions?

Can I borrow your pen?
Could I borrow your pen?

b) Ask suitable questions with *can* or *could*.

1 You want to borrow your mum's car.
Can I borrow your car, Mum?
2 You are at work and you want to ask your boss for permission to leave early.
3 You are at your best friend's house and you want to use the phone.
4 You call the waiter at an expensive restaurant because you want to see the menu.
5 You are in class at your school/college and you want permission to leave the room.
6 You want your dad's permission to go to the disco on Saturday.

• should/shouldn't (advice)

15 Fill in *should* or *shouldn't*. When do we use these forms?

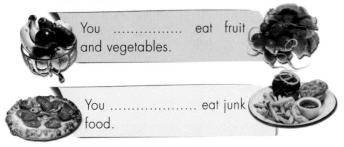

You .... eat fruit and vegetables.

You .... eat junk food.

16 The pictures show what someone should do if there is a fire in a hotel. Make sentences, as in the example.

1 set off/fire alarm
You should set off the fire alarm.

FIRE

2 close/all doors

3 use/fire extinguisher

4 cover/mouth/nose crawl along/floor

5 follow/escape route

17 Match the prompts to the pictures, then give each person advice, using *should/shouldn't*.

✓
... be careful with your money
... get more exercise
... stay in bed
... set your alarm clock

✗
... buy expensive things
... eat so many cakes
... go to school tomorrow
... go to bed so late

I can't manage to save any money.

1

I think I've got the flu.

2

I'm putting on weight.

3

I always oversleep in the mornings.

4

You should be careful with your money.
You shouldn't buy expensive things.

18 Match the sentences (1-8) to the responses (a-h).

1		Do I have to clean my room?
2		You don't have to wash up. I'll do it later.
3		You must study hard for the exams.
4		You mustn't be late for your interview.
5		Can I borrow your blue jacket?
6		You can't go in. The sign says 'Do not enter'.
7		You look ill. You should see a doctor.
8		You shouldn't go to bed so late.

a I know. I've got a lot to revise.
b Oh, yes, you're right! I didn't see it!
c Well ... all right, then.
d Yes, you do.
e You're right.
f Actually, I've got an appointment this afternoon.
g Great! Thanks, Dad!
h Don't worry — there's plenty of time.

Lesson 3 (pp. 80 - 81)

* Check Ss' HW (10').

14 a) Read out the examples and help Ss answer the questions. Check that Ss understand the meaning by giving further examples.
Suggested list: use the phone, borrow this notepad, open the window etc
e.g. T: use the phone – your boss
S1: Could I use the phone?
T: use the phone – your friend
S2: Can I use the phone?   etc

ANSWER KEY

Could is more formal. We use **can** and **could** when we want to ask for permission.

b) Explain the task, then read out the example. Allow Ss two minutes to do the exercise. Check Ss' answers orally in class.

ANSWER KEY

2 Could I leave early?
3 Can I use the phone?
4 Could I see the menu?
5 Could I leave the room?
6 Can I go to the disco on Saturday, Dad?

15 Read out the examples. Ss fill in the appropriate verb form. Check that Ss understand the meaning. Ask: *When would we say these? (To give advice to someone about eating healthily.)* Ask Ss to give more advice about healthy eating using *should/shouldn't*. Give prompts if necessary.
Suggested list: eat fatty foods, drink a lot of water, drink fizzy drinks, eat wholemeal bread etc
e.g. You shouldn't eat fatty foods.
You should drink a lot of water.
You shouldn't drink fizzy drinks.
You should eat wholemeal bread.   etc

ANSWER KEY

You **should** eat fruit and vegetables.
You **shouldn't** eat junk food.
We use **should/shouldn't** to give advice.

16 Explain the task. Read out the prompts. Ss make sentences orally.

ANSWER KEY

2 You should close all the doors.
3 You should use the fire extinguisher.
4 You should cover your mouth and nose and (you should) crawl along the floor.
5 You should follow the escape route.

17 Explain the task, then read out the prompts. Allow Ss two minutes to do the exercise. Check Ss' answers.

ANSWER KEY

1 You should be careful with your money.
   You shouldn't buy expensive things.
2 You should stay in bed.
   You shouldn't go to school tomorrow.
3 You should get more exercise.
   You shouldn't eat so many cakes.
4 You should set your alarm clock.
   You shouldn't go to bed so late.

18 Explain the task. Allow Ss two minutes to do the exercise. Check Ss' answers.

ANSWER KEY

1 d   4 h   7 f
2 g   5 c   8 e
3 a   6 b

19 a) Explain what **a rainforest** is (a thick forest of tall trees found in tropical areas where there is a lot of rain). Read out the prompts. Play the cassette. Ss listen and number. Check Ss' answers.

ANSWER KEY

3   cutting down trees
1   exotic animals, birds, reptiles and insects
2   clearing land / building roads
5   rain falling
4   an explosion

• I would expect to hear exotic animals, birds, reptiles and insects in a rainforest.

---

b) Read out the prompts. Play the cassette. Ss listen and match. Check Ss' answers.

ANSWER KEY

1 d   2 c   3 a   4 b

---

20 a) Allow Ss two minutes to read the article silently and do the exercise. Check Ss' answers.

ANSWER KEY

1 a   2 b   3 a   4 a   5 b

---

b) • Allow Ss two minutes to quickly scan the article and find the phrase/sentence which describes each picture. Check Ss' answers. Ss, then explain the words in bold by giving examples, synonyms etc. Help Ss where necessary.
   • Play the cassette for Ex. 19b again. Ss listen and follow the lines, then individual Ss read out from the article.

ANSWER KEY

A   ... and we build towns and roads where the forest used to be.
B   They are home to millions of kinds of exotic animals, birds, reptiles, and insects, ...
C   ... strange plants and beautiful flowers.
D   Logging companies cut down trees to sell the wood,...

---

21 Write the headings on the board. Elicit answers from Ss and write them under each heading. Ss copy the completed table into their notebooks. Ss, use the completed table to talk about rainforests.

SUGGESTED ANSWER KEY

• **Where they are:** south-east Asia, Africa, South America.
• **What lives there:** exotic animals, birds, reptiles, insects, strange plants, beautiful flowers
• **Why they are important:** reduce pollution levels in the atmosphere; affect the weather around the world
• **How do we destroy them:** cut down trees, clear land, build towns and roads.
• **The Amazon rainforest:** South America; the biggest and most important rainforest; home to rare undiscovered animal and plant species; plants could give medicines for cancer and AIDS.

The rainforests are near the equator, in south-east Asia, Africa, and South America. There are a lot of wonderful animals, birds, reptiles, insects, plants and flowers in the rainforests. Rainforests are very important for our planet because they help to reduce pollution levels in the atmosphere and they affect the weather all around the world. Although people know this, they destroy 30,000 hectares every day; they cut down trees, they clear land and build towns and roads where the forest used to be. The Amazon rainforest is the biggest and most important rainforest on our planet. This rainforest is home to rare and undiscovered animal and plant species. Experts say we have to take good care of this rainforest because there are plants which could give us medicines for cancer and AIDS.

(Suggested Homework)

1   **Copy:** any two paragraphs from the article in Ex. 20a (p. 81)
2   **Vocabulary:** words in bold in the article in Ex. 20a (p. 81)
3   **Reading aloud:** article in Ex. 20a (p. 81)
4   **Dictation:** same as in Vocabulary
5   **Speaking:** Ss look at their notes and talk about rainforests (Ex. 21, p. 81)

Listening and Reading

19 **a)** Listen and number the sounds in the order you hear them. Which sounds would you expect to hear in a rainforest?

..... cutting down trees
..... exotic animals, birds, reptiles and insects
..... clearing land/building roads
..... rain falling
..... an explosion

b) Listen to the article and match.

1	Rainforests help	a)	to grow crops.
2	Logging companies cut down trees	b)	could give us many new medicines.
3	Farmers clear land	c)	to sell the wood.
4	Plants from the forest	d)	to reduce pollution levels in the atmosphere.

20 **a)** Read the article, then choose what each numbered word in italics refers to.

1 *They* (para 2) = a the world's great rainforests
                     b Asia, Africa and S. America
2 *them* (para 2) = a rainforests
                     b the world's species
3 *They* (para 3) = a rainforests   b other ways
4 *They* (para 5) = a experts
                     b rare animal species
5 *them* (para 6) = a experts
                     b plant and animal species

b) Look at the pictures. Read the article again and find the phrase/sentence which best describes each picture. Then, explain the words in bold.

Speaking

21 Make notes under each heading, then use your notes to talk about rainforests.

- Where they are
- What lives there
- Why they are important
- How do we destroy them
- The Amazon rainforest

The World's Great Rainforests

1 The world's great rainforests are all near the **equator**, in south-east Asia, Africa and South America. These are huge areas of thick forest with very tall trees, where it rains almost every day.

2 ¹*They* are **home to** millions of kinds of exotic animals, birds, reptiles and insects, strange plants and beautiful flowers. Three quarters of the world's **species** live in rainforests. If we destroy their **habitat**, many of ²*them* will not survive.

3 The rainforests are important in other ways, too. ³*They* help to **reduce** pollution **levels** in the atmosphere, and **affect** the weather around the world. Without rainforests, our whole planet might not **survive**!

4 We know this — but we continue to destroy 30,000 hectares of rainforest every single day. **Logging companies** cut down trees to sell the wood, farmers **clear** the land to grow **crops**, and we build towns and roads where the forest used to be.

5 The biggest and most important of these forests is the Amazon rainforest in South America. Experts say that there are rare animal species in the forest which we have never seen. ⁴*They* also believe that plants from the forest could give us many important new medicines, such as **cures for cancer and AIDS**.

6 The Amazon rainforest is **disappearing** very quickly, though. Experts are afraid that many wonderful plant and animal species will become **extinct** before we have a chance to discover ⁵*them*.

Game

In teams, choose from the situations below and give advice using *should* or *shouldn't*. Each correct sentence gets one point. The team with the most points is the winner.

What advice would you give sb who wants to:

- lose weight? • meet new friends?
- buy a car? • learn English?
- save money? • make money?
- pass an exam? • get a job?
- help the environment? • get fit?

Team A S1: [sb wants to lose weight]
*You **shouldn't** eat cakes or chocolate.*

Communication

• Advice

asking	Could/Can you give/offer me some advice? What would you do in my place?
giving	Why don't you ... (+ inf)? You should ... (+ inf) How about ... (+ ing form)? The best thing you can do is (to) ... (+ inf) What you really need to do is (to) ... (+ inf)
accepting	
• Yes, that's a good idea. I'll take your advice. • Thanks for the advice. I'll do what you suggest.	

22 a) Complete the dialogues with expressions from the table, then listen and check your answers.

- A: Helen, 1) .... me some advice? I want to see my friend Jackie tonight, but there's a great film on TV.
  B: Well, 2) .... invite Jackie to come and watch the film with you?
  A: Yes, 3) ....

- A: Mary wants to go to the beach this weekend, but I want to go to the football match. What 1) .... ?
  B: Well, the 2) .... go to the beach this weekend and go to the football match next weekend.
  A: Well, thanks 3) ....
  –but I'd still rather go to the match this weekend!

b) In pairs, use the prompts, with phrases in the table, to act out similar dialogues.

- visit my grandparents tonight – a football match on TV
- visit your grandparents – video the football match

- John wants to go to Spain on holiday – I want to go to Italy
- go to Spain this year – Italy next year

Pronunciation

23 Listen and circle the letters in bold which are *not* pronounced. Listen again and repeat.

1	with	why	who	want
2	write	when	weather	woman
3	play	cold	look	talk
4	small	half	animal	sleep
5	brother	father	really	grow

Vocabulary Practice

24 Vocabulary Revision Game: In teams, make sentences with words/phrases from the list.

- naughty • pollute rivers • recycle • wildlife
- rare animal species • advertised • shore
- habitat • survive • reduce • become extinct
- affect the weather • cut down trees • shame
- thick forest • awful • disgusting

25 Fill in the correct word from the list, then make sentences.

- air • rubbish • grow • build • set • logging
- drop • pollution • endangered • unleaded

1	.... pollution	6	.... bags
2	...............species	7	.... levels
3	to .... litter	8	.... companies
4	a .... of rules	9	to .... crops
5	.... petrol	10	.... roads

26 Fill in: *to, in, of, off, at, for, on.*

1 to shout .... sb; 2 late .... night;
3 advertised .... a paper; 4 look forward .... sth; 5 cures .... cancer; 6 millions .... kinds .... exotic animals; 7 to drop litter .... beaches; 8 keep .... the grass

Lesson 4 (pp. 82 - 83)

* Check Ss' HW (10').

Game (p. 82)

Read out the prompts and present any unknown words in Ss' L1. Ss play the game as described in the Student's Book.

SUGGESTED ANSWER KEY

meet new friends: You should join a (tennis) club.
buy a car: You should start saving money.
learn English: You should take classes.
save money: You shouldn't spend a lot of money on clothes.
make money: You should find an evening job.
pass an exam: You should study hard.
get a job: You should look in the newspaper.
help the environment: You shouldn't leave your rubbish on the beach.
get fit: You should go cycling.

---

22 a) • Present the table, then allow Ss two minutes to complete the dialogue.
  • Play the cassette. Ss check their answers, then read out the completed dialogue.

ANSWER KEY

  • 1 can you give
  2 why don't you
  3 that's a good idea

  • 1 would you do in my place
  2 best thing you can do is (to)
  3 for the advice

---

b) Ss, in closed pairs, use the prompts to act out similar dialogues. Check Ss' performance round the class, then ask some pairs to report back to the class.

SUGGESTED ANSWER KEY

  • A: Bill, could you give me some advice? I want to visit my grandparents tonight, but there's a football match on TV.
    B: Well, the best thing to do is to visit your grandparents and video the football match.
    A: Yes, that's a good idea.

  • A: John wants to go to Spain on holiday, but I want to go to Italy. What would you do in my place?
    B: Well, how about going to Spain this year and going to Italy next year?
    A: Thanks for the advice – but I'd still rather go to Italy this year.

---

23 Explain the task. Play the cassette, twice if necessary. Ss listen and circle. Check Ss' answers. Play the cassette again with pauses for Ss to repeat either chorally or individually.

ANSWER KEY

  1 with why (who) want
  2 (write) when weather woman
  3 play cold look ta(l)k
  4 small ha(l)f animal sleep
  5 brother fathe(r) really grow

---

24 Ss, in teams, make sentences using the words/phrases in the order they appear in the list. Each correct sentence gets one point. The team with the most points wins.
  e.g. Team A S1: You are a very **naughty** boy.
    Team B S1: We should not **pollute rivers** or else the fish will die.   etc

25 Allow Ss two minutes to fill in the correct word. Check Ss' answers. Then, Ss in teams, make sentences using the completed phrases.
  e.g. Team A S1: Factories cause a lot of **air pollution**.
    Team B S1: Pandas are an **endangered species**.
    etc.

ANSWER KEY

  1 air   6 rubbish
  2 endangered   7 pollution
  3 drop   8 logging
  4 set   9 grow
  5 unleaded   10 build

---

26 Allow Ss two minutes to fill in the correct preposition. Check Ss' answers in class, then make sentences using the completed phrases.
  e.g. S1: You shouldn't **shout at** your parents.
    S2: Tim came back home **late at night**.etc

ANSWER KEY

  1 at   4 to   7 on
  2 at   5 for   8 off
  3 in   6 of, of

---

27 Allow Ss two minutes to do the exercise. Check Ss' answers orally in class.

> **ANSWER KEY**
>
> | | | | | | |
> |---|---|---|---|---|---|
> | 1 | cut down | 3 | protect | 5 | reduce |
> | 2 | survive | 4 | rare | | |

28 a) • Explain that Jenny has got a problem. Ask Ss to read the first paragraph and say what her problem is (she's got problems with her flatmate). Elicit what **flatmate** means (someone you share a flat with).

   • Present: **chore, take turns** in Ss' L1 or by giving examples. Allow Ss two minutes to read the text silently and fill in the phrases listed. Check Ss' answers.

> **ANSWER KEY**
>
> 1 why don't you   2 You should   3 how about

b) Read questions 1 to 4, one at a time and elicit answers from Ss..

> **ANSWER KEY**
>
> 1 David advises Jenny and her flatmate to:
>   a make a list of all the housework and agree who will do each chore.
>   b take turns to cook and wash up.
>   c hire a cleaner to come in once a week.
> 2 *reasons*
>   a/b That would be fairer for both of you.
>   c Neither of you will have to do the jobs you don't like.
> 3 Firstly, …, also … . Secondly, …
> 4 How's it going? **S**   I must go now. **E**
>   I'd better go now. **E**   Thanks for your letter. **S**
>   Hope to see you soon. **E**
>   How's everything with you? **S**
> 5 I was sorry to hear …

29 a) Ss read out the extract and answer the question.

> **SUGGESTED ANSWER KEY**
>
> He has problems with his neighbour, they're always arguing and he doesn't know what to do.

b) Explain the task. Read out the table and present these words/phrases by giving examples: **lose your temper, council, advisor**. Ss, in closed pairs do the exercise. Check Ss' answers.

> **ANSWER KEY**
>
> | | | | | |
> |---|---|---|---|---|
> | 1 b | | 2 c | | 3 a |

c) • Present the plan. Ask questions to make sure Ss understand it.
   e.g. T: What opening remarks would you write?
      S1: Dear John,
         Thanks for your letter.
      T: How would you express your sympathy to John?
      S2: I was sorry to hear you've got problems with your neighbour.

T: How would you offer help?
S3: I think I've got a couple of ideas which can help.
T: What advice would you give John?
S4: You shouldn't lose your temper when you talk to your neighbour.
T: What reason would you give to support your piece of advice?
S5: If you stay calm, your neighbour will do the same.
T: What other advice would you give John?
S6: You should agree to some of the changes your neighbour wants.
T: How would you support this advice?
S7: Then, your neighbour should agree to some of the changes you want.
T: What closing remarks would you write?
S8: I'd better go know.
   (Best wishes & my first name)

   • After Ss have done the task orally in class, assign it as written HW.

> **SUGGESTED ANSWER KEY**
>
> *Dear John,*
>   Thanks for your letter. I was sorry to hear that you and your neighbour are having problems and are always arguing. I've got a couple of ideas which I hope will help you.
>   Firstly, you should try never to lose your temper when you talk to your neighbour. If you stay calm, your neighbour will do the same. This way you'll both be able to listen to each other and be reasonable.
>   Secondly, why don't you agree to some of the changes your neighbour wants? Then, your neighbour should agree to some of the changes you want. This way you will both be happy!
>   Well, I must go now because I have a lot of things to do. I hope these ideas help. Write or give me a ring if there's anything else I can do.
> *Best wishes,*
> *Bill*

30 Explain the task, then allow Ss two minutes to do the exercise. Check Ss' answers.

> **ANSWER KEY**
>
> • 20   • minutes   • 80%

> (Suggested Homework)
>
> 1 Copy: Ex. 22a (p. 82)
> 2 Vocabulary: Exs 24, 25, 26 (p. 82) and table in Communication (p. 82)
> 3 Reading aloud: Ex. 28a (p. 83)
> 4 Dictation: same as for Vocabulary
> 5 Act out: first dialogue in Ex. 22a (p. 82)
> 6 Writing: Ex. 29c (p. 83)

> (Lesson 5)

• Check Ss' HW.
• Workbook: Unit 8
         Click on Grammar 8

27 Correct the sentences by replacing the words in bold with their opposites from the list.

• survive • cut down • rare • reduce • protect

1 Logging companies **grow** trees in the rainforest and sell the wood. ....
2 We should do whatever we can to make sure endangered species **become extinct**. ....
3 I think governments should pass laws to **destroy** the world's rainforests. ....
4 These animals are very **common** — you hardly ever see them in the wild. ....
5 Using less petrol helps to **increase** levels of air pollution. ....

Writing (a letter giving advice)

28 a) Read the letter and fill in the phrases:

• you should • why don't you • how about

Dear Jenny,

Thanks for your letter. I was sorry to hear that you and your flatmate are having problems getting along and sharing the housework. I've got a couple of ideas which I hope will help you.

Firstly, 1) .... make a list of all the housework and agree who will do each chore? 2) .... also take turns to cook and wash up. That would be fairer for both of you.

Secondly, **3)** .... hiring a cleaner to come in once a week? This way neither of you will have to do the jobs you don't like.

Well, I must go now, because I've got my own housework to do! I hope these ideas help. Write or give me a ring if there's anything else I can do.
Best wishes,
David

b) Answer the questions.

1 What is David's advice?
2 What reason does he give to support each piece of advice?
3 How does David list his points?
4 Which of these sentences can you use to start/end a letter of advice? Put *S* (start) or *E* (end) in the boxes.

• How's it going? ❑ • I must go now. ❑
• I'd better go now. ❑ • Thanks for your letter. ❑
• Hope to see you soon. ❑ • How's everything with you? ❑

5 Which words does David use to express his sympathy for Jenny?

29 a) Read part of John's letter to you. What is John's problem?

... I'm writing to ask you for advice. I'm having terrible problems with my neighbour — we are always arguing and I just don't know what to do.

b) Read the table and match the advice to the reason.

ADVICE	REASON
1 ☐ never lose your temper when you talk to your neighbour	a this person will try to solve your problems and stop the arguing
2 ☐ agree to some of the changes your neighbour wants	b if you stay calm, your neighbour will do the same
3 ☐ ask the council to send a special advisor to help	c your neighbour should agree to some of the changes *you* want

c) Now, use the plan below and any two of the points in the table to write your letter of advice to John. You can use the letter in Ex. 28 a) as a model (100 - 150 words).

Plan

Dear John,
Introduction
(Para 1) *opening remarks, express sympathy, offer help*
Main Body
(Para 2) *first piece of advice & reason*
(Para 3) *second piece of advice & reason*
Conclusion
(Para 4) *closing remarks*
Love from/Best wishes/etc
(+ your first name)

30 Read the sentences and choose the correct word/number in bold.

do you know...?

• In the next minute, people will destroy over **2/20/200** hectares of rainforest.
• In the next 10 **minutes/hours/weeks**, one more plant or animal species in the rainforest will become extinct.
• Rainforests provide about **8%/18%/80%** of the oxygen on our planet.

EPISODE 5
The Hound of the Baskervilles

The Hound Attacks

Dr Watson is about to shoot when he hears a familiar voice.

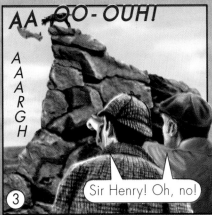

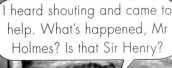

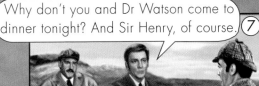

84

Pre-Reading Activities

1 a) **Look at the pictures and identify the characters, then answer the questions.**

1 Who's got: a moustache Dr Watson and Sir Henry; bushy eyebrows Dr Watson; short brown hair Dr Watson; grey sideburns Dr Watson; long wavy fair hair? Hugo Baskerville
2 Who wears: a deerstalker Holmes; a straw hat Stapleton; a cap Dr Watson; a cape Holmes; a raincoat? Dr Watson
3 Who's: middle-aged Dr Watson; in his early forties Holmes; rather plump Dr Watson; slim? Holmes and Stapleton

b) **Look at pictures 6 and 7 and describe each person.**

Dr Watson is middle-aged. He is rather plump. He's got ...
(Ss' own answers)

Listening and Reading Activities

2 **Listen and mark the sentences T (true) or F (false).**

1 Holmes has just arrived. F
2 Sir Henry is dead. F
3 The dog was chasing Sir Henry. F
4 Mrs Barrymore will be very upset. T
5 Stapleton isn't a Baskerville. F

3 **Read the episode, then read the sentences and replace the personal pronouns with the names in the list.**

• Holmes • The hound • Stapleton • Seldon • Dr Watson

1 He has been there from the very beginning. Holmes
2 He's wearing Sir Henry's old clothes. Seldon
3 It smelt Sir Henry's boot. The hound
4 He invites them to dinner. Stapleton
5 They must leave Dartmoor immediately. Holmes & Dr Watson
6 He is going to kill Sir Henry. Stapleton

Grammar

• **have been - have gone**

4 a) **Study the examples. Who is still in London? Who isn't in London now?**

*Paul **has been** to London twice.*
Paul isn't in London now.
*Sue **has gone** to London for the weekend.*
Sue is still in London.

b) **Fill in:** *have/has been **or** have/has gone.*

1 Tim has been to America three times.
2 Melanie has gone to bed.
3 The girls aren't here. They have gone to the shops.
4 I have been to Michelle's house many times.
5 Meg and Paul have gone to visit their parents.

• **someone/anyone/no one/etc**

5 **Study the table, then complete the sentences, as in the example.**

	Affirmative	Interrogative	Negative
People	someone somebody	anyone anybody	no one/not anyone nobody/not anybody
Things	something	anything	nothing/not anything
Places	somewhere	anywhere	nowhere/not anywhere

1 Does anyone know where Stapleton is?
2 Don't shout at me — I haven't done anything wrong!
3 I can't find my car keys anywhere!
4 I've got nothing to wear to Kay's party. I need to buy some clothes.
5 Has anyone/anybody seen my sunglasses?
6 Is there anything I can do to help?
7 The house was empty. There was nobody there.
8 Bob wants to go somewhere hot for his summer holiday.

6 **Listen to the episode again, then take roles and read out the episode.**

7 **Use the words in the list to give a summary of the episode using the past simple.**

Dr Watson met Holmes. The hound killed Seldon. He was wearing Sir Henry's old clothes. Stapleton appeared and helped Holmes and Watson. He invited them and Sir Henry to dinner. They refused because they had to return to London. Sir Henry told Mrs Barrymore about her brother's death. Holmes saw that the portrait of Hugo Baskerville without hair looked like Stapleton. He could be a Baskerville. They had to stop Stapleton before he murdered Sir Henry.

Vocabulary

1 Add to the lists.

- mammals: cow, horse, camel, dog, deer
- birds: parrot, goose, peacock, eagle
- herbivores: sheep, deer, cow, rabbit
- carnivores: bear, lion, leopard, tiger
- endangered species: leopard, eagle, tortoise, panda, tiger

(5 marks)

2 Fill in the correct word from the list.

• shore • tour • scary • culture • sample
• afford • naughty • reduce • crops
• crowded • become • affect

1 We watched a very scary film yesterday.
2 Sam's mum punished him for being naughty.
3 We had a picnic by the shore of Lake Tobey last Sunday.
4 I can't wait to sample John's cooking.
5 America has a very varied culture.
6 Using alternative forms of energy will reduce pollution levels.
7 We can't afford to go on holiday this year.
8 My brother is going to tour Europe next summer.
9 If endangered species are not protected, they will become extinct.
10 High pollution levels can affect the weather.
11 The shop was crowded with people.
12 Farmers shouldn't spray their crops with chemicals.

(12 marks)

3 Fill in: by, at, in, to, on.

1 A lot of animals live in the rainforest.
2 You can't put posters on the walls.
3 Don't shout at me.
4 We are looking forward to going on holiday.
5 New York was the last stop on our tour.
6 I hate travelling by boat.

(6 marks)

4 Underline the correct word.

1 It **took**/spent us two days to reach Scotland.
2 I feel as **fresh**/white as a daisy after my nap.
3 Dogs are very **loyal**/quiet animals.

4 New York has an impressive scenery/**skyline**.
5 Are there any boats in the accommodation/**harbour**?
6 Cats are not very **obedient**/funny animals.
7 You can't drive a car if you don't have a driving ticket/**licence**.
8 Forests are often destroyed when farmers clean/**clear** the land to grow crops.

(8 marks)

Grammar

5 Look at the table and write sentences, as in the example.

	The Ritz	The Carlton	The Park
expensive	* *	* * *	*
clean	*	* *	* * *
close to the beach	* * *	*	* *
good service	* *	* * *	*
crowded	* * *	* *	*

The Park is expensive. The Ritz is more expensive than the Park. The Carlton is the most expensive of all. (See Suggested Answers section)

(15 marks)

6 Complete the sentences using conditionals Type 0 or Type 1. (Suggested Answers)

1 If you go to the party, you'll have a good time.
2 If she passes her exams, she'll be very happy.
3 If you freeze water, it becomes ice.
4 If you heat ice, it melts.
5 If he misses the bus, he'll be late for work.
6 If you get a pet, you'll have to look after it.

(6 marks)

7 Underline the correct word.

1 You **should**/can use my hairdryer if you like.
2 You **shouldn't**/don't have to be rude to your parents.
3 You **don't have**/mustn't to wear a suit. It's an informal party.
4 I'm not going home yet. I **must**/should work late.
5 You **mustn't**/shouldn't play with matches. It's dangerous.
6 "I feel ill." "You **should**/can see a doctor."

(6 marks)

8 Make sentences, as in the example.

	Carol	Liz	Sandra
sing well	✔	✔✔✔	✔✔
work hard	✔✔✔	✔✔	✔
write neatly	✔✔	✔	✔✔✔
dress smartly	✔	✔✔	✔✔✔

Carol sings well. Sandra sings better than Carol. Liz sings the best of all. (See Suggested Answers section)

(18 marks)

Communication

9 Fill in the sentences. In pairs, read out the dialogues.

• How much are the white roses? • Certainly. That will be £30. • Yes, that's a good idea. • I'm afraid you can't.

1 A: I'll take a bouquet of lilies.
   B: Certainly. That will be £30.

2 A: Can I use the phone?
   B: I'm afraid you can't.

3 A: How much are the white roses?
   B: They're £1.50 each.

4 A: Why don't you wear your blue dress?
   B: Yes, that's a good idea.

(4 marks)

Reading (an article expressing an opinion)

10 a) Read the article and fill in the correct linking words. Then, replace them with other synonymous ones.

• All in all • However • Firstly • Secondly • Also

In recent years, people have started to move out of cities into the countryside. In my opinion, it is the best place to live.

1 Firstly, there is so much space in the countryside. The houses are further apart and you can go for walks in the fresh air. 2 Secondly, it is quieter in the countryside. You can listen to the birds singing while you are in your garden. People are friendly, too.

3 However, because the shops and entertainment are further away, you will need to have a car. 4 Also, houses in the countryside can often be very expensive.

5 All in all, I think that although living in the countryside can be more expensive, it is worth it. The air is clean, it is quiet and it is much more relaxed.

(5 marks)

b) Which reasons are in favour of the argument? Which is the opposing viewpoint? (See Suggested Answers section)

(5 marks)

Writing (an opinion essay)

11 Match the viewpoints to the reasons. Which are in favour? Which are against? Now write a short essay for your teacher about living in the city (100-110 words).

(See Suggested Answers section)

(20 marks)

viewpoint
• lots of shops
• variety of means of transport
• noisy and crowded

reason
can go wherever you want easily and quickly
lots of cars/people
wide choice of things to buy

(Total: 100 marks)

♪ Let's sing!

12 Listen and fill in. Listen again and sing.

Save the Planet

The fish in the 1) sea are dying
From the pollution we create
We've got to 2) stop polluting
Before it's too late
Before it's too late.

Our planet is in trouble
It gets worse every 3) day
We have to 4) help our planet
In every possible way.

In the woods and forests
They're cutting down the 5) trees
We've got to 6) save the forests
Everyone agrees
Everyone agrees.

The hole in the ozone layer
Is getting 7) bigger every day
We've got to stop 8) air pollution
We have to find a way
We have to find a way.

People & Places

◆ **Before you start...**

Can you name the planets in our solar system?
Would you rather live in a city, or in the countryside? Why?
What is your favourite animal? Why?
Have you given any advice to anyone lately? What was it?

◆ **Listen, read and talk about...**

Man-made Wonders

UNIT 9

- landmarks
- materials
- parts of a building
- furniture
- countries

Module 5
Units 9-10

Characters

◆ Learn how to ...

- talk about places
- describe landmarks
- give specific details about a place/landmark
- talk about currencies and languages
- talk about what things are made of
- describe the interior and exterior of a building
- describe sb's appearance
- describe sb's character
- express your preferences
- talk about likes/dislikes
- match hobbies to people's personalities

◆ Practise ...

- the definite article
- the passive (present simple and past simple)
- linkers (and, as well as, in addition to, also, but, however, although)
- too-enough
- to-infinitive, infinitive without to, -ing form

◆ Write ...

- a descriptive article about a landmark
- a narrative article about a visit to a place
- an article describing a person
- a letter of recommendation

9 Man-made Wonders

Lead-in

1 **a)** Look at the landmarks. Which is made of: marble, stone, concrete, iron, brick, steel, limestone?

The Colosseum is made of stone and concrete.

b) Look at the table and make true sentences about each landmark.

The Parthenon was designed by Ictinus and Callicrates.

c) Have you ever been to any of these landmarks? Can you name some of the landmarks in your country? Where are they located? When were they built?

The Parthenon		
The Eiffel Tower		by Ictinus and Callicrate
The Millennium Dome		in honour of a ruler's w...
Sydney Opera House	was/were built	by Egyptian Kings
The Colosseum	was completed	in Australia
The Taj Mahal	was designed	iron
The Great Wall of China	is located	to celebrate the new millennium
The Great Pyramids	is made of	in AD 82
Big Ben		for communication and protection
		in 1859

2 🎧 **Listen and repeat.**

- Oh, that's really sad.
- Why? What was that?
- He was imprisoned.
- I bet you had a brilliant time.
- It was amazing.
- What a strange-looking building!
- The more I look at it, the more it reminds me of something.
- On your right is the Clock Tower.
- When was the tower built?
- Does the clock always tell the right time?
- Oh dear!
- I was supposed to meet my wife half an hour ago.

Listening and Reading

3 🎧 **Listen to the dialogues and match the buildings to their designers.**

Taj Mahal	Jorn Utzon
Sydney Opera House	Edmund Beckett
Big Ben	Shah Jahan

4 **a)** **Read the dialogues and correct the sentences, then explain the words in bold.**

1 The Taj Mahal was built in honour of Shah Jahan's sister.
2 Sydney Opera House looks very old.
3 Sydney Opera House looks like fishing boats.
4 Big Ben weighs 30 tons.
5 The clock never tells the right time.

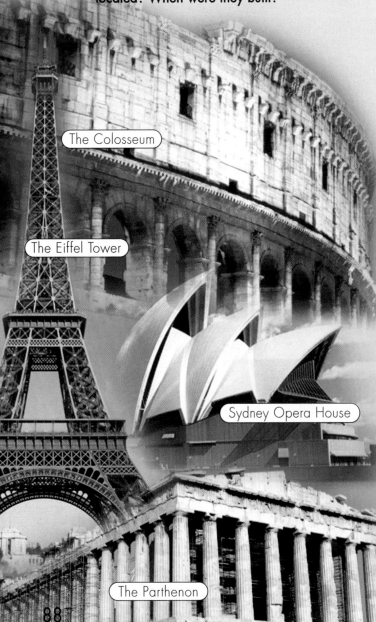

The Colosseum

The Eiffel Tower

Sydney Opera House

The Parthenon

Objectives

Vocabulary: landmarks; materials; parts of a building (interior - exterior); furniture; furnishings; countries
Reading: reading for gist; detailed comprehension; skimming & scanning skills
Listening: listening for specified information; identifying specific information
Speaking: talking about places; giving details; describing landmarks
Communication: asking about currency
Pronunciation: linked sounds
Grammar: the definite article "the"; the passive (present simple - past simple)
Project: a descriptive article about a landmark
Writing: an article about a visit to a building

Lesson 1 (pp. 88 - 89)

1 a) • Present the title *(landmarks made by man).* Elicit how the title is related to the unit *(all pictures on pp. 88 - 89 show famous landmarks made by man).*
    • Read out the name of each landmark. Elicit where each landmark is located *(Colosseum – Rome, Italy; Eiffel Tower – Paris, France; Sydney Opera House – Sydney, Australia; Parthenon – Athens, Greece; Big Ben – London, England; Taj Mahal – Agra, India; Millennium Dome – London, England; Great Wall of China – China; Great Pyramids – Cairo, Egypt).*
    • Present the materials using Ss' L1, then help Ss say what each landmark is made of.
    • Ask Ss to look at the example. Ask: *Do we know who built the Colosseum? (No).* Underline **is made of.** Explain that this is a passive tense form. Elicit the form of the passive (to be + past participle). Explain that we use the passive when we are more interested in the action rather than the person who did it.

ANSWER KEY

The Eiffel Tower is made of iron.
Sydney Opera House is made of concrete.
The Parthenon is made of marble.
The Taj Mahal is made of (sandstone and) marble.
Big Ben (The Clock Tower) is made of stone.
The Millennium Dome is made of (fabric and) steel.
The Great Wall of China is made of (earth and) brick.
The Great Pyramids are made of limestone.

   b) • Read out the table. Present these words in Ss' L1 or by giving examples: **completed, designed, honour, ruler, millennium, communication.**
       e.g. **completed:** finished
    • Help Ss make true sentences about the landmarks.

ANSWER KEY

The Eiffel Tower is made of iron.
The Millennium Dome was built to celebrate the new millennium.
Sydney Opera House is located in Australia.
The Colosseum was completed in AD 82.
The Taj Mahal was built in honour of a ruler's wife.
The Great Wall of China was built for communication and protection.
The Great Pyramids were built by Egyptian kings.
Big Ben (The Clock Tower) was completed in 1859.

   c) • Ask Ss the questions one at a time. Elicit answers. Help Ss where necessary.

       (Ss' own answers)

2 • Play the cassette. Ss listen and follow the lines. Play the cassette again. Ss listen and repeat either chorally or individually.
   • Present these phrases/sentences by giving examples, miming or using Ss' L1.
     e.g. **I bet you had a brilliant time.** (Go up to a S. Ask him: *Where did you go on holiday last summer? (I went to Paris.)* Say: *Paris!* **I bet you had a brilliant time.**)

3 Explain the task. Play the cassette. Ss do the exercise. Check Ss' answers.

ANSWER KEY

Taj Mahal → Shah Jahan
Sydney Opera House → Jorn Utzon
Big Ben → Edmund Beckett

4 a) • Explain the task, then read out the sentences 1 to 5. Allow Ss two minutes to read the dialogues silently and correct the sentences. Check Ss' answers around the class.

ANSWER KEY

1 *The Taj Mahal was built in honour of Shah Jahan's* **wife.**
2 *Sydney Opera House looks very* **modern.**
3 *Sydney Opera House looks like* **sailing** *boats.*
4 *Big Ben weighs* **13** *tons.*
5 *The clock* **always** *tells the right time.*

    • Help Ss explain the words in bold in Ss' L1 or by giving examples, synonyms or antonyms.
      e.g. **magnificent:** fantastic, great, fabulous, superb
            sad: unhappy   etc

9

b) Play the cassette for Ex. 3 again. Ss listen and follow the lines, then take roles and read out the dialogues.

c) Allow Ss three minutes to underline the phrases/ sentences, then Ss say who said each one.

ANSWER KEY

Pam said, "Oh, that's really sad."
Pam asked, "Why? What was that?"
Jo said, "He was imprisoned."
Mark said, "I bet you had a brilliant time."
Jean said, "It was amazing."
Mark said, "What a strange-looking building!"
Mark said, "The more I look at it, the more it reminds me of something."
The tour guide said, "On your right is the Clock Tower."
The tourist asked, "When was the tower built?"
The tourist asked, "Does the clock always tell the right time?"
The tourist said, "Oh dear!"
The tourist said, "I was supposed to meet my wife half an hour ago."

Memory Game

Ask Ss to look at the phrases/sentences in Ex. 2 again for two minutes. Ss close their books and, in teams, try to remember as many as possible. Each correct phrase/ sentence gets 1 point. The team with the most points is the winner.

e.g. Team A S1: It was amazing.
  Team B S1: On your right is the Clock Tower.   etc

(Suggested Homework)

1 **Copy:** dialogue A in Ex. 4a (p. 89)
2 **Vocabulary:** words in bold in dialogues A - C (p. 89)
3 **Reading aloud:** dialogues A - C in Ex. 4a (p. 89) (Point out that Ss practise *reading aloud* at home using the S's cassette/audio CD)
4 **Dictation:** any ten words from Vocabulary
5 **Speaking:** Ss memorise any five sentences from Ex. 2 (p. 88)

A

Jo: I think the Taj Mahal is the most beautiful building in the world.

Pam: Yes, it's **magnificent**. Do you know who it was built by?

Jo: An Indian ruler. His name was Shah Jahan. He built it in **honour** of his wife after she died.

Pam: Oh, that's really sad.

Jo: Not as **sad** as what happened to him in the end.

Pam: Why? What was that?

Jo: He was **imprisoned**.

Pam: Oh dear.

Jo: Yes and the only thing that he could see out of his **cell window** was the Taj Mahal!

B

Mark: Wow, Jean, these pictures are great! I bet you had a brilliant time in Australia.

Jean: Oh, I did. It was **amazing**. Look – this is the Sydney Opera House.

Mark: What a **strange-looking** building!

Jean: I know. It was designed by a Danish architect called Jorn Utzon.

Mark: Oh, It looks very modern. When was it built?

Jean: Well, it **was opened** in 1973, so it's not that new.

Mark: It's very big, isn't it?

Jean: Yes. There's a concert hall, two theatres, a cinema and a recording studio inside.

Mark: The more I look at it, the more it **reminds** me of something ...

Jean: Well, it's supposed to look like **sailing boats**.

Mark: Oh yes, you're right, it does.

C

Tour Guide: On your right is the Clock Tower, which was designed by Edmund Beckett.

Tourist : I thought the tower was called 'Big Ben'.

Tour Guide: Well actually, the biggest bell, which **weighs** 13 tons, is called Big Ben. It was named after Sir Benjamin Hall, who was the **Commissioner for works** when it was put in.

Tourist : When was the **tower** built?

Tour Guide: Well, **building** was started in 1858 and completed in 1859.

Tourist : Does the clock always tell the right time?

Tour Guide: Yes. In fact it's famous for its **accuracy**.

Tourist : Oh dear! I was supposed to meet my wife half an hour ago. Excuse me!

b) In pairs read out the dialogues.

Speaking

c) **Read the dialogues again and underline the phrases/sentences used in Ex. 2. Who said each phrase/sentence?**

Big Ben

The Taj Mahal

The Millennium Dome

The Great Wall of China

The Great Pyramids

Vocabulary

• **Landmarks & Material**

5 **a)** Look at the pictures. In pairs, use the prompts to ask and answer questions, as in the example.

Materials:
- stone
- brick
- marble
- steel
- concrete
- wood
- glass

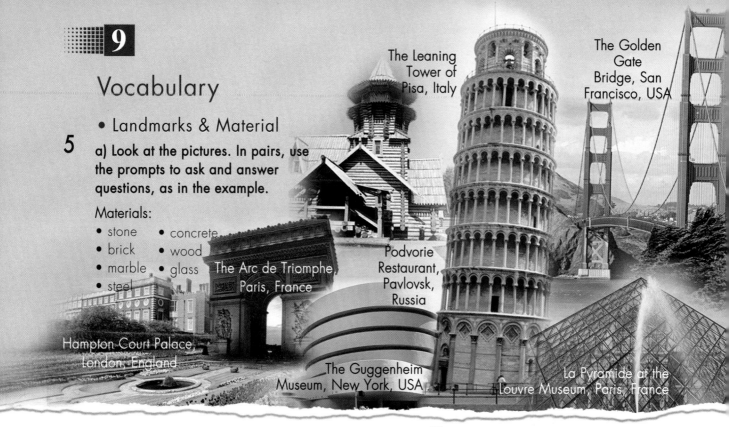

The Leaning Tower of Pisa, Italy

The Golden Gate Bridge, San Francisco, USA

The Arc de Triomphe, Paris, France

Podvorie Restaurant, Pavlovsk, Russia

Hampton Court Palace, London, England

The Guggenheim Museum, New York, USA

La Pyramide at the Louvre Museum, Paris, France

A: What is Hampton Court Palace made of?
B: It's made of brick.

b) What is the most famous landmark in your country? What is it made of?

• **Parts of a building**

6 Look at the picture and tick (✓) what you can see, then describe the exterior.

The White House

garden		chimney	
fountain		fence	
balcony		path	
roof		portico	

7 **a)** What types of rooms/furniture/furnishings do you think there are in the White House? Choose from the list, then listen and circle the words you hear.

rooms: office, entrance hall, sitting room, bedroom, bathroom, dining room, basement, library, ballroom, billiard room, attic

furniture: desks, wooden armchairs, bookcases, fitted wardrobes, dressing tables, mahogany tables, silk sofas, chests of drawers, coffee tables, bedside tables, antique beds

furnishings: silver-plated lamps, cushions, soft carpets, portraits

b) Listen and write down the numbers, then use your answers in Exs 6 and 7 to talk about the White House.

...... rooms, ... bathrooms, ... doors, ... windows, ... fireplaces, ... staircases, ... lifts, ... cinema

Grammar

• **The Passive**

8 Study the examples, then complete the rule.

Active	Passive
Millions of people **visit** the Statue of Liberty every year.	The Statue of Liberty **is visited** by millions of people every year.
They **opened** the Statue of Liberty in 1886.	The Statue of Liberty **was opened** in 1886.

We form the passive with the appropriate tense of the verb .... and the p...............
p............... of the main verb.
We use the passive when the action is more important than the agent (the person or thing doing the action)

Changing from Active into Passive
The object of the active verb becomes the subject of the passive verb. The subject of the active verb becomes the agent of the passive verb. We usually introduce the agent with **by**.

	subject	active verb	object
Active	*Fleming*	*discovered*	*penicillin.*

	subject	passive verb	object
Passive	*Penicillin*	*was discovered*	*by Fleming.*

Lesson 2 (pp. 90 - 91)

* • Check Ss' HW (10').
  • Play the Memory Game as described in Ex. 4c p. 89(T).

5 • Present the landmarks in the pictures. Read out their names. Ss repeat after you. Pay special attention to the pronunciation of the **Arc de Triomphe** /'ɑːk də'triːɒmf/, the **Guggenheim Museum** /'gʊgənhaɪm/ and the **Podvorie Restaurant** /ɒd'vɔːri/. Ask about the location of each landmark.

   e.g. T: Where is Hampton Court Palace located?
         S1: It's located in London, England.   etc
  • Present the unknown materials by giving examples. Elicit from Ss what each landmark is made of.
  • Read out the example. Then, Ss, in open pairs ask and answer questions about the rest of the monuments.

ANSWER KEY

- • A: What is the Arc de Triomphe made of?
    B: It's made of stone.
- • A: What is the Leaning Tower of Pisa made of?
    B: It's made of marble.
- • A: What is the Podvorie Restaurant made of?
    B: It's made of wood.
- • A: What is the Guggenheim Museum made of?
    B: It's made of concrete.
- • A: What is the Golden Gate Bridge made of?
    B: It's made of steel.
- • A: What is La Pyramide at the Louvre Museum made of?
    B: It's made of glass.

b) Elicit answers to the questions. Help Ss where necessary. (Ss' own answers)

6 • Ask Ss to look at the picture. Explain/Elicit that this is the White House – the residence of the president of the USA in Washington DC.
  • Read out the prompts. Ss tick what they can see. As Ss mark their answers, explain what each word means.

ANSWER KEY

| garden | balcony | chimney |
| fountain | roof | portico |

  • Ss now describe the exterior.

SUGGESTED ANSWER KEY

Outside the White House there is a big garden with a fountain. At the front of the White House there is a portico with a big balcony. On the roof there are a lot of chimneys.

7 a) • Present the words in the list, then Ss, in closed pairs, decide what there is inside the White House.
  • Play the cassette. Ss listen and check their answers. Check Ss' answers on the board.

ANSWER KEY

rooms: *bathroom, office, entrance hall, sitting room, bedroom, ballroom, dining room, library, billiard room*
furniture: *desks, wooden armchairs, mahogany tables, silk sofas, chests of drawers, antique beds, fitted wardrobes, dressing tables, grand piano, bookcases*
furnishings: *portraits, soft carpets, silver-plated lamps*

TAPESCRIPT

For two hundred years, the White House has stood as the symbol of the Presidency, the United States government, and the American people. Its construction began in October, 1792 and it was completed in 1800, when President John Adams and his wife Abigail moved in. Since that time, each President has made his own changes and additions.

Inside this national monument there are a total of **132 rooms** and **32 bathrooms**. You might be surprised to learn that the White House has 6 different levels. This is why there are **7 staircases** and **3 lifts**. There are also **412 doors** and **147 windows** and **28 fireplaces**. The President works here as well as lives here and there are plenty of different <u>offices</u> in the White House. The most famous, though, is the oval office which has a large <u>desk</u> in the middle of it.

There are two <u>entrance halls</u> with marble floors and walls, bronze lamps and Italian furniture. There are luxurious <u>sitting rooms</u> and <u>wooden armchairs</u>, round <u>mahogany tables</u>, cut-glass chandeliers, <u>silk sofas</u>, <u>chests of drawers</u> and fireplaces. On the walls there are beautiful paintings and <u>portraits</u> of all the American presidents. The many <u>bedrooms</u> are beautiful, too, with <u>antique beds</u>, huge <u>fitted wardrobes</u>, elegant <u>dressing tables</u>, thick <u>soft carpets</u> and heavy curtains.

The East Room is the name of the <u>ballroom</u>. It has a beautiful oak floor, three Bohemian cut-glass chandeliers and a Steinway <u>grand piano</u>. It is used for dances, concerts, parties and weddings.

The State <u>Dining Room</u> seats as many as 140 guests. There are round <u>mahogany tables</u>, surrounded by Queen-Anne style chairs as well as a carefully-carved frieze. Above the fireplace there is the <u>portrait</u> of President Lincoln. On the floor there is a <u>soft</u> green and brown Persian <u>carpet</u>.

The <u>Library</u> is often used for teas and meetings. On the fireplace you can see a pair of <u>silver-plated lamps</u> whereas <u>portraits</u> hang on the walls. In the <u>bookcases</u> there are hundreds of books.

For entertainment the Presidential family can use the <u>billiard room</u>, a bowling alley, <u>a cinema</u> and an inside swimming pool.

The White House is open for tours every Tuesday to Saturday from 10 am to 12 noon except for national holidays. All tours are free. For more information call 202 - 456 - 7041.

b) • Play the cassette for Ex. 7a again. Ss listen and write down the numbers.

ANSWER KEY

132 rooms, 32 bathrooms, 412 doors, 147 windows, 28 fireplaces, 7 staircases, 3 lifts, 1 cinema

  • Explain that when we describe a building we first describe its exterior, then its interior. Allow Ss two minutes to think of a description of the White House. Individual Ss describe the building. As an extension, Ss can describe their own houses.

SUGGESTED ANSWER KEY

From the outside of the White House you can see a big portico with a balcony. You can also see the roof with lots of chimneys. In front of the White House is a big garden with a fountain in it. Inside there are 6 different levels. There is an elegant ballroom, a state dining room and a library with hundreds of books. There are lots of offices and sitting rooms with mahogany tables and silk sofas. There is even a cinema and a swimming pool.

8 • Read out the examples. Help Ss complete the rule. Then, explain how we turn an active sentence into a passive sentence.
  • Drill your Ss to check they understand how the passive is formed. Write on the board sentences in the active. Ss turn them into the passive. Refer Ss to the Grammar Reference section for more details.

   e.g. T: Jim wrote a letter.
         S1: A letter was written by Jim.
         T: A fire destroyed the palace.
         S2: The palace was destroyed by a fire.
         T: They keep paintings in the Louvre.
         S3: Paintings are kept in the Louvre.   etc

ANSWER KEY: *to be ... past participle*

9

9 Explain the task. Help Ss find and underline the passive forms In the first dialogue. Then, Ss work on the other two dialogues. Check Ss' answers while Ss identify the tense form, then Ss make sentences using the passive forms.

> **ANSWER KEY**
>
> dialogue A: was built (past passive)
> was imprisoned (past passive)
> dialogue B: was designed (past passive)
> was it built (past passive)
> was opened (past passive)
> is supposed (present passive)
> dialogue C: was designed (past passive)
> was called (past passive)
> is called (present passive)
> was named after (past passive)
> was put in (past passive)
> was the tower built (past passive)
> was started/completed (past passive)
> was supposed (past passive)

10 • Present these words: **fortress, Crown Jewels, housed, executed, guarded** by giving examples or synonyms.
e.g. **fortress:** castle etc
• Allow Ss two minutes to read the text and do the exercise. Check Ss' answers while Ss read out from the text.

> **ANSWER KEY**
>
> 1 is 3 are 5 was 7 is
> 2 is 4 was 6 were 8 are

• As an extension Ss can ask and answer questions using the passive verbs.
e.g. S1: Where is the Tower of London located?
S2: It is located in the East End of London. What is it known as?
S3: It is known as a famous landmark, museum and fortress. What are housed there? etc

11 Read out the signs and present any unknown words. Help Ss expand them into full sentences, then say where they can find each one.

> **ANSWER KEY**
>
> 1 These seats are reserved for disabled passengers — Train
> 2 (The) Feeding of the animals is prohibited — Zoo
> 3 (The) Touching of the exhibits is forbidden — Museum
> 4 Dinner is served at 8 pm — Hotel

12 • Explain that the following are headlines from newspapers. Read out the headlines. Present these words: **Mayor, Grand Prix, blocks** by giving examples.
• Read out the example, then, Ss in closed pairs, do the rest of the exercise. Check Ss' answers.

> **ANSWER KEY**
>
> 2 A boy was saved by a dog last Monday.
> 3 A shopping centre was opened by the Mayor last Monday.
> 4 The Grand Prix was won by Smith last Monday.
> 5 Roads were blocked by snow last Monday.

13 Read out the prompts, then ask two Ss to read out the example. Ss, in open pairs, act out similar dialogues.

> **ANSWER KEY**
>
> • A: What is this vase made of?
> B: It's made of clay.
> A: Where was it found?
> B: It was found in Greece.
> • A: What is this cup made of?
> B: It's made of gold.
> A: Where was it found?
> B: It was found in Austria.
> • A: What is this plate made of?
> B: It's made of china.
> A: Where was it found?
> B: It was found in Germany.
> • A: What is this teapot made of?
> B: It's made of gold.
> A: Where was it found?
> B: It was found in Turkey.

14 • Read out the information, then ask two Ss to read out the example.
• Read out the information about the Little Mermaid. Ss, one after the other, ask and answer.

> **ANSWER KEY**
>
> S1: Where is the Little Mermaid located?
> S2: It is located in Copenhagen in Denmark. What is it made of?
> S3: It is made of bronze. When was it completed?
> S4: It was completed in 1913. Who was it sculpted by?
> S5: It was sculpted by Edward Eriksen. Why was it made?
> S6: It was made to honour the Royal Danish Ballet. How many people visit it per year?
> S7: It is visited by 1,000,000 people per year.

(Suggested Homework)

1 **Copy:** Ex. 12 (p. 91)
2 **Vocabulary:** words in Exs 5a & 6 (p. 90)
3 **Reading aloud:** Ex. 10 (p. 91)
4 **Dictation:** any ten words from Vocabulary
5 **Act out:** Exs 13 & 14 (p. 91)

9 Read the dialogues in Ex. 4 and underline all the passive forms. Which are in the present passive? Which are in the past passive? Close your books and make sentences using the passive forms.

10 Fill in: *is, are, was, were*.

The Tower of London 1) .... located in the East End of London. It 2) .... known as a famous landmark, museum and fortress. The Crown Jewels 3) .... housed there. The oldest building, the White Tower, 4) .... built by William the Conqueror in the 11th century. The Tower of London 5) .... used as a prison for many years. Many people 6) .... executed in the Tower. The Tower 7) .... guarded by the Yeoman Warders. They 8) .... also called Beefeaters.

11 Expand the signs into full sentences. Where can you find these signs?

1. THESE SEATS RESERVED FOR DISABLED PASSENGERS
2. FEEDING OF ANIMALS PROHIBITED
3. Touching of Exhibits Forbidden
4. Dinner served 8 pm

12 Use the headlines to complete the first sentence of the article.

1. FIRE Destroys National Museum
2. DOG saves BOY
3. Mayor Opens Shopping Centre
4. Smith Wins Grand Prix
5. Snow Blocks Roads

*The National Museum **was destroyed by a fire** last Monday.*

13 In pairs, ask and answer questions, as in the example.

china plate Germany
clay vase Greece
gold teapot Turkey
silver candlestick Poland
gold cup Austria

A: What is this candlestick made of?
B: It's made of silver.
A: Where was it found?
B: It was found in Poland.

14 In pairs, use the information to ask and answer questions, as in the example.

Name:	Lincoln Memorial, Washington DC, USA
Made of:	marble
Completed:	1922
Designer:	Henry Bacon
Reason Built:	to honour Abraham Lincoln
Number of visitors per year:	1,500,000

S1: **Where** is the Lincoln Memorial located?
S2: It is located in Washington DC, in the USA. **What** is it made of?
S3: It is made of marble. **When** was it completed?
S4: It was completed in 1922. **Who** was it designed by?
S5: It was designed by Henry Bacon. **Why** was it built?
S6: It was built to honour Abraham Lincoln. **How many** people visit it per year?
S7: It is visited by 1,500,000 people per year.

Name:	The Little Mermaid, Copenhagen, Denmark
Made of:	bronze
Completed:	1913
Sculptor:	Edward Eriksen
Reason Made:	to honour the Royal Danish Ballet
Number of visitors per year:	1,000,000

Listening

• The Bank of England Museum

15 Listen and choose the correct answers, then talk about the museum.

1 When was the bank founded?
  A 1654
  B 1684
  C 1694
  D 1644

2 What can't you see in this museum?
  A books
  B banknotes and coins
  C gold
  D calculators

3 The world's finest collection of coins includes items from:
  A the late 18th and late 19th centuries.
  B the early 18th and early 20th centuries.
  C the late 19th and early 20th centuries.
  D the early 18th and late 19th centuries.

4 There are many photographs from:
  A 1815
  B the 1860s
  C before the 1890s
  D after the 1890s

5 There are portraits of:
  A the inside of the bank
  B the outside of the bank
  C places in London
  D past Governors and Directors

6 The gold bars are from:
  A Stuart times
  B Roman times
  C Tudor times
  D the 1930s

• Project

Use the information in the Photo File section to write short descriptions of each monument.

16 Put the verbs in brackets into the correct passive tense, then ask questions which match the answers below.

The Pompidou Centre **1)** .... **(locate)** in Paris, France. It **2)** .... **(use)** as the National Museum of Modern Art and it **3)** .... **(complete)** in 1977. It **4)** .... **(design)** by Rogers and Piano and it **5)** .... **(make)** of glass and steel. It is a very modern building. It looks like it is inside out because the pipes, escalators and walkways are all on the outside. Inside, artwork by Picasso, Matisse, Duchamps and many other famous artists **6)** .... **(display)**. Outside the centre, there is a large open area where artists meet and performances

7) .... **(hold)**. There are lots of trendy shops and little cafés, too. The Pompidou Centre is an interesting place to visit. It is an exciting and modern building with lots to see and do inside and outside. No wonder it **8)** .... **(visit)** by millions of people every year.

1 Q: Where .... ?
  A: In Paris, France.
2 Q: What .... as?
  A: The National Museum of Modern Art.
3 Q: When .... ?
  A: 1977.
4 Q: Who .... ?
  A: Rogers and Piano.
5 Q: What .... ?
  A: Glass and steel.
6 Q: Whose works .... there?
  A: Picasso, Matisse, Duchamps and many others.

• The Definite Article *the*

17 Fill in *the* where necessary.

1 My friend wants to travel to 1) .... United States and 2) .... South America. She really wants to go to 3) .... Amazon. I would rather go to 4) .... China because I want to see 5) .... Great Wall.
2 1) .... capital city of 2) .... Republic of Ireland is 3) .... Dublin. 4) .... Dublin lies on 5) .... River Liffey not far from 6) .... Irish Sea.
3 1) .... Titanic was a huge ship which sank on its maiden voyage across 2) .... Atlantic in 3) .... April in 4) .... 1912.

Lesson 3 (pp. 92 - 93)

* Check Ss' HW (10').

15 • Explain that Ss are going to listen to a tour guide talking about the Bank of England Museum. Read out questions 1 to 6 along with the options to familiarise Ss with what they are going to listen to. Present these words: **founded, banknotes, coins, calculators, centuries, Governors, Directors, gold bars, Stuart times, Roman times, Tudor times** in Ss' L1 or by giving an example or synonym.

    e.g. **founded:** started, set up

        banknotes: show Ss a ten-pound note and say: *This is a banknote.*

        coins: show Ss a ten-pence piece and say: *This is a coin.* etc.

• Explain the task. Play the cassette. Ss listen and circle the correct answer. Check Ss' answers then Ss talk about the Bank of England Museum.

ANSWER KEY

1 C	3 C	5 D
2 A	4 D	6 B

Suggested answer: The Bank of England Museum was founded in 1694. In the museum you can see banknotes and coins, gold and calculators. It has the world's finest collection of coins which includes items from the late 19th and early 20th centuries. There are also many photographs from after the 1890s. At the museum you can see portraits of past Governors and Directors. There are also gold bars which are from the Roman times.

TAPESCRIPT

Museum Guide:

Welcome to the Bank of England Museum which was founded in 1694. Today the Bank of England, as you must all know, is the nation's central bank. Here, you will have the chance to see a great variety of exhibits. For example, you'll see some early writing equipment, official seals, calculators, gold, coins and banknotes and even some weapons which were used to defend the bank.

Here, on the right, you can see a large collection of notes. Together with each note, you can see the designer's drawings. The amazing thing is that there is also a collection of forgeries; these notes are so good that it's extremely difficult to tell they're not real.

On your left you can see the world's finest coin collection. This includes a wide selection of late 19th and early 20th century foreign gold coins. In the next room there are photographs, pictures, prints and drawings. The earliest photographs date from the 1850s, but there aren't really many of them until after the 1890s. As for the pictures and drawings these are mainly views of the bank, inside and outside, portraits of past Governors and Directors as well as many maps of London.

Now you're looking at some of the treasure that was found when the bank was rebuilt, from 1925 to 1939. These gold bars that you see here are Roman and extremely rare. There are also items from Tudor and Stuart times.

And now, let's go on *(fade)...*

Project (p. 92)

• Ask Ss to look at the Photo File section for Unit 9. Explain that the pictures show *rock legends* ie famous statues made of rock.

• Read out the prompts. Present these words: **Pacific Ocean, volcanic, islanders, memory, dead, ancestors, granite, symbol, power, temple** by giving examples or synonyms.
e.g. **islanders:** people who live on an island. etc.

• Read the short text for *Moai Statues* and explain what Ss should do. Ss use the prompts to do the exercise orally. Assign it as written HW. See Photo File section Unit 9 for the Answer Key.

16 • Explain that the Pompidou Centre is in Paris, France. Present these words: **pipes, escalators, walkways, artwork, display, trendy, no wonder** by giving examples or synonyms.
e.g. **trendy:** modern etc

• Explain the task. Allow Ss two minutes to complete the task. Check Ss' answers on the board while Ss read out from the text.

• Do question 1 with Ss. Then, Ss, in closed pairs, complete the exercise in writing. Check Ss' answers.

ANSWER KEY

1	is located	5	is made
2	is used	6	is displayed
3	was completed	7	are held
4	was designed	8	is visited

1	... is the Pompidou Centre located ...
2	... is it used ...
3	... was it completed ...
4	... was it designed by ...
5	... is it made of ...
6	... are displayed ...

---

17 Refer Ss to the Grammar Reference section. Present the theory from there, then allow Ss two minutes to do the exercise. Check Ss' answers.

ANSWER KEY

1	1 the	2 —	3 the	4 —	5 the
2	1 The	3 —		5 the	
	2 the	4 —		6 the	
3	1 The	2 the	3 —	4 —	

---

18 a) Ask Ss to look at the pictures. Read out sentences 1 to 7. Ss mark the sentences. While reading out the sentences present these words: **pavilions, pagodas, well-preserved, antiques** by giving examples, or showing pictures.

b) Play the cassette. Ss listen and check their answers.

> ANSWER KEY
>
> | | | | |
> |---|---|---|---|
> | 1 T | 3 F | 5 F | 7 T |
> | 2 T | 4 T | 6 T | |

19 a) Explain that Peking is another name for Beijing, the capital of China. Ss read out sentences 1 to 4. Allow Ss three minutes to read the text silently and circle the correct answer. Check Ss' answers, then help Ss explain the words in bold.

> ANSWER KEY
>
> | | | | |
> |---|---|---|---|
> | 1 C | 2 B | 3 D | 4 C |

b) • Play the cassette for Ex. 18b again. Ss listen and follow the lines, then read out from the text.
  • Write the headings on the board. Elicit answers from Ss to complete the table. Ss copy the completed table into their notebooks and use it to talk about the Summer Palace.

> SUGGESTED ANSWER KEY
>
> Name: The Summer Palace
> Location: outside Beijing, China
> Historical facts: began in the 13th cent. – completed in the 17th cent. destroyed by fire in 1860 - was rebuilt in 1865
> Things to see:
> • Marble Boat - two storeys high – 25m long with four dragon heads
> • Seventeen-Arch Bridge – white marble - over 500 lions carved on it
> • Suzhou Market Street – copy of a traditional street with shops
> • museum – antiques, priceless treasures
> • Long Corridor – world's longest handpainted covered walkway
>
> The Summer Palace is outside Beijing, China. It was begun in the 13th century and it was completed in the 17th century. The palace was destroyed by a fire in 1860, but it was rebuilt in 1865. There you can see the Marble Boat which is two storeys high and 25m long with four dragon heads. There is also the Seventeen-Arch Bridge which is made of white marble and has over 500 lions carved on it. You can also see Suzhou Market Street a copy of a traditional shopping street, and antiques and priceless treasures in the museum. Don't miss the Long Corridor, the world's longest handpainted covered walkway.

20 Play the cassette. Ss listen, then repeat individually.

> Suggested Homework
>
> 1 **Copy:** any two paragraphs from article in Ex. 19a (p. 93)
> 2 **Vocabulary:** words in bold in article in Ex. 19a (p. 93)
> 3 **Reading aloud:** article in Ex. 19a (p. 93)
> 4 **Dictation:** words in bold in article in Ex. 19a (p. 93)
> 5 **Speaking:** Ex. 19b (p. 93) Ss use their notes to talk about the Summer Palace
> 6 **Project:** (p. 92)

Listening and Reading

18 a) Look at the pictures. Which of the following do you think are true statements? Write T (true) or F (false).

1 The Summer Palace is in China. ....
2 It covers an area of more than 800 acres. ....
3 It includes a huge river. ....
4 There are pavilions, pagodas, towers and bridges. ....
5 The Summer Palace is not well-preserved. ....
6 The palace itself is a museum. ....
7 There is a rich collection of precious antiques in the palace. ....

b) Listen and check your answers.

19 a) Read the article and circle the correct answer A, B, C or D, then explain the words in bold.

1 The Summer Palace was used by the .... of China.
 A princes   B visitors
 C rulers   D presidents

2 The palace was .... in 1860.
 A preserved   B burnt down
 C rebuilt   D added

3 The Seventeen-Arch Bridge is made of ....
 A four dragon heads   B hills
 C colourful designs   D white marble

4 There are .... treasures in the palace.
 A expensive   B rich
 C valuable   D handpainted

Speaking

b) Make notes under the headings, then talk about the Summer Palace.
 • *name* • *location* • *historical facts*
 • *things to see*

A Peking Paradise

The Summer Palace is located just outside Beijing in China. It is one of the biggest and most famous **existing royal** gardens in the world. It covers an area of more than 800 acres including a huge lake called K'unming Lake.

The Palace was used by the **emperors** and **empresses** of China. It was begun in the 13th century, but it wasn't until the 17th century that man-made hills, halls, **pavilions**, **pagodas**, **towers** and bridges were **added**. Unfortunately, the palace was destroyed in 1860 by a fire, but was rebuilt in 1865.

The Summer Palace is so **well-preserved** that visitors can still enjoy its beautiful **features** today. One of the most famous sights is the Marble Boat which is two **storeys** high and 25m long with four dragon heads that **spout** water. There is also the magnificent white marble Seventeen-Arch Bridge which has over 500 lions **carved on** it, and Suzhou Market Street, a copy of a traditional street where the royal family used to do their shopping.

The palace itself is a museum with a rich collection of precious **antiques** and priceless **treasures** from various Chinese **dynasties**. It also contains the sight you must not miss; the world's longest **handpainted** covered **walkway**, known as the Long **Corridor**. Its walls are **covered** in **unique** handpainted images and colourful designs.

A visit to the Summer Palace and its gardens will **take up** the better part of a day, but it's **well worth** it. You shouldn't miss it if you travel to Beijing.

Pronunciation (linked sounds)

20 Listen and repeat.

The telephone was invented by Alexander Graham Bell.
The Colosseum in Rome was completed in 82 AD.
The Millennium Dome was built in 1999.

93

Game

Divide the class into two teams. Say words which do/don't require the definite article *the*. The teams take turns to add *the* where necessary. Each correct phrase gets 1 point. The team with the most points wins.

Teacher: Sahara Desert
Team A S1: the Sahara Desert
Teacher: Queen Elizabeth
Team B S1: Queen Elizabeth (no *the*)   etc

Vocabulary Practice

21 Fill in the correct word from the list, then make sentences using the collocations.

• dragon • white • spout • royal • open
• trendy • rich • priceless

1 the .... family
2 to .... water
3 a(n) .... area
4 .... collection
5 .... heads
6 .... shops
7 .... marble
8 .... treasures

22 Fill in: *in, after, for, of, to*.

1) It was named .... sb; 2) famous ....
sth; 3) .... honour .... sb; 4) ....
the end; 5) reminds me .... sth; 6) happen
.... sb; 7) made .... silver; 8) covered
.... sth; 9) a visit .... a place

23 Vocabulary Revision Game: In teams, make sentences with the words/ phrases in the list.

• rebuilt • was destroyed • imprisoned
• recording studio • weighs • accuracy
• was designed • was supposed • located
• strange-looking • amazing • was completed

24 Fill in: *say* or *tell*, then make sentences.

1) .... the time; 2) .... your name; 3) ....
one from the other; 4) .... the truth; 5) ....
good morning; 6) .... a story; 7) .... sb the
way; 8) .... a secret; 9) .... the difference

Writing (an article about a visit to a building)

25 a) Read the article and replace the adjectives in bold with the synonyms in the list.

• huge • breathtaking • well-known
• highest • cloudless

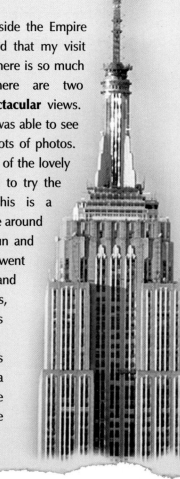

1 Last year I visited the Empire State Building in New York, USA. I had a fantastic time and I learnt a lot about this beautiful and **famous** landmark.

2 This modern-looking building was built in 1931 and it is one of the **tallest** buildings in the world. Many famous people have visited it, even royalty, such as the Queen of England and the King of Siam. No wonder Hollywood has used it in films such as 'King Kong' and 'Sleepless in Seattle'.

3 The first thing I noticed about the building is that it looks like a **giant** pencil, with a tall, pointed top. It is 443.2m high and has 102 floors. Looking at it from the ground made me feel very small. The style of the building is Art Deco and the architecture is beautiful.

4 As soon as I was inside the Empire State Building, I realised that my visit would be a long one. There is so much to see and do. There are two observatories with **spectacular** views. It was a **clear** day so I was able to see for 80 miles and take lots of photos. After I had lunch in one of the lovely coffee shops, I decided to try the New York Skyride. This is a simulated helicopter ride around the city. It was great fun and very exciting. Finally, I went to the souvenir shop and bought some postcards, so that I would always remember my visit.

5 I was sad when it was time to leave. I had a marvellous time there and I hope to go there again one day.

94

Lesson 4 (pp. 94 - 95)

* Check Ss' HW (10').

Game (p. 94)

Play the game as described in the Student's Book. Use words from the list below.

Suggested list: Sahara Desert, Queen Elizabeth, Amazon River, Lake Victoria, Niagara Falls, New York, Europe, Austria, moon, piano, sky, Picasso, Earth, North America, Ankara, United Kingdom, August, Titanic etc.

e.g.   Teacher: Amazon
      Team A S2: the Amazon
      Teacher: Lake Victoria
      Team B S2: Lake Victoria (no **the**) etc.

21 Allow Ss two minutes to fill in the words. Check Ss' answers, then Ss make sentences using the completed collocations.

> *ANSWER KEY*
>
> | | | | | | |
> |---|---|---|---|---|---|
> | 1 | royal | 4 | rich | 7 | white |
> | 2 | spout | 5 | dragon | 8 | priceless |
> | 3 | open | 6 | trendy | | |

e.g. S1: **The royal family** live in Buckingham Palace.
      S2: The dragons **spout water** from their mouths.
          etc.

22 Allow Ss two minutes to fill in the prepositions. Check Ss' answers, then Ss make sentences using these phrases.

> *ANSWER KEY*
>
> | | | | | | |
> |---|---|---|---|---|---|
> | 1 | after | 4 | in | 7 | of |
> | 2 | for | 5 | of | 8 | in |
> | 3 | in, of | 6 | to | 9 | to |

23 Ss, in teams, make sentences using the words/phrases in the order they appear in the S's Book. Each correct sentence gets 1 point. The team with the most points is the winner.
e.g. Team A S1: The palace was **rebuilt** in 1865.
      Team B S1: The palace **was destroyed** by a fire in
                 1860.   etc

24 Explain that **say/tell** can be used idiomatically. Allow Ss two minutes to do the exercise and make sentences.
e.g. When did you learn to **tell the time**?
Check Ss' answers. Ss should memorise these expressions. Check in the next lesson.

> *ANSWER KEY*
>
> | | | | | | |
> |---|---|---|---|---|---|
> | 1 | tell | 4 | tell | 7 | tell |
> | 2 | say | 5 | say | 8 | tell |
> | 3 | tell | 6 | tell | 9 | tell |

25 a) • Explain that the article is about the writer's visit to a place. Ask: *Which place did the writer go to?* *(Empire State Building, New York, USA)* etc. Present these words: **giant, pointed, observatories, architecture, spectacular, view, simulated** by giving examples or synonyms.
          e.g. **giant:** very big, huge etc.

    • Allow Ss three minutes to read the article, then do the exercise.

> *ANSWER KEY*
>
> | | |
> |---|---|
> | famous - well-known | spectacular - breathtaking |
> | tallest - highest | clear - cloudless |
> | giant - huge | |

b) Help Ss answer by asking questions.
e.g. T: Which paragraph gives information about the location of the building?
S1: The first paragraph.
T: What other information does para 1 give?
S2: The name of the building and when the writer visited it.
T: Which paragraph expresses the writer's feelings towards the building?
S3: The last paragraph.   etc.

ANSWER KEY

Para 1: what, where, when visited
Para 2: historical facts
Para 3: description of outside
Para 4: what you can see/do inside
Para 5: how writer felt

c) Read out the questions, one at a time. Ss answer. Check Ss' answers.

ANSWER KEY

— to talk about the name/location of the building
  past simple
— to talk about the historical facts
  past passive - present perfect simple
— to describe the interior/exterior of the building
  present simple - past simple
— to describe his/her feelings
  present simple - past simple

26 • Ask Ss to read out the extracts. Ss then do the exercise.
• Point out that extract A is not a recommendation; it expresses a negative opinion.

ANSWER KEY   B

27 a) • Present the writing tip.
• Read out the situation. Choose one building that everyone knows, then read out the questions. Ss answer the questions, first orally, then in writing. Ask individual Ss to read out their answers.
(Ss' own answers)

b) Explain the task. Read out the plan. Ss use their answers from Ex. 27a to talk about a famous building they have visited. After Ss have done the exercise orally in class, assign it as written HW.

SUGGESTED ANSWER KEY

Last summer I visited the Eiffel Tower in Paris, France. I had a wonderful time and I learnt a lot about this famous tourist attraction.
The Eiffel Tower was built in 1889 and it was named after the designer, Alexandre-Gustave Eiffel. It is made of iron and it was built for a world fair called the "Universal Exposition". It was the tallest building in the world until 1930.
The Tower has got four legs with arches in between each leg. These support the large tower. I felt very small standing at the bottom of it.

Inside the Tower there is plenty to see and do. I took a trip in a glass lift and saw some spectacular views of Paris. Then I visited the observation decks and I took some lovely photographs. I had a delicious lunch in one of the restaurants before I went to the souvenir shops to buy some postcards.
I didn't want the visit to end. I really enjoyed myself and I would love to visit it again one day.

28 • Play the cassette. Ss listen and follow the lines, then read out the dialogue.
• Ss, in closed pairs, use the prompts to act out similar dialogues. Check Ss' performance, then some pairs act out their dialogues in class.

ANSWER KEY

A: Excuse me. What currency is used in China?
B: Did you say in China?
A: Yes.
B: It's the yuan.
A: Thank you.

A: Excuse me. What currency is used in Japan?
B: Did you say in Japan?
A: Yes.
B: It's the yen.
A: Thank you.

A: Excuse me. What currency is used in Brazil?
B: Did you say in Brazil?
A: Yes.
B: It's the real.
A: Thank you.   etc

29 Explain the task. Allow Ss two minutes to complete the sentences. Check Ss' answers while individual Ss read out the completed sentences.

ANSWER KEY

• tallest
• largest
• longest
• oldest

Suggested Homework

1 **Copy:** any two paragraphs from the article in Ex. 25a (p. 94)
2 **Vocabulary:** Exs. 21, 22, 23, 24 (p. 94)
3 **Reading aloud:** article in Ex. 25a (p. 94)
4 **Dictation:** any ten words from vocabulary
5 **Act out:** Ex. 28 (p. 95)
6 **Writing:** Ex. 27b (p. 95)

Lesson 5

• Check Ss' HW.
• Workbook: Unit 9
    Click on Grammar 9

b) Read the article again. What information does each paragraph give?

c) What tenses has the writer used:

- to talk about the name/location of the building?
- to talk about the historical facts?
- to describe the interior/exterior of the building?
- to describe his/her feelings?

26 Which of the endings can replace the last paragraph?

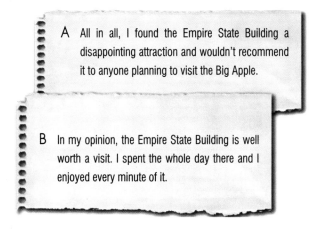

A All in all, I found the Empire State Building a disappointing attraction and wouldn't recommend it to anyone planning to visit the Big Apple.

B In my opinion, the Empire State Building is well worth a visit. I spent the whole day there and I enjoyed every minute of it.

To write a narrative-descriptive article about a visit to a building we can divide it into five paragraphs.
In the **first paragraph** we mention its **name**, **location** and **when** we **visited** it.
In the **second paragraph** we give **historical facts** about the building (e.g. who designed it, when it was built, etc) using past tenses.
In the **third paragraph** we describe the **exterior** of the building.
In the **fourth paragraph** we describe the **interior** of the building.
In the **last paragraph** we write how we felt.

27 a) Your teacher has asked you to write a short article for the school magazine describing a visit to a famous building.

1 What is the most famous building you have visited? When was it built? What kind of building is it? What is it famous for?
2 What does it look like from the outside? What is the inside like?
3 Why is it worth visiting?

b) Use your answers from Ex. 27a) as well as the plan below to write your article (100-150 words). You can use the article in Ex. 25a) as a model.

Plan

Introduction
Para 1 *name, location, when you visited it*
Main Body
Para 2 *historical facts*
Para 3 *exterior*
Para 4 *interior*
Conclusion
Para 5 *feelings*

Communication

- **Asking about currency**

28 Listen and repeat, then in pairs use the prompts to act out similar dialogues.

A: Excuse me. What currency is used in **France**?
B: Did you say in **France**?
A: Yes.
B: It's the **euro**.
A: Thank you.

- China/yuan
- Japan/yen
- Brazil/real
- Poland/zloty
- Russia/rouble

- the USA/dollar
- England/pound
- Mexico/new peso
- Chile/peso
- Portugal/euro

29 Fill in: *longest, tallest, oldest, largest.*

do you know...

- The Petronas Twin Towers in Malaysia is the world's .... building. It has 88 storeys and it is 451.9 metres high.
- The world's .... art gallery is the Winter Palace and Hermitage Museum in St Petersburg in Russia. It covers an area of 24 square km and contains about 3 million works of art.
- The Great Wall of China is the .... wall in the world at 3,460 km.
- The .... pyramid in the world is the Djoser Step Pyramid at Saqqâra, Egypt. It was built in 2630 BC.

The Hound of the Baskervilles

An Invitation to Murder

Holmes and Watson tell Sir Henry about Stapleton's invitation to dinner.

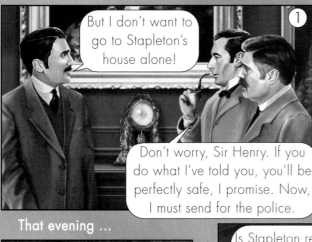

1 But I don't want to go to Stapleton's house alone!

Don't worry, Sir Henry. If you do what I've told you, you'll be perfectly safe, I promise. Now, I must send for the police.

2 I'd like to send a telegram to Inspector Lestrade of Scotland Yard in London, please. It's urgent.

COME TO BASKERVILLE HALL IMMEDIATELY * STOP * HOLMES

That evening …

3 Well, Sir Henry has arrived. I hope we can keep him safe!

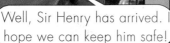

4 Is Stapleton really so dangerous?

Yes, Lestrade! Now get down!

5 Go and take a look, Watson, then come back and report.

Where is Beryl Stapleton? I can't see her anywhere.

7 … and I heard a strange noise from a shed in the garden. There's something in there …

6

8 Thank you for dinner, Stapleton. I say, what terrible fog!

Yes — don't get lost on the moor and end up in Grimpen Mire!

9 AA-OO-OUH!

HELP!!

WOO-OU-AHH!

Oh, no! If this fog gets thicker, it will ruin our plans. Are your guns ready, gentlemen?

It's the Baskerville hound! We have to save Sir Henry!

10 Watson, Lestrade — *SHOOT!!*

Pre-Reading Activities

1 Look at the pictures, then read the questions and circle the correct answer.

1 What is Holmes sending in picture 2?
a a letter   **(b)** a telegram

2 Where are Holmes & Watson in pictures 3 - 5?
a outside Sir Henry's house
(b) outside Stapleton's house

3 What is Watson doing in picture 6?
(a) looking through the window
b climbing the fence

4 What is the weather like in picture 8?
a It's cold and wet.
(b) It's foggy.

Listening and Reading Activities

2 🎧 Listen and tick (✓) the correct box A, B or C.

1 Sir Henry is invited to
[A] lunch
[B] ✓ dinner
[C] a party

2 Holmes sends for
[A] the hound
[B] a telegram
[C] ✓ the police

3 Watson hears a strange noise from
[A] ✓ a shed
[B] the house
[C] Baskerville Hall

3 Read the episode and find the name of the person who:

1 ... is visiting Stapleton. Sir Henry
2 ... receives a telegram. Inspector Lestrade
3 ... is dangerous. Stapleton
4 ... Watson can't see at all in Stapleton's house. Beryl Stapleton
5 ... is advised not to lose his way. Sir Henry

4 Read the episode again and find the words which mean:

- on my own alone
- without danger safe
- police chief inspector
- to be done at once urgent
- to spoil ruin
- to fire shoot

Grammar (prepositions of movement)

5 Match the pictures to the correct preposition, then use the phrases to say what Watson did.

• through • past • towards • over • along • into

over the wall

into the garden

along the garden path

past the fountain

towards the house

through the window

Watson and Holmes were behind the wall. Watson went over the wall and into the garden. He walked along the garden path and past the fountain towards the house. Then, he looked through the window.

6 🎧 Listen to the episode again and follow the lines, then take roles and act out the episode.

7 Read the episode again and correct the summary. What do you think is going to happen?

Sir Henry goes to Stapleton's house to have ~~lunch~~ dinner with him. ~~Watson~~ Holmes sends an urgent ~~letter~~ telegram to Inspector Lestrade in ~~Paris~~ London. That evening they go to Stapleton's house. Watson goes to see what is happening inside the house. He can't see Stapleton's ~~maid~~ wife anywhere, but he hears a strange noise from a garden shed. Sir Henry thanks Stapleton for the dinner and heads for his house. Holmes, Watson and Lestrade watch ~~Mrs Barrymore~~ Sir Henry. They can't see very well because it's ~~windy~~ foggy. Suddenly they hear the Baskerville ~~maid~~ hound.

97(T)

Lead-in

1 a) Look at the pictures on pp. 98 - 99 and choose words from the list to describe each person's appearance, as in the example.

- long/short - dark/fair/blond(e)/(light) brown hair
- big/small - blue/green/brown eyes
- a small/wide mouth
  - thin/full lips
    - a beard/moustache/wrinkles

Bob has got short light brown hair.

b) In pairs, ask and answer, as in the example.

A: *What does Bob look like?*
B: *He's got short light brown hair and wrinkles. He's also got a beard and a moustache.*

2 Read what each person says, then describe their character, using words from the list.

- hardworking • shy • sociable • forgetful
- patient • vain

Jamie: I hate talking to strangers.
Ann: I only wear designer clothes.
Bob: I like working long hours.
Ken: I don't mind waiting.
Sue: I never remember to send birthday cards.
Sally & Tina: We enjoy going out with our friends.

A: *What is Jamie like?*
B: *He's shy; he hates talking to strangers.*

3 🎧 **Listen and repeat.**

- You must be the new secretary.
- That's a lovely outfit you're wearing.
- Well, I must get to work.
- She's very vain, isn't she?
- I thought she looked very pretty.
- Typical man!
- Have a seat, Mr Walker.
- Tell me about yourself.
- I've got a lot of experience in management.
- The more you work, the more you learn – that's my motto.
- I'm sure you'll hear from us soon.
- Thank you for your time.
- Ready for what?
- You should be looking forward to it!
- I'd rather stay in tonight.
- That's fine by me.

Listening and Reading

4 🎧 **Listen and write the correct name from the list.**

- Ann • Mr Walker
- Jamie

Who is ...
1 at a job interview?
....
2 starting a new job today?
....
3 at home?
....

Bob

Ken

Sue

Jamie

Objectives

Vocabulary: facial features; character adjectives; sports; hobbies; types of films
Reading: reading for specific information; understanding main points, details and text structure
Listening: listening for gist; identifying people; multiple matching
Speaking: describing people; talking about films/ actors you like/dislike
Communication: expressing preferences
Pronunciation: stressed syllables
Grammar: linkers (and, as well as, in addition to, also, but, however, although), too - enough, to-infinitive, infinitive without to, -ing form
Project: a friendly letter describing a person
Writing: a letter of recommendation

Lesson 1 (pp. 98 - 99)

1 a) • Ask Ss to look at the pictures. Read out the prompts. Ask Ss questions.
e.g. T: Who's got short brown hair?
      S1: Bob.
      T: Who's got a beard and a moustache?
      S2: Bob and Ken.
      T: Who's got a round face?
      S3: Jamie.   etc.
• Ss, then make sentences about each person.

SUGGESTED ANSWER KEY

• Bob has got a beard and a moustache.
  Bob has got wrinkles.   etc.
• Ken has got short dark hair.
  Ken has got thin lips.
  Ken has got a beard and a moustache.   etc.
• Sue has got short dark hair.
  Sue has got a wide mouth.
  Sue has got full lips.   etc.
• Jamie has got short fair hair.
  Jamie has got blue eyes.
  Jamie has got thin lips.   etc.
• Ann has got long dark hair.
  Ann has got green eyes.
  Ann has got full lips.   etc.
• Sally and Tina have got long blonde hair.
  Sally and Tina have got blue eyes.
  Sally and Tina have got wide mouths.
  Sally and Tina have got full lips.   etc.

---

b) Ask two Ss to read out the example. Explain that we use: *What does ... look like?* to ask about a person's appearance. Then, Ss in open pairs, act out similar dialogues.

SUGGESTED ANSWER KEY

• A: What does Ken look like?
  B: He's got short dark hair and thin lips. He's also got a beard and a moustache.

• A: What does Sue look like?
  B: She's got short dark hair and blue eyes. She's also got a wide mouth and full lips.

• A: What does Jamie look like?
  B: He's got short fair hair and blue eyes. He's also got thin lips.

• A: What does Ann look like?
  B: She's got long dark brown hair and green eyes. She's also got full lips.

• A: What do Sally and Tina look like?
  B: They've got long blonde hair and blue eyes. They've also got wide mouths and full lips.

---

2 • Read out the prompts and present these words to Ss by giving examples, synonyms or miming.
e.g. hardworking: (Say: *John works very hard. He's hardworking.*)
shy: (Say: *Jackie is very nervous when she is with other people. She does not talk a lot. She blushes easily when someone talks to her. She's* **shy**.)
• Read out what each person says one at a time. Ss match the sentences to the adjectives in the list. Read out the example. Explain that we use: *What is ... like?* to ask about a person's character. Then Ss, in open pairs, act out similar dialogues.

ANSWER KEY

A: What is Ann like?
B: She's vain; she only wears designer clothes.

A: What is Bob like?
B: He's hardworking; he likes working long hours.

A: What is Ken like?
B: He's patient; he doesn't mind waiting.

A: What is Sue like?
B: She's forgetful; she never remembers to send birthday cards.

A: What are Sally and Tina like?
B: They are sociable; they enjoy going out with their friends.

---

3 Play the cassette. Ss listen and follow the lines. Play the cassette again. Ss repeat, either chorally or individually.

4 Explain the task. Play the cassette. Ss do the exercise. Check Ss' answers.

ANSWER KEY

1 Mr Walker   2 Ann   3 Jamie

---

5 a) Individual Ss read out the sentences. Allow Ss two minutes to read out the dialogues and mark the sentences accordingly. Check Ss' answers, then help Ss explain the words in bold.

ANSWER KEY

1 F	3 T	5 F
2 T	4 F	6 T

---

b) Play the cassette for Ex. 4 again. Ss listen and follow the lines, then take roles and read out the dialogues.

c) Allow Ss two minutes to read the dialogues and highlight using their text markers, the sentences/ phrases. Then, Ss say who said each one.

ANSWER KEY

Lizzie said, "You must be the new secretary."
Lizzie said, "That's a lovely outfit you're wearing."
Ann said, "Well, I must get to work."
Lizzie said, "She's very vain, isn't she?"
Mike said, "I thought she looked very pretty."
Lizzie said, "Typical man!"
The interviewer said, "Have a seat, Mr Walker."
The interviewer said, "Tell me about yourself."
Mr Walker said, "I've got a lot of experience in management."
Mr Walker said, "The more you work, the more you learn — that's my motto."
The interviewer said, " I'm sure you'll hear from us soon."
Mr Walker said, "Thank you for your time."
Jamie said, "Ready for what?"
Bill said, "You should be looking forward to it!"
Jamie said, "I'd rather stay in tonight."
Bill said, "That's fine by me."

Memory Game

Ss look at the phrases/sentences in Ex. 3 for two minutes, then close their books and, in teams, try to remember as many phrases/sentences as possible. Each correct phrase/ sentence gets 1 point. The team with the most points is the winner.

e.g. Team A S1: Have a seat, Mr Walker.
     Team B S1: Thank you for your time.   etc.

(Suggested Homework)

1 **Copy:** dialogue C Ex. 5a (p. 99)
2 **Vocabulary:** words in bold in dialogues A - C Ex. 5a (p. 99)
3 **Reading aloud:** dialogues A - C Ex. 5a (p. 99) (Point out that Ss practise *reading aloud* at home using the S's cassette/audio CD.)
4 **Dictation:** same as for Vocabulary
5 **Speaking:** a) Ss memorise any five sentences from Ex. 3 (p. 98);
                 b) Ss in pairs talk about the people in the pictures Ex. 1b (p. 98)

5 **a)** Read the dialogues and mark these sentences as *T* (true) or *F* (false), then explain the words in bold.

1 Ann is the new manager. ......
2 Ann is wearing designer clothes. ......
3 Mr Walker is very experienced. ......
4 Mr Walker does not work hard. ......
5 Jamie wants to go to Angie's party. ......
6 Jamie doesn't feel comfortable with strangers. ......

A
Ann: Good morning.
Mike: Hi!
Lizzie: You must be the new secretary.
Ann: That's right. I'm Ann.
Lizzie: Well, I'm Lizzie and this is Mike. That's a lovely **outfit** you're wearing.
Ann: Thank you. I only wear **designer clothes**. Well, I must get to work.
Lizzie: She's very **vain**, isn't she?
Mike: Vain?
Lizzie: Yes — she looks like she's going to a party, and she's wearing far too much **make-up**.
Mike: Oh. I thought she looked very pretty.
Lizzie: Huh! **Typical man**!

B
Interviewer: Good morning. Mr Walker, isn't it?
Mr Walker: Yes, that's right. Good morning.
Interviewer: **Have a seat**, Mr Walker.
Mr Walker: Thank you.
Interviewer: So, tell me about yourself.
Mr Walker: Well, I've just moved to London with my family. I've got a lot of **experience** in **management** and I'd like to work for your company.
Interviewer: Why our company?
Mr Walker: Because it's very successful and it has an excellent **reputation**.
Interviewer: That's true. We all work very hard here, you know. There can be a lot of **overtime**.
Mr Walker: Oh, I like working long hours. The more you work, the more you learn — that's my motto.
Interviewer: Well, you seem like a very **hardworking** and **determined** person, Mr Walker. I'm sure you'll **hear from** us soon.
Mr Walker: Thank you for your time.

C
Bill: Jamie, are you ready?
Jamie: Ready for what?
Bill: For Angie's party, of course.
Jamie: Oh, no! Do I have to go?
Bill: You should be **looking forward to** it!
Jamie: Why? I don't know any of Angie's friends.
Bill: Oh, Jamie! You shouldn't be so **shy**. You should meet some new people — you know, try to be more **sociable**.
Jamie: But I hate talking to **strangers**.
Bill: Well, if you *really* don't want to go ...
Jamie: I'd rather **stay in** tonight, have a cup of tea and watch TV.
Bill: That's **fine** by me, but you must call Angie and tell her.
Jamie: Oh, no! Can't *you* tell her?

b) In pairs, read out the dialogues.

c) Read the dialogues again and highlight the phrases/sentences used in Ex. 3. Who said each phrase/sentence?

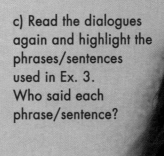

Ann

Sally and Tina

99

Vocabulary

- Describing people's appearance

6 a) **Fill in:** *plump, average, round, double, bald, full, big, build, moustache, glasses, thin, grey,* **then complete the table with these words.**

A *Max - 68 - 1.85 m - 60 kg*

Max is in his late sixties. He is tall and thin, with wavy **1)** .... hair, small blue eyes and quite a **2)** .... nose. He has got wrinkles and a grey **3)** .... He wears **4)** ....

B *Jan - 35 - 1.64 m - 60 kg*

Jan is in her mid thirties. She's of **1)** .... height and medium **2)** .... She's got straight dark hair, a round face, almond-shaped eyes, **3)** .... eyebrows and **4)** .... lips.

Age:	in his (early/mid/late) teens/twenties; young, middle-aged, old
Height:	tall, short, of .... height
Build:	thin, slim, ..., fat, of medium ....
Hair:	long, short; straight, curly, wavy; dark, fair, blond(e), ginger, ...; ....
Face:	long, narrow, ..., oval, thin
Forehead:	high, narrow, wide, square
Eyebrows:	long, arched, bushy, ...,
Eyes:	large/big, small; almond-shaped, round, narrow; blue, brown, green
Nose:	.........., small; pointed, wide, flat, button
Mouth/Lips:	wide, thin, ...
Chin/Jaw:	pointed, ..., square, strong
Special Features:	dimples, freckles, wrinkles; ...., beard; ....

C *Eddie - 41 - 1.51 m - 96 kg*

Eddie is in his early forties. He's short and **1)** .... He's got a(n) **2)** .... face with a wide forehead and thick, arched eyebrows and a **3)** .... chin. He is going **4)** ....

b) **Listen and write each person's name, then use words from the table to describe each person.**

Game

Choose a leader. The leader writes the name of one of the people in the photographs in Ex. 6 on a piece of paper. Students, in teams, ask questions to find out who the person is.
The team that finds the person gets one point. Choose a new leader, and the game continues. The team with the most points is the winner.

Team A S1: Is it a boy?
  Leader: Yes, it is.
Team B S1: Has he got fair hair?
  Leader: Yes, he has.   etc

100

Lesson 2 (pp. 100 - 101)

* • Check Ss' HW (10').
  • Play the Memory Game as described in Ex 5c p. 99(T).

6 a) • Present the words in the list by using the pictures in Ex. 6a. Explain the task, then do item A with Ss. Allow Ss three minutes to complete the blanks. Check Ss' answers by asking individual Ss to read out the completed texts.

ANSWER KEY

A 1 grey, 2 big, 3 moustache, 4 glasses
B 1 average, 2 build, 3 thin, 4 full
C 1 plump, 2 round, 3 double, 4 bald

  • Allow Ss two minutes to complete the table. Check Ss' answers. Then, present any unknown words using pictures.

ANSWER KEY

Age:	in his (early/mid/late) teens/twenties; young, middle-aged, old
Height:	tall, short, of **average** height
Build:	thin, slim, **plump**, fat, of medium **build**
Hair:	long, short; straight, curly, wavy; dark, fair, blond(e), ginger, **grey**; **bald**
Face:	long, narrow, **round**, thin
Forehead:	high, narrow, wide, square
Eyebrows:	long, arched, bushy, **thin**
Eyes:	large/big, small; almond-shaped, round, narrow; blue, brown, green
Nose:	**big**, small; pointed, wide, flat, button
Mouth/Lips:	wide, thin, **full**
Chin/Jaw:	pointed, **double**, square, strong
Special Features:	dimples, freckles, wrinkles; **moustache**, beard; **glasses**

b) • Ask Ss to look at the pictures. Explain that Ss are going to listen to a woman talking about her family. Point out that we use *blond* for men and *blonde* for women.
  • Play the cassette twice. Ss listen and write down the names. Check Ss' answers, then individual Ss describe each person.

ANSWER KEY

1 Jim	3 John	5 Bob
2 Tim	4 Pam	

SUGGESTED ANSWER KEY

1 Jim is about 6 years old. He's slim with short blond hair and small blue eyes. He's got an oval face and a button nose.
2 Ann is in her early thirties. She is of average height and slim build. She's got straight blonde hair and blue eyes. She's got an oval face, a wide mouth and dimples.
3 Tim is in his late thirties and he's got a slim build. He's got small eyes, a pointed nose and a strong jaw.
4 Sue is 8 years old. She has a slim build and long blonde hair. She's got small blue eyes and a button nose.
5 Tony is about 5 years old. He has a slim build and he's got short brown hair and brown eyes.
6 Peter is in his mid seventies. He's of average height and he's rather plump. He's got short grey hair and a wide forehead with bushy eyebrows.
7 John is ten years old. He's slim with short blond hair. He's got a long face.
8 Pam is about 9 years old. She is plump with long dark curly hair. She's got small eyes, a button nose and a wide mouth.
9 Mary is in her early forties. She is slim with blonde hair and blue eyes and a wide mouth.
10 Betty is in her mid sixties. She has got curly blonde hair, small eyes and a wide mouth.
11 Bob is about 10 years old with a slim build. He has short blond hair and blue eyes with a wide nose, thin lips and a pointed chin.

TAPESCRIPT

A: I've just got some photos developed. Do you want to see?
B: Yes, please. Oh, this woman must be your sister. She's got blonde hair and blue eyes and the same dimples as you.
A: Yes, that's my sister Ann and her son Jim. He's got blond hair, too, but he's got small eyes like his dad.
B: Which one is his dad?
A: Here. That's Tim with their daughter Sue. She's eight now.
B: Oh! He's handsome, isn't he? What a nice pointed nose and a strong jaw, too.
A: Julie, behave yourself! He's a married man.
B: Sorry. Haven't you got any pictures of Tony and John?
A: Oh, my boys. Yes, here we are. That's them with their grandad, Peter.
B: Ooh. Your dad looks well, doesn't he? I mean he may have white hair and a few wrinkles, but he looks very good for his age. What is he, 75 now?
A: Thanks. I'll tell him that. He'll be pleased. Anyway, here's a picture of my other sister, Mary, with her daughter Pam.
B: What lovely dark curly hair Pam's got!
A: Mm. And that's Mary's son Bob with my mother-in-law, Betty.
B: Wow! Bob and Pam are totally different, aren't they?
A: Yes, Bob takes after his mum, you know, blond hair, blue eyes and Pam's like her dad, but she's a real mummy's girl.
B: You're so lucky to have such a nice family and such a big one, too.
A: Well, we're having a party next month. Everyone will be there. You should come and meet them all ... (fade)

Game (p. 100)

Play the game as described in the Student's Book. As an alternative you can choose pictures of people from magazines, stick them on the board and play the game using these pictures.

7 • Explain that adjectives 1 to 10 are adjectives used to describe a person's character. Read out the adjectives and help Ss match them to the definitions. Check Ss' answers, then explain any unknown words.

• Ask a S to read out the example. Allow Ss three minutes to do the exercise. Check Ss' answers, then assign it as written HW.

ANSWER KEY

2 g	4 e	6 i	8 a	10 h
3 f	5 c	7 b	9 j	

2 An honest person is someone who tells the truth. *(positive)*

3 An ambitious person is someone who wants to be successful. *(positive)*

4 A stubborn person is someone who refuses to change their mind. *(negative)*

5 An aggressive person is someone who often behaves in an angry way. *(negative)*

6 A reliable person is someone who does what they promise to do. *(positive)*

7 A sensitive person is someone who gets upset easily. *(negative)*

8 An outgoing person is someone who likes meeting people. *(positive)*

9 A greedy person is someone who wants more than they need. *(negative)*

10 A polite person is someone who has good manners. *(positive)*

---

8 • Before Ss do the exercise, present linkers. Explain that we use specific words (linkers) to join two sentences.

• Read out the examples. Ask questions to check meaning and use.

   e.g. T: Which linkers do we use to talk about similar qualities ?
     S1: and, as well as.
      T: Thank you. Anyone else?
     S2: In addition to, also.   etc

• Explain the task, then do item 1 with Ss. Allow Ss two to three minutes to do the exercise in writing. Check Ss' answers by asking individual Ss to read out their sentences.

SUGGESTED ANSWER KEY

1 She is usually reliable, **but** she can be forgetful at times.

2 He is kind **and** generous.

3 She is outgoing. **However**, she can be stubborn at times.

4 **Although** she is hardworking, she has a tendency to be aggressive.

5 He is often rude, **but** he can sometimes be polite.

6 **In addition to** being vain, she is **also** greedy.

---

9 • Read out the prompts. Present the adjectives by giving examples, synonyms or antonyms.

   e.g. **daring**: having the courage to do dangerous things   etc

• Explain the task, then help Ss do the exercise.

ANSWER KEY

I think Tony would probably like mountaineering because he's daring and adventurous.

I think Jeff would probably like snowboarding because he's athletic and fun-loving.

I think Joan would probably like ice-skating because she's active and graceful.

I think Kevin would probably like painting because he's creative and artistic.

I think Sam would probably like boxing because he's strong and aggressive.

Project (p. 101)

• Ask Ss to look at the Photo File section. Explain that Ss must fill in the letter Anne sent to her friend, Sue. Read out the information, then ask questions to elicit answers.

   e.g. T: What does Rachel look like?
     S1: She's tall and slim with long dark hair and brown eyes.
      T: What is she like?   etc

• After Ss have completed the task orally in class, assign it as written HW.

Suggested Homework

1 **Copy:** Ex. 8 (p. 101)
2 **Vocabulary:** Ex. 6 (p. 100), Exs 7 & 9 (p. 101)
3 **Reading aloud:** Ex. 6a (p. 100)
4 **Dictation:** any ten words from Vocabulary
5 **Speaking:** Ss describe the people in the pictures in Ex. 6b (p. 100)
6 **Project:** (p. 101)

• Describing people's character

5 He is often rude. He is sometimes polite.
6 She is vain. She is greedy.

7 Match the character adjectives (1-10) to the descriptions (a-j), then make sentences, as in the example. Which of the adjectives are positive, and which of them are negative?

1	d	generous
2		honest
3		ambitious
4		stubborn
5		aggressive

6		reliable
7		sensitive
8		outgoing
9		greedy
10		polite

a likes meeting people
b gets upset easily
c often behaves in an angry way
d likes giving things to others
e refuses to change their mind

f wants to be successful
g tells the truth
h has good manners
i does what they promise to do
j wants more than they need

A generous person is someone who likes giving things to others.   *(positive)*

• Linkers

To join **similar qualities** (both positive or both negative), we use **and**, **as well as**, **also**, **In addition to**, etc.
She is generous. She is honest.
*She is generous **and** honest.*
*She is generous **as well as** (being) honest.*
***In addition to being** generous, she is **also** honest.*

To join **opposing qualities** (one positive, one negative), we use **but**, **However**, **Although**, etc.
He is shy. He can be sociable at times.
*He is shy, **but** he can be sociable at times.*
*He is shy. **However**, he can be sociable at times.*
***Although** he is shy, he can be sociable at times.*

8 Rewrite the following sentences using linking words/phrases from the table above.

1 She is usually reliable. She is forgetful at times.
2 He is kind. He is generous.
3 She is outgoing. She can be stubborn.
4 She is hardworking. She has a tendency to be aggressive.

9 Which sport/hobby do you think each of these people would choose? Make sentences, as in the example.

painting

mountaineering

Liza (quiet, intelligent)
Tony (daring, adventurous)
Jeff (athletic, fun-loving)
Joan (active, graceful)
Kevin (creative, artistic)
Sam (strong, aggressive)

ice-skating

boxing

snowboarding

chess

e.g. *I think Liza would probably like playing chess, because she's quiet and intelligent.*

• Project

Look at the Photo File section and complete the letter describing Rachel's appearance, character and hobbies.

10 Match the adjectives to the descriptions, then look at the picture and ask and answer, as in the example.

| 1 | | clumsy | 3 | | lazy | 5 | | miserable |
| 2 | | cheerful | 4 | | noisy | 6 | | bossy |

a keeps dropping things
b never smiles or laughs
c makes a lot of noise
d does very little work
e always tells people what to do
f always seems happy

S1: *Carl is very clumsy, isn't he?*
S2: *Yes, he keeps dropping things. Mandy is ... etc*

Grammar

• too - enough

11 Read the sentences and fill in *can* or *can't*, then answer the questions.

Tom's **too short** to become a firefighter. =
Tom .... become a firefighter.
Bob's **tall enough** to become a firefighter. =
Bob .... become a firefighter.

1 Which structure has a negative meaning?
2 Which structure has a positive meaning?

12 Complete the sentences, using the word in bold and *too* or *enough*, as in the example.

1 A: Shall we go out tonight?
 B: No, it's *too cold to go out tonight.* (cold)
2 A: Do you want to go out tonight?
 B: No, I'm .... (tired)
3 A: Shall we go for a swim?
 B: Yes, it's .... (warm)
4 A: Can you reach the top shelf?
 B: No, I'm .... (short)
5 A: Can you lift that box?
 B: Yes, I'm ....(strong)

• Verb + *to*-infinitive, *-ing* form or infinitive without *to*

13 Study the table, then put the verbs in brackets into the correct form.

+ *to*-infinitive	+ *-ing* form	+ infinitive without *to*
agree	can't help	let
begin	can't stand	make
decide	don't mind	can
expect	enjoy	could
refuse	hate	may
want	look forward to	might
		must
would like/love	like/love	will
would prefer	prefer	would
(on this occasion)	*(usually)*	would rather

1 A: Can you ....(help) me with the dishes, please?
 B: Yes, then we could .... (go) for a walk, what do you think?
 A: That would be great.

2 A: Do you enjoy .... (go) to parties?
 B: Yes — I love .... (meet) new people.

3 A: I expected .... (see) Tony here tonight.
 B: Well, he wanted .... (come), but he was busy.

4 A: Let's .... (go) to the cinema or would you rather .... (watch) TV?
 B: Well, I usually prefer .... (go) out to .... (stay) at home, but tonight I think I'd prefer .... (watch) TV.

5 A: Well, Terry, are you looking forward to .... (fly) to Paris?
 B: No – I hate .... (travel)!

6 A: Mum agreed .... (lend) me her car.
 B: You mean she's really going to let you .... (drive) her BMW?

7 A: Steve always makes me .... (laugh).
 B: Me too. I love .... (listen) to his funny stories.

8 A: Mr Harris, do you mind .... (work) long hours?
 B: No, not at all. Actually I was wondering if I could .... (do) some overtime.

Lesson 3 (pp. 102 - 103)

* Check Ss' HW (10').

10 • Read out the adjectives and help Ss match them to the definitions, then explain any unknown words.
   • Ask Ss to look at the picture and match the adjectives to the people.
   • Read out the example, then Ss ask and answer rolling questions.

ANSWER KEY

1	a	3	d	5	b
2	f	4	c	6	e

S2: ... very bossy isn't she?
S3: Yes, she always tells people what to do. John is very cheerful, isn't he?
S4: Yes, he always seems happy. Fiona is very miserable, isn't she?
S5: Yes, she never smiles or laughs. Dave is very lazy, isn't he?
S6: Yes, he does very little work. Sharon is very noisy, isn't she?
S7: Yes, she makes a lot of noise.
---

11 • Ss' books closed. Demonstrate the meaning and relationship between *too* and *enough*. Try to touch the light in the ceiling. Say, then write on the board: *I'm too short to reach the light. I'm not tall enough to reach the light.*
   • Ss' books open. Ss read out the examples and complete the sentences, then answer the questions.

ANSWER KEY

can't   can

1 **too** has a negative meaning
2 **enough** has a positive meaning
---

12 Do item 1 with Ss, then allow Ss two minutes to do the exercise. Check Ss' answers while they read out their sentences.

ANSWER KEY

2 ... too tired to go out tonight.
3 ... warm enough to go for a swim.
4 ... too short to reach the top shelf.
5 ... strong enough to lift that box.
---

13 • Say, then write on the board: *I like playing tennis. I hate fishing.* Underline: **playing** and **fishing**. Explain that these verb forms are -ing form. Ask Ss to make similar sentences about themselves.

• Say, then write on the board: *I would like to play tennis.* Underline **to play**. Explain that this verb form is a to-infinitive. Ask Ss to make similar sentences about themselves.

• Say, then write on the board: *I can play tennis well.* Underline **play**. Explain that this verb form is an infinitive without to. Ss make similar sentences about themselves.

• Read out the table in Ex. 13. Ask Ss to make sentences using the verbs in the table.

• Explain the task, then allow Ss two minutes to complete the exercise. Check Ss' answers.

ANSWER KEY

1 help, go
2 going, meeting
3 to see, to come
4 go, watch, going, staying, to watch
5 flying, travelling
6 to lend, drive
7 laugh, listening
8 working, do
---

10

14 • Present these words: **well-spaced eyes**, **strong jawline**, **high cheekbones** by giving examples.
   • Ask Ss to look at the pictures, and read out the actors' names. Read out the prompts and help Ss match them to the pictures.

> **ANSWER KEY**
>
> 2 D   4 F   6 E
> 3 B   5 C

15 Play the cassette. Ss listen and check their answers.

16 • Read out sentences 1 to 6. Allow Ss' three minutes to read the article silently and answer the questions. Check Ss' answers, then help Ss explain the words in bold.

> **ANSWER KEY**
>
> 1 a   3 b   5 b
> 2 a   4 b   6 a

   • Write these words on the board, then ask Ss to read questions 1 to 6 and fill in the appropriate nouns. Complete the table. Ss copy this table into their notebooks.

Adjective	Noun
honest	honesty
friendly	friendliness
creative	creativity
generous	generosity
sociable	sociability
ambitious	ambition
determined	determination

   • Play the cassette again. Ss listen and follow the lines, then read out from the article.
   • As an extension you ask Ss to cut out 3 to 4 pictures of their favourite actors, singers etc from magazines and write a short paragraph for each, similar to the ones in the article.

> **Suggested Homework**
>
> 1 **Copy:** any two paragraphs from the article in Ex. 16 (p. 103)
> 2 **Vocabulary:** table in Ex. 13 (p. 102)
> 3 **Reading aloud:** article Ex. 16 (p. 103)
> 4 **Dictation:** words in Ex. 14 (p. 103)
> 5 **Speaking:** Ss choose two of the famous people in Ex. 16 and talk about their characters.

Listening and Reading

14 Look at the pictures. Who's got:—

1 **A** short dark hair, a square forehead with wrinkles and blue eyes?

2 □ short fair hair, well-spaced eyes, an oval-shaped face and a wide mouth with thin lips?

3 □ long fair hair, long eyebrows and a small nose?

4 □ long curly brown hair, a wide mouth, full lips and long arched eyebrows?

5 □ short brown hair, a long oval face with full lips and a big nose?

6 □ shoulder-length curly brown hair, a strong jawline and high cheekbones?

15 🎧 Listen and check if your answers in Ex. 14 were correct.

16 Read the article and circle the correct answer for questions 1 to 6. Then, explain the words in bold using your dictionaries.

1 Laughter lines around the eyes suggest ...
   a a good sense of humour.
   b honesty.

2 Long eyebrows and a small nose suggest ...
   a friendliness.
   b creativity.

3 A high forehead and large, wide eyes suggest ...
   a a calm person.
   b generosity.

4 Wide, thin lips suggest someone who has got ...
   a a fun-loving nature.
   b ambition.

5 A strong jawline suggests ...
   a someone who is romantic.
   b determination.

6 A wide mouth and very full lips suggest ...
   a a desire to try everything.
   b friendliness.

Famous Faces

Face reading, or **personology**, is an old **art** that is becoming more and more popular. It is believed that a person's facial features can tell us a lot about what kind of person they are. Let's see what some famous faces tell us.

(A)

Mel Gibson
Mel's square forehead means he is honest and not **afraid** to say what he thinks. However, the **laughter lines** around his eyes show he's a very funny person who enjoys listening to and **telling jokes**.

(B)

Jodie Foster
Jodie has large eyes, which means she is very creative. She's also got long eyebrows and a small nose, which means she's a friendly person and very **gentle**, too.

(C)

Nicolas Cage
Nicolas has got a long oval face. That means he's quite active, but he's got full lips, so he is also a calm and **relaxed sort** of person. His very high forehead and large wide eyes tell us he is also **open-hearted** and very generous.

(D)

Meg Ryan
Meg's well-spaced eyes mean she's probably a very sociable person, and her oval-shaped face and wide thin lips show she's also quite ambitious. However, her small pretty nose **suggests** she can also be very gentle and kind. She probably loves children and animals.

(E)

Antonio Banderas
Antonio's strong jawline means he's a very determined kind of person. At the same time, he's probably quite **romantic**, because he's got a large nose with a **soft tip**. His high cheekbones are a **sign** that he loves to travel, likes **adventure** and **change**, and gets bored very easily.

Julia Roberts
Julia has a wide mouth and very full lips, which show she has a huge **appetite** for life and a **desire** to try everything. Her very long arched eyebrows show she is kind to others as well as being friendly and outgoing. **Unfortunately**, her fun-loving nature sometimes stops her from doing important things or from taking people more **seriously**.

(F)

Listening

17 a) **Listen and match the people (A-E) to the types of film they like (1-6). There is one type of film which does not match.**

Angela	A	1	science fiction
Charlie	B	2	romance
Sophie	C	3	adventure
Tony	D	4	thriller
Laura	E	5	comedy
		6	historical

Speaking

b) **Which types of film do *you* like watching? Who are your favourite actors? Describe their appearance and character.**

Communication

• **Expressing preferences**

18 **Listen to the dialogue and fill in the words. Then use the prompts to make similar dialogues.**

> A: What 1) .... we do today?
> B: I don't know.
> A: Do you like playing tennis?
> B: No. I 2) .... playing
> football 3) .... playing tennis.
> A: Oh. Do you like reading?
> B: Well, I'd 4) .... watch
> TV 5) .... read.
> A: Me too! Let's go and watch TV, then.
> B: Good idea!

• listen to **pop/rock** music – play **on the computer/outside**
• sunbathe/play volleyball – swim/sail
• take/paint pictures – play chess/cards
• skateboarding/rollerblading – watch comedies/thrillers

Pronunciation

19 **Listen and underline the stressed syllable. Listen again and repeat.**

1	pre - fer	→	pre - fe - rence
2	co - me - dy	→	co - me - di - an
3	ge - ne - rous	→	ge - ne - ro - si - ty
4	hi - sto - ry	→	hi - sto - ri - cal
5	ar - tist	→	ar - tis - tic
6	ath - lete	→	ath - le - tic

Vocabulary Practice

20 **Vocabulary Revision Game: In teams, make sentences with words/phrases from the list.**

• don't mind • wrinkles • outfit • reputation
• interview • vain • motto • fine by me
• forgetful • desire • is like • gentle • relaxed
• looks like • boxing • shy • ambitious
• stay in • I'd rather • overtime

21 **Fill in the correct word, then make sentences.**

• huge • double • facial • laughter • blonde • full
• science • wear • bushy • well-spaced

1	.... hair	6	to .... make-up
2	.... lips	7	a .... appetite
3	.... eyebrows	8	.... lines
4	.... features	9	.... eyes
5	.... chin	10	.... fiction

22 **Fill in: *at, for, in, to, with, from.***

1 to hear .... sb; 2 to look forward ....
sth; 3 to talk .... strangers; 4 to work .... a
company; 5 to stay .... home; 6 to go out
.... sb; 7 to be kind .... sb; 8 to stop sb
.... doing sth; 9 to move .... London; 10 to
have experience .... sth

Game

In teams, choose verbs/modals from the list and make sentences using *to*-infinitive, *-ing* form or infinitive without *to*. Each correct sentence gets one point. The team with the most points is the winner.

• like • decide • begin • look forward to
• would like • must • manage • want • hate
• make • would rather • enjoy • let • prefer
• can't stand • don't mind • can • expect

Lesson 4 (pp. 104 - 105)

* Check Ss' HW (10').

17 a) Explain the task. Point out that one type of film does not match any of the speakers. Play the cassette twice. Ss listen and match. Check Ss' answers.

ANSWER KEY: A 4, B 6, C 5, D 2, E 3

TAPESCRIPT

1 *Angela:* I don't usually enjoy science-fiction films, but I thought Jodie Foster was brilliant in "Contact". I usually prefer watching thrillers because they're so exciting.

2 *Charlie:* I'm quite a romantic person, but I can't stand watching romantic films. I like historical films, though. I loved Mel Gibson in "Braveheart". He always plays such adventurous characters.

3 *Sophie:* I hate adventure films normally, but I quite liked "Zorro" with Antonio Banderas. I'm quite a fun - loving person, though, so I prefer watching comedies.

4 *Tony:* I don't really like historical films because I find them boring. I enjoy romance films. Anything with Julia Roberts in it suits me!

5 *Laura:* I love adventure films. Nicholas Cage usually plays quite aggressive characters, but I think he's great. I can't stand thrillers - I get too scared!

b) Individual Ss answer the questions.

SUGGESTED ANSWER KEY

I mostly like comedies and adventure films. My favourite actor is Jim Carrey. Jim is in his mid thirties. He's of average height and he's slim. He's got an oval face and short brown hair. He's also got blue eyes and a wide mouth. He's kind and generous.

18 Ss read the dialogue. Play the cassette. Ss listen and fill in. Check Ss' answers, then play the cassette again. Ss listen and follow the lines, then take roles and read out the dialogue. Focus Ss' attention on **rather/prefer**. Write the structures on the board.

prefer + -ing form ... to + -ing form
'd rather + infinitive without to ... than + infinitive without to

Give prompts for Ss to make sentences using either *prefer* or *'d rather*. **Suggested list:** watch a comedy/a thriller, read science fiction/romance, go to the cinema/theatre, eat fish/meat, play basketball/squash etc
e.g. S1: I'd rather go to the cinema than go to the theatre.
    S2: I prefer eating fish to eating meat. etc
Ss, in closed pairs, use the prompts to act out dialogues. Check Ss' answers then some pairs report back to the class.

ANSWER KEY

1 shall, 2 prefer, 3 to, 4 rather, 5 than

• A: What shall we do today?
  B: I don't know.
  A: Do you like listening to pop music?
  B: No, I prefer listening to rock music to listening to pop music.
  A: Oh. Do you like playing on the computer?
  B: Well, I'd rather play outside than play on the computer.
  A: Me too! Let's go and play outside then.
  B: Good Idea!

• A: What shall we do today?
  B: I don't know.
  A: Do you like sunbathing?
  B: No, I prefer playing volleyball to sunbathing.
  A: Oh. Do you like swimming?
  B: Well, I'd rather go sailing than swimming.
  A: Me too! Let's go sailing then.
  B: Good idea! etc

19 Explain the task. Play the cassette. Ss listen and underline accordingly. Check Ss' answers.

ANSWER KEY

1	pre - **fer**	→	**pre** - fe - rence
2	**co** - me - dy	→	co - **me** - di - an
3	**ge** - ne - rous	→	ge - ne - **ro** - si - ty
4	**hi** - sto - ry	→	hi - **sto** - ri - cal
5	**ar** - tist	→	ar - **tis** - tic
6	**ath** - lete	→	ath - **le** - tic

20 Ss, in teams, make sentences using the words/phrases in the order in which they appear. Each correct sentence gets one point. The team with the most points is the winner.
e.g. Team A S1: I **don't mind** working long hours.
    Team B S1: My grandad's got **wrinkles**.

21 Allow Ss two minutes to do the exercise. Check Ss' answers, then Ss, in teams, make sentences using the collocations.
e.g. Team A S1: My mum has got long **blonde hair**.
    Team B S1: Jim hasn't got thin lips. He's got **full lips**.

ANSWER KEY

1 blonde	5 double	8 laughter
2 full	6 wear	9 well-spaced
3 bushy	7 huge	10 science
4 facial		

22 Allow Ss two minutes to fill in the correct preposition. Check Ss' answers. As an extension Ss can make sentences using the phrases.

ANSWER KEY:

1 from, 2 to, 3 to, 4 for, 5 at,
6 with, 7 to, 8 from, 9 to 10 in/(with)

Game (p. 104)

Play the game as described in the Student's Book.

SUGGESTED ANSWER KEY

Team A S1: I **like** travelling abroad.
Team B S1: She **decided** to move to London.
Team A S2: He **began** to tidy his room an hour ago.
Team B S2: We **are looking forward** to going on holiday.
Team A S3: I**'d like** to eat a sandwich.
Team B S3: We **must** go now.
Team A S4: He **managed** to reach the station on time.
Team B S4: She **wants** to become a nurse.
Team A S5: I **hate** skiing.
Team B S5: He **made** me cry.
Team A S6: I**'d rather** watch TV.
Team B S6: He **enjoys** listening to music.
Team A S7: **Let** me go out.
Team B S7: He **prefers** swimming to sailing.
Team A S8: I **can't stand** walking in the rain.
Team B S8: I **don't mind** working overtime.
Team A S9: She **can** type fast.
Team B S9: She **expects** to get a promotion.

104(T)

23 Explain the task. Allow Ss two minutes to do the exercise. Check Ss' answers.

ANSWER KEY

1 mean	3 polite	5 lazy
2 shy	4 aggressive	
---

24 • Present these words: **in reply to, reference, rose to position, staff** by giving examples.
  e.g. **in reply to:** when sb has written a letter and we write back, then we write a letter **in reply to** his/her letter.

  • Explain that Ss are going to read a letter of recommendation i.e. a letter which is sent by a person's previous employer to his/her future employer, commenting on the person's behaviour while at work. Ask Ss to look at the letter. Point out that this is a formal letter sent to a person whose name is known to us therefore we start with Dear + the person's last name, and sign off "Yours sincerely" + our full name.

  • Allow Ss two minutes to read the letter silently and underline the correct word/phrase. Then, Ss answer questions 1 to 5.

ANSWER KEY

Although, In addition, In conclusion

1 The letter is from Jean Greenwood. She starts with **Dear Mr Milton** and she ends with **Yours sincerely**. Because this is a formal letter and she knows the name of the person she is writing to.
2 It is a letter of recommendation.
3 The second paragraph.
4 *Positive qualities:*
   hardworking
   responsible
   kind and helpful
   polite
   Negative qualities:
   stubborn
5 It is not required as this is a character reference.
---

25 • Explain the situation. Read out the prompts, then ask questions to check Ss' understanding.
  e.g. T: Who is going to write the letter?
    S1: David Grey.
    T: Who is going to read the letter?
    S2: Ms Page.
    T: Who is the letter about?
    S3: Miss Miller.
    T: What experience does Miss Miller have?
    S4: She worked for Mr Grey's company as a secretary for three years. She rose to the position of Head Secretary.
    T: Why did she leave Mr Grey's company?
    S5: She moved house.
    T: What are Miss Miller's positive qualities?
    S6: She is intelligent; she was quick to understand things.

S7: She was also reliable and worked well.
S8: She was also hardworking as she often worked overtime and always polite to customers.
T: What are Miss Miller's negative qualities?
S9: She was rather bossy at times, but she was always polite to customers.
T: Do you think Mr Grey should recommend her for the position?
S10: Yes, because she's got the right qualifications.

• Present the plan, then Ss do the task orally. Assign it as written HW.

SUGGESTED ANSWER KEY

Dear Ms Page,
    I am writing in reply to your recent letter asking for a reference for Lisa Miller. Ms Miller worked for this company for three years and rose to the position of Head Secretary. She left the company when she moved house.
    Ms Miller was an intelligent, reliable employee who was quick to understand and always worked well. Although she was sometimes rather bossy, she was always polite to staff and customers. In addition, she was hardworking and often worked overtime.
    In conclusion, Ms Miller was an excellent employee. I strongly recommend her for the position she has applied for.
    Yours sincerely
    David Grey
---

26 • Present these words: **tribe, toes, necks, fitting, copper, extend, adult twins** by giving examples. You can ask Ss to look up these words in their dictionaries.

  • Explain the task. Ss do the exercise. Check Ss' answers.

ANSWER KEY

The world's shortest adult twins are John and Greg Rice of Florida. They are both **86** cm tall.

Suggested Homework

1 Copy: dialogue in Ex. 18 (p. 104)
2 **Vocabulary:** Exs 20, 21, 22 (p. 104) and Ex. 23 (p. 105)
3 **Reading aloud:** Ex. 24 (p. 105)
4 **Dictation:** any ten words from Vocabulary
5 **Act out:** Ex. 18 (p. 104)
6 **Writing:** Ex. 25 (p. 105)

Lesson 5

• Check Ss' HW.
• Workbook: Unit 10
         Click on Grammar 10

23 Correct the sentences by replacing the words in bold with their opposites from the list.

• aggressive • lazy • mean • polite • shy

1 He is so **generous** that he doesn't even give his best friends birthday presents.
2 She's very **outgoing**, so she finds it difficult to talk to strangers and make new friends.
3 You should always be **rude** in class, and put your hand up before you speak.
4 Ben is a very **gentle** person — he keeps arguing and shouting at people.
5 Sally isn't a good employee, because she's **hardworking** and never gets to work on time.

Writing (a letter of recommendation)

24 Read the letter and underline the correct words/phrases, then answer the questions.

Dear Mr Milton,
I am writing in reply to your recent letter asking for a reference for John Baker. Mr Baker worked for this company for five years and rose to the position of Department Manager. He left the company when he moved to Scotland.

Mr Baker was a hardworking, responsible employee who always did his job very well. **However/Although** he was sometimes rather stubborn, he was kind and helpful towards the other staff. **In addition/Too**, he was always very polite to everyone he met.

In conclusion/To start with, Mr Baker was an excellent employee. I strongly recommend him for the position he has applied for.

Yours sincerely,
Jean Greenwood
Jean Greenwood

1 Who is the letter from? How does she start/end the letter? Why doesn't she use "Best wishes", "Love", etc to end the letter?
2 What is the letter about?
3 Which paragraph gives a description of the employee's character?
4 What positive/negative qualities does the writer mention?
5 Why is there no physical description?

25 David Grey has received a letter from Ms Page, asking for a reference for Miss Miller, who worked for his company. She left when she moved house, and she has now applied for a job in Ms Page's company. Look at the notes Mr Grey has made, then write his letter to Ms Page, using the plan below. You can use the letter in Ex. 24 as a model.

Full name:
Lisa Miller
Experience:
• worked as secretary - three years
- rose to position of Head Secretary
Qualities:
• intelligent - quick to understand, reliable - always worked well
• rather bossy at times - always polite to customers
• hardworking - often worked overtime

Plan

Dear Ms Page,
Introduction
(Para 1) *reason for writing, name of person, position in company, reason for leaving*
Main Body
(Para 2) *character, qualities*
Conclusion
(Para 3) *general comments about person, closing remarks*
Yours sincerely,
David Grey

26 Read the sentences. Find which one contains a mistake and try to correct the mistake.

do you know...

• Some members of the Wadomo tribe of Zimbabwe have only two toes on each foot.
• Women of the Padaung tribe in Myanmar make their necks longer by fitting copper rings around them. They can extend their necks by as much as 40 centimetres.
• The world's shortest adult twins are John and Greg Rice of Florida. They are both 1 metre 86 centimetres tall.

The Hound of the Baskervilles

The Case is Closed

A hound with eyes of fire was chasing Sir Henry in the thick fog.

Is Sir Henry alive?

Yes — we shot the hound just in time. It was a real dog …

1

Look — phosphorus! Stapleton painted this dog's eyes to make it look like the hound in the legend.

2

Thank you for saving my life!

Quickly, back to the house! We must catch Stapleton before he gets away.

3

4

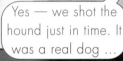

There's someone upstairs in the attic!

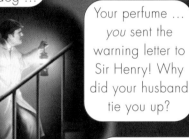

Your perfume … *you* sent the warning letter to Sir Henry! Why did your husband tie you up?

I wanted to stop him from killing Sir Henry. He used the dog before, to kill Sir Charles.

5

6

But why?

He's Rodger Baskerville's son. With Sir Henry dead, Baskerville Hall would be his.

Where is he now?

In Grimpen Mire. You won't catch him tonight in this fog.

Then we'll wait until morning.

7

In the morning … **8**

Jack put these sticks here. They show the only safe way through the mire.

There are no footprints in this mud, Holmes — and I'm afraid of getting caught in the quicksand!

9

Don't worry, Lestrade. If he's still alive, we'll find him!

10

Look, Holmes! Stapleton's scarf, in the middle of the quicksand!

Obviously he lost his way in the fog and fell in.

We'll never find his body in there …

11

Thank you again, Mr Holmes. And you, too, Dr Watson.

12

Our pleasure, Sir Henry.

Well, Watson — the case is closed.

Pre-Reading Activities

1 **Look at the pictures and underline the correct word.**

1 Watson has got <u>phosphorus</u>/blood on his fingers. (pict. 2)
2 Stapleton/<u>Beryl</u> is tied up in the attic. (pict. 5)
3 Trees/<u>Sticks</u> show the way through the mire. (pict. 8)
4 Stapleton's scarf is in the middle of the <u>quicksand</u>/mire. (pict. 10)

Listening and Reading Activities

2 **Listen and mark the sentences Yes or No.**

1 Sir Henry is alive. Yes
2 Stapleton sent the warning letter. No
3 Stapleton is Rodger Baskerville's nephew. No
4 Stapleton fell into the quicksand. Yes

3 **Read the episode and answer the questions.**

1 How did Holmes manage to save Sir Henry? He shot the hound just in time.
2 Why did Stapleton paint the dog's eyes? To make it look like the hound in the legend.
3 Why did Stapleton tie up his wife? Because she wanted to stop him from killing Sir Henry.
4 Why did Stapleton want Sir Henry dead? So Baskerville Hall would be his.
5 What happened to Stapleton? He lost his way in the fog and fell in the quicksand.

4 **Which of the adjectives in the list best describe Holmes, Stapleton, Beryl? Can you justify your choice?**

- honest • brave • mean • selfish
- intelligent • responsible • friendly
- polite • careful

Grammar
- Time Clauses

5 **Fill in: before, when, until, after or while. Which tense form is used with these words?** (The present simple)

1 We can go when you are ready.
2 You can read a magazine while you wait.
3 I usually walk home with my friends after school.
4 Don't forget to lock the door before you go to bed.
5 Don't speak to me now. Wait until the film finishes.

- Indirect Questions

6 **a) Study the examples. Which is a direct question? Which is an indirect question? How do these questions differ?**

Where does he work? – direct question
Do you know where he works? – indirect question

b) Rewrite the direct questions as indirect questions.

1 Why did he want to kill Sir Henry? Do you know why he wanted to kill Sir Henry?
2 Where is he hiding? Can you tell me where he is hiding?
3 What is he holding? Do you know what he is holding?
4 Who sent this letter? Do you know who sent this letter?
5 Who is Sir Charles' nephew? Can you tell me who Sir Charles' nephew is?

- Question Tags

7 **Underline the correct question tag. How do we form question tags?**

1 There aren't any footprints in this mud, <u>are there</u>/aren't there?
2 He has made a mistake, has he/<u>hasn't he</u>?
3 She didn't call, <u>did she</u>/didn't she?
4 They are missing, are they/<u>aren't they</u>?
5 You'll be on time, will you/<u>won't you</u>?
6 He can't do that, <u>can he</u>/can't he?
7 They didn't lie, <u>did they</u>/didn't they?
8 He is alive, is he/<u>isn't he</u>?

8 **Listen to the episode again and follow the lines, then take roles and act out the episode.**

9 **Chain story. Students, one after the other, tell the story of The Hound of the Baskervilles. Start with: *One day Dr Mortimer came to visit Holmes in his house.*** (Ss' own answers)

Holmes: intelligent – he solved the case
Stapleton: mean and selfish – he tried to kill Sir Henry and have Baskerville Hall for himself
Beryl: brave/honest – she tried to stop her husband from killing Sir Henry

Vocabulary

1 **Fill in the correct word.**

• lines • designed • overtime • located
• weighs • imprisoned • carved • support
• stunning • reputation

1 The palace is located on a hill overlooking the River Severn.
2 Jim weighs the same as Mark, but Mark looks much heavier than Jim.
3 This company has an excellent reputation.
4 The bridge is covered with carved dragon heads.
5 What a stunning outfit! Is it a designer label?
6 I can see from the laughter lines around her eyes that she has a great sense of humour.
7 The owner of the art gallery was imprisoned for selling forgeries.
8 I'll be late tonight; I have to work overtime.
9 Bridges are made of steel so they can support the weight of the traffic.
10 Who designed that new office block by the river? It's so strange-looking!

(10 marks)

2 **Underline the correct word.**

1 Tom is an <u>honest</u>/reliable person. He always tells the truth.
2 Audrey is very lazy/<u>hardworking</u>. She does a lot of overtime.
3 Tamara is so <u>vain</u>/forgetful! She never goes out without make-up.
4 Paul never remembers our anniversary. He's so reliable/<u>forgetful</u>!
5 Kelly finds it hard to make friends because she's so sociable/<u>shy</u>.
6 Mr Wallis is a great teacher. He's so <u>patient</u>/aggressive with the children!
7 Dad won't change his mind. You know how outgoing/<u>stubborn</u> he is!
8 If you want to succeed as a fashion designer, you have to be athletic/<u>creative</u>.

(8 marks)

3 **Fill in two more adjectives which can describe the following. Then describe your classmates.**

1	high,	wide, narrow	forehead
2	curly,	straight, wavy	hair
3	long,	round, oval	face
4	arched,	long, bushy	eyebrows
5	pointed,	big, button	nose
6	square,	pointed, double	chin/jaw

(See Suggested Answers section)   *(11 marks)*

4 **Fill in the correct preposition.**

1 The Pyramids were built for Egyptian Kings.
2 The Eiffel Tower was named after its designer.
3 That song reminds me of my childhood.
4 What's the Parthenon made of?
5 I expect to hear from them on my birthday.
6 I'm really looking forward to my summer holiday.
7 His wife stopped him from taking the job abroad.
8 The police say the thief is in his late teens.

(8 marks)

Grammar

5 **Put the verbs in brackets into the correct passive form.**

1 The concert hall is located in the city centre. (locate)
2 The company was founded in 1962. (found)
3 The palace was completed in 1795. (complete)
4 The statue is made of pure gold. (make)
5 The hotel is often used for business conferences. (use)
6 The Crown Jewels are housed in the Tower of London. (house)

(6 marks)

6 **Fill in the correct form of the verb: to – infinitive, -ing form or infinitive without to.**

1 A: I won't stay until 6 o'clock! (stay)
   B: Oh – I thought you didn't mind working late at the office! (work)
2 A: Will you water the plants while I'm away? (water)
   B: Don't worry. I can feed the cat, too if you want me to. (feed)
3 A: I decided to take the job in South America. (take)
   B: So, are you looking forward to living abroad? (live)
4 A: I'd love to go to the Bahamas! (go)
   B: I thought you hated travelling! (travel)
5 A: I can't stand listening to loud music! (listen)
   B: Would you prefer to go somewhere quieter? (go)

(10 marks)

7 Underline the correct question tag.

1 You won't forget to call me, **won't you/<u>will you</u>?**
2 Linda lives at no. 42, **does she/<u>doesn't she</u>?**
3 Brian isn't coming tonight, **<u>is he</u>/isn't he?**
4 They didn't lose their jobs, **didn't they/<u>did they</u>?**
5 She won a prize, **did she/<u>didn't she</u>?**

(5 marks)

Communication

8 Fill in the correct sentence, then in pairs, read out the short dialogues.

> • What is the statue made of • Why was it built

* A: Excuse me. **1)** What is the statue made of?
  B: Bronze and gold.
  A: **2)** Why was it built?
  B: To honour the people who died in the war.

> • So, tell me about yourself • Thank you for coming

* A: Good morning, Mr Taylor. **1)** Thank you for coming.
  B: Thank you for seeing me.
  A: **2)** So, tell me about yourself.
  B: Well, I have a lot of experience in sales.

(8 marks)

Reading

9 a) Read the article and put the paragraphs into the correct order.

[3] Neil was an interesting person. He was friendly and patient. He was also well-educated. He didn't like going out much. He preferred to stay at home and read or write poetry and the only sport he ever played was golf.

[4] Neil helped me to pass my driving test. We stayed friends for a while afterwards, then I moved away and we lost touch. Still, each time I start my car. I always remember him.

[1] I met Neil ten years ago at a driving school. I was learning to drive and he was my third instructor. After many lessons I still couldn't drive and it was Neil who eventually taught me.

[2] I wasn't very keen on having him as my instructor at first, as he was rather strange-looking. He was very tall and slim with short ginger hair and a moustache. He always wore jeans and a T-shirt.

(4 marks)

b) Which paragraph: gives us the person's name and job? tells us how the writer and the person met? gives a physical description of the person? describes the person's character? includes the writer's feelings towards the person? (See Suggested Answers section)

(10 marks)

Writing (an article describing a person)

10 Use the plan below to write a short article about someone you like a lot.

(20 marks)

> **Plan**
>
> (See Suggested Answers section)
> Introduction
> (Para 1) *name, how you met*
> Main Body
> (Para 2) *looks like, clothes etc.*
> (Para 3) *likes, free-time activities/sports*
> Conclusion
> (Para 4) *how you feel towards him/her*

(Total = 100 marks)

11 Listen and fill in. Listen and sing.

Our Wonderful World

There are so many wonderful things to **1)** see
In our world, in our world
Look around and I'm sure you'll **2)** agree
It's a great big wonderful world.

Have you ever **3)** been up the Eiffel Tower?
It's so very high it would take you an hour
It's made of **4)** iron which is very strong
That's why it has lasted so long.

The Pyramids in Egypt are really a sight
5) Built by slaves to a hair-raising height
They're made of **6)** stone and they look very grand
Standing there on the desert sand.

The Great Wall of China is so very **7)** long
Built by the Chinese to keep China strong
It can even be **8)** seen from high up in space
It's truly a wonderful place.

Grammar Reference Section

UNIT 1

PRESENT SIMPLE

Affirmative	Interrogative
I like	Do I like?
you like	Do you like?
he likes	Does he like?
she likes	Does she like?
it likes	Does it like?
we like	Do we like?
you like	Do you like?
they like	Do they like?

Negative	
Long form	Short form
I do not like	I don't like
you do not like	you don't like
he does not like	he doesn't like
she does not like	she doesn't like
it does not like	it doesn't like
we do not like	we don't like
you do not like	you don't like
they do not like	they don't like

Form

- We form the **present simple** with the **subject (noun or personal pronoun)** and the **verb**.
  Affirmative
- The third person singular takes **-s** or **-es** in the affirmative.
  Interrogative
- We use **do + subject + verb** in all persons except for the third person singular. We use **does + subject + verb** in this person.
  Do you like ice cream? Does he like ice cream?
  Negative
- We form the third person singular in the negative with **does not/doesn't + main verb**.
- We form all other persons in the negative with **do not/don't + main verb**.

Spelling: 3rd person singular affirmative

- Most verbs take **-s** in the third person singular.
  I run - he runs
- Verbs ending in -ss, -sh, -ch, -x or -o take **-es**.
  I pass - he passes, I wash - he washes

- Verbs ending in a **consonant + y** drop the -y and take **-ies**. *I cry - he cries*
- Verbs ending in a **vowel + y** take **-s**. *I stay - he stays*

Pronunciation (third person singular)

-s or -es ending is pronounced:
- /s/ with verbs ending in /f/, /k/, /p/ or /t/ sounds. *he eats*
- /ɪz/ with verbs ending in /s/, /ʃ/, /tʃ/, /dʒ/ or /z/ sounds. *he watches*
- /z/ with verbs ending in all other sounds. *he runs*

Use

We use the **present simple** for:
- daily routines, repeated actions or habits.
  I eat lunch at 12 o'clock every day.
- permanent states. *He lives in New York.*

Time expressions used with present simple: *every hour/day/week/month/summer/year* etc, *usually, always, every morning/evening/afternoon/night, in the morning/afternoon* etc.

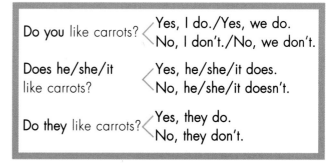

Do you like carrots?	Yes, I do./Yes, we do. / No, I don't./No, we don't.
Does he/she/it like carrots?	Yes, he/she/it does. / No, he/she/it doesn't.
Do they like carrots?	Yes, they do. / No, they don't.

PRESENT CONTINUOUS

Affirmative	Interrogative	Negative
I'm eating	Am I eating?	I'm not eating
you're eating	Are you eating?	you aren't eating
he's eating	Is he eating?	he isn't eating
she's eating	Is she eating?	she isn't eating
it's eating	Is it eating?	it isn't eating
we're eating	Are we eating?	we aren't eating
you're eating	Are you eating?	you aren't eating
they're eating	Are they eating?	they aren't eating

Form

- We form the **present continuous** with the verb **to be** and the **main verb + ing**.
  I am playing tennis now.

Use

We use the **present continuous** for:

- actions happening now, at the moment of speaking.
  I'm reading a book now.
- actions happening around the moment of speaking.
  Andy is looking for a new house these days.
- fixed arrangements in the near future.
  The invitations are ready. They're getting married next month.

Time expressions used with the present continuous:
now, at the moment, at present (tomorrow, next month/week etc, in a week etc)

Short Answers

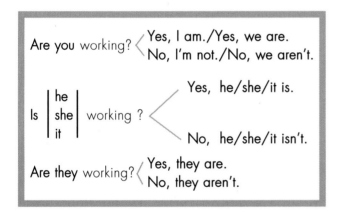

| Are you working? | Yes, I am./Yes, we are.
No, I'm not./No, we aren't. |

| Is he/she/it working? | Yes, he/she/it is.
No, he/she/it isn't. |

| Are they working? | Yes, they are.
No, they aren't. |

In short answers we use **Yes** or **No**, the **subject pronoun** and the verb **to be** in the correct form. We do not repeat the main verb + -ing.

ADVERBS OF FREQUENCY

Adverbs of frequency **(always, often, never, rarely, sometimes, usually)** tell us how often something happens. They come **before** the **main verb**, but **after** **auxiliary verbs** (do, does etc) and the verb **to be**.

always (100%)	sometimes (25%)
usually (75%)	rarely (10%)
often (50%)	never (0%)

*He **often** cycles to work.*
*He is **rarely** late for school.*

PREPOSITIONS OF TIME

Use

We use **prepositions of time** to say **when** something happens.

AT	time:	at 6 o'clock
	holidays:	at Easter
	expressions:	at noon, at daybreak, at the moment, at the weekend etc
IN	months:	in June, in August etc
	seasons:	in the summer/autumn etc
	years:	in 2001, in 1969 etc
	expressions:	in the afternoon/evening etc
ON	days:	on Monday, on New Year's Day
	dates:	on 26th May etc

UNIT 2

PAST SIMPLE

Regular verbs

Affirmative	Interrogative
I wait**ed**	**Did** I wait?
you wait**ed**	**Did** you wait?
he wait**ed**	**Did** he wait?
she wait**ed**	**Did** she wait?
it wait**ed**	**Did** it wait?
we wait**ed**	**Did** we wait?
you wait**ed**	**Did** you wait?
they wait**ed**	**Did** they wait?

Negative	
Long form	Short form
I **did not** wait	I **didn't** wait
you **did not** wait	you **didn't** wait
he **did not** wait	he **didn't** wait
she **did not** wait	she **didn't** wait
it **did not** wait	it **didn't** wait
we **did not** wait	we **didn't** wait
you **did not** wait	you **didn't** wait
they **did not** wait	they **didn't** wait

Irregular verbs

Affirmative	Interrogative	Negative
I saw	Did I see?	I did not see
you saw	Did you see?	you did not see
he saw	Did he see?	he did not see
she saw	Did she see?	she did not see
it saw	Did it see?	it did not see
we saw	Did we see?	we did not see
you saw	Did you see?	you did not see
they saw	Did they see?	they did not see

Form

- We form the **past simple** with the **subject (noun or personal pronoun)** and the appropriate form of the **verb**.
  Affirmative
- We form the affirmative of most regular verbs by adding **-ed** to the verb. *I play - I play**ed***
- Other verbs have irregular affirmative forms.
  *I **eat** - I **ate***
  Interrogative
- We form the interrogative with **did + subject personal pronoun + base form of the verb**.
  Did you play *tennis yesterday?* ***Did you eat*** *breakfast this morning?*
  Negative
- We form the negative of the past simple with **didn't + base form of the verb**. *I **didn't watch** television yesterday.* ***He didn't sleep*** *well last night.*
- We form **positive** short answers with **did** and **negative** short answers with **didn't**.
  *"**Did you phone** him?" "Yes, I **did**."*
  *"**Did you tell** her?" "No, I **didn't**."*

Spelling: affirmative of regular verbs

- We add **-d** to verbs ending in **-e**. *I live - I liv**ed***
- Verbs ending in **consonant +y** drop the -y and add **-ied**. *I study - I stud**ied***
- Verbs ending in one stressed vowel between **two consonants** double the last consonant and take **-ed**. *I slip - I slip**ped***

Use

We use the **past simple** for:
- **past habits**
  *He **wore** glasses when he was young.*

- **actions** which **started and ended** in the past.
  *Sir Arthur Conan Doyle **was born** in 1859 and **died** in 1930.*
- **actions** which happened **at a specific time** in the past.
  *He **moved** to England from Australia in 1984.*

Time expressions used with the past simple: *yesterday, last night/week etc, two weeks/a month ago, in 1988 etc* .

Short Answers

Did I/you/he etc work ...?	Yes, I/you/he etc did. No, I/you/he etc didn't.

USED TO

- We use **used to** or the **past simple** to talk about past habits or things that do not happen/exist any more. It has the same form in all persons and it is followed by the infinitive.
  *I **used to play/played** the guitar in a band. (I don't play the guitar in a band any more.)*
- We form the interrogative and negative with the auxiliary verb **did/did not (didn't)**, the subject and the verb **use** without -d.
  ***Did** you **use to go** to the cinema very often?*
  *Robert **didn't use to** eat junk food.*
- We use the **past simple** for an action which happened at a specific time in the past.
  *He **went** to Paris last month. (NOT: He ~~used to go~~ to Paris last month.*

AT - ON - IN

We use **at**:
- in the expressions:
  at school, **at** college, **at** work, **at** home etc.
- in addresses when we mention the house number.
  ***at** 36, Pine Road BUT **in** Pine Road*

We use **on**:
- in the expressions:
  on the right, **on** the left, **on** the ground/first etc floor, **on** a chair BUT **in** an armchair

We use **in**:
* in the expressions:
  in bed, **in** hospital, **in** prison, **in** a newspaper/ magazine/book, **in** a street, **in** the world
* with the names of cities, countries and continents.
  in London, in France, in Asia

Personal Pronouns

Subject Personal Pronouns   Object Personal Pronouns

Singular	Plural	Singular	Plural
I	we	me	us
you	you	you	you
he		him	
she	they	her	them
it		it	

* We use **subject personal pronouns** in front of **verbs** instead of a name or noun as subjects. *She is beautiful.*
* We use **object personal pronouns** after verbs or **prepositions** as objects. *John loves her. Listen to them.*

POSSESSIVES

Possessive adjectives

Singular	Plural
my	ours
your	yours
his	
her	their
its	

* Possessive adjectives show:
  - that something belongs to somebody.
    I am Steve. This is my car.
  - the relationship between two or more people.
    Jennifer is my sister.
* We use **your** both for the second person singular and plural.
  That is your pencil. Those are your books.
* We put possessive adjectives **before nouns**.
  This is my car. That is your jacket.

Possessive pronouns

Singular	Plural
mine	ours
yours	yours
his	
hers	theirs
— *	

* There is no possessive pronoun for "it."
* Possessive pronouns show that something belongs to someone. They do not take a noun after them.
  *That's **her** hat.* (possessive adjective)
  *It's **hers**.* (possessive pronoun)

The Possessive Case

To show possession we add:
* **'s** to a noun in the singular and to irregular plural nouns. *It is the girl's hat. (It is her hat; the hat belongs to her.) It is the women's house. (It is their house; the house belongs to them.)*
* **'** to regular plural nouns.
  This is the boys' computer. (It is their computer; the computer belongs to them.)
* **'s** to the last noun of a phrase to show that something belongs to two or more people.
  This is Jim and Jack's dog. (It is their dog.)
* We use **of** with: a) inanimate things or abstract nouns (*The windows of the house are broken.*) b) with a/the/this/that + noun + of + possessive (*He's a friend of mine.*)

UNIT 3

PRESENT PERFECT

Regular verbs

Affirmative		Interrogative
Long form	Short form	
I **have** played	I**'ve** played	**Have** I played?
you **have** played	you**'ve** played	**Have** you played?
he **has** played	he**'s** played	**Has** he played?
she **has** played	she**'s** played	**Has** she played?
it **has** played	it**'s** played	**Has** it played?
we **have** played	we**'ve** played	**Have** we played?
you **have** played	you**'ve** played	**Have** you played?
they **have** played	they**'ve** played	**Have** they played?

Negative	
Long form	Short form
I **have not** played	I **haven't** played
you **have not** played	you **haven't** played
he **has not** played	he **hasn't** played
she **has not** played	she **hasn't** played
it **has not** played	it **hasn't** played
we **have not** played	we **haven't** played
you **have not** played	you **haven't** played
they **have not** played	they **haven't** played

Irregular verbs

Affirmative		Interrogative
Long form	Short form	
I **have** caught	I**'ve** caught	**Have** I caught?
you **have** caught	you**'ve** caught	**Have** you caught?
he **has** caught	he**'s** caught	**Has** he caught?
she **has** caught	she**'s** caught	**Has** she caught?
it **has** caught	it**'s** caught	**Has** it caught?
we **have** caught	we**'ve** caught	**Have** we caught?
you **have** caught	you**'ve** caught	**Have** you caught?
they **have** caught	they**'ve** caught	**Have** they caught?

Negative	
Long form	Short form
I **have not** caught	I **haven't** caught
you **have not** caught	you **haven't** caught
he **has not** caught	he **hasn't** caught
she **has not** caught	she **hasn't** caught
it **has not** caught	it **hasn't** caught
we **have not** caught	we **haven't** caught
you **have not** caught	you **haven't** caught
they **have not** caught	they **haven't** caught

Form

- We form the **present perfect** with the auxiliary verb **have/has** and the **past participle** of the main verb.

- We usually form the past participle of regular verbs by adding **-ed** to the verb. *look - look**ed*** Other verbs have irregular forms. *catch - **caught***
- We form questions by putting **have/has** before the subject. *Has she checked her tickets?* *Have you washed the dishes?*
- We form negations by putting **not** between **have/has** and the past participle. *She **has not/hasn't checked** her tickets.* *You **have not/haven't washed** the dishes.*

Use

We use the **present perfect** to:

- talk about **an action** which **started in the past** and **continues up to the present**. *I **have worked** here for the last four months. (=I still work here.)*
- talk about **a past action which has a visible result in the present**. *Look at her. She is sad. She **has failed** the exam.*
- refer to an **experience**. *Have you **ever been** to Prague?*
- refer to **an action which happened at an unstated time in the past**. The action is more important than the time. *I've **been** to England twice. (When? We don't know.)*

Time expressions used with the present perfect: *just, already, yet, for, since, ever, never, etc.*

EVER/NEVER

- We use **ever** in questions and statements with the present perfect. *Have you **ever** visited Budapest? Budapest is the best city I've **ever** visited.*
- We use **never** in statements with the present perfect. *I've **never** visited Hungary. (I haven't visited Hungary.)*

ALREADY/YET

- We use **already** in positive statements and questions. *"Have you cleaned the kitchen **already**?" "Yes, I have. I've **already** cleaned it."*

- We use **yet** in questions and negations.
  *"Have you done your homework **yet**?"*
  *"**No**, I haven't. I have**n't** done my homework **yet**."*

JUST

- We use **just** in statements to show that an action finished only a few minutes earlier.
  "Have you finished your lunch yet?"
  *"Yes, I've **just** finished it."*

FOR/SINCE

- We use **for** to express duration.
  *He has lived here **for** five years.*

- We use **since** to state a starting point.
  *She has lived here **since** 1992.*

PRESENT PERFECT vs PAST SIMPLE

- We use the **present perfect** for an action which started in the past and continues to the present.
  *He **has been** in Lisbon for ten years. (He went to Lisbon ten years ago and he is still there.)*

- We use the **past simple** for an action which started and finished in the past.
  *She **was** in Lisbon for ten years. (She went to Lisbon ten years ago but she left. She isn't in Lisbon any more.)*

PREPOSITIONS OF PLACE

- We use **prepositions of place** to say where somebody or something is.

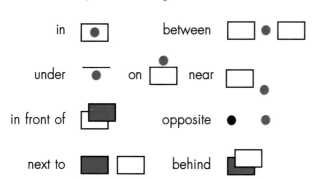

UNIT 4

PAST CONTINUOUS

Form

- We form the **past continuous** with **was/were** (past tense of the verb "to be") and add **-ing** to the base form of the main verb.

Affirmative:	I **was** standing, you **were** standing, he **was** standing etc
Negative:	I **wasn't** standing, you **weren't** standing, he **wasn't** standing etc
Interrogative:	**Was** I standing?, **Were** you standing?, **Was** he standing? etc
Short answers:	Yes, I/he/she/it **was**. Yes, you/we/they **were**. No, I/he/she/it **wasn't**. No, you/we/they **weren't**.

Use

We use the **past continuous** for:

- two or more actions happening at the same time in the past. *I **was reading** a book while John **was watching** television.*
- an action which was in progress when another action interrupted it. We use the past continuous for the action in progress (longer action) and the past simple for the action that interrupted it. (shorter action) *She **was leaving** the house when the telephone **rang**.*
- an action in progress at a stated time in the past. *Jane **was watching** television at 8 o'clock last night.*
- background information in a story. *It **was snowing** heavily when Tom left home yesterday morning.*

> Time expressions used with the past continuous: *while, when, as, all day/night/morning, all day, yesterday, etc*

ADJECTIVES/ADVERBS
Adjectives

Form

- **Adjectives** have the **same** form in the singular and plural. *a **red** car - two **red** cars*

Use

- **Adjectives** describe nouns. *a hot day, a perfect plan* Adjectives **go before nouns**. They can also be **used after** the verb **to be** and **after verbs** such as: **look, smell, sound, feel, taste**, etc. *Jane is slim. John looks happy.*
  Something smells good.

Adverbs

Form

- We usually form **adverbs** by adding **-ly** to the adjective. *beautiful - beautifully*
- When the adjective ends with a **consonant + y**, we drop **-y** and add **-ily** to form the adverb. *lucky - luckily*
- When the adjective ends in **-le** we drop **-e** and **- y**. *simple - simply*.
- Some adverbs have the same form as their adjectives.
  long ➡ *long, fast* ➡ *fast, early* ➡ *early*
  Note: *good* ➡ *well*

Use

- **Adverbs** usually describe verbs. *He walks slowly.* Adverbs can **show manner** (how), **place** (where), **time** (when) and **frequency** (how often). Adverbs usually **go after verbs**.
  He speaks *loudly*. *(How does he speak? Loudly-manner)*
  He went *upstairs*. *(Where did he go? Upstairs - place)*
  She left *early*. *(When did she leave? Early - time)*
  He visits us *every week*. *(How often does he visit us? Every week - frequency)*

CAN/MAY (permission)

- We use **can** to **ask for** or **give permission** when we **know the person well**.
  Can I leave now? You can leave now.
- We use **may** to **ask for** or **give permission** when we **don't know the person well**.
  May I come in? You may come in.

UNIT 5

BE GOING TO

Affirmative:	I am/You are/He is etc going to cross the road.
Negative:	I'm not/You aren't/He isn't etc going to cross the road.
Interrogative:	Am I/Are you/Is he etc going to to cross the road?
Short answers:	Yes, I am/you are/he is etc. No, I'm not/you aren't/he isn't etc.

Form

- We form the affirmative with the verb **to be + going to** and the **base form of the verb**.
  She is going to write a book.
- We form questions by putting the verb **to be** before the subject pronoun.
  Is she going to write a book?
- We form negations by putting **not** after the verb to be. *She is not/isn't going to write a book.*

Use

We use **be going to**:
- for **plans** and **intentions**.
  I am going to fly to Barbados next week.
  What are you going to wear tonight, Jean?
- for **predictions** based on what we see or we know.
  She is going to have an accident. (She is driving very fast.)

WILL

Affirmative		Interrogative
Long form	**Short form**	
I will go	I'll go	Will I go?
you will go	you'll go	Will you go?
he will go	he'll go	Will he go?
she will go	she'll go	Will she go?
it will go	it'll go	Will it go?
we will go	we'll go	Will we go?
you will go	you'll go	Will you go?
they will go	they'll go	Will they go?

Negative	
Long form	Short form
I will not go	I won't go
you will not go	you won't go
he will not go	he won't go
she will not go	she won't go
it will not go	it won't go
we will not go	we won't go
you will not go	you won't go
they will not go	they won't go

Short Answers

Will I/you/he etc help me?	Yes, I/you/he etc will.
	No, I/you/he etc won't.

Form

- We form the **future simple** with **will** and the **base form of the verb**. *He will go to the supermarket.*
- We form questions by putting **will** before the subject pronoun. *Will he go to the supermarket? Will they go to the cinema?*
- We form negations by putting **not** after will. *They will not/won't go to the cinema.*

Use

We use **will**:
- to make **predictions** based on what we believe or think. We usually use **will** with **I think, I believe, I expect** and **probably**. *I expect she'll be here at 9 o'clock tomorrow morning.*
- to make **on-the-spot decisions**. *"The phone is ringing." "I'll answer it."*
- to make a **promise**. *I'll buy you a computer.*

Time expressions used with the future simple: *tomorrow, soon, next week/month/etc, the day after tomorrow etc.*

PRESENT CONTINUOUS (future meaning)

We can use the **present continuous** for **actions we have already arranged to do in the near future** (fixed arrangements). *I am seeing the dentist tomorrow. I've already made an appointment.*

UNIT 6

COUNTABLE - UNCOUNTABLE NOUNS

- **Countable nouns** are nouns which we **can count**. They have singular and plural forms. *one apple - two apples - three apples etc*
- **Uncountable nouns** are nouns which we **cannot count**. Uncountable nouns have only singular forms. These nouns include:
  food: salt, cream, bread, cereal, rice, cheese etc
  drinks: tea, lemonade, water, milk, coffee etc
- We can use the following nouns in front of some uncountable nouns to show quantity:

> a **bottle** of water, a **glass** of milk, a **carton** of orange juice, a **cup** of tea, a **bowl** of soup, a **packet** of crisps, a **slice** of cake, a **loaf** of bread, a **kilo** of potatoes

A/AN/SOME/ANY

	Singular	Plural	Uncountable Nouns
Affirmative	There is **an** orange.	There are **some** apples.	There is **some** milk.
Negative	There isn't **an** orange.	There aren't **any** apples.	There isn't **any** milk.
Interrogative	Is there **an** orange?	Are there **any** apples?	Is there **any** milk?

- We use **a/an** in all forms (affirmative, negative and interrogative) with countable nouns in the singular.
  There is a horse. There isn't a cat. Is there a dog?
- We use **some** in the **affirmative** with **countable nouns in the plural** and with **uncountable nouns**.
  I want some oranges and some milk.
- We use **any** in the **negative** and the **interrogative** with both **countable nouns in the plural** and **uncountable nouns**.
  Are there any lemons in the fridge?
  There isn't any salt.

Note: We use **some** in the interrogative for **offers** or **requests**.
Would you like some coffee? (offer)
Can I have some sugar, please? (request)

A FEW/A LITTLE

- We use **a few** (=not many; some) with countable nouns. *She took **a few days** off work.*
- We use **a little** (=not much; some) with uncountable nouns. *Can I have **a little cream** in my coffee?*

PLURALS

- Most nouns take **-s** to form their plural. *book → books, teacher → teachers*
- Nouns ending in **-s, -ss** or **-x** take **-es** to form their plural. *bus → buses, dress → dresses*
- Nouns ending in a **vowel + y** take **-s** in the plural. *boy → boys, toy → toys*
- Nouns ending in a **consonant + y** drop the **-y** and take **-ies**. *diary → diaries, fairy → fairies*
- Nouns ending in **-f** or **-fe**, drop the -f or -fe and take **-ves** in the plural. *wolf → wolves, knife → knives*
  However, some nouns ending in -f or -fe take only **-s**. *roof → roofs, giraffe → giraffes*

Irregular Forms			
Singular	Plural	Singular	Plural
man	men	foot	feet
woman	women	tooth	teeth
child	children	goose	geese
person	people		

THIS - THESE / THAT - THOSE

- We use **this/these** to talk about or point to people, animals or things which are near us.
- We use **that/those** to talk about or point to people, animals or things which are far away from us.
  This is my book and that is my pencil box.

UNIT 7

CONDITIONAL - TYPE 0/TYPE 1

Form

If clause		main clause	
If + present simple	→	present simple	Type 0
*If you **heat** water to 100°C, it **boils**.*			

If clause	main clause	
If + present simple	→ will/can/must/etc + bare infinitive **or** imperative	Type 1
*If you **study** hard, you'**ll pass** the exam.*		
*If you **don't like** it, **don't eat** it.*		

Use

- We use the **conditional Type 0** to say something which is always true (law of nature), or to talk about something that always happens as a result of something else.
  We can use **when** instead of **if**.
  *If/When the temperature **drops** below 0°C, water **becomes** ice. (law of nature)*
  *If/When I have a big lunch, I always **feel** sleepy.*
- We use the **conditional Type 1** to talk about **a real or very probable situation in the present or future.**
- We can use **unless** instead of **if ... not** in the -if-clause. The verb is always in the affirmative after unless.
  *If you **don't** hurry up, we'll be late.*
  Unless you hurry up, we'll be late.
  When the if-clause comes before the **main clause**, we separate them with a comma. When the **main clause** comes before the **if-clause** then we do not separate them with a comma.

COMPARISONS OF ADJECTIVES/ADVERBS

	Adjective	Comparative	Superlative
one - syllable adjectives	fast / long / thin	faster / longer / thinner	the fastest / the longest / the thinnest
-y adjectives	busy	busier	the busiest
adjectives with two or more syllables	beautiful	more beautiful	the most beautiful
irregular forms	good / bad / much / many / little / far	better / worse / more / less / farther/ further	the best / the worst / the most / the least / the farthest/ the furthest

Form

- One-syllable adjectives add -(e)r/-(e)st to form their comparative and superlative forms.
  *small - smaller (than) - **the smallest** (of/in),*
  *rare - rarer (than) - **the rarest** (of/in)*
- Adjectives of two or more syllables take **more/most**.
  *useful - **more useful** (than) - **the most** useful (of/in)*
- Adverbs having the same form as their adjectives add **-er/-est**. *fast - faster (than) - **the fastest** (of/in)*

Spelling

- **One-syllable** adjectives **ending in a vowel + a consonant double the consonant.**
  thin - thinner (than) - the thinnest (of/in)
- **Two-syllable** adjectives **ending in a consonant + y replace -y with -ie.** *crazy - crazier (than) - the craziest (of/in)*
- **Two-syllable** adjectives **ending in -w add -er/-est.**
  *shallow - shallower (than) - **the shallowest** (of/in)*

Use

- We use **the comparative form** to compare two **people, things, places** etc. We usually use **than** with comparative adjectives.
  *Aeroplanes are **faster than** trains.*
- We use **the superlative form** to compare one **person or thing with more than one person or thing in the same group.** We use **the ... of/in** with superlative adjectives. *Everest is **the highest** mountain **of** all. He is **the tallest student in** the class.*
- We use **(not) as + adjective + as** to say that **two people, places or things are/are not similar.** *My mother **is not as old as** my father.*
- We also use **much + comparative form + than**.
  *A lorry is **much bigger than** a car.*
- We use **less + adjective + than** for two persons, things or places. *The red dress is **less expensive than** the blue one.*

- **Adverbs** form their comparative and superlative forms in the same way as adjectives. Study the table.

	Adverb	Comparative	Superlative
short adverbs	soon early	sooner earlier	soonest earliest
longer adverbs	carefully	more carefully	most carefully
irregular forms	badly well many/much little	worse better more less	worst best most least

RELATIVES - WHO/WHICH/THAT/WHERE/WHOSE

- We use **who** to refer to **people**.
  *I met a man **who** was a scientist.*
- We use **which/that** to refer to **things**. *This is the necklace **which** John bought me.*
- We use **where** to refer to **places**. *I want to live in a place **where** it's hot and sunny.*
- We use the relative pronoun **whose** to refer to **possession**. *"**Whose** is this coat?" "It's Jane's."*

UNIT 8

IMPERATIVE

Form

- We form the **imperative** with the main verb without a subject. ***Close** the window!*
- We form the **negative imperative** with **do not/don't** and the main verb. ***Don't sit** there!*

Use

We use the **imperative** to:
- give orders: *Put that down!*
- give instructions: *Sign here.*
- offer something: *Have a biscuit.*
- make a request: *Sit down, please.*

SHOULD/SHOULDN'T

- We use **should/shouldn't** to give advice.
  *You **should** eat healthily.*
  *You **shouldn't** eat lots of sweets.*

HAVE TO/DON'T HAVE TO

- We use **have to** to express necessity.
  *You **have to** tidy your room. (It's necessary.)*
- We use **do not have to** to say that it is not necessary for something to happen. (absence of necessity) *You **don't have to** come to the theatre. (It isn't necessary for you to come to the theatre, but you can if you want to.)*

MUST/MUSTN'T

- We use **must** to express a rule. (obligation)
  *You **must** come to class on time.*
- We use **must/mustn't** to express very strong advice.
  *You **must** wear a seat belt. (It's very important that you wear a seat belt).*
  *You **mustn't** swim in the lake. (It's very important that you don't swim in the lake.)*
- We also use **mustn't** to express prohibition.
  *You **mustn't** drive fast on this road. (It's illegal.)*

CAN/CAN'T

- We use **can** to **ask for** or **give permission**.
  *Can I borrow this? You **can** leave now.*
- We use **can't** to **refuse permission**.
  *I'm afraid you **can't** come in here.*
- We also use **can** to **make a request** or **make a suggestion**.
  Can you help me carry this box, please?
  *We **can** go to the cinema later.*
- We use **could** to **ask for permission, make a request** or **make a suggestion** when we want to be more polite.
  Could I ask you a question? (asking for permission)
  Could you tell him I called. (making a request)
  *You **could** talk to the manager about it. (making a suggestion)*

SOME/ANY/NO + COMPOUNDS

Affirmative			
Determiners	Pronouns		Adverbs
	people	things	places
some	someone/ somebody	something	somewhere

Interrogative			
Determiners	Pronouns		Adverbs
	people	things	places
any	anyone/ anybody	anything	anywhere

Negative			
Determiners	Pronouns		Adverbs
	people	things	places
no/not any	no one/ anyone/ nobody/ anybody	nothing/ anything	nowhere/ anywhere

- We normally use **some** and **its compounds** (someone, something, etc.) in **affirmative** sentences. We can also use them in questions to **make an offer** or **a request**. *There's **something** on the chair.*
  *Would you like **some** coffee? (offer)*
  *Can I have **some** biscuits? (request)*
- We use **any** and **its compounds** (anyone, anything, etc) in **questions** and **negative** sentences.
  *Is **anybody** here? Is there **any** milk left in the fridge?*
  *I don't think there's **anything** on the table.*
  Note: We can use **some** and its compounds in questions when we expect a positive answer.
  Compare: *Is **someone** there? (I expect there is.)*
  but: *Is **anyone** there? (I'm asking in general.)*
- When we use **any, anyone/anybody, anything** and **anywhere** in affirmative statements, there is a difference in meaning.
  a) *You can take **any** book you want. (It doesn't matter which.)*
  b) ***Anyone/Anybody** can ride a bicycle. (Everybody can do it because it's easy.)*
  c) *You can buy **anything** you want. (It doesn't matter what.)*
  d) *We can travel **anywhere** you want. (It doesn't matter where.)*
- We can use **any** and **its compounds** after **if** in affirmative sentences. *Call me **if anybody** comes.*
- We can also use **any** and **its compounds** with **negative words** (hardly, never, without, seldom, rarely, etc)
  *I **hardly** know **anybody** in the neighbourhood.*

HAVE BEEN/HAVE GONE

- The present perfect of the verb **go** has two forms: **have gone** and **have been**.
- We use **have gone** to express the fact that a person went somewhere and is **still there**.
  *Martha **has gone** to Paris. (She is still there.)*
- We use **have been** to express the fact that a person went somewhere, but is **not there now**.
  *Bill **has been** to Paris. (He went to Paris, but now he has left; he isn't there any more.)*

UNIT 9

THE PASSIVE

Form

- We form **the passive** with the verb **to be** and the past participle of the main verb.

Active	Passive
They **make** cars in Japan.	Cars **are made** in Japan.
They **made** a speech.	A speech **was made**.

- We form negations with the word **not**.
  *The door **wasn't locked** this morning.*
- We form questions by putting the verb **to be** before the subject.
  ***Is this cheese** made in Holland?*

Use

- We use **the passive** when we want **to show that the action of the verb is more important than the person who carries out the action** (the agent).
  *The lost dog **was found** yesterday.*
- The agent is introduced with **by** and is mentioned only when it is important.
  *E.T. was directed **by Steven Spielberg**.*
  We do not mention the agent when:
  - it is unknown. *The picture was stolen last night.*
  - it is unimportant. *Dinner is served at 5pm.*
  - it is obvious. *He was arrested.* (obviously by the police)

Changing from Active into Passive

- The object of the active sentence becomes the subject in the passive sentence.
- The active verb changes into a passive form.
- The subject of the active sentence becomes the agent.

	Subject	Verb	Object
Active	Tim	broke	the vase.
	Subject	Verb	Agent
Passive	The vase	was broken	by Tim.

THE DEFINITE ARTICLE

We use **the** with:
- nouns that are mentioned for a second time or are already known.
  *I bought a jumper yesterday. **The** jumper is black.*
- nouns which are unique.
  *the Eiffel Tower, **the** Earth, **the** sky, etc*
- the names of rivers, seas, oceans, mountain ranges, deserts, groups of islands and countries that include the words 'state', 'kingdom' etc. *the Seine, **the** Atlantic, **the** Sahara, **the** United Kingdom, etc*
- the names of musical instruments.
  *the piano, **the** trumpet, etc*
- the names of hotels, theatres, cinemas, ships, organisations, newspapers and museums.
  *the Ritz, **the** Titanic, **the** Times, etc*
- nationality words and family names.
  *the Dutch, **the** Browns, etc*
- titles when the person's name is not mentioned.
  *the Queen, **the** President, etc*
- the words *morning, afternoon* and *evening*.
  *I get up at 6 o'clock in **the** morning every day.*

We don't use **the** with:
- proper nouns (names of people, places, organisations, etc). *This is John. He's from London.* [Note: common nouns are nouns such as book, tree, etc which are not the names of particular people or things.]
- plural nouns when talking in general.
  Leopards live in the wild.
- names of countries, cities, streets, parks, mountains, islands, lakes and continents.
  Spain, Moss Road, Everest, Lake Superior, etc
- names of meals and games or sports.
  breakfast, football, etc
- the words *this/that/these/those*. *This is my mum.*
- possessive adjectives or the possessive case.
- titles when the person's name is mentioned.
  Queen Elizabeth, President Bush, etc
- the words *school, church, bed, hospital, prison, home*, when talking about their purpose.
  *Jane is in **hospital**. (She is a patient.) Paul went to **the hospital** to visit Jane. (He isn't a patient.)*

PREPOSITIONS OF MOVEMENT

Use

- We use **prepositions of movement** to **show the direction** in which somebody or something is moving.

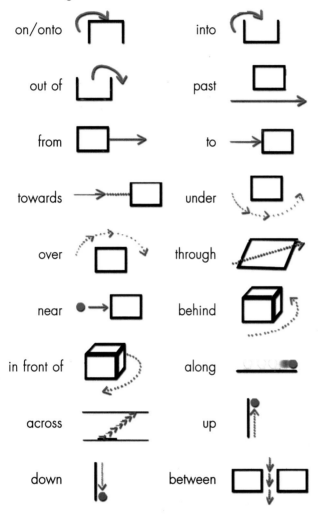

on/onto

out of

from

towards

over

near

in front of

across

down

into

past

to

under

through

behind

along

up

between

Note: When we talk about a means of transport, we use the preposition **by** e.g. *by plane, car, bus, train, boat,* BUT **on foot**.

When there is an article (**a, an, the**), a possessive adjective (**my, your,** etc.) or the possessive case before the means of transport, we do not use the preposition **by**.

e.g. *on the plane* (**Not:** ~~by~~ *the plane*),
in my car (**Not:** ~~by~~ *my car*)
on the 4 o' clock bus/in a taxi/
on the plane/in Jane's car

UNIT 10

TO-INFINITIVE/-ING FORM
Form

- We use **to -infinitive** after these verbs:
decide, want, would like, would love, etc
I'd like to go to the party.
- We use the **-ing form** after these verbs: **love, enjoy, like, hate, don't, mind,** etc
I hate dancing.
- We use **infinitive** without **to** after modal verbs **might, can,** etc and the verbs **let** and **make.** (in the active voice.)
We can go to the cinema tonight.
She let me borrow her jacket.
John made me watch the film.

TOO - ENOUGH

- **Too** goes **before adjectives** or **adverbs**. It has a negative meaning and **shows that something is more than enough, more than necessary or more than wanted.**
too+adjective/adverb+to - infinitive.
*Janice is **too small to ride** that bicycle. (She can't ride that bicycle.)*
*He speaks **too quickly** for me **to understand** him.*
- **Enough** goes **before nouns** but **after adjectives** or **adverbs**. It has a positive meaning and **shows that there is as much of something as is wanted or needed.**
*She's **old enough to make** her own decisions.*
*I've got **enough money to start** my own business.*
- **enough + to -infinitive** (positive meaning)
*He is **clever enough to** solve the problem. (He can solve the problem.)*
- **not enough... + to -infinitive** (negative meaning)
*He was **not fast enough to win** the race.*
- **too.... + to -infinitive** (negative meaning).
*It is **too late to change** your mind. (You can't change your mind.)*
- **too... for somebody/something + to - infinitive** (negative meaning)
*The bag is **too heavy for you to carry.***

EXPRESSING PREFERENCES

- We use:
  - prefer + -ing + to + -ing
  - prefer + full infinitive + rather than + bare infinitive
  - prefer + noun + to + noun to express a **general preference**.

  I prefer cooking to ironing.
  I prefer to cook rather than iron.
  I prefer coffee to tea.
- We use **would prefer + full infinitive + rather than + (bare infinitive)** to express a **specific preference**.
  I'd prefer to eat out rather than cook.
- We also use **would rather + bare infinitive + than + (bare infinitive)** to express **preference**.
  *Peter **would rather watch** TV **than listen** to music.*

LINKERS

- We use **linkers** to **show the relationship between sentences or parts of a sentence**.
- We use **and, as well as, In addition, also,** etc to join sentences, parts of sentences or ideas that **express similar qualities**. *John is kind **and** patient.*
  *John is kind **as well as** (being) patient.*
  ***In addition to** being kind, John is **also** patient.*
- We use **but, However, Although,** etc to join sentences, parts of sentences or ideas that **express opposing qualities.**
  *John is quiet, **but** he has a good sense of humour.*
  *John is quiet. **However,** he has a good sense of humour.*
  ***Although** John is quiet, he has a good sense of humour.*

TIME WORDS

- We express **time** with the words: **when, while, before, after, until,** etc. We do not use future tenses with these words.
  *I'll wash the dishes **before** I **go** to bed.*
  (Not: ... before I will go to bed)

- When the time word comes at the beginning of a sentence, we use a comma.
  ***Before** you go to bed, please lock the door.*
- When the time word comes in the middle of a sentence, we don't use a comma.
  *Please lock the door **before** you go to bed.*

INDIRECT QUESTIONS

- We use **indirect questions** to **ask for information in a polite way.** We use indirect questions after expressions such as: *Do you know ..., Could you tell me ..., I wonder ...,* etc.
- When the indirect question is part of a question we use a question mark.
  *Could you tell me **what the time is?***
- When the indirect question is part of a statement we use a full stop. *I wonder **what the time is.***

QUESTION TAGS

- **Question tags** are **short questions at the end of statements.** We form them with the auxiliary verb from the main sentence and the appropriate subject pronoun. *She is clever, **isn't she?***
- When the verb of the sentence is in the present simple we use **do/does** in the question tag.
  *You live in England, **don't you?***
- When the verb of the sentence is in the past simple we use **did** in the question tag.
  *They waited, **didn't they?***
- A **positive** statement takes a **negative** question tag. *He **is** French, **isn't** he?*
- A **negative** statement takes a **positive** question tag. *You **haven't** got any money, **have you?***

Intonation

- When we are sure of the answer, the voice goes down in the question tag. (↘)
  They've just moved house, haven't (↘) they?
- When we are not sure of the answer, the voice goes up in the question tag. (↗)
  You've got two brothers, haven't (↗) you?

123

Irregular Verbs

Infinitive	Past	Past Participle
be	was	been
bear	bore	born(e)
beat	beat	beaten
become	became	become
begin	began	begun
bite	bit	bitten
blow	blew	blown
break	broke	broken
bring	brought	brought
build	built	built
burn	burnt (burned)	burnt (burned)
burst	burst	burst
buy	bought	bought
can	could	(been able to)
catch	caught	caught
choose	chose	chosen
come	came	come
cost	cost	cost
cut	cut	cut
deal	dealt	dealt
dig	dug	dug
do	did	done
dream	dreamt (dreamed)	dreamt (dreamed)
drink	drank	drunk
drive	drove	driven
eat	ate	eaten
fall	fell	fallen
feed	fed	fed
feel	felt	felt
fight	fought	fought
find	found	found
flee	fled	fled
fly	flew	flown
forbid	forbade	forbidden
forget	forgot	forgotten
forgive	forgave	forgiven
freeze	froze	frozen
get	got	got
give	gave	given
go	went	gone
grow	grew	grown
hang	hung (hanged)	hung (hanged)
have	had	had
hear	heard	heard
hide	hid	hidden
hit	hit	hit
hold	held	held
hurt	hurt	hurt
keep	kept	kept
know	knew	known
lay	laid	laid
lead	led	led
learn	learnt (learned)	learnt (learned)
leave	left	left
lend	lent	lent
let	let	let

Infinitive	Past	Past Participle
lie	lay	lain
light	lit	lit
lose	lost	lost
make	made	made
mean	meant	meant
meet	met	met
pay	paid	paid
put	put	put
read	read	read
ride	rode	ridden
ring	rang	rung
rise	rose	risen
run	ran	run
say	said	said
see	saw	seen
seek	sought	sought
sell	sold	sold
send	sent	sent
set	set	set
sew	sewed	sewn (sewed)
shake	shook	shaken
shine	shone	shone
shoot	shot	shot
show	showed	shown
shut	shut	shut
sing	sang	sung
sit	sat	sat
sleep	slept	slept
smell	smelt (smelled)	smelt (smelled)
speak	spoke	spoken
spell	spelt (spelled)	spelt (spelled)
spend	spent	spent
split	split	split
spread	spread	spread
spring	sprang	sprung
stand	stood	stood
steal	stole	stolen
stick	stuck	stuck
sting	stung	stung
stink	stank	stunk
strike	struck	struck
swear	swore	sworn
sweep	swept	swept
swim	swam	swum
take	took	taken
teach	taught	taught
tear	tore	torn
tell	told	told
think	thought	thought
throw	threw	thrown
understand	understood	understood
wake	woke	woken
wear	wore	worn
win	won	won
write	wrote	written

Word List

UNIT 1

accountant /əkaʊntənt/
achievement /ətʃiːvmənt/
after you /aːftəʳ juː/
appropriate /əproʊpriət/
architect /aːʳkitekt/
art /aːʳt/
barbecue /baːʳbɪkjuː/
bark /baːʳk/
be from /bi frɒm/
blow /bloʊ/
building /bɪldɪŋ/
camp /kæmp/
camp coach /kæmp koʊtʃ/
campfire /kæmp-faɪəʳ/
can't stand /kaːnt stænd/
can't wait /kaːnt weɪt/
canoeing /kənuːɪŋ/
(the) Caribbean /kærəbɪən/
carpenter /kaːʳpintəʳ/
circus /sɜːʳkəs/
clerical work /klerɪkəl wɜːʳk/
climbing /klaɪmɪŋ/
come on /kʌm ɒn/
couple /kʌpəl/
daily routine /deɪli ruːtiːn/
design clothes /dɪzaɪn
    kloʊðz/
diving equipment /daɪvɪŋ
    /kwɪpmənt/
double life /dʌbəl laɪf/
drama /draːmə/
duck /dʌk/
energy /enəʳdʒi/
equipment /ɪkwɪpmənt/
fancy /fænsi/
fashion designer /fæʃən
    dɪzaɪnəʳ/
financial accounts /faɪnænʃəl
    əkaʊnts/
fixed arrangement /fɪkst
    əreɪndʒmənt/
flat /flæt/
flight attendant /flaɪt
    ətendənt/
fly /flaɪ/
footballer /fʊtbɔːləʳ/
full (of) /fʊl əv/
furniture /fɜːʳnɪtʃəʳ/
garage sale /gæraːʒ seɪl/

gardener /gaːʳdənəʳ/
good at /gʊd ət/
grass /graːs/
hairdresser /heəʳdresəʳ/
half past /haːf paːst/
hate /heɪt/
helmet /helmɪt/
horse riding /hɔːʳs raɪdɪŋ/
I don't mind /aɪ doʊnt maɪnd/
ice-skating /aɪs-skeɪtɪŋ/
insurance /ɪnʃʊərəns/
introduce /ɪntrədjuːs/
journalist /dʒɜːʳnəlɪst/
kayaking /kaɪækɪŋ/
laugh /laːf/
length of time /leŋθ əv taɪm/
live music /laɪv mjuːzik/
look for /lʊk fəʳ/
look forward to /lʊk
    fɔːʳwəʳd tuː/
lunchtime /lʌntʃtaɪm/
magazine /mægeziːn/
nanny /næni/
neither /naɪðəʳ/
normal life /nɔːʳməl laɪf/
not really /nɒt riːəli/
nurse /nɜːʳs/
o'clock /əklɒk/
on foot /ɒn fʊt/
on holiday /ɒn hɒlɪdeɪ/
ourselves /aʊəʳselvz/
pack /pæk/
part - time /paːʳt - taɪm/
passenger /pæsɪndʒəʳ/
past /paːst/
permanent state /pɜːʳmənənt
    steɪt/
photo shoot /foʊtoʊ ʃuːt/
plant flowers /plaːnt flaʊəʳz/
play records /pleɪ rekɔːʳdz/
quack /kwæk/
quarter past /kwɔːʳtəʳ paːst/
quarter to /kwɔːʳtəʳ tu/
rafting /raːftɪŋ/
receptionist /rɪsepʃənɪst/
report the news /rɪpɔːʳt ðə
    njuːz/
right /raɪt/
rollerblading /roʊləʳbleɪdɪŋ/
sailing /seɪlɪŋ/
scuba diving /skuːbə daɪvɪŋ/

secretary /sekrətrɪ/
security guard /sɪkjʊəʳɪti
    gaːʳd/
see you then /siː juː ðen/
seldom /seldəm/
sense /sens/
serve customers /sɜːʳv
    kʌstəməʳz/
set off /set ɒf/
shares /ʃeəʳz/
shop assistant /ʃɒp əsɪstənt/
sick /sik/
snorkelling /snɔːʳkəlɪŋ/
so /soʊ/
spare time /speəʳ taɪm/
stockbroker /stɒkbroʊkəʳ/
stocks /stɒks/
stunt /stʌnt/
summer time /sʌməʳ taɪm/
surf the net /sɜːʳf ðə net/
surveying office /səʳveɪɪŋ
    ɒfɪs/
this way /ðɪs weɪ/
to /tu/
training /treɪnɪŋ/
type /taɪp/
typical /tipɪkəl/
underwater /ʌndəʳwɔːtəʳ/
underwater stuntman
    /ʌndəʳwɔːtəʳ stʌntmæn/
wait /weɪt/
water sports /wɔːtəʳ spɔːʳts/
water-skiing /wɔːtəʳ-skiːɪŋ/
weekend /wiːkend/
wind /wɪnd/
wooden /wʊdən/

UNIT 2

achievements /ətʃiːvmənts/
after all /aːftəʳ ɔːl/
angry /æŋgri/
arm /aːʳm/
article /aːʳtɪkəl/
author /ɔːθəʳ/
be around /bi əraʊnd/
be used to /bi juːst tu/
because of /bɪkʌz əv/
believe in /bɪliːv in/
bet /bet/
block of flats /blɒk əv flæts/

break /breɪk/
brush /brʌʃ/
bus station /bʌs steɪʃən/
celebrated /selɪbreɪtɪd/
childhood /tʃaɪldhʊd/
coach /koʊtʃ/
comments /kɒmentz/
composer /kəmpoʊzeʳ/
contact lens(es) /kɒntækt
    lenziz/
dangerous /deɪndʒərəs/
death /deθ/
designer clothes /dɪzaɪnəʳ
    kloʊðz/
detective /dɪtektiv/
fairy /feəri/
fairy tale /feəri teɪl/
famous /feɪməs/
farm /faːʳm/
feed /fiːd/
five-star /faɪv-staːʳ/
for fun /fəʳ fʌn/
foxhunting /fɒkshʌntɪŋ/
free-time activities /friː-taɪm
    æktɪvɪtiz/
game /geɪm/
ghost /goʊst/
grow up /groʊ ʌp/
Guess what! /ges ʰwɒt/
happily /hæpɪli/
hide - and - seek /haɪd-ənd-
    siːk/
historical /hɪstɒrɪkəl/
hit /hɪt/
hobby /hɒbi/
hopscotch /hɒpskɒtʃ/
horrible /hɒrɪbəl/
huge /hjuːdʒ/
imagine /ɪmædʒɪn/
intelligent /ɪntelɪdʒənt/
interview /ɪntəʳvjuː/
jeans /dʒiːnz/
jet-skiing /dʒet-skiːɪŋ/
join /dʒɔɪn/
joke /dʒoʊk/
keen /kiːn/
kind to /kaɪnd tu/
ladder /lædəʳ/
lake /leɪk/
later /leɪtəʳ/
law /lɔː/

125

Word List _____

leg /leg/
lend /lend/
lies /laɪz/
lifestyle /laɪfstaɪl/
light /laɪt/
lose /luːz/
lucky /lʌki/
marriage /mærɪdʒ/
maybe /meɪbi/
mean /miːn/
medicine /medsᵊn/
miss /mɪs/
mouth /maʊθ/
moved /muːvd/
navy /neɪvi/
neighbour /neɪbəʳ/
nephew /nefjuː/
nickname /nɪkneɪm/
niece /niːs/
nowadays /naʊədeɪz/
original /ərɪdʒɪnᵊl/
painter /peɪntəʳ/
pet /pet/
play tricks /pleɪ trɪks/
pollution /pəluːʃᵊn/
poor health /pɔːʳ helθ/
popular /pɒpjʊləʳ/
present /prezᵊnt/
pure /pjʊəʳ/
related /rɪleɪtɪd/
rent /rent/
reporter /rɪpɔːʳtəʳ/
rest /rest/
sail /seɪl/
save /seɪv/
science fiction /saɪəns fɪkʃᵊn/
seaside /siːsaɪd/
second-hand /sekənd-hænd/
send /send/
snakes and ladders /sneɪks-
   ənd-lædəʳz/
social occasions /soʊʃᵊl
   əkeɪʒnz/
socks /sɒks/
sportsman /spɔːʳtsmən/
stay away /steɪ əweɪ/
stream /striːm/
study /stʌdi/
subject /sʌbdʒɪkt/
sunshine /sʌnʃaɪn/
surprising /səʳpraɪzɪŋ/

talented /tæləntɪd/
tidy /taɪdi/
times /taɪmz/
toy /tɔɪ/
tough /tʌf/
travel /trævᵊl/
true /truː/
video games /vɪdioʊ geɪmz/
village /vɪlɪdʒ/
was born /wəz bɔːʳn/
washing machine /wɒʃɪŋ
   məʃiːn/
wet /wet/
woods /wʊdz/
world /wɜːʳld/
wrong /rɒŋ/

Episode 1
A New Case for
Sherlock Holmes

case /keɪs/
catch /kætʃ/
chase /tʃeɪs/
curse /kɜːʳs/
escape /ɪskeɪp/
evil /iːvᵊl/
fear /fɪəʳ/
frightening /fraɪtənɪŋ/
grassland /grɑːslænd/
hound /haʊnd/
inherit /ɪnherɪt/
kidnap /kɪdnæp/
land /lænd/
legend /ledʒᵊnd/
manage /mænɪdʒ/
moor /mʊəʳ/
property /prɒpəʳti/
protect /prətekt/
receive /rɪsiːv/
run after /rʌn ɑːftəʳ/
scary /skeəri/
supernatural power
   /suːpəʳnætʃrəl paʊəʳ/

UNIT 3

acre /eɪkəʳ/
adventure /ædventʃəʳ/
allow /əlaʊ/
amazing /əmeɪzɪŋ/

amethyst /æməθɪst/
amusement park /əmjuːzmənt
   pɑːʳk/
ankle /æŋkᵊl/
aquarium /əkweəriəm/
ashtray /æʃtreɪ/
attractions /ətrækʃᵊnz/
back in time /bæk ɪn taɪm/
based on /beɪst ɒn/
bed /bed/
borrow /bɒroʊ/
box /bɒks/
bracelet /breɪslɪt/
breath /breθ/
brooch /broʊtʃ/
bruise /bruːz/
brush /brʌʃ/
canvas /kænvəs/
carefree /keəʳfriː/
carpet /kɑːʳpɪt/
cartoon characters /kɑːʳtuːn
   kærɪktəʳ/
catch a cold /kætʃ ə koʊld/
century /sentʃəri/
chance /tʃɑːns/
charm /tʃɑːʳm/
childhood /tʃaɪldhʊd/
china /tʃaɪnə/
clasp /klɑːsp/
comb /koʊm/
comedian /kəmiːdiən/
credit card /kredɪt kɑːʳd/
cruise /kruːz/
diamond /daɪəmənd/
disappear /dɪsəpɪəʳ/
dot /dɒt/
dream of /driːm əv/
dust /dʌst/
earring /ɪərɪŋ/
elegant /elɪgənt/
emerald /emərəld/
experience /ɪkspɪəriəns/
faded /feɪdɪd/
fare /feəʳ/
fasten /fɑːsᵊn/
ferry /feri/
finger /fɪŋgəʳ/
firework display /faɪəʳwɜːʳk
   dɪspleɪ/
fun /fʌn/
furniture /fɜːʳnitʃəʳ/

glass /glɑːs/
gold /goʊld/
hair /heəʳ/
handle /hændᵊl/
hang /hæŋ/
haunted house /hɔːntɪd haʊs/
heart-shaped /hɑːʳt-ʃeɪpt/
hoover /huːvəʳ/
hurt /hɜːʳt/
innocent /ɪnəsənt/
jewellery /dʒuːəlri/
kingdom /kɪŋdəm/
knee /niː/
last /lɑːst/
lay /leɪ/
leather strap /leðəʳ stræp/
lifetime /laɪftaɪm/
live shows /laɪv ʃoʊz/
location /loʊkeɪʃᵊn/
lock /lɒk/
look /lʊk/
lost property /lɒst prɒpəʳti/
magical /mædʒɪkᵊl/
mango /mæŋgoʊ/
marvellous /mɑːʳvələs/
merry /meri/
necklace /neklɪs/
nervous /nɜːʳvəs/
out of this world /aʊt əv
   ðɪs wɜːʳld/
paperweight /peɪpəʳweɪt/
parade /pəreɪd/
pear /peəʳ/
pencil case /pensᵊl keɪs/
plastic frame /plæstɪk freɪm/
pleasure /pleʒəʳ/
pool /puːl/
possession /pəzeʃᵊn/
probably /prɒbəbli/
put away /pʊt əweɪ/
relief /rɪliːf/
remind /rɪmaɪnd/
rides /raɪdz/
riverboat /rɪvəʳboʊt/
rollercoaster /roʊləʳkoʊstəʳ/
ruby /ruːbi/
rucksack /rʌksæk/
sapphire /sæfaɪəʳ/
scarf /skɑːʳf/
sea turtle /siː tɜːʳtᵊl/
set /set/

shape /ʃeɪp/
shiny /ʃaɪni/
silk /sɪlk/
since then /sɪns ðen/
stare /steər/
sticker /stɪkər/
suit /suːt/
taste /teɪst/
teeth /tiːθ/
theme park /θiːm pɑːrk/
thrill /θrɪl/
ticket /tɪkɪt/
touch /tʌtʃ/
trip /trɪp/
trip over /trɪp oʊvər/
wallet /wɒlɪt/
What's the matter? /ʰwɒts
    ðə mætər/

UNIT 4

ache /eɪk/
ambulance /æmbjʊləns/
angry at /æŋgi ət/
ankle /æŋkəl/
annoyed /ənɔɪd/
answer the phone /ɑːnsər
    ðə foʊn/
approach /əproʊtʃ/
arm /ɑːrm/
at least /ət liːst/
bandage /bændɪdʒ/
bang /bæŋ/
be alive /bi əlaɪv/
beat /biːt/
Bedouin /bedʊɪn/
blow /bloʊ/
bored /bɔːrd/
burn down /bɜːrn daʊn/
bus stop /bʌs stɒp/
camel /kæməl/
cheer /tʃɪər/
clap /klæp/
crack /kræk/
cracked /krækt/
crash /kræʃ/
creak /kriːk/
cross /krɒs/
darkness /dɑːrknəs/
desert /dezərt/

desperately /despərətli/
dessert /dɪzɜːrt/
develop /dɪveləp/
distance /dɪstəns/
doorbell /dɔːrbel/
dressing /dresɪŋ/
dry /draɪ/
emergency /ɪmɜːrdʒⁿnci/
engine /endʒɪn/
enthusiastically
    /ɪnθjuːziæstikli/
excited /ɪksaɪtɪd/
exhausted /ɪgzɔːstɪd/
explode /ɪksploʊd/
fasten /fɑːsⁿn/
ferryboat /feriboʊt/
final /faɪnəl/
fine /faɪn/
finger /fɪŋgər/
fire engine /faɪər endʒɪn/
fish /fɪʃ/
fix /fɪks/
flame /fleɪm/
flash /flæʃ/
flood /flʌd/
footprint /fʊtprɪnt/
footstep /fʊtstep/
for ages /fər eɪdʒɪz/
grateful /greɪtfʊl/
gratefully /greɪtfʊli/
guess /ges/
hand /hænd/
hang out /hæŋ aʊt/
have a snack /hæv ə snæk/
hoovering /huːvərɪŋ/
hour after hour /aʊər ɑːftər
    aʊər/
hovercraft /hɒvərkrɑːft/
hurt /hɜːrt/
immediately /ɪmiːdiətli/
improper /ɪmprɒpər/
jog /dʒɒg/
kite /kaɪt/
knee /niː/
land /lænd/
leg /leg/
life jacket /laɪf dʒækɪt/
lift /lɪft/
lip /lɪp/
lonely /loʊnli/
lose altitude /luːz æltɪtjuːd/

mile /maɪl/
miserable /mɪzərəbəl/
mistaken /mɪsteɪkən/
mud /mʌd/
muddy /mʌdi/
nearby /nɪərbaɪ/
nest /nest/
newspaper /njuːspeɪpər/
notice /noʊtɪs/
passenger /pæsɪndʒər/
photo file section /foʊtoʊ
    faɪl sekʃⁿn/
plaster /plɑːstər/
pleased /pliːzd/
plug in /plʌg ɪn/
practise /præktɪs/
prize /praɪz/
race /reɪs/
radio /reɪdioʊ/
realise /riːəlaɪz/
relieved /rɪliːvd/
report /rɪpɔːrt/
rescue /reskjuː/
rock /rɒk/
rollerblade /roʊlərbleɪd/
rub sth on (a surface) /rʌb
    ɒn/
rumble /rʌmbəl/
run a bath /rʌn ə bɑːθ/
run after /rʌn ɑːftər/
save /seɪv/
scene /siːn/
scrape /skreɪp/
scratch /skrætʃ/
seat belt /siːt belt/
set off /set ɒf/
shocking /ʃɒkɪŋ/
silly /sɪli/
sink /sɪŋk/
skateboard /skeɪtbɔːrd/
skin /skɪn/
slam /slæm/
slice /slaɪs/
slip /slɪp/
smoke /smoʊk/
soaking wet /soʊkɪŋ wet/
spectator /spekteɪtər/
sprain (ankle/wrist) /spreɪn
    æŋkəl rɪst/
stadium /steɪdiəm/
surprised /sərpraɪzd/

survive /sərvaɪv/
survivor /sərvaɪvər/
tear /teər/
tent /tent/
think of /θɪŋk əv/
thunder /θʌndər/
tie /taɪ/
tooth /tuːθ/
yell /jel/
up in flames /ʌp ɪn fleɪmz/
use /juːs/
washing /wɒʃɪŋ/
wave /weɪv/
whistle /ʰwɪsəl/

Episode 2
Strange Happenings

arrive /əraɪv/
boot /buːt/
by all means /baɪ ɔːl miːnz/
cab /kæb/
danger /deɪndʒər/
follow /fɒloʊ/
happening /hæpənɪŋ/
never mind /nevər maɪnd/
perfume /pɜːrfjuːm/
pleased /pliːzd/
reach /riːtʃ/
report /rɪpɔːrt/
since /sɪns/

UNIT 5

accessories /æksesəriz/
accommodation
    /əkɒmədeɪʃⁿn/
air pollution /eər pəluːʃⁿn/
also /ɔːlsoʊ/
animal rescue shelter
    /ænɪməl reskjuː ʃeltər/
apply for /əplaɪ fər/
baggy /bægi/
bargain /bɑːrgɪn/
be away /bi əweɪ/
breathing mask /briːðɪŋ
    mɑːsk/
brightly-coloured /braɪtli-
    kʌlərd/
business trip /bɪznɪs trɪp/

127

Word List _____

cardigan /kɑːrdɪgənr/
change your mind /tʃeɪndʒ
    jɔːr maɪnd/
checked /tʃekt/
chilly /tʃɪli/
city centre /sɪti sentər/
click /klɪk/
cloudy /klaʊdi/
collect /kəlekt/
comfort /kʌmfərt/
credit card /kredɪt kɑːrd/
cruise /kruːz/
cybershopping /saɪbərʃɒpɪŋ/
daytime /deɪtaɪm/
denim /denɪm/
designer label /dɪzaɪnər
    leɪbəl/
downtown /daʊntaʊn/
dress up /dres ʌp/
expect /ɪkspekt/
experience /ɪkspɪəriəns/
fashion /fæʃən/
feed /fiːd/
fence /fens/
flashing light /flæʃɪŋ laɪt/
footwear /fʊtweər/
forecast /fɔːrkɑːst/
furthermore /fɜːrðərmɔːr/
give sb a lift /gɪv ə lɪft/
glove /glʌv/
goggles /gɒgəlz/
grow up /groʊ ʌp/
high-heeled /haɪ-hiːld/
homework /hoʊmwɜːrk/
in addition /ɪn ədɪʃən/
in that case /ɪn ðæt keɪs/
Internet /ɪntərnet/
jumper /dʒʌmpər/
ladder /lædər/
ladies' wear /leɪdiz weər/
lamp post /læmp poʊst/
lastly /lɑːstli/
leggings /legɪŋz/
long-sleeved /lɒŋ-sliːvd/
low /loʊ/
main /meɪn/
make money /meɪk mʌni/
menswear /menzweər/
microchip /maɪkroʊtʃɪp/
moreover /mɔːroʊvər/
mouse /maʊs/

need /niːd/
no way /noʊ weɪ/
occupy /ɒkjʊpaɪ/
on my way /ɒn maɪ weɪ/
online /ɒnlaɪn/
order form /ɔːrdər fɔːrm/
outfit /aʊtfɪt/
pack /pæk/
plain /pleɪn/
planet /plænɪt/
platform shoes /plætfɔːrm
    ʃuːz/
polo-neck /poʊloʊ-nek/
prediction /prɪdɪkʃən/
price /praɪs/
promise /prɒmɪs/
protect /prətekt/
queue /kjuː/
reach /riːtʃ/
record /rekɔːrd/
rubbish /rʌbɪʃ/
run out of /rʌn aʊt əv/
second-hand /sekənd-hænd/
share /ʃeər/
shop /ʃɒp/
shopping area /ʃɒpɪŋ eəriə/
short-sleeved /ʃɔːrt-sliːvd/
size /saɪz/
sightseeing /saɪtsiːɪŋ/
site /saɪt/
skin /skɪn/
slip /slɪp/
souvenir /suːvənɪər/
spotted /spɒtɪd/
square foot /skweər fʊt/
stock /stɒk/
storey /stɔːri/
straw /strɔː/
striped /straɪpt/
sunny /sʌni/
suppose /səpoʊz/
there's no point /ðərz noʊ
    pɔɪnt/
top designer /tɒp dɪzaɪnər/
treat /triːt/
trip /trɪp/
V-neck /viː-nek/
waistcoat /weɪstkoʊt/
water /wɔːtər/
website /websaɪt/
wet /wet/

what a pity /ʰwɒt ə pɪti/
whether /ʰweðər/
windy /wɪndi/
world tour /wɜːrld tʊər/

UNIT 6

amazing /əmeɪzɪŋ/
annual /ænjuəl/
bag /bæg/
bake /beɪk/
bar /bɑːr/
barbecue /bɑːrbɪkjuː/
be full /bi fʊl/
beef /biːf/
bottle /bɒtəl/
bowl /boʊl/
box /bɒks/
broccoli /brɒkəli/
buffet /bʊfeɪ/
carbohydrate
    /kɑːrboʊhaɪdreɪt/
carton /kɑːrtən/
cauliflower /kɒliflaʊər/
celebrate /selɪbreɪt/
chicken curry /tʃɪkɪn kʌri/
chicken wing /tʃɪkɪn wɪŋ/
chilli /tʃɪli/
chop /tʃɒp/
colourful /kʌlərfʊl/
corner shop /kɔːrnər ʃɒp/
cornflakes /kɔːrnfleɪks/
3-course meal /θriː kɔːrs
    miːl/
crisps /krɪsps/
cup /kʌp/
cupboard /kʌpbərd/
dessert /dɪzɜːrt/
double /dʌbəl/
dragon /drægən/
drink /drɪŋk/
fat /fæt/
fry /fraɪ/
ginger /dʒɪndʒər/
glass /glɑːs/
grill /grɪl/
grilled /grɪld/
happiness /hæpines/
health /helθ/
healthy diet /helθi daɪət/
hold /hoʊld/

include /ɪnkluːd/
Independence Day
    /ɪndɪpendəns deɪ/
independent from
    /ɪndɪpendənt frəm/
ingredient /ɪngriːdiənt/
it's all gone /ɪts ɔːl gɒn/
jam /dʒæm/
jar /dʒɑːr/
junk food /dʒʌŋk fuːd/
ketchup /ketʃʌp/
left over /left oʊvər/
lentils /lentɪlz/
lettuce /letɪs/
live on /lɪv ɒn/
loaf /loʊf/
local /loʊkəl/
main course /meɪn kɔːrs/
maypole /meɪpoʊl/
memory /meməri/
mineral water /mɪnərəl
    wɔːtər/
mix /mɪks/
national /næʃənəl/
oil /ɔɪl/
order /ɔːrdər/
packet /pækɪt/
pass /pɑːs/
pasta /pæstə/
peanuts /piːnʌts/
pear /peər/
peas /piːz/
pickle /pɪkəl/
piece /piːs/
plate /pleɪt/
pole /poʊl/
pretzel /pretsəl/
protein /proʊtiːn/
pudding /pʊdɪŋ/
pulses /pʌlsɪz/
ribbon /rɪbən/
roast beef /roʊst biːf/
saffron /sæfrɒn/
salty /sɔːlti/
sardine /sɑːrdiːn/
sauce /sɔːs/
sesame seed balls /sesəmi
    siːd bɔːlz/
side salad /saɪd sæləd/
slice /slaɪs/
soap /soʊp/

sour /saʊəʳ/
special occasion /speʃəl
    əkeɪʒ°n/
spice /spaɪs/
spicy /spaɪsi/
spring onion /sprɪŋ ʌnjən/
starter /stɑːʳtəʳ/
starve /stɑːʳv/
steak /steɪk/
stray /streɪ/
street parade /striːt pəreɪd/
stuffed /stʌft/
suitable for /suːtəbəl fəʳ/
sweet /swiːt/
take part in /teɪk pɑːʳt ɪn/
tasty /teɪsti/
tin /tɪn/
ton /tʌn/
traditional /trədɪʃənəl/
vegetable /vedʒtəbəl/
vegetarian /vedʒɪteərɪən/
village hall /vɪlɪdʒ hɔːl/
vinegar /vɪnɪgəʳ/
vitamin /vɪtəmɪn/
wait for /weɪt fəʳ/
wealth /welθ/
weigh /weɪ/
welcome /welkəm/

Episode 3
Danger on Dartmoor

accompanied /əkʌmpənid/
alone /əloʊn/
apron /eɪprən/
at once /ət wʌns/
awful /ɔːfʊl/
backgammon /bækgæmən/
bow tie /boʊ taɪ/
bowler hat /boʊləʳ hæt/
called /kɔːld/
capture /kæptʃəʳ/
chess /tʃes/
close to /kloʊs tu/
coat /koʊt/
danger /deɪndʒəʳ/
darts /dɑːʳts/
do our hair /du aʊəʳ heəʳ/
escape from /ɪskeɪp frəm/
far from /fɑːʳ frəm/
glove /glʌv/

hound /haʊnd/
in danger /ɪn deɪndʒəʳ/
in the middle of /ɪn ðə
    mɪdəl əv/
join /dʒɔɪn/
later /leɪtəʳ/
legend /ledʒ°nd/
noise /nɔɪz/
post /poʊst/
quicksand /kwɪksænd/
release /rɪliːs/
Sergeant /sɑːʳdʒ°nt/
servant /sɜːʳvənt/
shall we /ʃæl wɪ/
signal /sɪgnəl/
station /steɪʃ°n/
tie /taɪ/
top hat /tɒp hæt/
tuxedo /tʌksiːdoʊ/
wonder /wʌndəʳ/

UNIT 7

accommodation
    /əkɒmədeɪʃ°n/
afford /əfɔːʳd/
antler /æntləʳ/
as fresh as daisies /əz freʃ
    əz deɪziz/
attraction /ətrækʃ°n/
available /əveɪləbəl/
bank /bæŋk/
beak /biːk/
below /bɪloʊ/
bird /bɜːʳd/
bite /baɪt/
blue whale /bluː weɪl/
book /bʊk/
bouquet /boʊkeɪ/
break down /breɪk daʊn/
brochure /broʊʃəʳ/
bunch /bʌntʃ/
business class /bɪznɪs klɑːs/
cabin /kæbɪn/
careful /keəʳfʊl/
carnivore /kɑːʳnɪvɔːʳ/
casino /kəsiːnoʊ/
catch /kætʃ/
chance /tʃɑːns/
claw /klɔː/
colourful /kʌləʳfʊl/

comfort /kʌmfəʳt/
comfortable /kʌmftəbəl/
community /kəmjuːnɪti/
complex /kɒmpleks/
concerned /kənsɜːʳnd/
concert hall /kɒnsəʳt hɔːl/
contain /kənteɪn/
convenience /kənviːnɪəns/
convenient /kənviːnɪənt/
cope with /koʊp wɪð/
cosmopolitan /kɒzməpɒlɪtən/
cost /kɒst/
crowded /kraʊdɪd/
danger /deɪndʒəʳ/
departure /dɪpɑːʳtʃəʳ/
destination /destɪneɪʃ°n/
difference /dɪfrəns/
distance /dɪstəns/
do tricks /du trɪks/
dozen /dʌz°n/
(the) Earth /(ði) ɜːʳθ/
economy /ɪkɒnəmi/
endangered /ɪndeɪndʒəʳd/
excursion /ɪkskɜːʳʃ°n/
expand /ɪkspænd/
farm animal /fɑːʳm ænɪməl/
feather /feðəʳ/
fleet /fliːt/
florist's /flɒrɪsts/
fond of /fɒnd əv/
foot /fʊt/
freeze /friːz/
freeze to death /friːz tə deθ/
fur /fɜːʳ/
furthermore /fɜːʳðəʳmɔːʳ/
giraffe /dʒɪrɑːf/
good point /gʊd pɔɪnt/
guinea pig /gɪni pɪg/
harbour /hɑːʳbəʳ/
have a look /hæv ə lʊk/
heat /hiːt/
height /haɪt/
herbivore /hɜːʳbɪvɔːʳ/
hill /hɪl/
home /hoʊm/
however /haʊevəʳ/
hurry up /hʌri ʌp/
I'd rather /aɪd rɑːðəʳ/
ice /aɪs/
in addition /ɪn ədɪʃ°n/
in advance /ɪn ædvɑːns/

in conclusion /ɪn kənkluːʒən/
in fact /ɪn fækt/
information /ɪnfəʳmeɪʃ°n/
insect /ɪnsekt/
intelligent /ɪntelɪdʒ°nt/
itinerary /aɪtɪnərəri/
journey /dʒɜːʳni/
Jupiter /dʒuːpɪtɜːʳ/
kid /kɪd/
kitten /kɪt°n/
leaflet /liːflət/
lifetime /laɪftaɪm/
liner /laɪnəʳ/
lizard /lɪzəʳd/
located on /loʊkeɪtɪd ɒn/
loyal /lɔɪəl/
luxurious /lʌgʒʊərɪəs/
magnificent /mægnɪfɪsənt/
mammal /mæməl/
Mars /mɑːʳz/
melt /melt/
memorial /mɪmɔːrɪəl/
Mercury /mɜːʳkjʊəri/
metal /metəl/
motorway /moʊtəʳweɪ/
Neptune /neptjuːn/
noisy /nɔɪzi/
obedient /oʊbiːdɪənt/
oh dear /oʊ dɪəʳ/
open park /oʊpən pɑːʳk/
opposing /əpoʊzɪŋ/
orchestra /ɔːʳkɪstrə/
orchid /ɔːʳkɪd/
ostrich /ɒstrɪtʃ/
oversleep /oʊvəʳsliːp/
owner /oʊnəʳ/
parrot /pærət/
peaceful /piːsfʊl/
playful /pleɪfʊl/
plenty /plenti/
Pluto /pluːtoʊ/
public building /pʌblɪk bɪldɪŋ/
recipe /resɪpi/
reptile /reptaɪl/
resort /rɪzɔːʳt/
restate /riːsteɪt/
rose /roʊz/
safe /seɪf/
safety /seɪfti/
sample /sɑːmpəl/
Saturn /sætəʳn/

scales /skeɪlz/
scary /skeəri/
scenery /siːnəri/
sharp /ʃɑːrp/
shore /ʃɔːr/
skyline /skaɪlaɪn/
species /spiːʃiz/
speed /spiːd/
stare at /steər ət/
statue /stætʃuː/
steam /stiːm/
swimming pool /swɪmɪŋ puːl/
tail /teɪl/
take the strain /teɪk ðe
    streɪn/
tame /teɪm/
temperature /temprətʃər/
that's settled /ðæts setəld/
the moon /ðe muːn/
to start with /tə stɑːrt wɪð/
ton /tʌn/
tour /tʊər/
traffic jam /træfɪk dʒæm/
travel /trævəl/
travel agent's /trævəl
    eɪdʒənts/
tulip /tjuːlɪp/
unless /ʌnles/
Uranus /jɔːrænəs/
varied culture /veərɪd kʌltʃər/
Venus /viːnəs/
viewpoint /vjuːpɔɪnt/
violinist /vaɪəlɪnɪst/
wedding /wedɪŋ/
what is more /hwɒt ɪz mɔːr/
wild /waɪld/
wing /wɪŋ/

Episode 4
The Midnight Watcher

acrobat /ækrəbæt/
bark /bɑːrk/
blanket /blæŋkɪt/
catch /kætʃ/
daily /deɪli/
dangerous /deɪndʒərəs/
deliver /dɪlɪvər/
fault /fɔːlt/
find out /faɪnd aʊt/

first light /fɜːrst laɪt/
footstep /fʊtstep/
hiding place /haɪdɪŋ pleɪs/
midnight watcher /mɪdnaɪt
    wɒtʃər/
poor /pʊər/
shoot /ʃuːt/
signal /sɪgnəl/
society /səsaɪti/
watch /wɒtʃ/

UNIT 8

advertised /ædvərtaɪzd/
affect /əfekt/
AIDS /eɪdz/
air pollution /eər pəluːʃən/
alligator /ælɪgeɪtər/
appointment /əpɔɪntmənt/
argue /ɑːrgjuː/
atmosphere /ætməsfɪər/
awful /ɔːful/
be polite to /bi pəlaɪt tə/
behind /bɪhaɪnd/
bin /bɪn/
borrow /bɒroʊ/
boss /bɒs/
cancer /kænsər/
chore /tʃɔːr/
clear land /klɪər lænd/
common /kɒmən/
corridor /kɒridɔːr/
council /kaʊnsəl/
cover /kʌvər/
crawl /krɔːl/
create /krieɪt/
cure /kjʊər/
cut down /kʌt doʊn/
disappear /dɪsəpɪər/
disgusting /dɪsgʌstɪŋ/
driving licence /draɪvɪŋ
    laɪsəns/
environment
    /ɪnvaɪərənmənt/
equator /ɪkweɪtər/
escape route /ɪskeɪp ruːt/
exhibit /ɪgzɪbɪt/
expert /ekspɜːrt/
explosion /ɪksploʊʒən/
extinct /ɪkstɪŋkt/
factory /fæktri/

fair /feər/
fire extinguisher /faɪər
    ɪkstɪŋgwɪʃər/
follow /fɒloʊ/
forest /fɒrɪst/
fortunately /fɔːrtʃʊnɪtli/
get fit /get fɪt/
grow crops /groʊ krɒps/
habitat /hæbɪtæt/
have to /hæv tuː/
hectare /hekteər/
home to /hoʊm tuː/
housework /haʊswɜːrk/
How's it going? /haʊz ɪt
    goʊɪŋ/
I see /aɪ siː/
jungle /dʒʌngəl/
life /laɪf/
list /lɪst/
litter /lɪtər/
logging company /lɒgɪŋ
    kʌmpəni/
look forward to /lʊk
    fɔːrwərd tuː/
lose your temper /luːz jɔːr
    tempər/
medicine /medsən/
naughty /nɔːti/
neighbour /neɪbər/
on time /ɒn taɪm/
oxygen /ɒksɪdʒən/
packed lunch /pækd lʌntʃ/
permission /pərmɪʃən/
plenty of /plenti əv/
pollute /pəluːt/
pollution level /pəluːʃən
    levəl/
poster /poʊstər/
protect /prətekt/
provide /prəvaɪd/
rainforest /reɪnfɒrɪst/
rare /reər/
recycle (paper) /riːsaɪkəl/
reduce /rɪdjuːs/
rent /rent/
reptile /reptaɪl/
resource /rɪzɔːrs/
rest /rest/
rubbish /rʌbɪʃ/
rubbish bag /rʌbɪʃ bæg/
rule /ruːl/

same /seɪm/
save money /seɪv mʌni/
set /set/
set off /set ɒf/
share /ʃeər/
shout at /ʃaʊt ət/
suggest /sədʒest/
survive /sərvaɪv/
take turns /teɪk tɜːrnz/
try /traɪ/
understand /ʌndərstænd/
uniform /juːnɪfɔːrm/
unleaded petrol /ʌnledɪd
    petrəl/
vote /voʊt/
wildlife /waɪldlaɪf/
without /wɪðaʊt/

Episode 5
The Hound Attacks

afraid /əfreɪd/
attack /ətæk/
bushy /bʊʃi/
cape /keɪp/
chase /tʃeɪs/
deerstalker /dɪərstɔːkər/
elementary /elɪmentri/
eyebrow /aɪbraʊ/
ever since /evər sɪns/
familiar /fəmɪliər/
invitation /ɪnvɪteɪʃən/
kind /kaɪnd/
moustache /məstɑːʃ/
murder /mɜːrdər/
plump /plʌmp/
return /rɪtɜːrn/
sideburns /saɪdbɜːrnz/
straw hat /strɔː hæt/
though /ðoʊ/
wavy /weɪvi/

UNIT 9

accuracy /ækjʊrəsi/
AD /eɪ diː/
agent /eɪdʒənt/
all in all /ɔːl ɪn ɔːl/
antique /æntiːk/
architecture /ɑːrkɪtektʃər/
area /eəriə/

Art Deco /ɑːʳt dekoʊ/
artwork /ɑːʳt wɜːʳk/
attic /ætɪk/
attraction /ətrækʃən/
balcony /bælkəni/
ballroom /bɔːlruːm/
banknote /bæŋknoʊt/
basement /beɪsmənt/
bedside table /bedsaɪd
    teɪbəl/
brick /brɪk/
brilliant /brɪliənt/
building /bɪldɪŋ/
calculator /kælkjʊleɪtəʳ/
candlestick /kændəlstɪk/
carved /kɑːʳvd/
celebrate /selɪbreɪt/
cell window /sel wɪndoʊ/
chest of drawers /tʃest əv
    drɔːəʳz/
chimney /tʃɪmni/
china /tʃaɪnə/
clay /kleɪ/
clear /klɪəʳ/
coin /kɔɪn/
collection /kəlekʃən/
colourful /kʌləʳfʊl/
Commissioner /kəmɪʃənəʳ/
communication
    /kəmjuːnɪkeɪʃən/
complete /kəmpliːt/
concrete /kɒŋkriːt/
conqueror /kɒŋkərəʳ/
contain /kənteɪn/
cover /kʌvəʳ/
currency /kʌrənsi/
design /dɪzaɪn/
director /daɪrektəʳ/
disappointing /dɪsəpɔɪntɪŋ/
display /dɪspleɪ/
dragon /drægən/
dressing table /dresɪŋ/
emperor /empərəʳ/
empress /emprɪs/
entrance hall /ɪntrɑːns hɔːl/
escalator /eskəleɪtəʳ/
excuse me /ɪksjuːz mi/
executed /eksɪkjuːtɪd/
exterior /ɪkstɪəriəʳ/
famous for /feɪməs fɔːʳ/
features /fiːtʃəʳz/

fence /fens/
fine /faɪn/
fitted /fɪtɪd/
fortress /fɔːʳtrɪs/
fountain /faʊntɪn/
furnishings /fɜːʳnɪʃɪŋz/
giant /dʒaɪənt/
glass /glɑːs/
gold bar /goʊld bɑːʳ/
governor /gʌvəʳnəʳ/
grandeur /grændʒəʳ/
ground /graʊnd/
guard /gɑːd/
hall /hɔːl/
handpainted /hændpeɪntɪd/
historical facts /hɪstɒrɪkəl
    fækts/
honour /ɒnəʳ/
housed /haʊzd/
imprisoned /ɪmprɪzənd/
in the end /ɪn ðɪ end/
include /ɪnkluːd/
interior /ɪntɪəriəʳ/
introduce /ɪntrədjuːs/
iron /aɪəʳn/
item /aɪtəm/
landmark /lændmɑːʳk/
lie on /laɪ ɒn/
lift /lɪft/
limestone /laɪmstoʊn/
made of /meɪd əv/
magnificent /mægnɪfɪsənt/
mahogany /məhɒgəni/
maiden /meɪdən/
man-made /mæn meɪd/
marble /mɑːʳbəl/
marvellous /mɑːʳvələs/
mayor /meəʳ/
millennium /mɪleniəm/
name after /neɪm ɑːftəʳ/
no wonder /noʊ wʌndəʳ/
notice /noʊtɪs/
object /ɒbdʒɪkt/
observatory /əbzɜːʳvətri/
Oh dear! /oʊ dɪəʳ/
open area /oʊpən eəria/
pagoda /pəgoʊda/
past /pɑːst/
path /pɑːθ/
pavilion /pəvɪliən/
performance /pəʳfɔːʳməns/

pipes /paɪps/
pointed top /pɔɪntɪd tɒp/
porch /pɔːʳtʃ/
portico /pɔːʳtɪkoʊ/
precious /preʃəs/
priceless /praɪsləs/
prison /prɪzən/
protection /prətekʃən/
put in /pʊt ɪn/
rebuild /riːbɪld/
recommend /rekəmend/
recording studio /rɪkɔːʳdɪŋ
    stjuːdɪoʊ/
remind of /rɪmaɪnd əv/
republic /rɪpʌblɪk/
reserve /rɪzɜːʳv/
rich /rɪtʃ/
right /raɪt/
Roman times /roʊmən
    taɪmz/
royal /rɔɪəl/
royalty /rɔɪəti/
ruler /ruːləʳ/
sad /sæd/
shopping centre /ʃɒpɪŋ
    sentəʳ/
sight /saɪt/
silver-plated /sɪlvəʳ pleɪtɪd/
simulated /sɪmjʊleɪtɪd/
spectacular /spektækjʊləʳ/
spout /spaʊt/
star /stɑːʳ/
steel /stiːl/
stone /stoʊn/
storey /stɔːriː/
strange-looking /streɪndʒ
    lʊkɪŋ/
style /staɪl/
Stuart times /stjuːəʳt taɪmz/
subject /sʌbdʒɪkt/
surprising /səʳpraɪzɪŋ/
take up /teɪk ʌp/
teapot /tiːpɒt/
the Big Apple /ðə bɪg æpəl/
to be located /tə bɪ
    loʊkeɪtɪd/
to be supposed to /tə bɪ
    səpoʊzd tu/
tower /taʊəʳ/
treasure /treʒəʳ/
Tudor times /tjuːdəʳ taɪmz/

unique /juːniːk/
view /vjuː/
voyage /vɔɪɪdʒ/
walkway /wɔːkweɪ/
weigh /weɪ/
well-preserved /wel
    prɪzɜːʳvd/
wonder /wʌndəʳ/
wood /wuːd/
work /wɜːʳk/

Episode 6
An Invitation to
Murder

advise /ædvaɪz/
alone /aloʊn/
anywhere /eniʰweəʳ/
climb /klaɪm/
end up /end ʌp/
fence /fens/
fire /faɪəʳ/
fog /fɒg/
get down /get daʊn/
inspector /ɪnspektəʳ/
invitation /ɪnvɪteɪʃən/
on my own /ɒn maɪ oʊn/
perfectly /pɜːʳfɪktli/
police chief /pəliːs tʃiːf/
promise /prɒmɪs/
ruin /ruːɪn/
safe /seɪf/
send for /send fɔːʳ/
shed /ʃed/
spoil /spɔɪl/
take a look /teɪk ə lʊk/
telegram /telɪgræm/
urgent /ɜːʳdʒənt/
worry /wʌri/

UNIT 10

active /æktɪv/
adult /ædʌlt/
adventure /ædventʃəʳ/
adventurous /ædventʃərəs/
afraid /əfreɪd/
aggressive /əgresɪv/
almond-shaped /ɑːmənd
    ʃeɪpt/

although /ɔːlðoʊ/
ambition /æmbɪʃən/
ambitious /æmbɪʃəs/
appearance /əpɪərəns/
appetite /æpɪtaɪt/
apply for /əplaɪ fɔːr/
arched /ɑːrtʃt/
artistic /ɑːrtɪstɪk/
athletic /æθletɪk/
beard /bɪərd/
begin /bɪgɪn/
behave /bɪheɪv/
birthday card /bɜːrθdeɪ kɑːrd/
blond(e) /blɒnd/
bored /bɔːrd/
bossy /bɒsi/
briefly /briːfli/
build /bɪld/
bushy /boʃi/
but /bʌt/
button /bʌtən/
calm /kɑːm/
can't help /kɑːnt help/
can't stand /kɑːnt stænd/
change /tʃeɪndʒ/
change (their) mind /tʃeɪndʒ ðeər maɪnd/
cheekbones /tʃiːkboʊnz/
cheerful /tʃɪərfʊl/
clumsy /klʌmzi/
comedy /kɒmədi/
comfortable /kʌmftəbəl/
copper /kɒpər/
creative /kriːeɪtɪv/
creativity /kriːeɪtɪvɪti/
curly /kɜːrli/
customer /kʌstəmər/
daring /deərɪŋ/
decide /dɪsaɪd/
desire /dɪzaɪər/
determination /dɪtɜːrmɪneɪʃən/
determined /dɪtɜːrmɪnd/
dimples /dɪmpəls/
don't mind /doʊnt maɪnd/
drop /drɒp/
employee /ɪmplɔɪiː/
enough /ɪnʌf/
expect /ɪkspekt/
experience /ɪkspɪəriəns/

experienced /ɪkspɪəriənst/
extend /ɪkstend/
face reading /feɪs riːdɪŋ/
fair /feər/
fine /faɪn/
flat /flæt/
forehead /fɔːrhed/
forgetful /fərgetfʊl/
freckles /frekəls/
friendliness /frendlinəs/
full lips /fʊl lɪps/
fun-loving /fʌn lʌvɪŋ/
generosity /dʒenərɒsɪti/
generous /dʒenərəs/
gentle /dʒentəl/
good manners /gʊd mænərz/
graceful /greɪsfʊl/
greedy /griːdi/
hardworking /hɑːrdwɔːrkɪŋ/
have a seat /həv ə siːt/
hear from /hɪər frəm/
historical /hɪstɒrɪkəl/
honest /ɒnɪst/
honesty /ɒnɪsti/
however /haʊevər/
huge /hjuːdʒ/
in addition /ɪn ədɪʃən/
in conclusion /ɪn kənkluːʒən/
in reply to /ɪn rɪplaɪ tu/
intelligent /ɪnteliːdʒənt/
jawline /dʒɔːlaɪn/
job interview /dʒɒb ɪntərvjuː/
justification /dʒʌstɪfɪkeɪʃən/
laughter /lɑːftər/
lazy /leɪzi/
letter of recommendation /letər əv rekəmendeɪʃən/
lift /lɪft/
line /laɪn/
long hours /lɒŋ aʊərz/
look forward to /lʊk fɔːrwərd tʊ/
make-up /meɪk ʌp/
management /mænɪdʒmənt/
manager /mænɪdʒər/
middle-aged /mɪdəl eɪdʒd/
miserable /mɪzərəbəl/
moustache /məstɑːʃ/
nature /neɪtʃər/

neck /nek/
noisy /nɔɪzi/
occasion /əkeɪʒən/
open-hearted /oʊpen hɑːrtɪd/
outfit /aʊtfɪt/
outgoing /aʊtgoʊɪŋ/
oval /oʊvəl/
overtime /oʊvərtaɪm/
patient /peɪʃənt/
personality /pɜːrsənælɪti/
personology /pɜːrsənɒlədʒi/
physical description /fɪzɪkəl dɪskrɪpʃən/
play cards /pleɪ kɑːrdz/
pointed /pɔɪntɪd/
polite /pəlaɪt/
position /pəzɪʃən/
promise /prɒmɪs/
quality /kwɒlɪti/
quiet /kwaɪət/
reference /refərəns/
refuse /rɪfjuːz/
relaxed /rɪlækst/
reliable /rɪlaɪəbəl/
remember /rɪmembər/
reputation /repjʊteɪʃən/
responsible /rɪspɒnsɪbəl/
rise /raɪz/
romance /rəmæns/
romantic /roʊmæntɪk/
rude /ruːd/
sail /seɪl/
science fiction /saɪəns fɪkʃən/
sense of humour /sens əv hjuːmər/
sensitive /sensɪtɪv/
seriously /sɪəriəsli/
Shall we...? /ʃæl wɪ/
share /ʃeər/
shoulder-length /ʃoʊldər leŋθ/
shy /ʃaɪ/
sign /saɪn/
sincerely /sɪnsɪərli/
sociable /soʊʃəbəl/
sort /sɔːrt/
staff /stɑːf/
stay in /steɪ ɪn/
stranger /streɪndʒər/

strong /strɒŋ/
structure /strʌktʃər/
stubborn /stʌbərn/
successful /səksesfʊl/
suggest /sədʒest/
sunbathe /sʌnbeɪθ/
tell jokes /tel dʒoʊks/
tendency /tendənsi/
the more ... the more /ðə mɔːr... ðə mɔːr/
thriller /θrɪlər/
tip /tɪp/
toe /toʊ/
too /tuː/
top shelf /tɒp ʃelf/
trusted /trʌstɪd/
typical /tɪpɪkəl/
vain /veɪn/
wavy /weɪvi/
well-spaced /wel speɪst/
What does ... look like? /ʰwɒt dəz... lʊk laɪk/
wrinkles /rɪŋkəls/

Episode 7
The Case is Closed

alive /əlaɪv/
attic /ætɪk/
case /keɪs/
chased /tʃeɪst/
closed /kloʊzd/
footprint /fʊtstep/
get away /get əweɪ/
get caught /get kɔːt/
in time /ɪn taɪm/
lock /lɒk/
magazine /mægəziːn/
mire /maɪər/
missing /mɪsɪŋ/
obviously /ɒbviəsli/
on time /ɒn taɪm/
perfume /pɜːrfjuːm/
phosphorus /fɒsfərəs/
pleasure /pleʒər/
save /seɪv/
stick /stɪk/
tie up /taɪ ʌp/
warning /wɔːrnɪŋ/

My Daily Routine

Julie Baker is a secretary. She has a busy daily routine. She gets up at half past seven every day. She catches the bus to work at half past eight. Julie arrives at the office at nine o'clock. She works at her computer until 1 o'clock, then she has her lunch in the park.

In the afternoon, she goes back to the office and finishes typing her letters. She leaves work at 5 o'clock and goes home.

In the evening, she usually watches TV or reads a book.

In her free time, Julie has dinner with her friends on Saturday evenings and rides her bike on Sundays.

at the weekend

in the evening

BUS STOP 29/6/14

Dear Diary,

This weekend was just great. On Saturday I woke up early. I **1)** ....had/made...............

 a cup of tea, then I **2)** ....did............... my

homework. When I finished, I **3)** ....listened............... to some music, then

I had lunch. In the afternoon, Josh came round and we **4)** ....went...............

 rollerblading. It was just great. When I came back home, I

5) ....drank............... 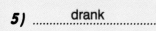 some milk, then I went straight to bed. I was

very tired.

On Sunday morning I **6)** ....painted............... my room. It was fun. In

the afternoon I **7)** ....played............... tennis with my brother. I had a

shower, then I **8)** ....read...............  my favourite comic before I went to

bed. It was a lovely weekend.

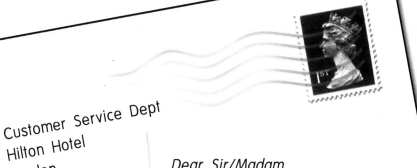

Customer Service Dept
Hilton Hotel
London
W12 8QX

Dear Sir/Madam,

I am writing to inquire about an item which I left at your hotel. On Sunday, 8th May, I left the Hilton Hotel. When I got home, I realised that my handbag was missing.

It is a black leather handbag with leather straps. There are five items inside the bag. There is a black camera, a brown leather wallet, a gold watch with a black leather strap, a pair of brown woollen gloves and a gold ring with small round diamonds.

Should you find the bag, I can be contacted on 01284 673892 from 9am to 5pm every day.

Yours faithfully,
Mrs J Mills

handbag

camera

gloves

wallet

watch

ring

- be a warm sunny Saturday afternoon last summer
- Roger Black / be at stadium / get ready run in the 5,000m final
- be an hour before the big race / reporters / approach him / they start asking questions and taking photographs
- Roger / feel very nervous / he know / he have to win

It was a warm sunny Saturday afternoon last summer. Roger Black was at the stadium. He was getting ready to run in the 5,000 metre final. It was an hour before the big race. The reporters approached him. They started asking questions and taking photographs. Roger felt very nervous. He knew he had to win.

- Roger / lift his arms / as he / cross the line
- the spectators / clap and cheer enthusiastically
- he / feel excited / happy
- he / cannot believe the gold medal / be his / at last

Roger lifted his arms as he crossed the line. The spectators clapped and cheered enthusiastically. He felt excited and happy. He couldn't believe that the gold medal was his at last.

- You should have seen what was in the box when I opened it
- I am very disappointed
- or a full refund
- I am writing to complain about

- I can't stand this any more
- Yours faithfully
- The one I received was size small
- I ordered a black woollen jumper, size large
- Best wishes

Dear Sir/Madam,

1) **I am writing to complain about** .... the goods

I have recently received.

2) **I ordered a black woollen jumper, size large** .... However,

I received a blue one. I also ordered a medium checked cotton blouse. 3) .... **The one** ....

.... **I received was size small** ....

4) **I am very disappointed** .... because I wanted

to take these items on holiday with me. I would appreciate replacement items 5) .... **or a** ....

.... **full refund** .... as soon as possible.

6) .. **Yours faithfully** .... ,

Jane Johnson (Mrs)

customer number 278-349 Z

Riverside Restaurant

7 Wyre Road

Open Mon - Fri 6pm - 12pm, Sat and Sun 11am - 12pm

Traditional Sunday Lunch

3-course meal for £15

Menu

— Starter: —

1) .... vegetable soup .... and fresh

2) .... bread ....

— Main Course: —

Choose from: roast   3) .... chicken .... and chips, grilled

4) .... fish .... with   5) .... rice ....

or roast beef and boiled potatoes.

All served with a selection of fresh   6) .... vegetables ....

— Dessert: —

A choice of: chocolate   7) .... cake ....

8) .... fruit salad .... or

9) .... ice cream ....

tiger - largest member of the cat family	
has got:	orange, black & white fur with stripes, very long tail
lives in:	forests, swamps Asia, China, Russia, India
is:	up to 2.2 metres long
eats:	deer, peacocks, wild hogs
can:	swim well, climb trees

The tiger is the largest member of the cat family. It has got orange, black and white fur with stripes and a very long tail. The tiger lives in forests and swamps in Asia, China, Russia and India. It is up to 2.2 metres long. It eats deer, peacocks, and wild hogs. It can swim well and climb trees.

crocodile - largest living reptile	
has got:	short legs, long tail, tough skin, sharp teeth
lives in:	shallow water, rivers Africa, America, Australia, Asia
is:	up to 9 metres long
eats:	small animals, fish, birds, turtles
can:	swim very well, breathe under water

The crocodile is the largest living reptile. It has got short legs, a long tail, tough skin and sharp teeth. The crocodile lives in Africa, America, Australia, and Asia. It is up to 9 metres long. It eats small animals, fish, birds and turtles. It can swim very well and breathe under water.

- drive faster than 45 kilometres per hour
- turn left
- enter here

- stop here
- park here
- give way to other drivers

1 You must turn left.

2 You must stop here.

3 You mustn't drive faster than 45 kilometres per hour.

4 You mustn't park here.

5 You mustn't enter here.

6 You must give way to other drivers.

Rock Legends

Moai Statues

location:	Rapa Nui (Easter Island), Pacific Ocean
size:	3-6 metres high
made of:	volcanic stone
when built:	1000-1600 AD
who built by:	islanders
why built:	in memory of their ancestors

The Moai Statues are located on Rapa Nui in the Pacific Ocean. They are 3 to 6 metres high. They are made of volcanic stone. The statues were built between 1000 - 1600 AD. They were built by the islanders in memory of their ancestors.

Colossi of Ramses II

location:	Luxor, Egypt
size:	around 10 metres high
made of:	granite
when built:	1304-1237 BC
who built by:	Ramses II
why built:	as a symbol of power

The Colossi of Ramses II are located in Luxor, Egypt. They are around 10 metres high and they are made of granite. They were built between 1304 - 1237 B.C. They were built by Ramses II as a symbol of power.

Chac Mool

location:	Chichen Itza, southern Mexico
size:	somewhat larger than human size
made of:	stone
when built:	11th century
who built by:	Mayan people
why built:	as part of an ancient temple

Chac Mool is located in Chichen Itza in southern Mexico. It is somewhat larger than human size and it is made of stone. It was built in the 11th century by the Mayan people. It was built as part of an ancient temple.

Rachel Blake

Appearance

early twenties – tall – slim
long dark hair – high forehead
– brown eyes – full lips

Personality

outgoing (goes to parties) –
sociable (has a lot of friends) –
generous (likes giving things to
others) – bossy at times

Free-time activities

hockey – meets friends – plays
with dog (Henry)

Dear Sue,

How's it going? Life here is very nice. I've already made lots of friends. The best one is my neighbour Rachel. Rachel is a student. She is in her early twenties. She is tall and slim with long straight dark hair. She also has a high forehead, brown eyes and full lips.

Rachel has got an interesting personality. She is outgoing. She likes going to parties. She is also very sociable; she has a lot of friends and enjoys meeting new people. In addition to being sociable, she is also generous. She likes giving things to others. However, she can be a bit bossy at times.

Rachel hasn't got much free time. When she has time though, she likes playing hockey and meeting friends. She also loves playing with her dog, Henry.

You must come and visit me. Just give me a ring a couple of days before you come so that I'm free to show you round.

Lots of love,

Anne

Guide to UK & USA Culture

Islands

tic
Ocean

Northern
Ireland
Bel

Ireland

Dublin ✪

1 Education

Listening

Listen and mark the sentences T (true) or F (false).

1 British schools start in September.   T
2 All British children finish school at 4.00 pm.   F
3 American students start school at 8.00 am every weekend.   F
4 American students don't wear school uniforms.   T

Reading

Read the texts and answer the questions. Write B (for Britain) or A (for America). In some sentences both B and A are correct. Then, explain the words in bold.

British children must go to school from the age of 5 to 16. Most children go to nursery school or **playschool** before they start school. Children attend primary school from age 5 to 11 and secondary or high school from age 11 to 16. Some students leave school at 16. Others stay another two years to **attend** sixth form.

School **runs** from September until June or July for five days a week. School starts at 9 am and finishes at 3 pm for younger students and 4 pm for older ones. Most secondary school pupils wear a **school uniform**. Most schools have **clubs** and **societies**. Students can play sports, music or visit places of interest.

American children go to school from the age of 5 to 18, but as in Britain, many children attend nursery school first. Children attend elementary school from kindergarten to **grade** six and secondary school from grades seven to twelve.

The school year is the same as in Britain, as is the school week. The hours are **slightly** different though. American students attend school from 8:30 am to 3:30 pm. They don't have to wear school uniforms **either**.

Children in America can go to summer school during the holidays to **catch up with** their work or take an extra **course**. There are also clubs and societies for students to join as in Britain.

In which country or countries ...

1 can children leave school at 16?   B   .....
2 do most pupils wear a uniform?   B   .....
3 do children have classes in the summer?   A   .....
4 are there after-school clubs?   A   B

Speaking

- What time do children finish school in your country?
- Are there any clubs and societies for children?
- At what age do you leave school?
  (Ss' own answers)

Listening

 Listen and underline the correct word/ number.

1 The Celts came to Britain about <u>500</u>/5000 BC.
2 Celts made beautiful pottery/<u>jewellery</u>.
3 Native Americans lived in <u>tribes</u>/towns.
4 Native Americans made tools from <u>stone</u>/ pottery.

Reading

Read the texts and choose A, B or C, then explain the words in bold.

The Celts

The Celts are an ancient European people. They came to Britain about 500 BC. Their **traditions** and languages still **survive** today in Scotland, Ireland, Wales and Cornwall.

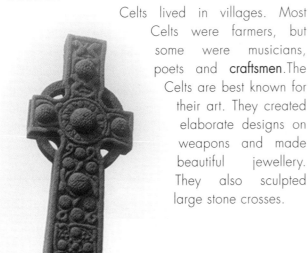

Celts lived in villages. Most Celts were farmers, but some were musicians, poets and **craftsmen**. The Celts are best known for their art. They created elaborate designs on weapons and made beautiful jewellery. They also sculpted large stone crosses.

The Native Americans

Thousands of years before Europeans arrived in America the people now called Native Americans lived there. The Native American people lived in different groups all over America. They had many different ways of life and spoke hundreds of different languages. Native Americans **lived off** the land. They **hunted** animals such as deer and buffalo and they were farmers, too. They made tools and weapons from stone and wood. They also made beautiful pottery and ornaments. Sadly, today there are only 2 million Native Americans left. Many tribes, languages and traditions have **disappeared**.

1 The Celts moved to Britain from northern Europe.
   A Right   B Wrong   Ⓒ Doesn't say
2 Celtic people lived in tribes.
   A Right   B Wrong   Ⓒ Doesn't say
3 Native Americans were very tall.
   A Right   B Wrong   Ⓒ Doesn't say
4 Native Americans were hunters and farmers.
   Ⓐ Right   B Wrong   C Doesn't say

Speaking

• What were the people of your country like in the past?
• Where did they live? How did they live?
(Ss' own answers)

155(T)

Popular Places

Listening

 Listen and choose A, B, C or D.

1 There are about .... different kinds of plants in Kew Gardens.
   A 1,600   C 230,000
   (B) 40,000   D 6,500,000

2 There is a pagoda in ....
   A Southern Florida   C Key Largo
   (B) Kew Gardens   D Key West

3 The Florida Keys is ....
   A an island   C a special road
   B a tropical plant   (D) a chain of islands

4 Key Largo is .... long.
   (A) 50 km   C 40 km
   B 309 km   D 23 km

Reading

Read the texts and mark the sentences C (correct) or I (incorrect), then explain the words in bold.

Kew Gardens

One of the most beautiful places **to visit** in London is Kew Gardens. Its **official** name is the Royal Botanic Gardens and it was once part of a royal **estate**.
Lord Capel started the plant collection in the 1600s and today there are over 40,000 different kinds of plants at Kew Gardens. There are three museums with amazing collections of rare and beautiful flowers and plants, as well as an **exhibition** which tells the story of the **evolution** of plants.
There is so much to see and the gardens are so large that it is easy for visitors to **get lost**. Luckily, the pagoda – a tall, Chinese-style building – acts as a landmark for those exploring the gardens. If you love plants and flowers, Kew Gardens is the perfect place to visit.

Florida Keys

The Florida Keys is a **chain** of islands off southern Florida in the USA. It **stretches** for over 309 km into the Atlantic Ocean.
There are beautiful tropical plants all over the islands. The largest island in the chain is Key Largo, which is 50 km long. Along its east coast lies the John Pennekamp Coral Reef State Park, which was the first **undersea** park in the US. The Overseas Highway, the longest **over-water** road in the US, joins Key Largo to Key West. It is over 200 km long. Key West is the most important island in the chain, and probably the most famous.
It is easy to see why the Keys were the setting for so many romantic films and songs. Nowadays, they provide the perfect **location** for holidays, water sports or just relaxing in the sun.

1 Lord Capel started the collection of plants in Kew Gardens.   C
2 There are beautiful plants both at Kew Gardens and the Florida Keys.   C
3 There are three undersea parks in Kew Gardens.   I
4 Key West is the largest of the Florida Keys.   I

Speaking

- What are some popular places in your country?
- What can visitors see there? (Ss' own anwers)

Commuting

Listening

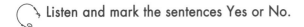

Listen and mark the sentences Yes or No.

1 In Britain the most popular form
of transport is the train.   No

2 In most cities in Britain it is difficult
to park.   Yes

3 Many American families have two
cars.   Yes

4 When visiting friends in another state
Americans prefer to travel by car.   No

Reading

**Read the texts and circle A, B or C, then
explain the words in bold.**

In Britain the most popular form of transport
is the car. People use it for everyday
activities such as getting to work, going to
the supermarket and taking the children to and from
school.

However, in busy city centres, where there are not
many parking spaces, people prefer to use public
transport such as taxis, buses and trains. In London,
the **Underground** is the fastest and most convenient
way of **getting around**.

In the countryside things are not quite the same.
People travel by car everywhere as buses and trains
are not very frequent.

The Americans, like the British, prefer
travelling by car. Families often have two
cars and many high school students drive
themselves to school.

In large cities such as Boston, New York and
Washington DC public transport is very good. There
are **overhead** and **underground rail systems** and a
regular bus service. In the countryside, Americans
prefer to use their cars to get around because they
often have to drive a long **distance** to get to school or
work.

When visiting friends or relatives in another state,
Americans usually prefer to travel by aeroplane. This
is because the USA is so huge that it can take many
days to travel by road or rail.

1 In Britain people prefer to use public transport in
busy city centres.
   (A) Right   B Wrong   C Doesn't say
2 In London, buses are the fastest way to travel.
   A Right   (B) Wrong   C Doesn't say
3 American cars are faster than British cars.
   A Right   B Wrong   (C) Doesn't say
4 Large American cities don't have an
underground rail system.
   A Right   (B) Wrong   C Doesn't say
5 You can travel across the USA quickly by road.
   A Right   (B) Wrong   C Doesn't say

Speaking

• What are the most popular forms of transport in
your country?
• How do you prefer to travel?
• Is there any form of transport that you don't like
using? Why? (Ss' own answers)

DOCKLANDS

Shopping

Listening

Listen and circle A, B, C or D.

1 Selfridges is situated in ....
A Herald Square C London
B New York D Oxford

2 Selfridges opened in ....
A 1900 C 1809
B 1908 D 1909

3 The Cellar is Macy's ....
A kids' department C boutique
B clothes department D food department

4 Macy's organises many .... each year.
A parades C exhibitions
B parties D competitions

Reading

a) Read the texts and answer the questions. Write S (for Selfridges) and M (for Macy's). In some sentences both S and M are correct.

 Selfridges

Selfridges in Oxford Street in the heart of London is one of the oldest and largest department stores in Britain. It opened in 1909 and is now a household name.
Its **fame** and **popularity came about** because of the excellent service, the huge variety of goods for sale and Selfridge's ability to **delight** its **customers**. It sells over 3,000 different **brands** over 7 floors and also has more than 10 restaurants, cafés and bars. The Food Halls are famous for their homemade dishes, fresh salads and delicious cakes. The clothes departments sell everything from the **latest fashions** to the **top designer labels** and the toy department is out of this world. So next time you're in the area make sure you **pay a visit** – you're sure to have a wonderful time.

Macy's

No trip to New York is complete without a visit to the world's largest department store. Macy's in Herald Square is right in the city centre and has everything you could ever want to buy.

There are a lot of wonderful departments to visit so you'll be spoilt for choice. The Cellar, which is the food and cooking department, sells **pots** and **pans** and delicious foods from all over the world. The clothes departments offer a **huge selection** of men's and women's clothing. There are many designer boutiques **within** each section to visit, too. Macy's Kids has got beautiful clothes and wonderful toys from all over the world. You can even shop online at Macys.com.

All year round Macy's organises events and exhibitions. The biggest event each year, though, is the Annual Thanksgiving Day Parade, famous for its giant balloons, **floats**, celebrities and clowns. Why not see for yourself?

Which department store(s)
1 has a parade every year? M .....
2 sells toys? S M
3 is in the centre of the city? S M
4 offers online shopping? M .....
5 has many places to eat? S .....

b) Explain the words in bold.

Speaking

- Are there any big department stores in your country? What can you find there?
- Do you like shopping in department stores?
- What do you usually shop for?

pumpkin lantern

toffee apples

Listening

 Listen and write one world only.

1 On Halloween children dress up as witches, ghosts and monsters.
2 On Halloween people play 'trick or treat'.
3 Thanksgiving is on the fourth Thursday in November.
4 The Americans celebrate Thanksgiving by eating a traditional dinner of turkey.

Reading

Read the texts and mark the sentences H (for Halloween) and T (for Thanksgiving) or B (for both). Then, explain the words in bold.

Halloween

The British **celebrate** Halloween every 31st October. It is also known as All Hallow's Eve, which means the day before All Saints' Day. People believed that **ghosts** and **evil creatures** came out on this night and so they tried to **scare** them **away**.
Today children dress up as witches, ghosts and monsters. They make lanterns from pumpkins and play 'trick or treat' with their neighbours. The **neighbour** can choose to give the children sweets or money as a 'treat' or have a 'trick', **played on** them. Everyone has a lot of fun.
Many people hold Halloween parties and eat sweets such as toffee apples.

Thanksgiving

The Americans celebrate Thanksgiving on the fourth Thursday in November each year. **Early settlers** in America couldn't find enough food to eat and many of them died in the first **winter**.

The Native Americans helped them the next year and they had enough to eat. They had a celebration to **give thanks** for their **survival**.
Today people remember those difficult **times** and celebrate by eating a traditional dinner of turkey, stuffing, cranberries, sweet potatoes and pumpkin pie. It is a national holiday and schools, offices and many businesses are **closed**. Families get together and many towns and cities have parades with balloons, **floats** and people in **fancy dress costumes**.

sweet potatoes

turkey

stuffing

cranberries

1 Children don't go to school on that day.   T
2 People have parades in the streets.   T
3 Children go from door to door.   H
4 Pumpkins are part of the celebrations.   B
5 It takes place in autumn.   B

Speaking

• What are the national holidays in your country?
• What do you celebrate on these days?
• Are there any special customs?
• What traditional foods do you eat?
  (Ss' own anwers)

Ben Nevis

Listening

 Listen and underline the correct word.

1 Ben Nevis is a river/<u>mountain</u>.
2 The Severn is a <u>river</u>/lake.
3 Lake Superior is in the UK/<u>USA</u>.
4 Lake Pontchartrain Causeway is a <u>bridge</u>/lake.

Reading

Read the texts and match the places to the statements, then explain the words in bold.

Ben Nevis, in the Highlands of Scotland, is the highest mountain in Britain. It is 1,343 metres high. Some parts of Ben Nevis are **covered** with snow all year round.
The Severn is Britain's longest river. It is 290 km long. It starts in north Wales and **flows** to the Bristol Channel. The Severn Bridge, which **crosses** the river, is one of the longest **suspension** bridges in the world.

Lake Superior is the largest lake in the United States and one of the largest in the world. It is 616 km long, and 258 km wide. The **deepest** part of the lake is 405 m. It is one of the five Great Lakes of North America. Its name comes from French and means 'upper' lake.
Lake Pontchartrain Causeway in Louisiana is the longest bridge in the world. It is 39 km long and it was completed in 1956.

1 It is the longest bridge in the world.   D
2 It is the largest of its kind in America.   C
3 It is the longest in Britain.   A
4 It is located in Scotland.   B
5 It is one the longest of its kind.   E

A The River Severn

B Ben Nevis

C Lake Superior

D Lake Pontchartrain Causeway

E The Severn Bridge

Speaking

- Are there any unusual places in your country?
- Which is the highest mountain?/largest lake?/ longest river?/longest bridge?
  (Ss' own anwers)

Passport or Visa?

Listening

Listen and mark the sentences T (true) or F (false).

1 People who live within the EEA only need a passport to get into the UK.   T
2 Americans need a visa to get into the UK.   F
3 People from most European countries need a visa to visit the USA.   F
4 Some people need a passport from the American Embassy to visit the USA. T

Reading

Read the texts and answer the questions, then explain the words in bold.

Thousands of people visit the UK every year. They come to have a holiday, to see the sights, to study, or to work.
People who live within the EEA (European Economic Area) only need a passport to get into the UK, but the passport must be **valid** for at least six months.
People who live outside the EEA may need to apply for a visa to enter the UK. To apply for a visa, you need your passport, an extra passport photo, and a

return ticket. You will also need to prove that you have a **permanent** address in your own country. Americans, Australians and people from Commonwealth countries do not need a visa.
(Note: Commonwealth countries are countries that used to be British colonies.)

Visiting the USA has also become easier recently. Anyone who is from Argentina, Australia, Britain, Canada, Japan, Singapore, Uruguay and most European countries do not need a visa to visit the USA. They can visit for 90 days or less. All they need is a current passport and a return ticket.
Other visitors need a visa which they can **apply for** at the American Consulate or Embassy in their own country. This is a slightly more **complicated** procedure, but not too difficult and certainly worth the effort.

1 What do people who live outside the EEA need to get into the UK? **a visa**
2 What do you need to apply for a visa to visit the UK? **passport, photo, return ticket**
3 How long can someone from Japan stay in the USA as a visitor? **90 days**
4 Where can one apply for a visa for the USA? **the American Consulate/Embassy in their country**

Speaking

- Have you got a passport?
- Have you ever travelled abroad? Where?
- Where would you like to travel? What would you need? A passport or a visa?
- Are there words in the texts which are the same as words in your language? Use these to make sentences.
(Ss' own answers)

9 Famous Landmarks

Listening

 Listen and underline the correct word.

1 Stonehenge is a large stone square/<u>circle</u>.
2 It is thought that the builders of Stonehenge were farmers/<u>sun worshippers</u>.
3 Mount Rushmore National Memorial is in <u>South Dakota</u>/Wiltshire.
4 Each head in the Mount Rushmore National Memorial is <u>18 m</u>/80 m high.

Reading

Read the texts and correct the sentences, then explain the words in bold.

Mount Rushmore National Memorial

Mount Rushmore National Memorial is in the Black Hills of South Dakota, USA. It is an enormous **sculpture carved** in **granite** on the side of Mount Rushmore.

The Memorial shows the faces of four American Presidents: George Washington, Thomas Jefferson, Theodore Roosevelt and Abraham Lincoln. Each head is about 18 metres high.

It was carved by the American sculptor, Gutzon Borglum. It was started in 1927 and completed in 1941.

About 2,000,000 people visit this spectacular **memorial** every year.

1 Stonehenge was originally built in ~~2100~~ 3100 BC.
2 The stones weigh ~~5~~ 50 tons.
3 Mount Rushmore National Memorial is a huge ~~building~~ sculpture.
4 About ~~2,000~~ 2 million people visit Mount Rushmore National Memorial every year.

Stonehenge

 Stonehenge is a **circle** of large **standing** stones on Salisbury Plain in Wiltshire, England. It was built in prehistoric times.
Work on the stone circle began in about 3100 BC. About a century later, the large circle of stones around a smaller semi-circle was **added**. These stones are 9 m long and weigh 50 tons.
It is not known exactly why Stonehenge was built, but it is thought that the builders were sun **worshippers**. What is surprising about Stonehenge is the fact that some of the stones were brought from as far as 385 km away! Today, thousands of tourists travel to see Stonehenge.

Speaking

• Are there any famous landmarks in your country? What are they?
• When were they built? Why?
• Do you like visiting historic places? Why?/ Why not? (Ss' own answers)

Listening

Listen and fill in one word only.

1 Britain has had a royal family for hundreds of years.
2 Today, the royal family is not as powerful as it used to be.
3 The president of the USA lives and works in Washington.
4 The president can serve a maximum of two terms.

Reading

Read the texts and circle A, B or C, then explain the words in bold.

In the United Kingdom the **head of state** is the **ruling** king or queen and the head of government is the prime minister.

Britain has had a royal family for hundreds of years. When a king or queen dies, his or her oldest living male relative takes the **crown**. If there are no male relatives to **take over**, the crown passes to the oldest female relative. The new monarch receives the crown at a **coronation** ceremony in Westminster Abbey.

The ruling monarch's **residence** is Buckingham Palace. His or her official duties include opening **parliament** and attending **state occasions** as well as **representing** the UK abroad on state visits.

Today, the royal family is not as powerful as it used to be, but they still have a great deal of influence over the British public.

In the USA the head of state and **government** is the president.

The president lives and works in the White House in Washington DC. Camp David is his second home and office in the Catoctin Mountains in Maryland.

The president has to perform many different **roles**. He has to make important decisions, meet with the **leaders** of other countries and control the US **army**.

The president can **serve** a maximum of two **terms**, which is a total of eight years, then he must **step down**.

1 The ruling monarch's residence is ....
   A parliament   B Westminster Abbey
   Ⓒ Buckingham Palace

2 When a king or queen dies, his/her oldest .... takes the crown.
   A female relative   B living relative
   Ⓒ male relative

3 The president is the head of the ....
   A government   B army
   Ⓒ government and state

4 The president can serve for up to ....
   A two years   Ⓑ eight years   C four years

Speaking

- Who is the head of state in your country?
- Where does he/she live and work?
- What are his/her official duties?
(Ss' own answers)

American English–British English Guide

American English	British English
A	
account	bill/account
band aid	sticking plaster
airplane	aeroplane
antenna	aerial
anyplace, anywhere	anywhere
apartment	flat
area code	dialling code (phone)
B	
bathrobe	dressing gown
bathtub	bath
bill	banknote
billion=thousand million	billion=million million
broil	grill
bureau	chest of drawers
busy	engaged (phone)
C	
cab	taxi
call/phone	ring up/phone
can	tin
candy	sweets
candy store	sweet shop/confectioner
check	bill (restaurant)
closet	cupboard
closet (hanging clothes)	wardrobe
connect (telephone)	put through
cookie	biscuit
corn	sweetcorn, maize
crazy	mad
D	
davenport/sofa	sofa
delivery truck	van
desk clerk	receptionist
dessert	pudding/dessert/sweet
downtown	centre (city/business)
drapes	curtains
dresser	chest of drawers
druggist	chemist
drugstore/pharmacy	chemist's (shop)
dungarees	jeans/overalls
duplex	semi-detached
E	
eggplant	aubergine
elevator	lift
eraser	rubber, eraser

American English	British English
F	
fall	autumn
faucet	tap
first floor, second floor etc.	ground floor, first floor etc
flashlight	torch
flat (tire)	flat tyre, puncture
freeway/highway	motorway
french fries	chips
freshman (at university)	1st year undergraduate
front desk (hotel)	reception
G	
garbage/trash	rubbish
garbage can/ash can/ trash can	dustbin/bin
gas	petrol
gas station	petrol station/garage
grade	class/form
I	
intermission	interval
intersection	crossroads
J	
janitor	caretaker/porter
jello	jelly
jump rope	skipping rope
K	
kerosene	paraffin
L	
lawyer/attorney	solicitor
lost and found	lost property
M	
mail	post
mailman	postman
make a reservation	book
motorcycle	motorbike/motorcycle
movie	film
movie house/theater	cinema
N	
news stand	newsagent

American English	British English
O	
office (doctor's/dentist's)	surgery
one-way (ticket)	single (ticket)
overalls	dungarees
P	
pants, trousers	trousers
pantyhose/nylons	tights
parka	anorak
parking lot	car park
pass (vehicle, etc)	overtake/pass
pavement	road surface
pedestrian crossing	zebra crossing
(potato) chips	crisps
public school	state school
purse	handbag
pocketbook	purse
R	
railroad	railway
rest room	toilet/cloakroom/public convenience
round trip (ticket)	return (ticket)
S	
sack lunch	packed lunch
sales clerk/sales girl	shop assistant
schedule	timetable
Scotch tape	Sellotape
shorts (underwear)	pants
sidewalk	pavement
stand in line	queue
store, shop	shop
subway	underground
T	
truck	lorry, van
two weeks	fortnight, two weeks
V	
vacation	holiday(s)
vacuum (v.)	hoover
vacuum cleaner	hoover
vest	waistcoat
W	
with or without (milk/cream in coffee)	black or white

American English	British English
Y	
yard	garden
Z	
(pronounced "zee")	(pronounced "zed")
zero	nought
zip code	postcode

Grammar

She just went out./ She has just gone out.	She has just gone out.
Hello, is this Ann?	Hello, is that Ann?
Do you have a car?/ Have you got a car?	Have you got a car?

Spelling

American English	British English
aluminum	aluminium
analyze	analyse
center	centre
check	cheque
color	colour
defense	defence
honor	honour
jewelry	jewellery
labor	labour
practice(n,v)	practice(n) practise(v)
program	programme
realize	realise
theater	theatre
tire	tyre
trave(l)ler	traveller

Expressions with prepositions and particles

different from/than	different from/to
live on X street	live in X street
on a team	in a team

Rules for Punctuation

Capital Letters

A capital letter is used:
- to begin a sentence.
  This is my father.
- for days of the week, months and public holidays.
  Sunday, December, Christmas
- for names of people and places.
  My teacher's name is Mary and she's from Cardiff, Wales.
- for people's titles. *Mr and Mrs Smith; Dr Stevens; Professor Brown; etc.*
- for nationalities and languages.
  They are Portuguese.
  He's fluent in Spanish and German.
  Note: The personal pronoun I is always a capital letter. *Tom and I are going to the park.*

Full Stop (.)

A full stop is used:
- to end a sentence that is not a question or an exclamation.
  We're having a great time. There's so much to do here in Madrid.

Comma (,)

A comma is used:
- to separate words in a list.
  We need milk, cheese, butter and orange juice.
- to separate a non-identifying relative clause (i.e. a clause giving extra information which is not essential to the meaning of the main clause) from the main clause.
  Anna, who is a singer, lives in Moscow.
- after certain linking words/phrases (e.g. in addition to this, for example, however, in conclusion, etc).
  In addition to this, Tom is a generous person.
- when if-clauses begin sentences.
  If you take her advice, you won't get lost.
  Note: No comma is used, however, when the if-clause follows the main clause.
- to separate question tags from the rest of the sentence.
  Ms Jones is your history teacher, isn't she?

Question Mark (?)

A question mark is used:
- to end a direct question. *What time is it?*

Exclamation Mark (!)

An exclamation mark is used:
- to end an exclamatory sentence, i.e. a sentence showing admiration, surprise, joy, anger, etc.
  That's great!   What a nice dress!

Quotation Marks (' ' " ")

Quotation marks are used:
- in direct speech to report the exact words someone said.
  'We are leaving at 10am,' said John.
  "How old are you?" he asked me.

Colon (:)

A colon is used:
- to introduce a list.
  There were four of us on the boat : my mother, my father, my cousin Tony and me.

Brackets ( )

Brackets are used:
- to separate extra information from the rest of the sentence.
  These days, you can buy popular newspapers (i.e. The New York Times, The Observer, etc) almost anywhere in the world.

Apostrophe (')

An apostrophe is used:
- in short forms to show that one or more letters or numbers have been left out.
  I'm (= I am) writing to tell you about ...
  He left for Spain in the summer of '99. (=1999)
- before or after the possessive -s to show ownership or the relationship between people.
  Tim's house, my sister's husband (singular noun + 's)
  my parents' friends (plural noun + ')
  men's hats (Irregular plural + 's)

Suggested Answers Section

Self-Assessment Module 1 (Units 1 - 2)

Ex. 1 p. 24 (T)

- It's three o'clock.
- It's (a) quarter past four.
  It's four fifteen.
- It's a quarter to eight.
  It's seven forty-five.
- It's ten past eight.
  It's eight ten.
- It's twenty past nine.
  It's nine twenty.

Ex. 2 p. 24 (T)

a) I always get up at 7 o'clock on Mondays. I have breakfast, then I catch the bus to work. I start work at 9:00 am. I usually have a break for lunch at 1:00 pm. for an hour. I finish work at 5:00 pm. I do the shopping, then I go back home. I have dinner, then I surf the net. Sometimes I meet my friends or visit relatives. I usually go to bed at around 10:30 pm.

b) In my free time, I play on my computer and surf the net. I also meet my friends.
On Saturdays, I usually sleep late and then I go shopping. Sometimes I have lunch in a café with my friends. In the evenings, I often go to the cinema.
On Sundays, I usually visit my grandparents. Then, I do my homework and go to bed early.

Ex. 6 p. 24 (T)

There used to be some nice houses in Winnipeg. Today, there are huge blocks of flats. There used to be lots of trees then and nice gardens. Today, there aren't any trees or gardens. The air used to be clean then. Today the air is polluted.

Ex. 10 p. 25 (T)

Lynn Smith is a DJ. She works for Chicago Radio. Lynn gets up at 3:30 am. She has a shower, then she goes to the studio. She starts work at 5:30 am. Lynn is on air until 10 am. She plays records and talks to her listeners.

Lynn finishes work at 12 am. Her afternoons are free. She usually spends time with her family. In the evenings, she usually goes to parties.

In her free time, Lynn likes driving her car. She also likes being with her family and playing tennis.

Lynn loves her job. She says, "I love radio - I have fun while I work."

Self-Assessment Module 2 (Units 3 - 4)

Ex. 3 p. 44 (T)

It's a gold watch with a black leather strap and a black face.
It's a silver necklace with a pearl.
It's a silver ring with blue and red glass stones.

Ex. 6 p. 44 (T)

- I have already eaten lunch.
  I have already tidied my room.
  I have already made my bed.   etc
- I haven't done my homework yet.
  I haven't walked the dog yet.
  I haven't watered the plants yet.   etc
- I have never been to a theme park.
  I have never eaten octopus.
  I have never travelled by plane.   etc

Ex. 9 p. 45 (T)

S3: It's quite good. Where are they staying?
S4: In a nice hotel near the train station. Which places have they visited so far?
S5: The Collosseum, the Fontana di Trevi and Piazza d' España. Have they visited the Vatican yet?
S6: No, they haven't. Where did they eat yesterday?
S7: At a wonderful restaurant by the river. What happened while they were having lunch?
S8: It started raining so they left. What are they doing tomorrow?
S9: They are going shopping in the famous Via Veneto.

Ex. 10 p. 45 (T)

Dear Tom,
  I'm having a great time here in New York. I'm staying with a friend of mine.
  So far we've been to Manhattan and we have done some shopping on 5th Avenue. Unfortunately, while I was shopping, I lost my camera. We haven't visited Liberty Island yet. Tomorrow we are going to see a concert at Carnegie Hall.
  I'm coming back next Monday. I hope you are OK.

  See you,
  Bill

Self-Assessment Module 3 (Units 5 - 6)

Ex. 4 p. 64 (T)

- Jim is wearing a suit, a shirt and a tie and flat shoes.
- John is wearing a shirt with a tie, a blue V-neck pullover and dark blue trousers. He's also wearing trainers. (It is a school uniform.)
- Ted is wearing a white T-shirt and striped shorts. He's also wearing socks and trainers.
- Kim is wearing a yellow dress and a straw hat. She's also wearing socks and flat shoes.
- Today I'm wearing a white polo neck pullover and black trousers. I'm also wearing flat black shoes.

Ex. 9 p. 65 (T)

1 To complain to the manager of *The Salmon's Leap* restaurant.
2 a The table was next to the kitchen and they couldn't change to another one.
   b It was noisy and waiters were pushing past them all the time.
   c The waiter spilled cola on her new dress and ruined it.
   d Her steak was burnt and the coffee was cold.
   e The bill was much more than she expected.
3 To pay to clean the dress and apologise for spoiling her special day.

Ex. 10 p. 65 (T)

Dear Sir/Madam,

I'm writing to complain about the service, food and prices at your restaurant, *The Rosebowl*.

I took my friends out to your restaurant on Monday 27th January and we had an awful meal. The waiters were very slow. We waited an hour for our meal. The pasta was too spicy and the pizza was cold. When I got the bill, I was surprised to see how much it cost.

I expect an apology for spoiling our evening. I hope you will improve your service and reduce your prices or else you will lose your customers.

Yours faithfully,
Tom Smart

Self-Assessment Module 4 (Units 7 - 8)

Ex. 5 p. 86 (T)

The Ritz is clean. The Carlton is cleaner than the Ritz. The Park is the cleanest of all.
The Carlton is close to the beach. The Park is closer to the beach than the Carlton. The Ritz is the closest of all to the beach.
The Park has good service. The Ritz has better service than the Park. The Carlton has the best service of all.
The Park is crowded. The Carlton is more crowded than the Park. The Ritz is the most crowded of all.

Ex. 8 p. 87 (T)

Sandra works hard. Liz works harder than Sandra. Carol works the hardest of all.
Liz writes neatly. Carol writes more neatly than Liz. Sandra writes the most neatly of all.
Carol dresses smartly. Liz dresses more smartly than Carol. Sandra dresses the most smartly of all.

Ex. 10a p. 87 (T)

1 To begin with/To start with
2 Next/Also
3 Nevertheless/On the other hand
4 Furthermore/In addition
5 To sum up/In conclusion

Ex. 10b p. 87 (T)

reasons in favour	opposing viewpoint
so much space	you will need a car
quieter	houses can be expensive
friendly people	

Ex. 11 p. 87 (T)

lots of shops - wide choice of things to buy (in favour)
variety of means of transport - can go wherever you want easily and quickly (in favour)
noisy and crowded - lots of cars/people (against)

In my opinion, living in the city has a number of benefits.

To begin with, there are lots of shops in the city. You can always find what you need and there is a wide choice of things to buy. Also, the city offers a wide variety of different means of transport. You can go wherever you want easily and quickly.

However, the city is often noisy and crowded. Lots of people live in the city and so there are lots of cars, too.

All in all, I think that although living in the city can be noisy and crowded, it is worth it. There is lots to see and do, lots of shops and good public transport.

Self-Assessment Module 5 (Units 9 - 10)

Ex. 3 p. 108 (T)

Natalie is quite pretty. She's got long straight dark hair and a round face with a narrow forehead. She's got big eyes with long eyebrows, a small button nose and a pointed chin.   etc.

Ex. 9b p. 109 (T)

person's name and job	–	Para 1
how they met	–	Para 1
physical description	–	Para 2
describes person's character	–	Para 3
writer's feelings	–	Para 4

Ex. 10 p. 109 (T)

Lynne is my best friend. We met on my first day at a new school when I was 6 years old and we have been good friends ever since.

She is slim and attractive with dark hair and skin. She's got brown eyes and she's always smiling. She likes to wear fashionable clothes.

Lynne is good fun. She's very sociable and she's got a great sense of humour. She's also generous and kind. She likes to be outdoors and often goes for bike rides and walks in the countryside.

We don't live close to each other anymore, but we write, talk on the phone and meet whenever we can. It's great to have such a good friend. I really like her a lot.

Test Booklet - Key

Test 1 A (Units 1, 2)

A

1	A	3	C	5	B	7	A	9	A
2	B	4	A	6	C	8	B	10	B

B
11 two o'clock.
12 (a) quarter past six.
13 (a) quarter to ten.
14 ten past ten.
15 twenty past one.

C
16 had
17 read
18 walked
19 fed
20 cooked/made
21 watched
22 surfed
23 played
24 listened
25 met

D
26 typical
27 missed
28 complete
29 spare
30 play
31 five-star
32 believe
33 sense
34 occasions
35 tell

E
36 Johan is German. He's a footballer
37 Anita is Portuguese. She's a nurse
38 Jacek is Polish. He's a receptionist
39 Kate is British. She's an accountant
40 Pauline is French. She's a gardener

F
41 at
42 to
43 on
44 at
45 for

G
46 rides
47 am writing
48 is not talking
49 loses
50 have

H

51	A	53	B	55	B	57	C	59	B
52	A	54	A	56	A	58	B	60	A

I
61 Do
62 is
63 did
64 are
65 does

J
66 How long did he spend there
67 On a farm
68 Yes, he does
69 Did you have a good time
70 At six o'clock

K
71 Yes
72 No
73 No
74 Yes
75 Yes

L (Suggested answer)

... a famous American composer, song writer and producer of musicals. He was born in 1895 and died in 1960. Hammerstein wrote over forty-five musicals for theatre, film and TV. He worked with many composers, and in 1943 he began working with Richard Rodgers. They wrote some famous musicals, *South Pacific*, *The King and I* and *The Sound of Music*. Some of their musicals became films and they won awards.

Rogers and Hammerstein musicals are still popular today.

Test 1 B (Units 1, 2)

A

1	C	3	B	5	C	7	B	9	C
2	B	4	C	6	B	8	A	10	C

B
11 five o'clock.
12 (a) quarter past two.
13 (a) quarter to eleven.
14 ten past one.
15 twenty past four.

C
16 had/drank
17 had
18 fed
19 did
20 made
21 watched
22 talked
23 wrote
24 had/ate
25 read

D
26 leads
27 part-time
28 introduce
29 playing
30 fell
31 fairy
32 midday
33 way
34 hit
35 looks

E
36 Fernando and Arturo are Portuguese. They are architects
37 Marie-Claire is French. She's a shop assistant
38 Joanne is English. She's a secretary
39 José is Spanish. He's a vet
40 Daniella is Italian. She's a teacher

F
41 in
42 for
43 after
44 with
45 to

G
46 plays
47 catches
48 is making
49 washes
50 isn't talking

H

51	B	53	B	55	A	57	A	59	A
52	A	54	C	56	B	58	C	60	A

I
61 did
62 do
63 are
64 does
65 is

J
66 Two weeks
67 Does she like her new boss
68 Ten o'clock
69 She types letters
70 Did you enjoy it

K
71 No
72 Yes
73 Yes
74 Yes
75 No

L (Suggested answer)

... a famous American rock and roll singer, guitarist, and song writer. He was born in 1936 and died in 1959. He made only three albums before he died in an aircrash. He was the first person to mix rock and roll music with country music. He played with a band called *The Crickets*. His most famous hits were *Peggy Sue*, *That'll be the Day* and *It Doesn't Matter Anymore*.

Musicians today still copy his style of music.

Test 2 A (Units 3, 4)

A
1 cartoon	5 rollercoaster	9 softly
2 lifetime	6 ages	10 wrong
3 matter	7 set	
4 gratefully	8 yelled	

B
11 They are cotton shorts with dots.
12 It's a gold necklace with sapphires and diamonds.
13 It's a gold watch with a leather strap.
14 It's a wooden chest with metal handles.
15 It's a platinum ring with rubies and diamonds.

C
16 He has hurt his leg.
17 He has lost a tooth.
18 She has crashed her car into a tree.
19 He has cut his finger.
20 He has broken his arm.

D
21 surprised   24 relieved
22 exhausted   25 lonely
23 bored

E
26 on   28 for   30 out
27 into   29 of

F
31 since   33 yet   35 never
32 for   34 just

G
36 didn't go   39 opened
37 was doing   40 was cooking
38 was blowing

H
41 A   43 A   45 B   47 C   49 A
42 C   44 B   46 C   48 B   50 B

I
51 washed   54 haven't spoken
52 Have you ever met ...?   55 left
53 enjoyed

J
56 nervously   59 beautiful
57 patient   60 Suddenly
58 well

K
61 What's the problem
62 I have no idea
63 We had a great time, thanks
64 Yes, I've just finished
65 I left my books on the bus

L 66 C   67 B   68 A   69 C   70 A

M (Suggested answer)

... The sun was shining and it was a perfect day for skiing.

Jenny was waiting for the ski lift when she heard a rumbling noise. She looked up and saw lots of snow falling down the mountain. It was an avalanche.

Jenny was looking desperately for somewhere to hide, when she saw a wooden house close by. She ran quickly and hid inside until the avalanche stopped. After a few minutes, she looked for a way out but the door wouldn't open. Finally, she managed to break a window and escaped.

Jenny was still shaking with fear when the rescue team arrived. They took her down the mountain to the village. She felt happy and relieved to be safe, but she decided to go to an island for her holidays next year!

Test 2 B (Units 3, 4)

A
1 realise	5 leather	9 wild
2 relieved	6 running	10 lost
3 cotton	7 hoovering	
4 trip	8 boiling	

B
11 It's a porcelain lamp with a floral design.
12 It's a leather handbag with a long strap.
13 It's a wooden box with a metal handle.
14 It's a plastic ball with dots.
15 It's a gold necklace with a pearl.

C
16 He has caught a cold.
17 He has broken his arm.
18 He has burnt his hands.
19 She has cut her finger.
20 He has broken/lost his tooth.

D
21 lonely   23 pleased   25 relieved
22 exhausted   24 miserable

E
26 at   28 into   30 in
27 on   29 over

F
31 already   33 never   35 for
32 since   34 just

G
36 got   39 were singing
37 was talking   40 happened
38 Did you stay

H
41 A   43 A   45 C   47 C   49 C
42 B   44 C   46 B   48 B   50 C

I
51 haven't seen   53 Have you eaten   55 flew
52 loved   54 heard

J
56 patiently   58 carefully   60 softly
57 happily   59 good

K
61 Yes, it does
62 Has anyone seen my handbag
63 It was out of this world
64 What's wrong with him
65 How shocking

L 66 B   67 C   68 A   69 C   70 A

M (Suggested answer)

... They were both exhausted after climbing to the top of the volcano. They put up their tent for the night and went straight to sleep.

They were sleeping peacefully when they heard a loud rumbling noise. They looked up and saw thick smoke coming out of the volcano. They ran down the mountain as fast as they could.

They arrived at the village at the bottom of the mountain and ran through the streets. They were shouting to the villagers to wake them up. The people realised what was happening and quickly jumped into their cars and left the village. As they were driving out of the village, they looked back and saw the volcano erupt.

Afterwards, the villagers were very grateful to Eric and Lars. They gave them medals. The climbers were happy that they were able to warn the villagers in time.

Test 3 A (Units 5,6)

A
1 B	3 B	5 C	7 A	9 A
2 C	4 A	6 B	8 C	10 B

B
11 belt	15 jumper	19 raincoat
12 jeans	16 trousers	20 boots
13 tie	17 dress	
14 jacket	18 cardigan	

C
21 fit	24 traditional	27 latest
22 main	25 display	28 take
23 slice	26 up	

D
29 for	31 of	33 to
30 on	32 in	

E
34 accessories	36 countries	38 wolves
35 men	37 mice	

F
39 much	41 jar
40 bowl	42 a lot of

G
43 will	47 will	51 is going to
44 am going to	48 will	52 are going to
45 willl	49 will	
46 is going to	50 will	

H
53 He is going to blow the candles out.
54 He is going to fall down.
55 He is going to eat the cake.

56 He is going to swim.
57 She is going to go on a trip.

I
58 piece	62 any	66 much
59 an	63 are leaving	67 any
60 a	64 going to visit	
61 children	65 will	

J
68 Where does it take place
69 May I take your order
70 Of course. Here you are
71 Really? I'll buy some then
72 Yes, I suppose so

K
73 The writer went to the restaurant in the evening.
74 The writer booked a table for 8 o'clock.
75 The writer ordered a drink.
76 Mrs Stevens' favourite dish is Chicken à la creme.
77 The restaurant doesn't have a lot of waiters.

L (Suggested answer)

...

I am writing to complain about the service at your restaurant last Saturday lunchtime.

The waiter looked untidy. He was wearing torn jeans and a dirty T-shirt and he wasn't friendly. We ordered the fish but it was too salty and it was cold. Also, I ordered boiled potatoes, but the waiter brought me chips.

I would like to suggest that your staff wear uniforms and be friendlier. I hope your service gets better or you will lose your customers.

...

Barbara Turner

Test 3 B (Units 5, 6)

A
1 B	3 C	5 B	7 B	9 C
2 A	4 B	6 B	8 C	10 A

B
11 tie	15 coat	19 T-shirt
12 trousers	16 boots	20 jeans
13 hat	17 cap	
14 jumper	18 dress	

C
21 special	24 weather	27 over
22 electronic	25 baked	28 suit
23 website	26 bowl	

D
29 about	31 for	33 at
30 of	32 on	

E
34 women	36 sandwiches	38 children
35 tomatoes	37 knives	

F
39 much	41 many
40 kilos	42 a little

G
43 is going to	47 am going to	51 are going to
44 will	48 am going to	52 will
45 will	49 will	
46 will	50 will	

H
53 They are going to take the bus.
54 She is going to have a rest.
55 He is going to fall out of the tree.
56 She is going to buy some new clothes.

57 They are going to see a film.

I 58 bowl   62 much   66 a little
    59 bar   63 a few   67 am going to
    60 will   64 some
    61 many   65 some

J 68 Oh, do you think so? Thank you
    69 I'm starving
    70 And for dessert
    71 We've run out of fruit
    72 It's hot and sunny

K 73 The writer had lunch at the café.
    74 The knives and forks were dirty.
    75 The waitress was rude.
    76 The writer ordered a Coke.
    77 The fish was very salty.

L (Suggested answer)

...

I am writing to complain about the service at your restaurant last Sunday lunch time.

The service was very slow, we waited for 45 minutes for the waiter to take our order. When the food came, the soup was cold and the bread rolls were old. Also, we ordered chicken wings but they weren't available. Finally, we chose something else but we were very annoyed.

I suggest that you have more waiters working on busy nights and that all the dishes on the menu are available. I hope your service gets better or else you will lose your customers.

...

John Dobson

Test 4 A (Units 7, 8)

A 1 shame   3 trip   5 habitat
    2 protect   4 pass

B 6 crowded   10 licence   14 endangered
    7 equator   11 fit   15 memorials
    8 naughty   12 common
    9 crops   13 loyal

C 16 of   18 from   20 by
    17 at   19 to

D 21 kitten   23 fishing   25 comfortable
    22 scales   24 litter

E 26 which   28 which   30 whose
    27 where   29 who

F 31 A   33 C   35 C   37 B   39 B
    32 C   34 C   36 A   38 A   40 B

G 41 beautiful   44 safely
    42 careful   45 happy
    43 nicer

H 46 If   48 don't have to   50 laziest
    47 tidier 49 can

I 51 No, we'll freeze to death
    52 Yes, they're obedient, too
    53 Where do you fancy going, to the cinema or the theatre
    54 Can I use the phone
    55 You should take an aspirin

J 56 C   57 E   58 F   59 A   60 D

K (Suggested answer)

...

Firstly, you can make your own timetable. You can get up early and set off whenever you want. You can even set off the night before.

Secondly, you can plan your route. You can stop along the way at different places of interest and enjoy the countryside. You can drive on quiet roads and not just on motorways. *In addition*, you can stop whenever you want. If you are tired you can have a rest or if you are hungry or thirsty you can stop at a café or restaurant and have something to eat or drink.

On the other hand, driving is not as fast as flying or travelling by train. Also, it can be expensive because you have to pay for petrol, food and drinks. *As far as I'm concerned*, there is nothing better than the open road and the freedom of setting your own schedule.

...

Test 4 B (Units 7, 8)

A 1 cosmopolitan   3 accommodation   5 exotic
    2 daisy   4 intelligent

B 6 afford   10 furthermore   14 peaceful
    7 book   11 advertised   15 cure
    8 litter   12 levels
    9 cultures   13 extinct

C 16 off   18 of   20 to
    17 on   19 for

D 21 deer   23 beak   25 chores
    22 Asia   24 Europe

E 26 which   28 who   30 who
    27 where   29 whose

F 31 A   33 B   35 C   37 C   39 A
    32 A   34 B   36 B   38 B   40 A

G 41 playful   44 clearly
    42 luckiest   45 beautifully
    43 peacefully

H 46 nicest   48 least   50 unless
    47 naughtier   49 should

I 51 What would you do in my place
    52 Do I have to
    53 I'd like to book a flight to Rome
    54 You mustn't be late for work
    55 That's a good idea

J 56 B   57 E   58 D   59 C   60 A

K (Suggested answer)

...

To start with, we should use public transport and leave our cars at home. This way we could reduce the number of cars on the roads. Also, we could ask a few colleagues to share cars. We could take turns to drive each one to work. This way we would cut down on pollution, and we would save money, too.

In addition, we could write to the council and make some suggestions. For example, using unleaded petrol in town buses or providing cheap transport to places with a lot of people working there.

On the other hand, some people think that people cannot reduce pollution by themselves. They believe the government should solve the problem. However, I believe every little helps and we can reduce pollution levels if we all do something to help and the sooner the better.

...

H 51 wonder where John is going.
    52 too heavy (for us) to carry.
    53 know when the train leaves for York?
    54 clever enough to find the answer
    55 tell me what the problem is?

I 56 What is this vase made of
    57 When was this house built
    58 That's fine by me
    59 That's right
    60 I keep dropping things

J 61 F   62 T   63 F   64 F   65 T

K (Suggested answer)

Courteney Cox is a famous actress. She was born in Alabama, USA, in 1964. She first appeared in a TV show in 1983. She is famous for the TV show "Friends", but she has also acted in several films.

Courteney Cox is tall and slim, with blue eyes. She has got a wide mouth and thin lips. She prefers wearing designer clothes. She is hardworking and open-hearted as well as funloving and friendly.

In her spare time, she enjoys designing houses and going for walks with her husband, David.

Courteney Cox is my favourite actress because she is very funny. I always watch her show on TV.

Test 5 A (Units 9, 10)

A 1 vain   6 unfortunately   11 artistic
    2 accuracy   7 manager   12 basement
    3 features   8 carved   13 nose
    4 imprisoned   9 quick   14 reputation
    5 appetite   10 outfit   15 priceless

B 16 marble   18 held   20 science
    17 balcony   19 straight

C 21 of   23 at   25 after
    22 to   24 in

D 26 A   28 B   30 A
    27 C   29 C

E 31 tidy   33 meeting   35 watch
    32 sunbathing   34 to move

F 36 B   38 C   40 C   42 A   44 B
    37 B   39 A   41 C   43 B   45 A

G 46 The living room was decorated by Jenny last week.
    47 The Colosseum is visited by many tourists every year.
    48 The city was destroyed by a volcano eruption.
    49 The office is cleaned every morning.
    50 This play was written by T. Williams.

Test 5 B (Units 9, 10)

A 1 clay   6 seriously   11 trendy
    2 designer   7 fitted   12 overtime
    3 laughter   8 display   13 aggressive
    4 weigh   9 freckles   14 interview
    5 remind   10 lazy   15 daring

B 16 ambitious   18 chimney   20 arched
    17 stone   19 well-preserved

C 21 of   23 from   25 with
    22 with   24 to

D 26 A   28 C   30 C
    27 C   29 B

E 31 to come   33 stay   35 to go
    32 playing   34 know

F 36 C   38 C   40 A   42 C   44 B
    37 A   39 A   41 B   43 C   45 C

G 46 Cars are made in Japan.
    47 The President's car is driven by a chauffeur.
    48 Many buildings were destroyed by the earthquake.
    49 The plants were watered yesterday by the gardener.
    50 All the roads were blocked by snow.

H 51 too young to drive a car.
52 know when Lisa's birthday is?
53 is good enough to win an Oscar.
54 tell me who you have invited to the party?
55 talented enough to become an artist.

I 56 Yes, he's very lazy
57 These bags are too heavy for me
58 What shall we do today
59 What currency is used in Japan
60 Who was the museum designed by

J 61 T   62 F   63 T   64 F   65 T

K (Suggested answer)

David Beckham is a famous football player. He was born in Essex in 1975. He started playing football for Manchester United when he was only 19 years old. He also plays football for England.

David Beckham is very athletic. He is tall, strong and of medium-build. He has got short, blond hair and blue eyes. He has also got an oval-shaped face and full lips. When he's not playing football he prefers wearing expensive fashionable clothes.

In his free time, he enjoys going out with his wife Victoria or playing with his son, Brooklyn.

David Beckham is my favourite football player. I like him because he is sociable and cheerful.

EXIT TEST

A 1 B   6 A   11 C   16 A
2 A   7 B   12 A   17 A
3 B   8 A   13 C   18 C
4 C   9 C   14 B   19 A
5 C   10 B   15 C   20 C

B 21 A   26 B   31 A   36 C
22 C   27 A   32 C   37 B
23 A   28 A   33 A   38 A
24 C   29 B   34 C   39 B
25 A   30 A   35 B   40 C

C 41 I'm looking for the Art teacher
42 Very intelligent
43 Do you know what you should do
44 What's the problem
45 Medium
46 Is there any cake left
47 That pizza looks nice
48 Great! Thanks, Mum
49 Oh dear
50 This company is very successful

D 51 F   54 F   57 T   60 F
52 T   55 F   58 T
53 F   56 F   59 F

E (Suggested answer)

...

Firstly, why don't you write down any new vocabulary in a special notebook? That way you can study the vocabulary better and remember new words more easily.

Secondly, you should listen to music in English and try to understand the songs' words. If you sing along it will probably help you speak better English.

Finally, how about sendng e-mails to British children? That way, you will make new friends and you will practise your English.

...

Listening Test 1

1 nine   4 camp office
2 horse riding   5 Wednesday
3 swimming

Listening Test 2

1 c   2 b   3 c   4 b   5 b

Listening Test 3

1 fifteen minutes   4 chopped
2 four   5 pepper
3 carrots

Listening Test 4

1 A   2 E   3 B   4 C   5 D

Listening Test 5

1 C   2 B   3 A   4 C   5 B

Listening Exit Test

1 b   2 a   3 a   4 b   5 c

175

Video Activity - Key

1 2 A: What's John's job?
      B: He's an accountant.
      A: What does he do at work?
      B: He keeps financial accounts.
      A: What is he doing now?
      B: He is reading a newspaper.

   3 A: What's Paula's job?
      B: She's a secretary.
      A: What does she do at work?
      B: She types letters.
      A: What is she doing now?
      B: She is driving to work.

   4 A: What's Peter's job?
      B: He's an architect.
      A: What does he do at work?
      B: He designs buildings.
      A: What is he doing now?
      B: He is taking the dog for a walk.

2 a) 2 He is brushing his teeth.   - everyday
       3 He is cycling.   - free-time
       4 They are eating out.   - free-time
       5 He is hanging out the washing.   - everyday

   b) Ss' own answers.

3 1 Jim   3 Glyn   5 Glyn
   2 Richard   4 Scott   6 Jim

4 1 a   2 b   3 b

5 **Job:** Teacher, writer
   Starts work at: nine, eight
   Finishes work at: four, five
   Likes: restaurants, watching TV

6 1 b   2 b   3 a   4 c

7 1 A: ... does Anne get up ...
      B: ... seven fifteen/quarter past seven ...
   2 A: ... is John cooking ...
      B: ... are coming .../... six thirty/half past six ...
   3 A: ... are you flying ...
      B: ... twenty past five .../ five twenty ...
   4 A: ... do you have ...
      B: ... always have .../... nine forty five/quarter to ten
      ...

8 Ss' own answers.

9 Can you spell your surname?
   And where are you from?
   Thank you. And your address?
   Hello.

Of course. Let me take some details. What's your name?
That's fine. Do you need an appointment now?
And what do you do Miss Perez?
And your telephone number?
We'll do that then, thank you.

P – E – R – E – Z.
Hello. I'd like to register.
I'm a student.
Thanks very much.
Lisa Perez.
01603927.
No, thank you. I just wanted to register.
41, Malborne Road.
Spain.

10 Ss' own answers.

1 2 In the past women used to wear long dresses but today they wear jeans.
   3 In the past rivers used to be clean but now they are dirty.
   4 In the past the air used to be clean but today it is polluted.

2 Ss' own answers.

3 1 T   3 T   5 F   7 T
   2 F   4 T   6 F

   2 People used to travel on foot or by horse.
   3 Today men wear jackets.
   6 The air is polluted.

4 1 D, E   3 B, D   5 B
   2 A   4 A   6 C

5 1 a   3 c   5 b
   2 a   4 b

6 changed the weather
   could make travellers lose their way
   knocked over things in people's homes

7 People travelled by coach 300 years ago, but today they travel by car.
   People cooked on real fires 300 years ago, but today they eat out.
   People had picnics by the river 300 years ago, but today they play on computers.
   People did not have electricity 300 years ago, but today they do not have pure air.

8 1 c   2 a   3 a   4 a

9 Ss' own answers.

10 a) 1 How   4 do
      2 Where   5 After
      3 went to

   b) 1 heard   6 did   11 Listen
      2 going   7 met   12 Call
      3 got   8 Are   13 Talk
      4 living   9 finished
      5 moved   10 working

11 Ss' own answers.

Unit 3 – Having fun

1 1 e   2 c   3 a   4 b   5 d

2 Ss' own answers.

3 1 F   3 F   5 T
   2 T   4 F   6 F

   1 Rich visited Pleasurewood Hills.
   3 You can get wet on the water ride.
   4 Woody Bear has his photograph taken with children.
   6 Rich had a burger, some chips and a coke.

4 1 c   2 e   3 b   4 a

5 1 b, Square
   2 e, Triangle/Triangular
   3 c, Rectangle/Rectangular
   4 a, Circle/round
   5 d, Oval

6 1 a   2 c   3 c

8 **Suggested Answer**
   Rich says that Pleasurewood Hills is a huge theme park. There are lots of things that you can see and do there. For example you can go on a train ride round the park. You can also race go-carts on a track. Finally you can go on a water ride although you might get wet.
   The park mascot is called Woody Bear and you can get someone to take a photograph of him with you, if you like. If you get hungry when you are in the park there are lots of different places where you can buy food. On the whole Pleasurewood hills is a wonderful place and Rich had a great time when he was there.

9 1 b   2 a   3 c   4 b

10 a 1 purse   2 black   3 money
   b 1 handbag   2 gold   3 keys
   c 1 rucksack   2 straps   3 wallet

---

11 **Suggested Answers**

   S1: Hello. I've lost my bag.
   S2: Right. What does it look like?
   S1: It's big and blue, with blue straps.
   S2: OK. What was in it?
   S1: My camera, my keys and a scarf.

   S2: Hello. I've lost my backpack.
   S1: OK. What does it look like?
   S2: It's black with two straps and a front pocket.
   S1: And what was in it?
   S2: My watch and a pen.

   S1: Hello. I've lost my suitcase.
   S2: Right. What does it look like?
   S1: It's blue, with a brown stripe and a label on it.
   S2: What was in it?
   S1: My wallet, a pair of shoes and an alarm clock.

Unit 4 – Experiences

1 **Suggested Answer**
   Rich was driving to work when he heard a funny noise. The car spluttered and came to a stop. Rich tried to restart the engine but it wasn't working. Then he tried to ring the studio but his phone wasn't working either.
   Rich decided to walk the rest of the way to work but before long he realised that he was lost. By this time he was also feeling very tired, in fact he was so tired that he started to fall asleep. Suddenly he heard a noise, someone was saying 'Rich, Rich, wake up! Time to film your report!'. Rich realised that it had all been a bizarre dream and that he had been in the studio the whole time.

2 2 He is exhausted because he has been working all day.
   3 He's bored because he has nothing to do.
   4 He is frustrated because he can't play the song.
   5 He is annoyed because his computer has got a bug.

3   As he was sleeping, somebody woke him up.
      He decided to walk to work.
      Rich was driving to work.
      Rich realised he had been dreaming.
      He was so tired that he fell asleep.
      His car engine wasn't working.
      Rich was in the studio.
      His phone wasn't working.

4 1 d   2 a   3 e   4 c

5 1 play   6 red
   2 motorway   7 open
   3 lanes   8 cheap
   4 M25   9 efficient
   5 sightseeing 10 city

6 Ss' own answers.

7 1 c   2 b   3 a   4 a

8 Ss' own answer.

9 a) 1 ticket
     2 Single
     3 time
     4 Twelve

   b) 5 send
     6 spell
     7 10
     8 Taxi
     9 much
     10 There
     11 change

10 Ss' own answers.

Unit 5 – Fashion in all Seasons

1 a) **Chris** is wearing black shoes and beige trousers. He's wearing a white short-sleeved shirt, woollen waistcoat and a striped tie.
   Amanda is wearing a long black formal dress and black high-heeled shoes.
   Paul is wearing a white cap and a blue and white checked shirt. He's also wearing red trousers and blue boots.
   Fiona is wearing a long blue dress and a straw hat.
   Sally is wearing a grey jacket and a white blouse. She is also wearing a patterned silk scarf.
   Mike is wearing a grey jacket, a white shirt and patterned tie.
   Jenny is wearing a blue and red checked skirt with a black belt. She is also wearing a blue blouse and a green cardigan.

   b) Paul is properly dressed to go on an excursion.
   Amanda is properly dressed to go to a dinner party.
   Sally and Mike are properly dressed for work.
   Jenny and Fiona are properly dressed to go for a walk.
   Mike, Sally and Amanda are all properly dressed to go to an expensive restaurant.

2 Ss' own answers.

3 a) 1 T   3 F   5 T
     2 F   4 T

     2 Lots of people order their clothes from catalogues.
     3 People who buy from catalogues order their clothes on the phone.
   b) 1 shirt   3 shorts   5 woollen suit
     2 jumper   4 T-shirt   6 evening dress

4 1 B, C   3 B   5 A
     2 A   4 C

5 Early morning: **Frosty**
   Late morning: **sunny** and **dry**
   Temperature: **-1°** C in the **morning**
   Later in the day: **14°**C by the **afternoon**
   Wind Force: **4**

7 1 b   2 a   3 a   4 c   5 b

8 a) 1 cold and wet
     2 freezing cold
     3 chilly
     4 boiling hot
     5 windy

   b) A 1   C 2   E 3
     B 4   D 5

9 Ss' own answers.

10 1 be   5 to
     2 late   6 feel
     3 Temperatures 7 Lows
     4 from   8 highs

11 Suggested Answers

   Our international weather report this week starts off in Europe where most places are enjoying fairly good weather at the moment. For example in Madrid tomorrow it will be sunny with high temperatures of 20°C that's 68°F. It will also be sunny in France although the temperatures will be slightly lower. We expect there to be highs of 15°C in Nice and 10°C in Paris.
   Next we will move on to Asia where it is much hotter and also wetter. Both New Delhi and Singapore are expecting showers tomorrow, with high temperatures of 35°C and 33°C respectively. That's 95°F and 91°F by the way.
   Finally today we'll have a quick look at North America where they are experiencing a cold spell at the moment. Tomorrow in Toronto it is going to be cloudy with temperatures of just 3°C and in Chicago there might even be some snow, as temperatures there are not expected to get any higher than 2°C.

12 a) 1 satisfied   4 I'm very sorry about this
     2 Is there a problem 5 As you wish
     3 label   6 receipt

   b) Ss' own answers.

Unit 6 – Food and celebration

1 1 lentils   4 bread rolls   7 cauliflower
     2 pasta   5 strawberries   8 broccoli
     3 cheese   6 spring onions   9 grapes

2 Ss' own answers.

3 **Fruit:** peaches, pears, strawberries, grapes
Pulses: beans, peas, lentils
Vegetables: cauliflower, peppers, spring onions, broccoli, artichokes

4   1   a, f   2   b, d   3   c, e

5   1   T   3   T   5   F
    2   F   4   F

2   On Bonfire night people light big fires in their gardens.
4   Shrove Tuesday is in February.
5   On Shrove Tuesday people eat pancakes with lemon juice.

6   1   soup, chicken
    2   pasta, fruit salad
    3   burger, chips, apple pie

8   1   b   3   a   5   c
    2   c   4   c

9   1   book   4   luck   7   expecting
    2   check   5   available   8   Thanks
    3   table   6   have

10 a) 1   start   5   something
        2   main   6   glass
        3   roast   7   have
        4   grilled   8   Certainly

    b) 1   How's   4   can
        2   on   5   Will
        3   Can   6   so

11 Ss' own answers.

Unit 7 – The World around Us

1   a) **Suggested Answer**
    Crocodiles are large reptiles. Their bodies are covered in scales and they have long, heavy tails. They have big mouths filled with sharp teeth.
    Bears are large mammals. They are covered in thick fur and they have big heavy bodies. They also have sharp teeth and claws.
    Donkeys are mammals. They have long ears and tails. They stand on four legs and their bodies are covered in fur.
    Peacocks are birds. They have sharp beaks and long tails made up of beautiful, colourful feathers.
    Rabbits are small mammals. They are covered in fur and have long ears. They have small tails and are often kept as family pets.
    Zebras are large mammals usually found in the wild in Africa. They have striped bodies and four legs.

b) **Suggested Answer**
I think a bear would be the strongest of these animals, it would also probably be the most intelligent. The most dangerous animal might be the crocodile or a snake. The quietest animal might be the rabbit or the snake and the noisiest would probably be the donkey. I think the donkey would also be the most obedient of the animals and the strangest one to have as a pet would be the zebra.

2   1   d   2   c   3   a   4   b

3   **Pet:** cat, pony, sheep
    Name: Jasper
    Description: black, big/neck, white/head

4   1   A, C   3   B, D   5   D
    2   B, D   4   C   6   E

5   1   F   3   T   5   F
    2   T   4   F

1   Some people travel by road.
4   To take a plane, first go to the airport.
5   They tell you your seat number when you check in.

6   1   Seven   5   8th
    2   August 1st   6   battles
    3   Stratford upon Avon   7   Romans
    4   Dover   8   hotels

8   Ss' own answers.

9   Ss' own answers.

10 a) 1   London   3   12th   5   £189
        2   Milan   4   19th   6   £139

    b) 1   may
        2   double
        3   22nd
        4   forward

    c) Um. Well, I'm afraid I'll have to cancel.
        Hello. My name is Mike Giles. I booked a single room for three nights on the 22nd.
        Yes, I hope so. Thank you very much.Goodbye.
        Oh, that's a shame! Thanks for letting us know. We hope to see you some other time.
        Dublin Hilton. How may I help you?
        Yes, Mr Giles. I found your booking. Can I help?

Unit 8 – Earth SOS

1 a)
| 1 | c | 3 | d | 5 | a |
| 2 | e | 4 | f | 6 | b |

b)
2 If we protect wildlife, we will save endangered species.
3 If we protect the rainforests, rare plants will survive.
4 If we use unleaded petrol, we will reduce air pollution.
5 If we don't drop litter, we will live in a cleaner environment.
6 If we recycle paper and glass, we will save resources.

2 a)
| 1 | F | 3 | D | 5 | C |
| 2 | A | 4 | B | 6 | E |

b) You might find notices B and D near a school.
You might find notice A in a library.
You might find notices C and F outside a factory.
You might find notice A in a restaurant.
You might find notices E and F on a road outside a hospital.

3
| 1 | a | 3 | b | 5 | a |
| 2 | b | 4 | a | | |

4
1 If you want to **lose** weight, you should try eating healthier food.
3 You should avoid sweets and **fatty** foods.
2 You should eat more fruit and **vegetables**.
4 You should try to think about **why** you don't have any friends.
6 The best thing you can do is to **change** your job.
5 Perhaps you ask too many **questions**.

5
| 1 | F | 3 | F | 5 | T |
| 2 | T | 4 | T | 6 | F |

1 Part of the world's coastline is being lost.
3 People are the cause of the changes in the world's climate.
6 The ice in the arctic and the antarctic is melting.

7
| 1 | b | 3 | a | 5 | e |
| 2 | d | 4 | c | | |

8 a)
| 1 | a | 3 | a | 5 | b |
| 2 | b | 4 | a | 6 | a |

9 Suggested Answers

1 You shouldn't work so hard, if I were you I would go and lie down for a bit.
2 You should have started it earlier, why don't you ask someone to help you?
3 Why don't you go and call your friends to see what they are doing?
4 You should leave that work until later, why don't you take an aspirin?
5 If I were you I would try and take out a loan.
6 You should try getting up earlier in the morning, why don't you buy an alarm clock.
7 If I were you I would try to get more exercise, you should probably go on a diet as well.

10
| 1 | c | 3 | b | 5 | d |
| 2 | a | 4 | e | | |

11
| 1 | study | 3 | really | 5 | were |
| 2 | better | 4 | Why | | |

Unit 9 – Man's Achievements

1 a) Suggested Answers
A: Where was Crystal Palace located?
B: It was located in London. What was it made of?
A: It was made of iron and glass. When was completed?
B: It was completed in 1851. Who was it designed by?
A: It was designed by Joseph Paxton. Why was it built?
B: It was built to display the country's achievements. How was it destroyed?
A: It was destroyed by fire.

b) A: Where is Tower Bridge located?
B: It is located in London. What is it made of?
A: It is made of stone and steel. When was it completed?
B: It was completed in 1894. Who was it designed by?
A: It was designed by Sir Horace Jones and John Wolfe Barry. Why was it built?
B: It was built to cross the river Thames.

2 Ss' own answers.

3 a
| 1 | bell | 3 | Designed |
| 2 | tower | 4 | weighs |

b
| 1 | Nelson's | 3 | 55 metres |
| 2 | statue | 4 | stone |

c
| 1 | 30 minutes | 2 | steel | 3 | glass |

d
| 1 | 400 | 2 | wood |

4 a
| 1 | d | 2 | c | 3 | a | 4 | b |
| **b** A | 1 | B | 4 | C | 3 | D | 2 |

6
1 was designed, was opened
2 is made, was completed
3 is located, is not known

| a | 1 | b | 3 | c | 2 |

7 Ss' own answers.

8 There you are. Your sterling and your **receipt**.

Can I help you?

Certainly. How many US **dollars** would you like to exchange?

It's 1.44 dollar to the **pound**. So that will give you **£69.44**.

$100. What's the exchange **rate**?

Thank you.

Yes, I'd like to **exchange** these US dollars for pound sterling, please.

Thank you very much.

9 Ss' own answers.

Unit 10 – Characters

1 1 d   3 b   5 e
   2 c   4 a

2 I think Mike would probably like boxing because he is strong and energetic.
3 I think Susan would probably like chess because she is quiet and enjoys a mental challenge.
4 I think Laura would probably like painting because she is sensitive and creative.
5 I think Simon would probably like climbing because he is daring and adventurous.

2 Ss' own answers

3 a daring, climbing   c graceful, ice skating
   b sensitive, painting   d intelligent, chess

   1 a   2 d   3 b   4 c

5 2 ✓

6 1 F   3 F   5 T
   2 T   4 F   6 T

   1 Rich knows who Lindsey is.
   2 Lindsey has just moved to Cambridge.
   3 Lindsey has a lot of experience as a weather reporter.

7 a 4   c 5   e 2
   b 1   d 3

8 1 b   3 c   5 a
   2 a   4 b   6 c

9 1 g   3 h   5 d   7 c
   2 f   4 e   6 a   8 b

Ss' own answers.

10 1 adventurous   4 hardworking
    2 indecisive   5 stubborn
    3 sociable

11 a) 1 Have a seat   4 work
        2 tell me about   5 learn
        3 would you like   6 for your time

    b) 1 employees   3 applied
        2 know   4 kind

12 Ss' own answers.

The Hound of the Baskervilles

A New Case for Sherlock Homes: Episode 1

1 1 b   2 a   3 a   4 b

2 1 A   3 C   5 A   7 A
   2 C   4 B   6 C

3 1 frightening   3 curse   5 legend
   2 moor   4 inherit

The **Hound** killed Sir Charles Baskerville.

4 1 Yes   3 No   5 No
   2 No   4 No   6 Yes

2 He took the girl to Baskerville Hall.
3 The girl died of fear.
4 Sir Hugo Baskerville was the first to be killed by the hound.
5 Sir Henry Baskerville is Sir Charles' nephew.

5 1 curse   6 black
   2 kidnapped   7 killed
   3 escape   8 protect
   4 chased   9 inherit
   5 fear   10 property

6 Suggested Answers
Who do you suspect? What reasons does he/she have to do so? etc

Strange Happenings: Episode 2

1 1 c   2 b   3 a

2 a 4   c 2   e 3
   b 5   d 1

3 1 a   3 b   5 e
   2 d   4 c

4 1 Since he was a boy.
   2 Dartmoor/Baskerville Hall.
   3 He smells perfume on it.
   4 At a hotel.
   5 A boot.
   6 To Baskerville Hall.

5 1 arrived, Canada   3 know, staying
   2 received, stay   4 report

Danger on Dartmoor: Episode 3

1 1 d   2 e   3 c   4 a   5 b

2 1 bow tie   3 tuxedo   5 top hat
   2 apron   4 tie

3 1 b   2 a   3 a   4 b   5 b

4 1 quicksand   4 stranger   7 post
   2 alone   5 mire   8 dangerous
   3 murderer   6 howl

This episode takes place in **Dartmoor**.

5 a) There are a lot of policemen at the station.

    Dr Watson decides to go to the village to send his
    report to Holmes.

    Dr Watson arrives in Dartmoor with Sir Henry and
    Dr Mortimer.

    Sir Henry meets his uncle's servants.

    Dr Watson meets Jack Stapleton.

    Jack Stapleton tells Dr Watson that it's dangerous
    to walk through Grimpen Mire.

    A policeman tells them they're looking for Seldon -
    an escaped murderer.

    Beryl Stapleton mistakes Dr Watson for Sir Henry.

    They hear the Hound of the Baskervilles howling.

    b) **Suggested Answers**
    Dr Watson sees Barrymore signalling with a light.

The Midnight Watcher: Episode 4

1 1 a   2 b   3 b   4 a

2 1 C   3 B   5 A
   2 C   4 B   6 A

3 1 Every day.
   2 To tell him they're bringing him food.
   3 He is dangerous to society.
   4 Early in the morning.
   5 Food and blankets.
   6 Footsteps.

4 Ss' own answers.

5 1 fault, prisoner   4 blankets, hiding
   2 catch, dangerous   5 Footsteps
   3 policeman

The Hound Attacks: Episode 5

1 1 cap   3 tie   5 sideburns
   2 moustache   4 deerstalker 6 bow tie

3 1 T   3 F   5 T   7 T   9 T
   2 F   4 T   6 F   8 F   10 T

4 2 Holmes knows who wants to kill Sir Henry.
   3 Holmes and Watson hear someone shouting.
   6 The hound thought it was chasing Sir Henry.
   8 Holmes turns down Stapleton's invitation.

5 a howling   g appeared
   b invited   h death
   c realised   i portrait
   d killed   j invitation
   e –   k murderer
   f met

   a 2   d 3   g 5   j 7
   b 6   e 4   h 8   k 11
   c 10   f 1   i 9

6 1 c   3 d   5 b
   2 a   4 e   7 f

   1 H   3 H   5 H
   2 W   4 H   7 W

7 Ss' own answers.

An Invitation to Murder: Episode 6

1 1 alone   2 a telegram

2 1 send   3 get   5 noise
   2 safe   4 take   6 thicker

3 1 To Stapleton's for dinner.
   2 To send a telegram to Lestrade.
   3 Behind a wall.
   4 Lestrade.
   5 Stapleton.
   6 He hears a noise coming from the shed.
   7 Don't get lost on the moor.
   8 It's very foggy.

4 1 shoot   4 urgent   7 safe
   2 shed   5 fog   8 promise
   3 alone   6 ruin
   Holmes sent a **telegram** to London.

5 a) 1 D Holmes and Watson tell Sir Henry about Stapleton's invitation to dinner.
   2 E Holmes sends a telegram to Lestrade of Scotland Yard.
   3 B Holmes and Lestrade watch Stapleton's house.
   4 C Watson reports hearing a strange noise coming from a shed in the garden.
   5 A Sir Henry leaves Stapleton's house and sets off across the moor.
   6 F The hound chases Sir Henry.

b) Suggested Answers
Holmes and Watson tell Sir Henry about Stapleton's invitation to dinner. Sir Henry doesn't want to go but Holmes tells him that he will be perfectly safe. Next Holmes goes to the village to send a telegram to Inspector Lestrade of Scotland Yard. He asks the Inspector to come to Dartmoor right away. Sir Henry goes to dinner with Stapleton while Holmes, Watson and Lestrade watch the house. Holmes sends Watson to go and take a look to see what is happening. When Watson returns he reports that he heard a strange noise coming from a shed in the garden. All this time the fog on the moor is getting thicker and thicker and when Sir Henry leaves Stapleton warns him not to get lost and end up in Grimpen Mire. As Sir Henry sets off for home the hound appears and starts to chase him.

The Case in Closed: Episode 7

1 1 d   2 a   3 c   4 b

3 1 F   3 F   5 T
   2 F   4 F

4 1 They shoot the hound before it kills Sir Henry.
   2 There was phosphorus in the hound's eyes.
   3 They find Beryl Stapleton tied up in the attic.
   4 Stapleton put sticks to show him the safe way through the mire.

5 Ss' own answers.

6 Suggested Answer
Holmes and Watson could catch Stapleon before he escapes into Grimpen mire.

7 1 legend   2 attic   3 perfume   4 son
   5 sticks   6 footprints   7 quicksand

   1 W   2 W   3 H   4 B
   6 L   5 B   7 W